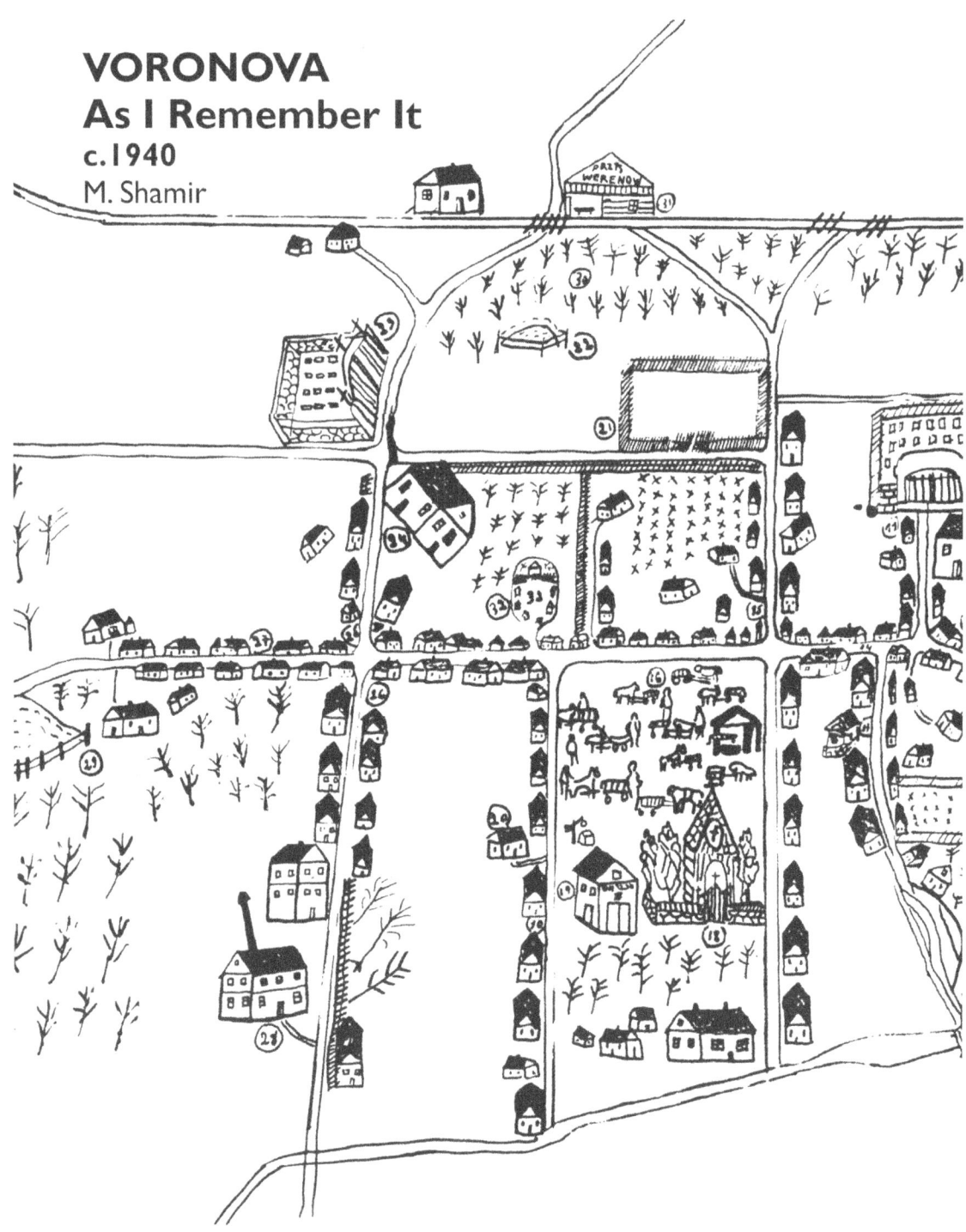

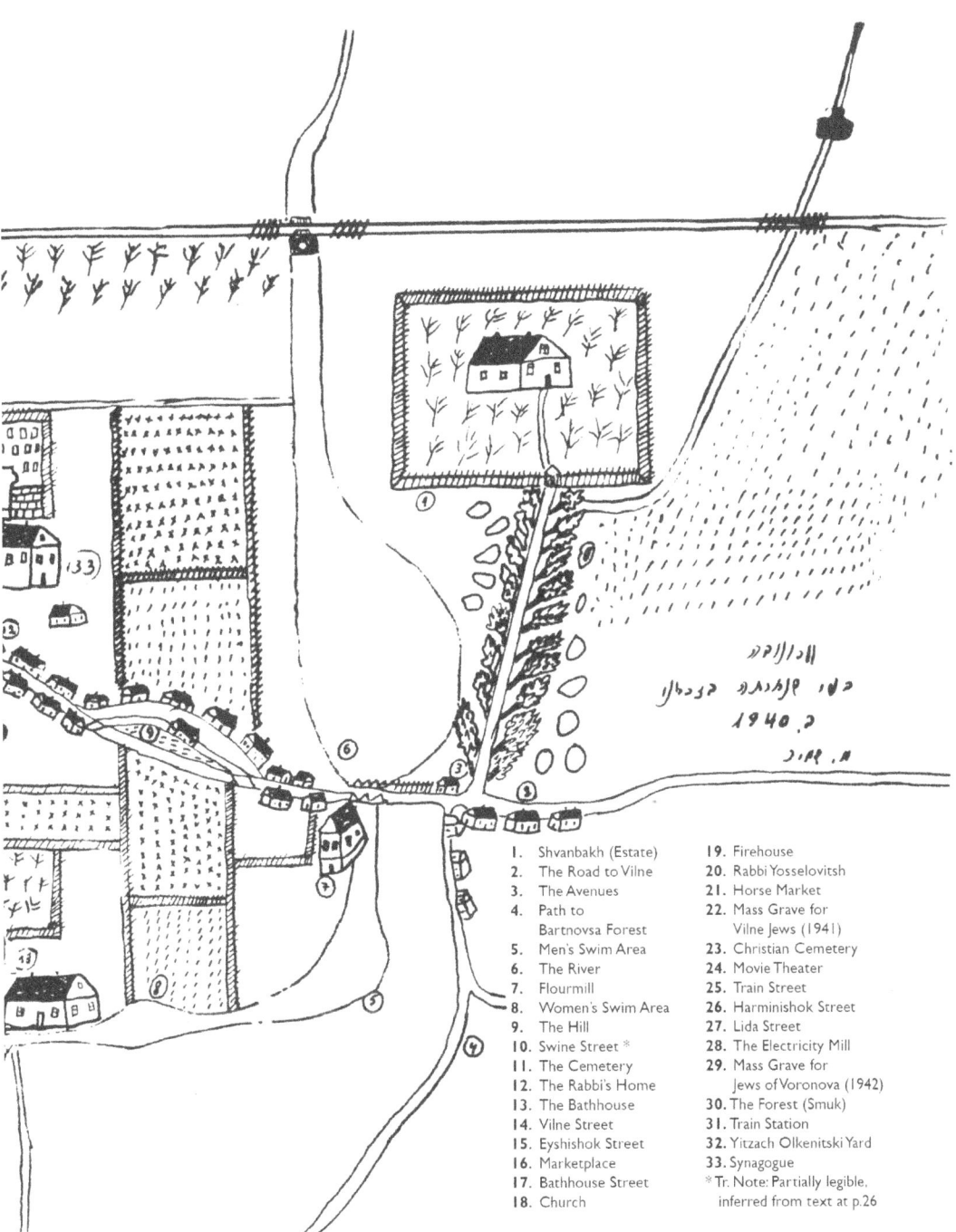

1. Shvanbakh (Estate)
2. The Road to Vilne
3. The Avenues
4. Path to Bartnovsa Forest
5. Men's Swim Area
6. The River
7. Flourmill
8. Women's Swim Area
9. The Hill
10. Swine Street *
11. The Cemetery
12. The Rabbi's Home
13. The Bathhouse
14. Vilne Street
15. Eyshishok Street
16. Marketplace
17. Bathhouse Street
18. Church
19. Firehouse
20. Rabbi Yosselovitsh
21. Horse Market
22. Mass Grave for Vilne Jews (1941)
23. Christian Cemetery
24. Movie Theater
25. Train Street
26. Harminishok Street
27. Lida Street
28. The Electricity Mill
29. Mass Grave for Jews of Voronova (1942)
30. The Forest (Smuk)
31. Train Station
32. Yitzach Olkenitski Yard
33. Synagogue

* Tr. Note: Partially legible, inferred from text at p.26

Memorial Book of Voronova
(Voranava, Belarus)

Translation of
*Voronova; sefer zikaron le-kedoshei Voronova
she-nispu be-shoat ha-natsim*

Memorial Book to the Martyrs of Voronova
Who Perished in the Nazi Holocaust

Original Yizkor Book Edited by: H. Rabin

Published by the Voronova Societies in Israel and the United States

Published in Israel, 1971

Published by JewishGen

An Affiliate of the Museum of Jewish Heritage—A Living Memorial to the Holocaust
New York

Memorial Book of Voronova (Voranava, Belarus)
Translation of: *Voronova; sefer zikaron le-kedoshei Voronova she-nispu be-shoat ha-natsim*
Memorial Book to the Martyrs of Voronova Who Perished in the Nazi Holocaust

Copyright © 2020 by JewishGen, Inc.
All rights reserved.
First Printing: October 2020, Tishrei 5781

Editor of the Original Yizkor Book: H. Rabin
Project Coordinator and Book Editor: Adam Cherson, Jack Gottleib (emeritus)
Layout: Jonathan Wind
Cover Design: Nina Schwartz, Impulse Graphics
Name and Place Indexing: Jonathan Wind

This book may not be reproduced, in whole or in part, including illustrations in any form (beyond that copying permitted by Sections 107 and 108 of the U.S. Copyright Law and except by reviewers for public press), without written permission from the publisher.

Published by JewishGen, Inc.
An Affiliate of the Museum of Jewish Heritage
A Living Memorial to the Holocaust
36 Battery Place, New York, NY 10280

JewishGen, Inc. is not responsible for inaccuracies or omissions in the original work and makes no representations regarding the accuracy of this translation. Digital images of the original book's contents can be seen online at the New York Public Library website.

The mission of the JewishGen organization is to produce a translation of the original work, and we cannot verify the accuracy of statements or alter facts cited.

Printed in the United States of America by Lightning Source, Inc.

Library of Congress Control Number (LCCN): 2020946705
ISBN: 978-1-939561-88-6 (hard cover: 528 pages, alk. paper)

Cover Credits:

Front cover, top left: *Esther Israel née Goldansky, c.1872, courtesy of Lawrence Burgheimer. The photo would have been taken after her marriage to Max Louis Israel.*

Top right: *Peisakh Tzigelnitzki (Siegel), from a June 6, 1926 Voronova postcard to his sister-in-law, Elke Siegel (née Meirowitz) in New York City. Courtesy of Laura Ann Levy.*

Bottom: *Rywa Szejman (Sheyman) with daughters Masha, Chaya, and Fruma, c.1927. Courtesy of Miriam Mehlman. Melhman is the daughter of Berel Szejman (Benny Simon), the girls' brother.*

Background: *1915 Map showing Voronów, from Karte des westlichen Russlands. Public domain. Source: Topographic Maps of Eastern Europe, easteuropetopo.org, held by Geography and Map Division, Library of Congress.*

Back cover, top: *Cantor, ritual slaughterer and inspector Yehuda Konopke, c.1965 in Israel. From the original book.*

Back cover, left: *Saul Goldansky, c.1872, courtesy of Larry Burgheimer. The photo would have been taken around the time of his marriage to Gisia (Jenny Grace) Wedlansky. The couple emigrated to the U.S. starting in 1881, and settled in Missouri.*

JewishGen and the Yizkor Books in Print Project

This book has been published by the **Yizkor Books in Print Project**, as part of the **Yizkor Book Project** of JewishGen, Inc.

JewishGen, Inc. is a non-profit organization founded in 1987 as a resource for Jewish genealogy. Its website [www.jewishgen.org] serves as an international clearinghouse and resource center to assist individuals who are researching the history of their Jewish families and the places where they lived. JewishGen provides databases, facilitates discussion groups, and coordinates projects relating to Jewish genealogy and the history of the Jewish people. In 2003, JewishGen became an affiliate of the **Museum of Jewish Heritage—A Living Memorial to the Holocaust** in New York.

The **JewishGen Yizkor Book Project** was organized to make more widely known the existence of Yizkor (Memorial) Books written by survivors and former residents of various Jewish communities throughout the world. Later, volunteers connected to the different destroyed communities began cooperating to have these books translated from the original language—usually Hebrew or Yiddish—into English, thus enabling a wider audience to have access to the valuable information contained within them. As each chapter of these books was translated, it was posted on the JewishGen website and made available to the general public.

The **Yizkor Books in Print Project** began in 2011 as an initiative to print and publish Yizkor Books that had been fully translated, so that hard copies would be available for purchase by the descendants of these communities and also by scholars, universities, synagogues, libraries, and museums.

These Yizkor books have been produced almost entirely through the volunteer effort of researchers from around the world, assisted by donations from private individuals. The books are printed and sold at near cost, so as to make them as affordable as possible. Our goal is to make this important genre of Jewish literature and history available in English in book form, so that people can have the personal histories of their ancestral towns on their bookshelves for themselves and for their children and grandchildren.

A list of all published translated Yizkor Books in the project with prices and ordering information can be found at:
http://www.jewishgen.org/Yizkor/ybip.html

Lance Ackerfeld, Yizkor Book Project Manager
Joel Alpert, Yizkor-Book-in-Print Project Coordinator
Susan Rosin, Yizkor-Book-in-Print Project Associate Coordinator

This book is presented by the
Yizkor-Books-In-Print Project
Project Coordinator: Joel Alpert

Part of the Yizkor Books Project of JewishGen. Inc.
Project Manager: Lance Ackerfeld

These books have been produced solely through efforts of volunteers from around the world. The books are printed using the Print-on-Demand technology and sold at near cost, to make them as affordable as possible.

Our goal is to make this intimate history of the destroyed Jewish shtetls of Eastern Europe available in book form in English, so that people can experience the near-personal histories of their ancestral town on their bookshelves and those of their children and grandchildren.

All donations to the Yizkor Books Project, which translated the books, are sincerely appreciated.

Please send donations to:

Yizkor Book Project
JewishGen, Inc.
36 Battery Place
New York, NY, 10280

JewishGen, Inc. is an affiliate of the
Museum of Jewish Heritage
A Living Memorial to the Holocaust

Notes to the Reader:

We apologize ahead of time for the poor quality of images in the book. Often these images had been scanned from the original Yizkor books, which were of poor quality to begin with, being copies of old photographs. Each transfer results in loss of quality. We have done the best we could, given the original material and the resources and technology at hand. Even though images often appear of higher quality on computer screens, that does not transfer to high quality images in print. A reader can view the original scans on the web sites listed below.

Within the text the reader will note "{34}" standing ahead of a paragraph. This indicates that the material translated below was on page 34 of the original book. However, when a paragraph was split between two pages in the original book, the marker is placed in this book after the end of the paragraph for ease of reading.

Also please note that all references within the text of the book to page numbers, refer to the page numbers of the original Yizkor Book.

The original book can be seen online at the New York Public Library site:

https://digitalcollections.nypl.org/items/07a1cbe0-28b8-0133-d172-58d385a7bbd0
or at the Yiddish Book Center web site:

https://www.yiddishbookcenter.org/collections/yizkor-books/yzk-nybc313666/rabin-h-voronovah-sefer-zikaron-li-kedoshe-voronovah-she-nispu-be-shoat

In order to obtain a list of all Shoah victims from Voronova, the reader should access the Yad Vashem web site listed below; one can also search for specific family names using family name option. These lists are continually updated by Yad Vashem, so it is worthwhile to periodically search these lists.

There is much valuable information available on this web site, including the Pages of Testimony, etc.
http://yvng.yadvashem.org

A list of this book and all books available in the Yizkor-Book-In-Print Project along with prices is available at:
http://www.jewishgen.org/Yizkor/ybip.html

Geopolitical Information:

Voranava, Belarus
The town is located at 54°09' N 25°20' E 92 miles West of Minsk

Period	Town	District	Province	Country
Before WWI (c. 1900):	Voronovo	Lida	Vilna	Russian Empire
Between the wars (c. 1930):	Woronów	Lida	Nowogródek	Poland
After WWII (c. 1950):	Voronovo			Soviet Union
Today (c. 2000):	Voranava			Belarus

Alternate names: Voranava [Belorussian], Voronovo [Russian], Woronów [Polish], Voronova [Yiddish], Varanavas [Lithuanian], Voranova, Voronov, Voronove, Werenów, Woronowo, Woranawa

Nearby Jewish Communities:
- Byenyakoni 7 miles N
- Šalčininkai, Lithuania 11 miles N
- Dieveniškės, Lithuania 12 miles ENE
- Eišiškes, Lithuania 14 miles W
- Radun 15 miles WSW
- Lipnishki 15 miles SE
- Lida 18 miles S
- Jašiunai, Lithuania 21 miles N
- Iwye 23 miles SE
- Gav'ya 23 miles SSE
- Traby 24 miles E
- Laibiškės, Lithuania 24 miles NNE
- Valkininkai, Lithuania 24 miles NW
- Degsnės, Lithuania 26 miles NW
- Halshany 28 miles ENE
- Rudamina, Lithuania 30 miles N
- Ashmyany 30 miles NE

Jewish Population in 1897: 1,432

Location of Voronova indicated

Voronova Memorial Book

Hebrew Title Page of Original Yizkor Book

ווֹרוֹנוֹבה
ספר זכרון לקדושי ווֹרוֹנוֹבה
שנספו בשואת הנאצים
בשנים 1941–1944

העורך:
ח. רבין

המערכת:
מאיר שמיר, יהושע שומרוני ז"ל, שלמה אביאל

ועדת הספר:
ש. אביאל, ז. דוקשטולסקי, ש. לוין, נ. צור, ג. קמנצקי,
ח. רוטברט, מ. שמיר, יהושע שומרוני ז"ל

Translation of the Title Page of the Original Yizkor Book

Voronova

Memorial Book to the Martyrs of Voronova Who Perished in the Nazi Holocaust
In the years 1941 - 1944

Editor:
H. Rabin

Editorial Board:
Meir Shamir, Yehoshua Shomroni z"l, Shlomo Aviel

Book Committee:
S. Aviel, Z. Dokshtolski, S. Levin, N. Tzur, G. Kaminetski,
H. Rotbard, M. Shamir, Yehoshua Shomroni z"l

הוצא על ידי ארגון עולי ורונובה בישראל
בתמיכת הסוסייטי בארצות הברית

עצוב השער והעטיפה רחל פרוסט
שנת התשל"א

Translation of previous page

Published by the Organization of Voronova Residents in Israel
With support of the Society in the US

Graphic Design of Title Page and Book Cover: Rachel Frost

In the year 5731 (1971)

Voronova: Memorial Book to the Martyrs of Voronova (Voranava, Belarus)
54°09' / 25°20'

Translation of

Voronova; sefer zikaron le-kedoshei Voronova she-nispu be-shoat ha-natsim

Edited by: H. Rabin, Voronova Societies in Israel and the United States

Published in Israel, 1971

Acknowledgments

Project Coordinator and Translation Editor: Adam Cherson

Emeritus Coordinator: Jack Gottlieb

This is a translation from: *Voronova; sefer zikaron le-kedoshei Voronova she-nispu be-shoat ha-natsim*

(Voronova: Memorial Book to the Martyrs of Voronova),

Editors: H. Rabin, Israel, Voronova Societies in Israel and the United States, 1971 (Hebrew and Yiddish, 440 pages).

וורונובה

ספר זכרון לקדושי ווראנובה
שנספו בשואת הנאצים
בשנים 1941 – 1944

העורך:

ח. רבין

המערכת:

טאיר שמיר, יהושע שומרוני ז"ל, שלמה אביאל

ועדת הספר:

ש. אביאל, ז. דולשטילסקי, ש. לוין, נ. צור, ג. קמנצקי,
ח. רוטברט, מ. טמיר, יהושע שומרוני ז"ל

Introduction to the Translation

The uncanny ability to make history real is the source of a Yizkor Book's power. This power is manifest in the Voronove book, an extraordinary resource for historians, genealogists, and scholars. When combined with the speed and accuracy of internet searching, the inherent values of the work are magnified and honored in precisely the way its original editors had in mind when they asked us to: "…make a place of honor for this book, that you'll look at it from time to time when your heart feels like remembering our special town and our holy martyrs, and that it may interest your children for generations to come."

I am forever grateful to the translators who have worked for pittances on this project. Their names may be found below the title of each of their articles and they should be treasured by the generations. We are likewise eternally indebted to the many generous, individual contributors whose funding made this translation possible, most notably Judy Baston, Jay D'Lugin, Mark Katz, and Anthony Rabin, and also to the project's initial director, Jack Gottlieb.

While I have made effort to remain faithful to the intent of the book's original authors, there are three areas in which an editorial decision has been made to departs from this principle:

- ➢ for the sake of indexing, the spellings of town names have been standardized throughout the book to conform with the Yiddish language versions of these names,

- ➢ similarly, the spellings of recurring names and surnames have been standardized to conform with the most commonly used versions of these names. An exception to this rule is the name of Voronove itself, which is standardized to Voronova in the Hebrew language portions of the book and to Voronove in the Yiddish language portions, and

> for the several articles which appear in both Hebrew and Yiddish language versions in the original book, only one translation is published here: in these instances, the article is placed where the original language version was placed (i.e., if the Hebrew version was used for the translation then the article appears in the Hebrew section, and vice versa); there also appears on the article's first page an "Editor's Note" detailing which of the language versions was used to make the translation.

I hope the public will find as much enlightenment, sustenance, pathos, and delight as I have in these pages.

Adam Benyakonski Cherson, 25 November 2020
Project Coordinator and Translation Editor

CONTENTS

TOC Hebrew translated by Sara Mages
TOC Yiddish translated by Yocheved Klausner

Town Map		10
Words from the Editorial Board		12
Additional Words and Appreciation	The Editor	18

Voronova – History and Importance

Voronova in the Sources and in the Voronova Book	H. Rabin	24
Image of Voronova, My Town	Shlomo Aviel Shmerkovitsh	34
Profile of a Town	Shlomo Pikovski	41

Holocaust and Heroism

From Bad to Worse	Meir Shamir (Shmerkovitsh)	46
My Holocaust Experience	Khenye Konopke	63
Thanks to Our Child	Moshe and Khayeh Kaplan	79
Final Days of Our Town	Keileh Grodzenchik (Shamir)	94
Ghettos and the Forest	M[eir] Shamir (Shmerkovitsh)	99
A Child's Gift During the Holocaust	K. Lisorski	155
A Son of Voronova's Heroism and Revenge	Zalmen Dukshtulski	155
Story of an Avenging Youth	Yekuthiel (Kushke) Boyarski	155
I Left for the Forest at Age 15	Ze'ev Kaplan	156
Unjust Regimes	Yitzach Ben-Ami	162
A Fifteen Year Old Boy in Fate's Hands	Yakov Olkenitski	162
My Miserable Russian Days	Bat Sheba Podesiuk (Kalmanovitsh)	169
Long is the Road to Zion	Yitzach Olkenitski	170
A Little More Revenge	Shmuel Kopelovitsh	174
My Revenge Against the Liquidator of Jews in Our Region	Moshe Kaplan	175
After the Underground	Y. Dvilianski	181
My Father is Summoning Me [Poem]	Shlomo Aviel (Shmerkovitsh)	185

Our Town – Memoirs, Images, Short Stories

Voronova: A Town of Blue and White	Yekhezkel Poz-Puziriski	189
A Town with a Marketplace and Neighborhoods	Shimon Levine	194
A Town of Unsettled Youth	Aharon Konikhovski (Krani)	199
"Chayei Adam"[1] Society and "Mishniyot" Society[2]	S. Levine	203

The Boulevards of Voronova [Poem]	Shlomo Aviel-Shmerkovitsh	207
The Rabbis and The Rabbinical Dispute	S. Levine	211
Yakov "Yankel" Kaminetski	M.S.V.	214
Illustrative Curiosities	Khaye Levine (Rothbart)	218
Women of Our Town	Aharon Karni (Konikhovski)	222
A Tale About a Telephone	Y. Poz (Puziriski)	223
A Tale About a Handshake	Y. Poz (Puziriski)	224

The Route to Redemption – Community, Movements, and Organizations

Hashomer HaTsair[3] Nest in Voronova	Abrashka Moltsadski (Sharid)	226
The Zionist and HeKhaluts[4] Movement in Voronova	M. Kuznets, of Blessed Memory	230
From the Memories of an Emissary	Yosef Bankover	234
Betar[5] in Voronova	A.A. Olkenitski, Khenyeh Konopke and Khaye Levine (Rothbart)	237
'Supplement' to the Image of *Betar*[5]	Shlomo Pikovski	241
Restless Youth (A Guide to Our Perplexed Town)	S. Levine	244
Impressions of a Teacher in Voronova	Tova Shomroni	249
Educators, Education, Educational Establishments, Educational Conditions, and *Melameds*	Shimon Levine	253
The Building and its Contents	Shimon Levine	258

Persons of Quality

The Zionist Veteran Nekhemye Shapira	Yehoshua Shomroni	263
Mr. Yosef Shmerkovitsh	M.S.V.	263
Reyzl Moltsadski	M.S.V.	269
The New Synagogue	Shimon Levine	272

Died in Israel

List of Voronova Residents Who Died in Israel		275
Eulogies For Those I Lament	S. Aviel	277
In Memory of Yehoshua, Of Blessed Memory	Aharon Karni	287
My Father Matisyahu, Of Blessed Memory	Prof. Moshe Kuznets	289
Reb Gottlieb Konikhovski, Of Blessed Memory	S. Aviel	291

The Yiddish Book

Our Shtete'le

I See You, My Little Town	V. Shomroni	295
Tsimes, Psalms, and Medicine	M. Kuznets	299

Little Memories	Y. Shomroni	302
To the First *Minyan* with the Cows	M. Kuznets	306
Voronove, Concept of Hospitality	A. Ginsburg	309
Let Us Recall	A. Konopke	310
The Zionist Veteran Nekhemye Shapira	Y. Shomroni	314
Memories, Types, and Victims	R. Gol	317
Direct and Indirect Paths to Zionism	Reuven Gol	321
The Society of Voronove in America – Isidore Dikson		328

Heroism and Destruction

Thanks to Our Child	Moshe and Khayeh Kaplan	332
Final Days of Our Town	K. Grodzenchik	332
In My Own "Partizanka"	Y. Konikhovski	333
An Involuntary Hero	Z. Dukshtulski	347
Our Child Saved Us	K. Lisorski	363
Exactly When It Rained	M. Konopke (Mutshnik)	369
A Child Partisan	Yekutiel (Kushke) Boyarski	379
Under Gentile Regimes	I. Ben–Ami	387
Death Before Our Eyes	R. Konopke–Mayortshik	404
Taking Some More Vengeance	S. Kopelovitsh	407
My Miserable Russian Days	Bat Sheba Podisiuk-Kalmanovitsh	414
In Memory of the Slaughtered Voronove Jews	H. Solodukha	419
This is How My Shtetl Marched to Death	M. Kaplan	422
Names of Voronove Martyrs		426
List of Voronove Immigrants to Israel		435

The Soletchnik (Šalčininkai) Book

The Tiny Town of "Great Soletchnik"	H. Kaplan	441
Soletchnik: Small but Great	K. Goldanski	447
Soletchnik on the Eve of Shoah	Chaim Kalai (Streletski)	453
A Home in Soletchnik	Yosef Krum	456
Velvele in Soletchnik	Chava Levine (Lieberman)	460
This is How My Mother Blessed Me	C. Levine (Lieberman)	461
How I Made *Aliyah*	Yosef Krum	463
Because of Wagner's Tractors	Chaim Kalai	464
List of Soletchnik People Living in the Diaspora and in Israel		467

The Great Soletchnik [Yiddish]

The Great Soletchnik [Y]	T. Krum	469
Generosity in My *Shtetl* [Y]	Esther Katz (Taibel)	475
Yakov Katz – Soletchnik's Poet [Y]	A.G. [Glikman]	481
A Silent Soul [Y]	A. Glikman	484

To Live I Want – to Live! [Y]	Yakov Katz	485
Flowers [Y]		486
Soletchnik and Soletchniker in Death [Y]	Tzemah Krum	487
Names of Soletchnik Martyrs		498
List of Soletchnik Residents Who Died in Israel		501

Book Indexes

Index of Names and Places	502

Translator's Footnotes:

1. The Life of Man
2. The first part of the *Talmud*, containing traditional oral interpretations of scriptural ordinances (Halakhot), compiled by the rabbis about 200, *From:* http://www.yourdictionary.com/mishnayot
3. The Pioneer - association of Jewish youth whose aim was to train its members to settle in Israel
4. Literally: Paths of Pleasantness
5. The initials of Brit Yosef Trumpeldor- The Covenant of Joseph Trumpeldor, the educational youth movement of the Revisionist Zionist Organization

[Unnumbered pages]

Voronova
As Etched in My Mind Near 1940
M. Shamir

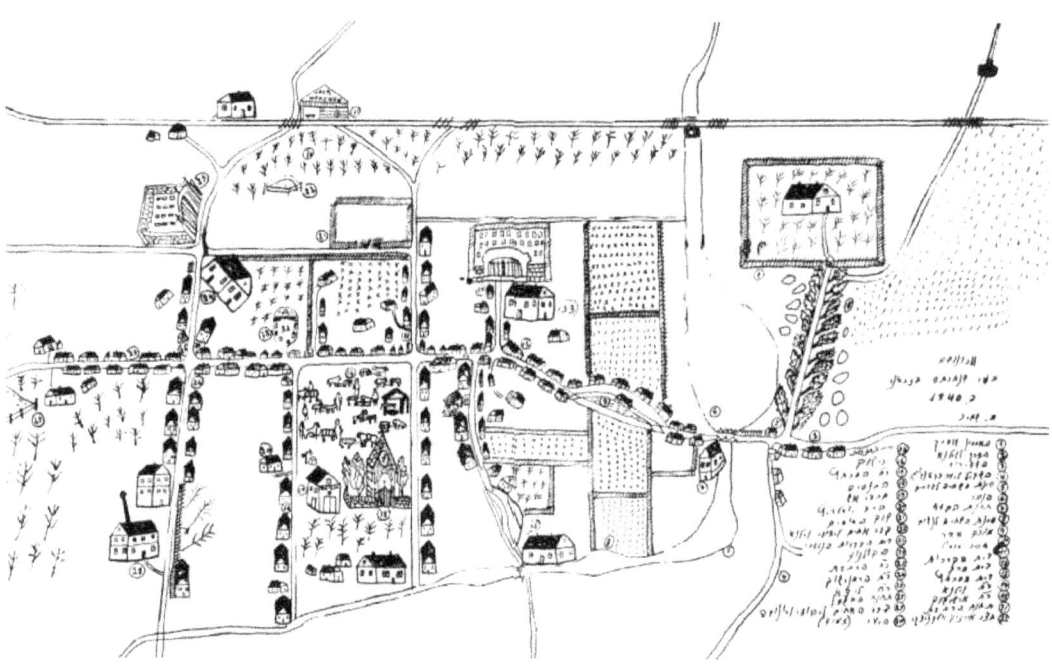

MAP KEY
Translation by Meir Bulman

1. Count Shvanbakh [Estate]
2. The road to Vilne
3. The avenues
4. The path to Bartnovsa Forest
5. Men's swim area
6. The river
7. The flourmill
8. Women's swim area
9. The hill
10. Swine St.*
11. The cemetery
12. The Rabbi's home
13. The bathhouse
14. Vilne Street
15. Eyshisok Street
16. The marketplace
17. The bathhouse street
18. The church
19. Firehouse
20. Rabbi Yosselovitsh
21. The Horse Market
22. Mass grave for Vilne Jews
23. The Christian cemetery
24. The movie theater
25. Train St.
26. Harminishok St.
27. Lida St.
28. The Electricity Mill
29. Mass grave for Jews of Voronova
30. The Forest (Smuk)
31. The train station
32. Yitzach Olkenitski yard
33. The Synagogue

*Tr. Note: partially legible, inferred from text at p.43

[Page 5]

Words from the Editorial Board

Translation by Emma Karabelnik

The Book of Voronova is being published now, 25 years after the end of the nightmare that brought our nation's extermination, followed by the purification of the world from the Nazi damage. This book is a symbol of the eternity of the nation of Israel, a tool to pass the torch from generation to generation, to continue to tell the story, and to prolong the chain.

The book's editorial committee stepped away from the quotidian, dedicating nights and vacations to the publication, seeing it as their privilege to bring to life the voices of their generation, and thus creating a memory and a monument to the martyrs buried in scattered mass graves without a gravestone and without a name.

We accepted the duty placed upon us by the Voronova Olim Community[1], and we did our best to accomplish the mission and to justify their trust. We know that no human is free from mistakes, and probably we also erred in our actions, our inter-relations, or the contents, but we hope that every member of the community can understand that any such inaccuracies or omissions were neither malicious nor deliberate. Those who act – make mistakes, but the fact and the outcome of the deed is greater than those small inaccuracies, and we hope to be forgiven.

***

And now to the contents of the book and its format:

We imagined our book as the last diary of the Voronova Community, whose Jews entered the history books in a most tragic way, and we, the survivors, must write down this history, the life and the annihilation.

We imagined our book as a testament to a most horrible crime committed by the world, which stood by while our blood spilled and did nothing for us; we, the survivors, must testify to and document the details of the crime for the sake of future generations and in order to bring this crime to the court of history.

We imagined our book as a monument to our dear ones, the victims of the terrible crimes, who have no gravestones or obituaries; we, their descendants, must raise a monument for them which to preserve their memories and their spirit.

And this is the format of the book: Community Diary, Monument, Historical Account, and Petition for Justice to all nations.

***

While writing the chapters about Voronova's history we discovered the town to have been under siege for all of its existence – a tale of closure and fortification. The physical enclosure brought upon us by the enemy, and the spiritual fortifications which the Jewish Community took upon itself to keep and preserve under any circumstances and at any price.

During its long wanderings our nation has always made an effort to detach itself from everyday realities in the Diaspora and to attach instead to the abstract idea of a distant homeland in Zion, thus developing an amazing ability to adapt to almost any condition by creating a magical circle in which to preserve the spirit and legacy of the forefathers, in which the outer world has no control or say. The town of Voronova was created in this spirit: a fortress for people to abstain from present-life worrying by remaining in a state of constant longing for a glorious former kingdom, while anticipating the glorious future which would one day come as a direct continuation of this past.

For this reason we dedicated a whole chapter to the history of the town's spirituality, its institutions for the education of younger generations, its community life, and its special events. In this chapter one may discover the marvelous organizational skills of our nation, which succeeds in creating a community life under any conditions and circumstances, in order to maintain a harmonic and organized society—with no need for a higher authority.

In this town, like in other Jewish towns, one finds several outstanding personalities standing out in their willingness to act publicly to preserve Community life, as well as idealists whose activity becomes their entire world while they live in anticipation and hope. That's why we saw a need to describe some of these persons, as much as our memory allowed us. In this way we preserve the memory of these people and of their positive values which should be passed on as a legacy to our new young nation, out of a feeling their examples will be needed in the future.

We allowed people to write their personal memories and experiences, thus revealing Voronova as a cultivator of warmth and heartiness, as well revealing the writers as individuals of ideals and vision, whose souls are torn between their love for the homeland where they were born and the homeland they long for now. The fact that they are drawn to their homeland and yet they ARE here, remembering their hometown and their old parents, proves that there was a conflict in their hearts which they succeeded in overcoming.

***

While writing the town's history for the last time, we had to recount its last days and those of its martyrs. These stories became chapters of blood and tears told by individuals who were victims of those awful atrocities – chapters of indescribable human suffering and human challenge. These chapters are additional live-evidence of the atrocities brought upon the Jewish nation, their detailed truth become a bill of indictment to the indifferent world which now walks on blood, an accusation against people who are deeply obliged to us. We won't be calm or rest until this obligation is fully fulfilled by the insurance of a future for our nation in its homeland.

From these chapters we learn extraordinary life stories of individuals who stuck to each other at every opportunity in order to gain strength and preserve their Judaism. Voronova was lucky to be surrounded by vast forests where Jews succeeding to escape from the ghettos found shelter. Their stories describe desperate suffering, depression, and humiliation, and also great moments of heroism and revenge which make this book special: it's not another depressing book of "like sheep to slaughter". It is about finding the last remnants of heroism and human spirit in the fight for dignity and existence conducted by self-appointed heroes who fought our enemies, and from the floors of their dugouts in the forests took revenge for Jewish lives on murderers of all nationalities.

We did not limit the number of pages in the book for these forest chapters, and compared to other chapters in the book we took special pride in them. It concerns not only the people of Voronova but all those Jews who saved what was left of our national dignity. This book is different from other distressing literature describing Jewish suffering, because it contains heroism and revenge. In these chapters of heroism we being to disprove the disgraceful image of weakness sometimes painted over our nation in *Galuth*.[2] No nation has withstood what we withstood, what the people of Voronova withstood. As editors of this book, we take great pride in this.

***

There are additional chapters in the book which may look out of place and too lighthearted for this book of sorrow, but at second glance they glimmer like gemstones or shining crystals describing our virtues. During the long years of Jewish ideological and tragic history, we developed unique qualities such as being satisfied with little, lowering one's head in public while remaining proud on the inside, being able to mock everyday worries, being able to belittle external cares while taking seriously matters of the soul, and other human characteristics deeply engraved by our nation's past and had to be described in our book.

We tried not to be tendentious and not to "edit history" when choosing the materials. We told everything. We wanted to show Voronova as it was – great in its smallness and rare in its events. Such are the chapters on Rabbinical conflicts, neighbors' relations, petty quarrels and their causes. All combined together to create a spectacular picture of their lives, small lives with great vision of their national legacy, showing a great, if flawed, humanity.

***

The last chapter is dedicated to names, according to our national custom. As it is known, our nation was the first to make graves for their dead and to honor them with a stone and a name.[3] In ancient times, when other nations buried their dead in family yards without any sign or name, our nation chose to designate a special area for all the deceased, thus recognizing the holiness of every single individual, emphasizing that there all are equal and together, but also that each one has his own name to be remembered forever.

Our book is a gravestone for those who were buried anonymously, for our loved ones who were buried alive where slaughtered with no headstone or name on their grave. The headstones engraved with names, as written on the pages of this book, are a great victory over those who tried to wipe out our names from the surface of the Earth. While our murderers' ashes are scattered by the winds and dispersed on the earth, the names of their victims are now written on the pages of this book to be remembered forever.

We wrote the names of our loved-ones in alphabetical order, to emphasize their, and our, togetherness. The common tragedy united us into one. The alphabetical list is available to and searchable by everyone. From A to Z they all belong to us, and from time to time we'll look and find them.

***

Dear friends and relatives we present you this book with a feeling of consummation in the task of saving our dear ones from their anonymity.

We feel that as People of the Book, in this tome we have established an eternal monument to our dear-ones, a monument that no winds can wipe of its inscriptions, and no human filth can ever pollute. It is a solid monument bringing the memory of the dead to us, to our homes, to our cities, and to the countries where we live.

We hope that you'll make a place of honor for this book, that you'll look at it from time to time when your heart feels like remembering our special town and our holy martyrs, and that it may interest your children for generations to come.

May the memory of our martyrs stay forever in our hearts.

Final remark: This book also includes chapters on "Big Soletchnik", our neighboring town, whose memory would be lost forever without our help to its last survivors. We have helped the people from Soletchnik to establish a monument for their martyrs, and it's our pleasure and satisfaction to take this initiative and willingness to assist them. And thus Soletchnik will not be lost.

All the above said about the Voronova book is true for Soletchnik, and though there are fewer chapters, the story is full and complete and that's why it's a great achievement.

The Book Committee: Standing, right to left: **H. Klei, G. Kaminetski, K. Rothbart-Levine, Z. Dukshtulski, M. Kaplan**; *Seated, right to left:* **E. Taibl-Katz, Y. Poz-Puziriski, N. Tsur-Shapira, M. Shamir-Shmerkovitsh, S. Aviel-Shmerkovitsh**

Footnotes:

1. Ed. Note: Community of persons from Voronova who made *aliyah* to Israel.
2. Ed. Note: i.e., living in exile
3. Ed. Note: The author here refers to the practice of marking graves

[Page 10]

Additional Words and Appreciation

From the Editor

Translation by Emma Karabelnik

During work on the Voronova book I had a feeling of excitement. For the first time I was able to add the word 'heroism' to the word 'shoah'. It is not a typical book. Besides being a monument to a lost community, to the town and its residents so dear to us all, this book became a symbol of dignity for the Jewish people who succeeded, in spite of those horrible conditions created by Nazism, in keeping the will to live, to escape to the forests, to fight the oppressors, and to survive.

To our knowledge, there is no other nation in history who has been able to withstand such conditions. Many other nations have surrendered to fate, been assimilated, and offered their necks under less cruel and oppressive conditions, only to perish.

Therefore, the people of Voronova, and others like them who escaped to the forests, took upon themselves the mission of preserving Judaism, because they didn't want to persist only as individuals. Their desire to survive was, in the name of "Am Israel Chai",[1] to return to the Motherland, to destroy the enemy, and to oppose physical violence with the powers of spirit and will.

We gained this power from the Book, the Bible, its continuity throughout generations. The books of Maccabim, Hashmonaim, and others as well, taught us to live for the sake of the idea of a Nation of the Book and of the human spirit. The Voronova book will teach succeeding generations to live in their homeland, to be cautious about leaving the homeland again, thereby putting us in danger of persecution, and to view the main goal of life as the nurturing of the Jewish nation after proving its heroism in the forests of Lida and Voronova.

The aspiration of all humanity is for the victory of the forces of heroism, and the spirit of the Book, over the forces of rape, aggression and cruelty; the heroism put to the test during the Holocaust gives such hope to all of humanity.

Therefore we must cherish those who created the book of Voronova, who sacrificed their nights and free time to establish a monument for your loved ones, and at the same time contributed tales of human heroism to the national literature.

Blessed be the members of the editorial committee: Yehoshua Shomroni OBM, who devoted his last days to this book, aware of his shortness of time, and may they live long, Meir Shamir Shmerkovitsh and Shlomo Aviel (Ed. Note: Shlomo Shamir-Shmerkovitsh), who put all his enthusiasm into this book and added his own impressions, and Meir Shamir who took over where others had failed, succeeding in the mission due to his energy and devotion. [He] took care of every small detail, from collecting money for publication, to collecting materials from people all over the country, and he served the Voronova Olim Association[2] in creating a meaningful monument for your loved ones.

The fact that a monument has been raised for our dear parents, beloved brothers, childhood friends, and others who don't have a gravestone or grave marker, and the fact that this book of testimony exists is thanks to them, and we should all be grateful to them.

As Editor, I take this opportunity to thank the Book Committee, who left behind their day-to-day cares and dedicated their nights and efforts to the cause. Their participation in the creation of the book added a public value to the work, and as members of the Voronova Association they honored that organization.

Editor's Footnotes:
1. Well known Hebrew phrase meaning: the Jewish nation lives
2. Association of persons from Voronova who made *aliyah* to Israel

[Page 12]

Book Portraits of Voronova Authors

Translation by Emma Karabelnik

For some reason these photos were not printed next to their articles as they were in other sections.

We understand and accept this oversight.

S. Aviel
Image of Voronova, My Town – 20

Y. Poz
Voronova: A Town of Blue and White – 169

A. Moltsadski
HaShomer HaTsair Nest in Voronova – 199

S. Levine
*A Town with a Marketplace
and Neighborhoods – 173*

K. Rothbart
Illustrative Curiosities – 190

A. Krani
A Town of Unsettled Youth – 177

S. Peyrovitsh [sic]
Profile of a Town – 25

[Page 13]

Voronova – History and Importance

[Pages 13-19]

Voronova in the Sources and in the Voronova Book

H. Rabin

Translation by Meir Bulman

A. Bibliography

I. *Slovnik Geographytshni*

Velveskli Publishing, 1884

Editors: Bronislav and Philip Hlibolinski,

"Voronov – a town and estate on the Blozianka Yovlo[1] of the Zhizmeh[2] is situated 32 versts[3] from Lida, 59 from Vilna,[4] and 20 from Eyshishok.[5] Part of the Lida District, Benakani Municipality.

… There are 42 homes in the town, 18 Russian Orthodox residents, 177 Catholics, and 333 Jews. There are two synagogues, 2 leather workshops, 12 shops and a wind mill operated by a stream and waterfall. V. is famous for its baked bagels.

… It is known that the town was under the complete ownership of the now defunct Geshtuld[6] dynasty. It is therefore inferred that Voronov existed before the 14th century, when those rulers ceased to exist. It is not mentioned in the royal certificate and judicial proceedings. 13 villages are a part of Voronov."

II. *Encyclopedia Pubshkhna*, 1867

"... named Voronov situated about 60 versts from Vilna,[7] a part of the Lida district and the Benakani municipality.

...V. does not appear in the royal ledgers and judicial proceeding, because, as is well known, was owned by the Shlohim[8] Family. In 1730, Yan Shlohim built a Collegium and schools for writing and accounting in Voronov.

...it was once a rich estate profitable for its owner. Today, it is a very poor town and has 52 houses and 334 residents."

III. *Yevreyskaya Encyclopedia*, 1908

Edited by Dr. A. Harkabi and Dr. L. Katznelson

"Vornovo – a town in the Lida district, Vilna region. In 1847, the "Vornovo Community" included 199 individuals.

In 1897, the whole of Vornovo included for 1574 individuals, 1432 of them Jews."

B. History and Order

We have quoted *Slovnik Geographychni* first, although *Pubshkhna* Encyclopedia was published earlier, because according to the *Slovnik* Voronova had already existed in the 14th century. Additionally, it is known that *Slovnik* was funded by the Polish Catholic Church, which conducted its research thoroughly; the objectivity of its conclusions is assured due to its primary editor (who was Jewish).

According to *Slovnik*, Voronova was "a town and estate", meaning a town center for village–estates founded by members of some dynasty. As is known, estate owners were warriors who received their estates as rewards for war efforts, and to maintain royal control over estate residents. As warriors, who knew nothing about agricultural administration and communal matters, estate owners always hired Jews as customs officials, tax collectors, and farm handlers, whose central focus was not agricultural planning but expanding production outcomes by encouraging work produced by contracted villagers.

It should be presumed that from its inception Voronova as a community was different from others as it was the center of 13 villages situated on the shores of a high river nourishing its surroundings. The presumption rises when one reads that in a community of 333 Jewish residents there was both a synagogue and a study house. Two conclusions follow: the financial ability of the community to establish two religious institutions, and its ability to maintain both. One also learns this way of the differences among community members: a class whose religion was manifested in prayer alone, and another whose religion is manifested in a study house where both prayer and study are mixed. Such religious groupings are also inferred from histories of other communities. What is unusual is that this was manifested in such a small community at that time. No sources mention small communities where there was such a differentiation — not in that century and not with that population size.

The distance between Voronova and the metropolitan areas and the length of forest between them indicate that it was a self-sustaining community. We add that the estate owners did not use Jewish workers from Lida or Vilna, instead they saw the need of establishing their own town. Therefore, we can infer that they were Jews [in Voronova] recognized as possessing the necessary skills. Such skills were also of a different kind, which is quite interesting: failures of estate owners stemmed from a lack of ability to maximize production from laborers in spite of the pressures of serfdom, or perhaps resulting from those methods. Thus, the Jews invited to [administer estates] were faced with a social/communal challenge. Jews were tasked with gaining control of apathetic human dust and motivating productivity. They did so by organizing villages and linking laborers to the land, so laborers looked upon these fields as a blessing. Jews had to change the historical relationship of masters and peasant by turning servants into tenant–farmers who received a share of the yield. By increasing workers' interests in the fields and the work, Jews also turned masters into partners who cared about the wellbeing and social spirit of the workers.

We add that those Jews were willing to uphold their Judaism even while detached from the world of central Torah and religion. Despite

Voronova's forest–covered conditions and the poor communication methods of the time, the Jews remained consciously firm in their faith.

Thus, Voronova originated as a planned settlement intended to change agricultural and social standards. We therefore infer the first Jews in Voronova were administratively talented men, just as from a Jewish perspective they were firm in their faith and adherents of a Jewish historical vision.

Residents and Employment

The sources are in dispute as to the population size. The cause of this inaccuracy is important, but we are not currently interested in exploring that here. Instead, we will contrast the figures and the conclusions arising from each.

The *Encyclopedia Pubsh.* notes that in 1867 "the town had 52 houses and 334 residents." In contrast, *Slovnik* notes that in 1884 there were 42 houses. Yet, the number of residents is 468, and the number of Jews is like the general population figures in *En. Pubsh.*

Moreover, the *Yevreyskaya Encyclopedia*, the sole Jewish source, states that in 1847, the community, meaning the Jews, numbered 199 and in 1897, fifty years later, 1432 Jews.

It is difficult to determine what is fact and what is hypothetical, and we will assist those seeking to draw conclusions with two pieces of information:

1. The *Y. Encyclopedia* editorial board based its figures on two censuses conducted in Czarist Russia in the territories annexed by the partitions of Poland. The first, in 1847, was done under rushed circumstances during regime changes and its figures are usually inaccurate. The census in 1897 was done under Russian control and was conducted and funded by Jews, mostly founded by the famed Baron Ginsburg, and should be assumed it is the correct one. The inaccuracy of the figure of 199 Jews in 1847 is also refuted by the two Gentile sources which are paralleled in their size and time. We are left to wonder only about the large increase of 333 Jews in 1884 (*Slov. Georg.*) to 1432 in 1897, a rapid 430% increase that we have not seen in

any other Jewish town.

We have no sources explaining the sudden increase. It is indicative of a local tragedy that caused wandering Jews to seek refuge in a sibling community, or of [economic] abundance in Voronova that attracted Jews. Demographic changes in Jewish towns always followed similar patterns. Seeking refuge or relief were always motives for wandering in the history of Jewish exile. We are uncertain about the reasons for the attraction. We have no sources documenting the abundance or the absorption capabilities in Voronova, and we are left solely with logical inferences, but not written facts.

2. A second fact on population size figures is that the two Christian versions were based solely on tax payer figures, and thus do not speak as to people but residents. Therefore, one should assume the final figure of the *Yevreyskaya Encyclopedia* (Russian) is correct, as 333 taxpayers mean a much larger number of people.

We emphasize the part about 12 flour mill stores, 2 leather processing workshops, and the famous bagel bakeries. Those figures serve as evidence of our assumption of the quality of the early Jewish residents of the town.

C. Voronova in this Book

This book is both a community ledger and an effort to complete the community's history for the sake of future generations. Voronova in its communal activities comes across as a town tired of activism where few jumped at the chance of community leadership as a means of quickly achieving fame or fortune. For many years, secular communal issues were determined by men of noble appearance who arrived to the town and were appointed as 'staroste'. The staroste was a quasi–mayor who the community did not choose nor was obligated to obey. At times, they were a positive force for their brethren and communal matters progressed due to their guidance.

Occasionally, people volunteered for certain projects, ceasing the activity once the task was completed. Yet, communal activism was not pronounced in Voronova.

Residents did not enthusiastically jump at the chance of maintaining Godly matters or of administering the synagogue. Even if people witnessed their houses of worship decaying, nobody paid any attention nor repaired them. It happened that at certain times there was a Gabbai who devoted himself to some issue and raised funds to repair the synagogues. The community did not examine him further and would pay him any amount levied upon them in his rounded, illegible handwriting in deep gratitude for a service which no other person had accepted. Sometimes the community was blessed with a respectable Gabbai, a man of many deeds who invested energy in quality administration. Such a man was respectable in a manner befitting the role and he and his image were honored by the community.

Unlike other communities, Voronova was inert concerning its future. Everything seemed on a downward path, and folks hoped for a change to come allowing redemption from the town, but nobody lifted a finger. Therefore, town elders were thrilled when the youth moved towards any activity promising redemption, and such activity won the support and encouragement of all.

The Voronova community was weary; no person worked on its behalf. As a town close to Vilna, it survived on Vilna's personal and cultural life. Voronova knew not of Hasidism and was unaware of the dispute concerning Hasidism. That lively rejuvenation passed over it. Voronova was spared the trickery of "miracle–working rabbis" and other such elements offering a mirage of redemption to the people. However, this lack of liveliness discouraged any desire for community activism. In most communities, activism was a main contributing factor to redemption and the search for a national path.

As stated, only the youth strove for such activism, and all others approved. However, most of the community was steeped in the depths of a difficult livelihood and most hearts were not veered towards matters such as the duties or privileges of community.

Occasionally, lone people rose and paved paths to redemption from their hearts and were pioneers of Zionism, but they were few: although they were admired, they did not become role models or leaders to follow.

The glory of Voronova in its older times attracted rabbis of fame and stature. Rabbis were honored to have the title of "Rabbi of Voronova," and the town was blessed to be led by noteworthy rabbis. As time passed, those rabbis were cured of the delusion called the 'Voronova community'. The community's apathy eventually discouraged them and they would leave.

Such events were repeated several times and caused something of a beneficial shock within the community. Of course, no Jew wants to stay without a rabbi present, because perhaps one's Judaism would be harmed, condemning one's soul, and delaying the footsteps of the messiah. Suddenly, the community would show great concern about appointing a rabbi and an emotional swirl would take place.

Disputes concerning rabbis were an unusual occurrence in the calm life of the Voronova community. Once such a dispute erupted, it was difficult to stop. It became a chance for town notables to examine their scholarliness. More than a mere concern for finding a rabbi befitting the town, these moments saw a tendency of town notables to face off against the nominated rabbi and his rivals for the crown of Torah. Men of Torah whose Torah skills had declined, suddenly found an opportunity to test themselves and see if their Torah within was still alive, and if the community still had any use for their knowledge. In the end, the Voronova community was 'blessed' by a startling awakening and had no other choice but to bear the financial burden of providing for two rabbis, for the sake of peace and to repair its previously harmed image. From then on, there was no "Rabbi of Voronova," and instead there was the Kletzker Rav and the Myadler Rav, and the town's diminishing glory fell even further.

Culture and Education

As in every Jewish town, Voronova too was a fortress of tradition where education was concerned. As regimes changed, the community withstood pressure from authorities for a dictated education, and the town remained loyal to the *cheder* education. When assessing the risk of educating children for a life fully devoted to heaven, obstructing any chance of professional and educational progress, there too they decided on siding with the heavens.

Children were educated in various institutions founded by individuals as a source of income. Here the great naïvete of the founders was reflected by the parents' inability to make crucial changes. Parents showed an amazingly strong will as to their children's fate, forming an unshakeable will to link their children to the nation's fate, a nation that rejected the nonsense of the Gentiles and accepted the burden of waiting for the messiah. The decision was made at the expense of the well-being of the children and of fortifying their future as individuals, and in spite of the fact that one still had to pass the national test. Without objection, the children were handed over to be educated by teachers who were loyal to the Torah but were disappointing as educators and path-setters.

As the Zionist awakening took place, a school was founded by *Tarbut* with the consent of the rabbi. Since then, the children of Voronova encountered a true education, including a concern for both the Jewish individual and the nation.

The cultural life of older generations of Voronovans was limited to a few classes studying *The Life of Man* and *Mishna*. Centuries passed like that until the awakening in the Jewish world arrived. As oppressed nations and exploited classes began awakening, Voronova too was affected by the spirit pf progress. The youth founded libraries, theater companies, and discussion groups. There was still no solid formation of views on worldly issues, but there was a curiosity and a search for a path, an examination of everything, and a move towards a new life and a new culture.

Since then, Voronova joined its counterparts and tied its liveliness to the liveliness of the Jewish nation and exited its cultural and national isolation.

Form this perspective the last days of Voronova were days of public alertness, cultural activism, and intensive Hebrew education. Matters in town continued as usual, but activism focused on redemption and the paths to redemption. Many groups formed; a common path led them all to Zion. There lies greatness and change.

Economy and Livelihood – Like all Jewish towns in Poland, Voronova struggled greatly for its livelihood. Poland, land of oversights and barren economic regimes, left its naturally rich land to remain in an agricultural slumber and Jewish territory continually decreased. Poland's hatred for Jews left no room allowing Jews to develop industry and trade, as they so diligently knew. Instead of encouraging the Jews, Poland imposed taxes on them and excluded them from existing industries. That situation left an even greater mark on Voronova. Voronova was a town hostile to Poland, which turned the exclusion of Jews into political necessity. The residents' anger at the authorities was turned towards the Jews, "the blood suckers," and instilled in the Gentile residents a sense of gratitude to the authorities. From that perspective the town's struggle was like that of other Jewish towns, but more difficult due to its Lithuanian location. Jews lived from crumbs of income as middlemen between the villages and Vilna, as the ground dropped beneath their own feet. Because of anti–Semitic economic discrimination, Voronova's status as a town gradually diminished, nearly disappeared, and remained a middle-point between villages and the city. Livelihood depended on a combination of trade, acting as a middleman, and delivery of goods. Tradesmen descended to the level of middlemen, middlemen became coachmen delivering merchandise, and coachmen searched for constructive use of any available, vacant horse. This was strengthened with some supporting income from minor agriculture, which many in town did for generations, increasing in the final years of the town.

The most depressing days in the town were market days. Those were days of economic activity with big hopes at the start and then big disappointments by their end.

The economic downturn signaled the end and was felt more and more strongly, causing all to think about emigration and *Aliyah*. But the poor odds of being able to emigrate erased the will or initiative for change. Voronova was split in its final years: on one side, a helpless older population, and on the other side, a lively and energetic youth jumping at the chance of desirable and crucial emigration.

As the Holocaust arrived, the Enemy found a town whose residents desirous of leaving the country and waited only for the chance to leave. If not for bloodlust, the Enemy could have "purified" Voronova of its Jews by allowing them to travel to Israel and this perceived problem would have been solved, but instead the choice was for massacre.

The criminal partnership between the Enemy and his collaborators is highlighted by the Holocaust of Voronova and other towns. The Enemy spilled the blood of Jews to intoxicate the occupied masses, and they drank our blood willingly to intoxication. It was murder for murder's sake without economic or demographic justification.

When Voronova stopped existing, it was a community of hard workers, living on the fruits of their labor, looking for a place to invest, to make a living, and wait for the day when they could leave the nation. Voronova was a community of pure and kind Jews who sacrificed generations at the altar of the great hope, remaining loyal to the nation, yet disappointed in their efforts.

For historians, Voronova will serve as a lesson and example, like a good man who remains loyal to leaders who are too weak to solve his problems. For anthropologists, Voronova will remain a social experiment of people who wanted to remain a society without government, army, or bloodshed but were mistaken and paid for that mistake with their existence.

Researchers of the Nazi crimes will find the tragic testament of a minority nation seeking to co-exist under an experimental social existence commanded by its own doctrines and morals. The existence of Voronova and communities like it posed a threat, so the Nazis destroyed them in a murderous rage.

Voronova was 600 years old when it ceased to exist.

Editor's Footnote

1. The word 'Yovlo' is spelled yud–vov–beyz (or veyz)–lamed–vov in the original text.
2. The word 'Zhizmeh' is spelled zayen–(apostrophe)–yid–zayen–mem–hey in the original text.
3. 32 versts is approximately 21.21 miles.

4. 59 versts is approximately 39.10 miles.
5. 20 versts is approximately 13.25 miles.
6. The word 'Geshtuld' is spelled giml–shin–tes–vov–lamed–daled in the original text.
7. 60 versts is approximately 39.77 miles.
8. The name 'Shlohim' is spelled shin–lamed–hey–mem in the original text.

[Pages 20-24]

Image of Voronova, My Town

Shlomo Aviel Shmerkovitsh

Translation by Meir Bulman

Voronova my home town: here are the roads, the pathways, the streets, the open fields and forests, rivers. A town where everyone is Jewish, except for a *Shabbos Goy*[1] or the pork salesman on market day, or a remnant of past nobility, or a few more, but the rest are Jews, sons of the covenant. Some are studious Torah scholars, some are educated, but most are ordinary Jews, hardworking, honest, innocent, god–fearing, lovers of the people and land of Israel.

We never had very wealthy people among us, but there were owners of nice homes, businessmen and the unique half–coachmen–half–businessmen, who traveled twice a week to Vilne and returned with various stocks of food items or sewing items for sale in exchange for cash or credit to the owners of small stores. There were also various manufacturing shops that sold products to the peasants of the area, and there were several Jews who received gifts from their relatives overseas – a few dollars before holidays who— there were the town's rich men. The vast majority, however, were limited merchants, in their stores they sold a mix of needles and threads, oil and sugar, flour and grain, candies and salt, oil for the coaches, etc.

Most of the income was generated on Tuesdays, which was the

market day, and some of it on Sundays, because on those days the peasants came in droves to the market and church. The town was very busy that day, and many had high hopes on that day. At dawn, the family would prepare for the big day, the day of livelihood. Some worked as salespeople, and others as assistant salespeople to aid against thieves and shoplifters. Jews traded everything at the marketplace: grains, various furs that were specially purchased from hunters in wintertime, swine hair, flax, dried mushrooms, and *zrza*[2] which was a type of plant the Gentiles gathered in the woods and, after drying, turned into a wound-healing powder that was also exported abroad. Animals such as horses were traded, as were dairy products, chickens, and eggs.

Many in town were craftsmen, among them blacksmiths whose bulk-work came from shoeing horses, and from fashioning plow blades, scythes, and sickles for harvesting grain. There were also cobblers, tailors, leather workers, seamstresses, carpenters, hatters, etc. There were some professions that were considered respectable because they involved trade, and less respectable ones that did not require trading.

That is how Jews made a living for many generations, and that is how they educated and raised children in the ways of Torah and civilization. In addition to the usual sources of livelihood, nearby to most homes in town there was a plot of land that assisted in providing nourishment to the family, on regular days and on troubled days.

Most had a cow or even two. The cow provided milk and many luxuries to the household, such as milk for the children, some sour milk, cheese, sour cream, and sometimes butter. Because of the vast amounts of fertilizer that piled up in the cowsheds over winter, plots of land were leased from the Gentiles to plant potatoes (an important food item for the Jews in the area). Many had their own plots that spanned 10–20 flowerbeds, 120 meters in length. Many vegetables were cultivated: carrots, onions, cucumbers, radishes, and other vegetables. All of those filled the basements and lasted, for men and animals, until the next season. Many had fruit gardens near their homes, and all made a living according to the will of God, some comfortably and others less so. The most pressing issue was clothing, as those cannot be planted in a field nor in a garden, and obtaining a golden coin was very difficult, especially for the youth.

As summer arrived, Voronova would be filled with happiness and laughter. Immediately following the Pentecost, many homes were filled with vacationers of all kinds who came from distant cities to rest and refresh, because Voronova was blessed with many surrounding forests. That too helped with making a living. A kingdom of youth would then take over the town and youthful cheers dominated Voronova.

Excerpt from *In the Tunnel*[3]

> Trubbe tunnel, Bezmuk in a foreign language
>
> I remember you from long ago [for the ages]
>
> Your cold water flowed in silence
>
> Gave life and quenched the wilderness
>
> On Sabbath, holiday, and festival [as we do]
>
> We would walk to you
>
> We would swim and float in your waters,
>
> Our youthful delight we brought with us
>
> The echo of laughing youths
>
> Was carried between your shade– providing woods
>
> We would collect A fistful of berries
>
> Wild grapes, blueberries, raspberries, strawberries
>
> As dessert to the joys of immersion
>
> While happy, silly, gleeful with delightful relaxation.

Evenings would then continue until midnight, with gleeful songs and sleeping in the barn on piles of fragrant hay. Those were days of forgetting school and other troubles.

But here comes fall, town is emptying out from guests and boredom takes over everything. The youth have nothing to do, there is no future or meaning. Continuing education in high school or university in the big city is reserved for a lucky few, because that was expensive, and the supposed rich men saw it as unfit to teach their children a trade. Still, many youths found employment, mainly in sewing. In those days, a number of factories were established in town, such as in clothing mass production, which employed many youths in exploitative conditions from dusk till dawn. Thus a workers uprising was organized. The communist ideal penetrated the hearts of many, Polish police watched them, and many were arrested, tortured, and sentenced to years in prison.

Excerpt from *In the Tunnel*

Once in The Tunnel in the dark of night

With silence surrounding

On the balcony they sat resting

Workers, laboring tailors called a meeting

Ben–Zion Alter's son of the cobbler's

spoke and said:

Dear friends! Laboring friends!

How long will we be exploited

How long will we sew them clothes

While we walk naked.

Kheikeh the seamstress asked to speak

And she had a proposal, to call a strike

That was accepted and implemented by all

And in town heaven and earth are moved

It is inconceivable, such a chutzpah!

In the synagogue opinions differ

In a discrete and silent tone, many then said

said many parents

They are laborers, they work

thus they are right.

A local meeting we held for *HaShomer HaTsair*

One day a messenger came with the message that redemption arrived. Hundreds of youths came to the meeting and his voice like that of the redeemer: laboring on the land of Israel, swamp–drying, conquering the wilderness, training, kibbutz, and Aliyah. There was enthusiasm that grew into large flames, therefore the *HaShomer HaTzair*[4] chapter took form and became a reality. There were conversations, debates, field trips. The town took on a new living form. As time passed, *Beitar*[5] was formed, *HaMizrachi*[6] and *HeKhalutz*[7] were strengthened, and the communist party was deserted by its members.

The library and the drama club were transferred to Zionist management, and all town residents, old and young, enjoyed the spirit of Zion and Jerusalem. Enthusiasm overtook all.

The ancient windmill

I remember some unusual episodes from that time: Motl the Leather Maker was glued to the eastern window at the *HaShomer HaTzair* branch— glued, attached, and did not let go, and said, "You will never know, will not understand how big my love for you is, when I see you in your uniforms and your enthusiasm, as you dance together while singing the lovely Hora, *lebn zal Bistritski mit zeyn horeh lebn zalt ir ale*,[8] how I love you, how much I envy you, I swear to God, I would fly there with you like on the wings of eagles, but unfortunately I am too old, so, take my Moshke, take my Rishkke, take my soul. *Lebn zal Bistritski mit zeyn horeh, lebn.*" And he left.

Before making Aliyah, while I was saying goodbye to friends, relatives, and strangers, Eliahu Dvilianski told me, "I know that I will not get to fulfill my dream, God did not bless me to reach the beloved land, to feel its earth beneath my feet and work it." "Indeed," said with a sigh his brother Ze'ev Dvilianski.

Many like those were left behind. When the holocaust arrived, many relatively young people managed to break the siege and escape to the woods, organized in Partisan squads, fought and avenged much of the blood of our fathers, brothers, and sisters, but the rest were mostly murdered by the cruel enemy and his assistants.

Voronova is now emptied of Jews, we will no longer hear their voices for they are gone. They are now silent forever.

Footnotes

1. Ed. Note: Gentile person able to do tasks forbidden to Jews on the Sabbath
2. Ed. Note: Possibly refers to zarza (Smilax ornata), a plant introduced to Europe from the Americas and then used there to treat various ailments including iills.
3. Tr. Note: Poem is written in rhyming couplets
4. Ed. Note: Zionist self-defense movement
5. Ed. Note: Revisionist Zionist youth movement
6. Ed. Note: One of two religious, Zionist parties that later in 1955 combined to form the National Religious Party, or Mafdal, in Israel (the other party being HaPoel HaMizrachi).
7. Ed. Note: a Zionist youth movement
8. Ed. Note: 'long live Bistriski and his hora, long live you all"; a hora is a type of Jewish dance; these are lyrics from a song often sung at *HaShomer HaTzair* gatherings; the identity of Bistriski has not yet been fully determined; possibly it is a reference to Nathan Bistriski, a director of Youth and Information at the Jewish National Fund in Jerusalem from 1922–1952, and who was also a playwright; in the 1930s his works were amongst the first Hebrew plays presented in Palestine. The rest if the lyric is as follows: *Nit keyn rekhter, nit keyn linker, nor a Mizrakhist a flinker*. 'not a right-winger, not a left-winger, but a deft [as in nimble or clever] Mizrachist'.

[Pages 25-30]

Profile of a Town

Shlomo Pikovski

Translation by Meir Bulman

Our town excelled in its lively youth which was alert to all world events and paid particular attention to events in the Jewish world, and so a variety of youth groups flourished in Voronova expressing a range of ideas. *HaShomer HaTsair*,[1] *Gordonia*[2] Zionists, and general *HeKhaluts*,[3] as well as *HeKhaluts HaTsair*. There was also no shortage of Bundists, Trotskyites, and other splintered movements.

Hebrew was spoken in town. It was one of the only towns in which there were Hebrew speaking households. On the school street, the language most spoken was that dead language resurrected with its nation. Interestingly, the plays produced by members of the various movements were purely in Hebrew though the target audience was the town's Jews, average people of *"sher u eisen"* [Tr. Note: shears and herbs].

A typical town in White Russia, it had also a special charm. It was a town where none fell to extremism. Its public charm was that all wanted the success of the Jewish People regardless of the movement one belonged to. Arguments and disagreements remained even–tempered and never reached the highest most dangerous level. Moves were made with everyone's participation, or at least with their blessing. With the abundance of energy among the youth and in spite of the arguments and activities separated according to faction, all joined together for general activities of mutual assistance, spreading education, and encouraging culture among the youth and general town population. Everyone searched for ways to study; be it in the yeshivas, seminaries, or secondary schools in local owns, and all helped one another with advice, congratulations, and more.

*

Given the general economic subsections, it can be said that Voronova was very diverse. Aside from the moderately rich people, most of the townspeople were small businesspeople and merchants, along with some laborers who made a difficult living while preserving their homey human dignity. It had all the roles typical for Jews in the diaspora such as tailors, cobblers, blacksmiths, and tinsmiths, alongside the freelancers like doctors and dental technicians, pharmacists, and more.

It was difficult to make a living in town. The market square at the center of town was empty all week aside from market day when it was filled with wagons loaded with agricultural products prepared by area Gentiles. Jews purchased a variety of products like butter and cheese, fruits and vegetables, grains, firewood and construction wood, goats and sheep, skins and furs, for self-consumption or resale.

Meeting of Voronova alumnae in Petach Tikva on Hanukah 1933

Most of the residents of Voronova spoke the local languages, so every person could speak to the Gentile he had dealings with. They spoke

Polish, Russian, Ukrainian, and Lithuanian, all on a basic level based on economic needs. Those were means of communication acquired not by formal study but absorbed through negotiations, and spoken only during those interactions, but the primary language was Yiddish. It was a language influenced by all languages and woven with idioms, proverbs, and metaphors from all languages, but our Yiddish was particularly decorated by Torah sayings and the eternal wisdom of the Mishna, *Talmud*, and lessons from musar, midrash, and prayers.

We are including language skills in the economic sub-section since the language in Voronova was used in a dual trading capacity; the Gentiles' languages in literal trade and Yiddish in a uniquely Jewish trading of wisdom, manners, relationships, good deeds, status and livelihood, contacts, and loans. Both served the desire to make a living and preserve relationships and respect across the stark class divides, and to subsist. Language offered physical support which may be why it was enjoyed by its speakers.

*

To erect a monument to that national institution that was the Voronova community, I will name the streets to paint a picture. I am not relating official names, as I do not remember such, and I think there were no signs. We called the streets Yiddish names and the generations knew those alone. And so I will be loyal to the reality that was and will commemorate it as it was. The exact list: *Vilner Gas, Lider Gas, Benakner Gessel, Eyshishoker Gessel, Zhreminer Gessel, Harminishker Gessel, der Nyer Plan, Bad Gessel, Ban Gessel, Der Mark, Nyer Mark, Der Galech, Khazerishe Gessel, Di Brick, Arap-Berg di Boyne, Zamak Veldel, Di Prasadis, Smoliarnia, Di Lanke* (*mit di balatess*).

*

Tradition was maintained in our town for many generations. Family meals took place on weekdays too, but that was not always possible due to financial troubles and work schedules. But on holidays and Shabbat, after family members returned from the houses of worship, the festive meals took place in their full traditional frame. The head of the household was at the head of the table, his wife beside him or facing him, and the children surrounding. When the main activity was not dining but rather the hymns, many songs were sung aside from the standard hymns, including Zionist songs, cantorial songs, and even Yiddish folk songs.

There were holidays on which joy was in the public domain and flowed outward. Those were Passover, Shavuot, and most of all Simchat Torah, when Jews expressed their joy in public and levity was permitted and honored. Hanukkah was very special since joy was accompanied by a lesson necessary to that small town surrounded by countless forests and villages, the lesson of the victory of the few over the many. It was a lesson relevant to the town and the entirety of the Nation of Israel, the small sheep among the wolves.

Without diminishing the rest of the Jewish holidays, it can be said we drew strength from Hanukkah more so than others, as faith in our revival and honor was elevated.

*

In summary and memoriam, Voronova was a fortress to preserve our national character and traditions and all descriptions of it are valuable to the world and to ourselves. It is important the world knows that we preserved small islands of prayer and longing for Zion and virtue among the kingdoms of blood and the cruelty of the nations. It is also important to remember that our uniqueness stems from that. Our parents who were born and raised among those dark and hopeless alleys nurtured much hope in the chance for a state of their own, full of light and horizons. Princes who dreamed of a kingdom and a state walked those narrow streets. There are few nations who can say they withstood the test of time in their attachment to a kingdom of their own while distant from the soil of that kingdom across space and many centuries of time. Voronova was destroyed and lost not only to our descendants but to the world and humanity as a social and national experiment. We cannot return what was lost but in writing our memorial books we can at least reconstruct its image which will stand forever within printed pages.

Our descendants will know how our ancestors were and will know there is something of which to be proud.

As the towns of Poland were engulfed in the flames of destruction, their descendants walked here on the walls of the State of Israel. The image of their parents being exterminated before their eyes gave them the strength to battle a foreign invader and be victorious. May we not forget that vision and armored in these memories we will draw a strength that will withstand any turmoil in our country and nation.

Voronova Once Upon A Time, 1971

Editor's Footnotes

1. *HaShomer HaTsair* ("The Young Guard") was a more left–leaning youth movement with the same Zionist goals as *HeKhaluts*
2. A youth Zionist movement based on the ideals and principles of Aaron David Gordon (non–Marxist).
3. An organization that prepared immigrants for Aliyah.

Holocaust and Heroism

[Page 31-45]

From Bad to Worse

Meir Shamir (Shmerkovitsh)

Translation by Emma Karabelnik

September 1939. Jews, as they usually do at the outset of a war between Gentiles, stood aside as if it didn't concern them, but the fear was showing. Everyone was in a hurry, everyone was a politician conducting discussions on state matters and strategies, guessing outcomes, gathering around public radio, and listening nervously to the surprising news and the course of fighting on the front. Tension was rising and the nervousness even more so. We were totally aware of what awaited us; we knew exactly what the arrival of Hitler would mean for us.

Meanwhile, general mobilization began: all sorts of soldiers were recruited. When it was my turn to be recruited, I decided to go back home to Voronova where I had left behind my parents and younger brother. I left Lida where I was working as an electrician and went back home. I stayed there for several days and then my turn came to report in Sokolka. We, the Jews, were eager to enlist and fight against Germans. I wanted to fight as soon as possible, but the road to Sokolka was already blocked. The railway was dysfunctional. I had to look for alternative ways to get to Vilne or Lida, and from there to my recruitment point.

In the evening an occasional train would pass and we [managed to] leave. Military life started there [on the train]. We lay on benches. At every station we received coffee and rolls from the Red Cross who welcomed the new recruits. The train proceeded slowly and with caution. From time to time when [passing] open fields with no hiding places we were attacked by German bombers throwing bombs and shells upon us. The number of victims was growing. One day in Grodno we were bombed by several formations of enemy planes and many were killed before we could jump out to find shelter. We lost faith that any of us would survive. There was no one to protect us. The whole anti-aircraft defense consisted of one machine gun hidden behind a tree at the station. That machine gun used to get stuck from time to time: before it was kind enough to shoot, enemy planes did what they wanted to us.

The railway station was destroyed almost to the ground and the train overturned. A small number of people managed to get out, but most were killed or wounded. A heavy train door torn from its hinges wounded my right leg. Only after the attack ended were we able to take care of the wounded and pull out the trapped from under the wagons.

At first I was unable to move my leg and I lay on the ground. Two people approached me with a stretcher, but I refused to be carried. I tried to stand up by myself. After I regained [some strength] and stood up, I saw a horrible site that didn't leave me until long after.

Near a pile of ruins there was a smashed woman with her child beside her, a two year old. For me it was the beginning of war and its [horrible] views. On many subsequent occasions my eyes saw human victims, the dead and the wounded, ripped and smashed, but again and again the site of this innocent woman with her little baby came back to me: unnecessary victims of a cruel war.

We couldn't continue until we had repaired the rails. We moved on after two days knowing for sure that the villain would return and repeat a blood bath.

Somehow we managed to get to Sokolka at three, after midnight. We were immediately enlisted and were taken to a mountain nearby. We stretched on the ground, took some imaginary cover, and fell into a deep sleep.

As sunrise we were awakened by loud sirens. Soon we saw the formations and the falling bombs exploding everywhere: Sokolka was under an air attack. For two days we walked around in civilian clothing. On the third day we got uniforms. We were divided into groups of up to 12, mostly Poles, according to our military professions. In the whole squad only two of us were Jews, the rest Poles from Warsaw and Poznan. We stayed in town as a guarding squadron. We were happy about it because the rumors from the frontline were not reassuring. The steady flow of wounded soldiers was increasing. Our company was ordered to defend the railway lines and station. We began digging trenches and prepared to fight the enemy.

Although we at the frontline suffered bitter losses every day, the radio transmitted news of the successes and victories of the Polish Army, in order to cheer up the fighters. It must be noted that we didn't lack courage. During each air attack we jumped into nearby gardens to appear to be picking fruit. But it didn't last for long. The Germans discovered us despite our disguise and conducted air raids on us from time to time. On one occasion, six formations appeared [in the sky]. The place turned into hell. The earth and the sky became one, heavy with grim smoke. When the attack stopped and all the dust sank, the earth and the sky were separated again. We found our friends scattered all around, crushed and laying in their own blood.

This went on for several days. We were ordered to prepare to move [retreat]. We knew the situation was getting worse. We knew we couldn't outlast them and that the end was coming near. There wasn't a single Polish plane on site. That was surprising and shocking. On one occasion, after an attack, one Polish airplane appeared in the sky for the first time. It flew low above our heads, looking miserable and pathetic like someone avoiding enemy airplanes.

We moved early in the evening. On the way we argued about the situation. The darkness became thicker and thicker. From time to time the sky would lighten up with air attacks, but that made our way seem even darker. It was more difficult to find our way through the darkness that fell after the lights of an air attack dazzled our eyes. We spent the night in the forest. We fell into a deep sleep.

When the morning came there were several scouts in the sky. After they disappeared, another plane appeared and someone from our group took a shot. The plane disappeared, but soon after a lot of bombers appeared and turned the forest into a mess. More than half of our people were dead or wounded. When the troops gathered together we discovered that out of 80 soldiers barely 25 to 30 survived. We knew that it had been treason: the shot wasn't fired by accident. There are traitors among us.

At night we were ordered to move on. Nobody knew yet where we are going. We traveled through the night packed together with our dead and wounded friends, while their final moans tore out our hearts. In the morning we recognized our destination. We were approaching Vilne. We didn't talk. Everyone knew what was going to happen. The mood was total depression. None of us could forget that treacherous shot in the forest, and it depressed us more and more. We realized that the war wouldn't last for long. The train stopped at the outskirts of Vilne and we soldiers were given the opportunity to wash and clean up the blood on our faces. They wanted us to look less depressing so that our entrance into town would not cause embarrassment or defeat.

In the train station a guard was put around us so that no one could get near us and see how miserable we looked. We found out later that local residents knew nothing about the real situation. They had heard from the radio only about victories and conquests

Meanwhile, the dead were buried, the wounded hospitalized, and the few remaining soldiers reorganized. There were very few of us left. To those few they wanted to add some reservists and send us all to the frontline. When we were ready to leave, news arrived that Hitler was approaching Vilne, and we were left to defend it. The Germans were supposed to arrive to Vilne from Klaipeda (Memel). That's why we didn't go to the front, and survived. We built the defense line, dug trenches, and established communication. I was appointed a sergeant. In my regiment there were White Russians [Belarusians]. I learned the differences favoring them when compared to treacherous Poles.

We stayed at the same spot for a week, and then we were astonished with news that the Russians were coming, crossing the Polish border in order to stop the Germans and prevent the occupation of all of Poland.

That was in November 1939. This information brought excitement to many of us, especially the Jews. It was [because of] the long history with the Poles who had caused a lot of suffering for the Jews. After the pogroms and harassments, the false arrests and heavy taxes, we finally took a breath of relief. [Not only us], but the Poles among us and the Belarusians from the worker class were also happy with the approach of the Communists. Then one day came the specific information that on the next day at 12 midnight the Russians would enter Vilne. This news bothered me because there were rumors that the Poles in town were preparing to resist the Russians. We [the Jews] and the Belarusians decided to run away. I put my trust in them and together we planned our desertion. The thought of continuing to serve in the treacherous anti-Semitic Polish Army frightened me. We didn't want to fight with them at the frontline.

That's how I imagined the Soviet regime - the savior of Polish Jews. I believed that this way we'd reach equality and eliminate anti-Semitism. In my head I still heard the voice of Moscow radio [speaking about the] brotherhood of nations and the equality of the working man. I remembered [stories] from the radio of rich Jewish cultural activity, the concerts, the lectures, and this made me enthusiastic to meet the Soviets— especially now, after the indescribable suffering, and the disorientation of the Polish authorities and commanders in battle, and the fear of falling into Nazi hands. The Soviet Army seemed like a miracle from heaven and our chance for salvation. Some soldiers danced for joy when discussing the politics. The Polish officers became angry. They were not pleased to see this. Probably resulting from the two occupations, they preferred the German, anti-Soviet, and anti-Semitic regime. I felt this in all of their behaviors so I decided it was time to act. Time was pressuring. I left a Belarusian soldier in my place and went away. I told him I was going to check the rumors and instructed him on what to do and say when the night control arrived.

A soldier who had relatives in town came with me. It was hard to sneak out of the trenches. Every movement had to be authorized and there were inspections everywhere, but our great excitement gave us great strength and we managed to overcome all obstacles. Under the cloak of darkness and the cover of bombings we managed to sneak away, pass unnoticed the bridge guards, and make it to town. I visited someone I knew and he confirmed the rumor that the Russians are arriving that night.

I stayed overnight at his [place]. He promised to organize civilian clothes for me so that I'd be able to walk around the town and not be arrested as a foreign soldier. My friends and I decided that if the Russians did not come during the night, we'd have no choice but to return to our base. He was supposed to wake me up.

I didn't shut my eyes the whole night in fear of being betrayed by my substitute. I didn't want to be court-martialed by the Polish anti-Semites on the verge of my salvation, only a moment before the expected final fall of their regime.

The Russians didn't arrive. The night ended and everything was quiet. The city's residents were enclosed in their homes. All the doors and windows were shut, and not one living soul was seen in the streets. I dressed up quickly while it was still dark and ran back to my regiment.

In my heart I regretted the whole night operation. My disappointment was great; again the illusion had blown up. Probably it was another of the false rumors spread during wars, with purposes known only to those who spread them.

In my regiment everything was quiet. The soldiers surrounded me, eager to hear everything I had to tell. In particular, they wanted to know how the Russian occupation would occur, if it would occur. Our hearts pounded with fear that the Russians would not come at all. Desperation was everywhere.

Meanwhile, the days went by and with them various rumors. Some said that the Poles and the Russians had come to an agreement, and that the Russians would not occupy Poland. But in the surrounding fields, sounds and echoes of shots and explosions could be heard.

In the afternoon I sent a soldier to the main barracks to bring food and mostly to bring new information.

At 2pm he came back running, without food, and said that in the main barracks there was turmoil and panic. The officers were packing their belongings, burning everything, and covering their footsteps. I decided to go to the barracks myself and check if this was true.

He was right and accurate. The officers ran around angrily and desperately. Turmoil and panic were everywhere. Piles of burnt papers, notebooks, and certificates were scattered all around. It was crystal clear to me that our saviors were on their way and maybe even at the outskirts of town. I decided to leave the base and never come back. This time I was sure that I would not return. When it became dark I started making my way to the city. I knew that from now on my place would be between friends and relatives, among those craving for change, and awaiting salvation like me. This time there was no need to fear control-points and guards. They also ran around and had deserted.

When I approached the green bridge I saw a strange sight: women and soldiers and ordinary civilians hugging and kissing in great joy. I didn't know yet what had happened. I stopped people and asked them about the big celebration. Someone who saw me wearing Polish uniform wanted to cheer me up and told me the whole story. Apparently it had been announced on the radio that Hitler was dead and that the Russians were not coming to Vilne, and that the Poles had come to an agreement with the Russians to withdraw to previous borders.

You have to realize – he explained to me - they would shoot us Poles to the last one.

I was naïve and confused, and my heart started beating hard. I couldn't decide: whether to leave or not? To return or no to return? I began slowly to make my way back. Heat and cold attacked me, each in its turn, but I couldn't make myself go back to the military base. Finally, I reached a bridge and heard again the news that the Pole told me. So I continued on my way— to the base of all places.

On my way I met terrified people on the run. The turmoil and confusion were immense, and my doubts grew even more.

Three times I re-crossed the bridge back and forth, and on the fourth time I decided to go back to town.

I told myself that it was only to check out the rumors with my friends. I'd find out everything from them. I continued to walk silently. Nobody noticed me. The night became darker with every minute.

I went on, and there I was in Zawolna Street. I saw a line of automobiles packed with women and small children. These were families of high rank, government servants, attempting to escape the Soviet regime and its expected cruelty against the Poles. This time they looked miserable and frightened. The heavy rain, the switched-off street lamps, and the solitude added to their misery. I waited impatiently for the cars to leave and then quickly crossed the street. I came to my friends' house, knocked on the door, but nobody replied. Everything was sealed and locked; nobody dared to approach the door.

I stood all alone in the night. Around me were only sounds of slamming doors. I had no desire to stay outside in the rainy night. I went to an inn owned by Itzek in Klein-Stephan-Street. My parents used to stay at this inn when they traveled to Vilne. Nobody replied to my knocking, but I knew that they were home. So I continued to knock until I heard a voice from inside:

"Who's there?"

I asked for someone from Itzek's [family] to come to the gate because I was an acquaintance. One of them came to the gate and recognized me. He had seen me here before, when I had come as a soldier to pick up packages sent from home.

The heavy gate opened. They had built barricades and they had to be dismantled.

When I entered the yard I saw a lot of people gathered together. They all surrounded me. Everybody wanted to hear from someone who had been outside. They took me to a big cellar. I saw lots of mothers with babies, some seated, and some lying on the floor. The men were outside with clubs, for protection. The atmosphere was full of fear and tribulation. Jewish Vilne was getting prepared for horrible attacks by the Jew-hating Poles. They accepted the rumor that Hitler was dead, and the Soviets were not coming etc., but they also saw it is a huge disaster, as unexpected trouble.

Later we found out that the Mayor who was sympathetic to Jews had spread this news deliberately to prevent a last-minute pogrom before Hitler or the Soviets entered the town.

At 7 we heard whistling bullets close to us and clear sounds of shootings. The Soviets lit up the town with huge spotlights, to force the Polish soldiers surrender before they could hide. They knew that the [Polish] army had decided to actively resist the entrance of Soviets. After the bullets came shells and bomb explosions. Vilne looked to be in shock and collapsing.

The assemblage left the yard and went down to the cellar. Everyone looked for a shelter and clung to Mother Earth for protection. I was used to the sounds of war and explosions so I lay on the ground and fell sound asleep.

At 12 everything went quiet. From time to time the rattling motor of a tank, or the sound of chains, could be heard from afar. I woke up and stood up and couldn't see anyone around me. Even those who had slept beside me weren't there anymore. I went to the room where the women were gathered and asked where the men were. My uniform scared them and my question confused them much. They started screaming. Then the men appeared and calmed them down. The situation was unclear. Were the Soviets here? Nobody had seen them yet.

I asked the inn workers to lend me civilian clothing. We hid my military uniform in the attic. I went outside. Jewish men were standing in groups, discussing the politics. Some assumed that the Russians had won. Others thought that they hadn't. In any case it was clear that the battle was ended. Nobody dared to get out into the street. The gate was still blocked and sealed. From the street one could hear the sound of approaching tanks. I found the courage to climb the stairs and look outside. It was still dark and it was hard to see what was going on. The window was broken so I stretched my head out and suddenly saw a person with something white on his back. I followed him with my eyes and saw more and more such images with white backs. Meanwhile as it became lighter I could see that these were Polish soldiers looking for shelter, from their fear. They are many, and the things on their backs were nothing more than their white army packs, which they had brought from their homes. I knew that they were done for. I knew the Soviets were coming in with zero resistance from our "heroes".

I climbed down and told the people what I had seen. We then heard noises outside the gate and people talking. We opened the gate slowly and went outside. The street was empty. From afar one could hear clear sound of the tanks. We ran towards the noise. Something told us those were Soviet tanks. A row of caterpillars appeared before our eyes, a heavy tank passed by and the earth was shaking under it, a second tank, and then a third. The third tank opened its hatch and the dusty head of a soldier appeared. He lifted his hand to us and said in pure Yiddish:

"Jews don't be afraid, we are with you!"

His words were like the password to salvation, like a magic word that had dispelled all doubts. We all were excited. In that moment a heavy stone had dropped from our hearts and [we felt] great relief.

Meanwhile the number of tanks was growing. They drove around along the streets, mounted kids on the turrets, and spread the spirit of liberty and comradeship. This tiny act filled our hearts with hope and relief.

And I...looked for a way to get back home to Voronova.

I found my cousin from Stephan Street; he loaned me his bicycle, so I could get to my family. I talked to another guy and we set out together, but at the last moment he changed his mind. He said they were catching people who wandered on the roads and were sending them to Russia as POWs. I couldn't stop myself. I missed home so much that I couldn't wait any longer.

I mounted the bike and drove home.

Outside the town I was arrested by a Russian patrol. There were many like me in custody. We were inspected, searched for weapons, asked about nationality, and then released. They treated the Jews with trust, unlike the Poles, and they were suspicious towards Poles.

On my way home I passed familiar soldiers dragging themselves home with their boots over the shoulders. After two and one half hours I arrived home to Voronova.

Our house was locked. Nobody was there. I waited for my parents. I stood impatiently leaning on a wall awaiting them. I was surrounded by a crowd who wanted to inquire about their sons, brothers, and relatives. Many of these didn't live to come back to their families, and there memory was lost forever.

On one occasion there was a need to install electricity in an estate which had been turned into a school, but there were no copper wires available. It was known that in Vilne one could find wires like this— not legally, with no receipts and no documents. I was appointed to go to Vilne to obtain the wires. I suggested to the accountant that he write an "act" [a protocol] for each transaction and thus we wouldn't have to submit orders, accounts, or receipts. He understood and wrote a [general] permit with which I succeeded in obtaining all that was needed, with a friend's help, and for a very cheap price. When I came back to the office and reported the details of the purchase, then suddenly he started with the game of checking the bills etc. I reminded him that he had written an "act" to avoid invoices and that I had acted under such an understanding, but it didn't help. He demanded that I submit invoices signed by me: it was the manager's orders.

I realized what was behind his words so I piled-on all the accusations he deserved. The office was full of people, but I couldn't control myself. I mentioned every sin of his known to me until he got angry and threatened to go to the police.

A week went by and Levinov kept on demanding. Meanwhile, the police gathered more evidence against me. One morning I was riding my bike on my way to work when I was met by the *politruk*[1] of the police, one of my first acquaintances, who was still there since the change of regimes. We spoke in detail about my conflict with Levinov and I asked him what they were cooking up for me at the police. In the course of our conversation, which started in a friendly way, I felt that he had turned on me, and then he invited me to come with him to the police station. I knew it was an ambush and that I needed to be careful.

At the police station I went through a long and harsh interrogation. I told the whole truth— which didn't serve their intentions. I was released. I rode to work but was stopped on the way and taken back to the police. I was ordered to sit near the officer on duty and not to talk to anyone. My brother-in-law, who came to check on me, was also arrested. Meanwhile the chief of police sent policemen to my home. All the equipment that I kept at my home for "black-market" jobs was taken as evidence. Only then was I officially arrested. The elation felt by my boss and the chief of police, my greatest enemies, was huge. My brother-in-law was released, but his bicycle was confiscated. He was still a boy. He cried bitterly because of his bike so they decided to give it up and let him go.

I was taken to prison with a convoy.

This was a new and sad chapter in my life. I spent nights sleeping on the floor. Food was brought to me from home, but no family members were allowed to see me. I looked out of a small window. I saw my wife leaning on an electric poll and crying. This clarified for me how the new regime could turn from white to black in a moment, how in one night a working and useful citizen could be turned into a convict, any connection with him forbidden.

The vengefulness didn't calm down until I was moved to Lida prison. Later I found out that is had been the Mayor who demanded my release.

On the morning of the third day in prison I was taken out together with 15 prisoners. We stood awaiting a vehicle that would take us to Lida. Town people gathered around us. Everyone expressed their sympathy to me, a son of this town. Some gave me cigarettes, some gave food or sweets.

In Lida we were conveyed with our hands cuffed behind our backs, like the worst criminals. The residents looked at us in the same manner. I was praying in my heart not to come across someone I knew.

At the prison entrance the heavy gate closed behind us and we were ordered to stand against the wall, our hands at the back, and not to look back. We were standing like people who stand before firing squad. Shortly we were called for an inspection one by one. At my [inspection] they even tore up my cigarettes. In the evening I was put in a tiny cell with a steel door and concrete floor. I was put in solitary confinement. I was told that it was temporary until they could find a proper cell for me. When it became dark my heart was heavy and depressed. I felt as if everyone had forgotten me.

I spent the night in solitary without sleep, standing on my feet. In the morning, when I was taken from there, I couldn't move my legs and the light bothered my eyes. They gave me back my stuff. The tobacco and the torn cigarettes were mixed in the food. I was given a blanket and taken to my cell as promised.

When I went in [to the cell] I was cut off and locked-in, with real prisoners surrounding me. They asked me a lot of questions. I didn't reply. Then I was approached by several Jews. They were from Ivye. They explained to me who all the prisoners were and how I should conduct myself. In our cell there were different people from different nationalities associated with different crimes in different states. Some were accused and under investigation, some convicted. Some were soldiers, some officers, and some were criminals serving long terms for heavy crimes. The latter were more interested in my belongings than in me. I explained to them that if anyone touched my things I'd reward him appropriately. They flinched and treated me with respect. I shared about 100 cigarettes with them and our relationship became better. They all invited me to take a place near them. Three of the old-timers were sleeping near the windows, enjoying the fresh air, while the newcomers suffered from the heat and the stench. We were 40 people in the cell. Our toilet was a common bucket- one for all equally- that spread the stench for all equally. Except for those three, all the rest slept on the floor. After a week one of them left and I was given the bunk near the window. My two neighbors, one a Pole and the other a Russian, befriended with me and I shared my food and smokes with them.

From time to time my friends were taken away for photos and fingerprints. I was impatient to be called because I wanted to know what was in store for me. I already knew the section of law. It was Section 55. I saw that when my fingerprints were taken during arrest.

My friends, who knew the law perfectly, told me that I was in for speculation [i.e., profiteering]: punishment 5 to 10 years.

When the day of my interrogation came, I wasn't taken to the scene of the crime. My manager had probably arranged for my interrogators to come to where I was imprisoned. My heart trembled when I was told about the interrogation. Finally, for the first time in my life I was going to be interrogated. My cellmates told me a lot about the process. They said that they would not be picky about using means of pressure and wouldn't hesitate to use them. I gathered all my courage and strength and decided to hold on, not to break down, and not to admit to all their accusations.

My interrogator was totally unknown to me. He welcomed me with courtesy and offered me a seat. There were just the two of us in the room. He asked me various questions and asked me to tell him my story. I told him the full history of my relationship with Levinov and all that had happened between me and the others. When he repeated the same questions, I kept silent. That made him angry. He pressed me in different ways to tell him where I had bought the wires, promising to release me [if I would tell him]. He appealed to my conscience and to my responsibilities towards my family. Nothing worked.

I was returned to my cell late that night. My cellmates waited impatiently. I fell asleep and had nightmares of the previous day. When I awoke I foresaw that more nightmares would occur on the following day. Several such days full of anxiety and nervousness passed.

One day, new prisoners were brought to our cell, and we learned from them that there was talk about a war between Russia and Germany. I didn't believe this: I was too deep inside my own nightmare.

On Friday night the prison guard came in suddenly and covered the windows with cloth so as to shut out electric light from the street.

We understood [why]. Nobody shut their eyes that night. At dawn we heard the noise of flying airplanes. We were not taken for our usual 15 minutes to the toilets. The door remained locked. Nobody came to open it. We began to communicate with other prisoners by clapping on walls. Slowly the uncertainty turned into fear: maybe the regime was going to kill us all inside these walls. At the same time we heard terrible screams coming from the minors' cell:

"God, people, help! Help!"

When people outside heard the children screaming they started to break open the prison gates. Somebody squeezed his head through the bars and shouted:

"The stork is not on the roof."

In prison language it meant that there were no more guards in the watch towers. Everybody started clapping on the walls, demanding to go to the toilets, but no one responded. We pressed the doors but they were made of iron. Prisoners of another cell managed to break free and they released us too.

We ran around to help each other. Meanwhile a crowd had gathered in the prison yard and we mingled with the crowd. The main gate was burst open with the help of those who had come to check on their children and relatives who had been turned into criminals by the "regime of justice".

We ran into the street. There was no sign of the military. We ran through fields and gardens to Voronova. Near the power station we were stopped by a Russian armed soldier. He probably was not aware [of events]. The road to Molodetchno was crowded with people terrified of the new regime and who were fleeing to Russia. Some of us climbed into vehicles heading for Russia. They offered me shelter but I didn't want any. I explained that I would not be leaving before learning the fate of my family.

People were wandering frightened in the fields, under attack from German bombers. We split into small groups. From Zhyrmun[2] to Voronova I went myself. On my way I came across Russian military units who took me back [wouldn't let me through]. They had evacuated the whole town to the countryside [villages]. While walking through the forest I met two Poles. We continued together and then were stopped at a Russian checkpoint. We were ordered to put our hands up and were searched – after a month without shaving, wearing our weird clothes, we looked suspicious to them. At that moment an officer came running and ordered them to leave us alone and to retreat.

On the way I asked children that I met whether there were Russians or Germans. I found out the road was clear so I continued, almost running. Time was short. I wanted to know what was [happening] in my town, with my family. Suddenly I felt my legs betraying me and I couldn't continue anymore. In a village about 4km from Bastuni I saw a group of Gentiles standing around talking. One of them invited me to spend the night with them, but the look in their eyes, and their good moods, made me suspicious so I decided to continue. The Gentile who was with me did stay with them for the night, but not me. I couldn't go much further so I moved 2km away, went into a forest, laid down in a ditch with my feet up, and fell asleep.

When I approached the town I heard explosions and saw distant flames of fire mounting up to the sky. We decided to enter the town anyway. We neared the first house and our hearts were beating. As the sun came up we could see the contours of the town. Hirshke Arkin opened the door of his house and intimated to us that near the Olkenitski house and the house of the Mayor, Germans had been seen. My Christian friend continued on his way. I stayed on the porch to see what would happen. A motorcycler [German] stopped him and then let him go. The Germans continued their ride. I followed them in the same direction. When they made a turn and disappeared I continued towards my home.

The house was closed and locked as if there were nobody at home. I punched and punched until my wife opened a shutter and peeked outside. She didn't recognize me with my wild beard, but when I opened my mouth and spoke, she screamed to her parents: "Meir is here!"

That's how I came back home from bad to worse.

Editor's Footnotes

1. A politruk is a political commissar, an officer responsible for ideological unity and organization in the unit under command. (http://www.wikiwand.com/en/Political_commissar, last accessed 3 Oct 2018)

2. The location of this town has not yet been identified. In the original text the town is spelled: zayen-reysh-mem-yud-langer nun

[Page 46]

My Holocaust Experience

Khenye Konopke (Blitter)

Translation by Emma Karabelnik

We Went From "*Anusim*"[1] to *Mar'anim*[2]

With the arrival of the Russians, the Voronova community took a breath of relief. We were saved from the economic repression, hatred of the goyim, and pogroms that had threatened us in the waning years of the Polish regime. The Jews were still worried about economic problems and *Yidishkeit*,[3] but they didn't have to worry about personal security anymore, and that was a relief. However the situation of *Beitar* people became worse, to us were attached the labels of nationalism and opportunism for revolution. We draw the attention of the Russian Secret Police and had to go hide our tracks, to disappear, and to somehow erase our past. We transformed ourselves into 'good–guys' enjoying the Russian light, and donned the appearance of being pure and devoted members of the "new society".

First of all we burned all the lists of members in the nest.[4] Before the Soviet immersion our headquarters were at Velvl the Blacksmith's house down the hill. The last commander had been Aharon Kalmanovitsh, but he was out of town, because for understandable reasons he had gone underground until danger had passed. So, we were ordered to do the job. I went to the nest together with Yitzach Olkenitski, we kindled the fire in the big oven, and we burned the lists of names of all the brothers and sisters, all the papers, and the pictures on the walls. Tears rolled down my cheeks as we did it. There was kind of bitterness in our hearts, a mixed feeling of self–betrayal, a total denial of our past and our identity, although we realized the necessity of this act for the safety of our brothers and sisters. We were not able to burn the flag. Yitzach took it with him, planning to hide it underground until better times.

Thus the nest was destroyed by those who had nourished it. Thus the world of our dreams was ruined— all the illusions and hopes that had filled our hearts with love and joy.

But it didn't end there.

The Russians opened their own club in town. We knew that everyone had "to show up" at the club. Every night the club was full of dancing and singing youth. Every night someone would appear and make a speech about "the happiness and freedom" brought by the new regime for the world and for us. The speech was always accepted with applause and a prolonged ovation.

We, the *Beitar*-ists, couldn't do it. Our hearts wouldn't let us go there. It wasn't a group decision, each one of us simple shared the same feelings, and we avoided the club. We didn't get together at all. We stayed away from each other, walking on opposite sidewalks, sending sad, affectionate looks to each other, understanding each other in silence. We developed our *"anusim"* skills, we used various methods of dissimulation, spent a lot of time with "*kosher*"[5] people, enjoying the air of their "*kashrut*".[6] But still our hearts wouldn't let us go to the club. I always tried to spend time with Khayke Gol. She had resigned from *Beitar* before the war, and was considered a 'leftie' opportunist, extraordinarily "kosher". Eventually, we [*Beitar*-ists] also had to attend the club. We realized that we were endangering ourselves and we had to go.

On the first night, when I heard one of their "big" speakers, tears dripped from my eyes and my heart shrank, realizing the mutual deceit, but Khaika touched my shoulder and whispered that people were paying attention to me and noticing my crying, and she ordered:

"Try to clap your hands in applause even more enthusiastically than others."

And so I did.

Aliyah B to Vilne

One night an emissary of the [Tr. Note: *Beitar*] movement arrived, bringing a secret message that today's Voronova, following the establishment of the new borders, being situated 15 km from Lithuanian border, would be a most convenient point for transferring Zionists to freedom and to *Eretz Israel*. Those of us who were loyal to the movement were assigned the mission of finding farmers whose farms were close to the border, and who would agree to allow the smuggling for money.

From that night, our house became a transition station for numerous people. Many *Beitar* members passed through our house, also yeshiva scholars and simple Jews. They came to us in order to leave here, to find a path to salvation. They were hungry, frozen, and covered with road mud and dust brought from afar. Mother, *Z"L*, used to welcome them with warm soup and a Jewish heart to warm their frozen bodies and to give them some encouragement and faith in another Jewish person. Chaim Balteriski who was born in a village, was appointed as contact man with all the smugglers. He kept the money, and as soon as a message arrived that people had been moved, Chaim'ke paid the fee to the Gentile. Chaim'ke's contribution was invaluable. Some people buy their world in an hour of turmoil by becoming a friend and a patron of need.[7] Such was Chaim Balteriski.

Those were dramatic days and life–endangering nights got us, taken for the sake of others. There is no bigger satisfaction. Although our home routine was gone, people sometimes stayed for several nights, and we all shared beds and resources. Crossing the border was not possible every night. Sometimes people would come back, interfering with our sleep and endangering our well–being, but my parents saw it as a big mitzvah of the "redemption of captives", and acted with enthusiasm and devotion.

When the groups became larger, we shared the work with our dear neighbors Moshe and Iytl Olkenitski and Iytl Poditvianski, and they collaborated. On Saturdays father used to take the men to the synagogue and made arrangements for them to sleep and eat at Jewish houses. Until then all the refugees, also those from the German side, were wearing poor clothing, and didn't have a dime in their pockets. My father used to collect money to mend their shoes, to give them new clothes, and a dime for the road. Yehezkhel and Feigeh Eishishki sold them shoes with a big discount and our good Jews generously contributed to the poor tragic souls.

We developed special precautionary skills to hide those refugees illegally crossing the border. Sometimes we took the refugees' youngsters into our club, as a proof that they were here to stay.

One evening Yakov Konikhovski came to us with information that the Russian secret police was getting suspicious. He said we were in great danger of being accused of serious crimes, the punishment for which was even more serious, and that we had to stop all our activity immediately. At that time, all the border checkpoints were being closed and the activity stopped anyhow. But even then our house remained suspicious in the eyes of the secret police. One day, we heard a rumor that there was a train in Bastuni ready to take all the "criminals" to Siberia. I was advised to flee and disappear so that all the blame would fall on me, while my family would be saved from constant danger and tension. I told this to Olkenitski. I left for Lida, and after several months he followed. With him came a group of *Beitar*-ists, and together we tried to find a way out, to get closer to the border, and to look for a chance to be smuggled out.

On the day that we went to the railway station to buy tickets to the border, I suddenly felt someone gently touch my hair. I turned my head. Beside me stood a very elegant man, he spoke Russian with exaggerated mildness:

"Will you please follow me for few moments to N.K.V.D."

From the expression in his eyes I understood that I had better obey.

Those few moments turned into several months in prison. I was lucky because the person who informed on me knew nothing about me, so they had only enough evidence to keep me for several months, and to interrogate me abusively. The rest of my friends were sentenced to years of imprisonment.

"Absorption" Difficulties in the New Life

After my release I came back to Voronova. Life there had already come to order. There were offices and workshops. Everybody worked, old and young. The Russians taught them that if they didn't work, they wouldn't eat.[8] My good friends advised me to start working: it would prove – so they said – that I was cleansed of all the nationalist "nonsense" and that I was becoming a part of the new life.

I looked for a job, but nobody wanted to hire me. At that time two new cooperatives of tailors and shoemakers were established in town. In the first worked the Levine brothers, in the second, the Dvilianski brothers, the Kaplan brothers, the old bachelor Volman, and the poor sickly Yankl Berl (later the story was told about Yankl Berl, who was sick and helpless, that when the Germans came to his house to take him to slaughter, he opposed, and threw a chair towards them, so they killed him right near his house). Several Poles also worked there. The accountant was Shmuel Berkovski. I turned to him in hopes of getting a job. He talked it over with the Dvilianskis and Kaplans, and they agreed to take a chance on hiring me as Shmuel's assistant. I was so well 'cleared' that on the 1st of May demonstration I was given the honor of carrying the red flag.

Yet, my suffering didn't stop. When the Russians ordered that the free day would be Monday, and that we would have to work on Saturdays, my doubts, and those of my religious parents, grew. Many times I thought of quitting, whatever the consequences. Luckily our cooperative burnt down in a fire, together with all the houses in the same street. Our synagogue burnt down too, but at least it was saved from desecration. They hadn't enough time to turn it into a stable or a warehouse. The fire started on Saturday, and even the Gentiles saw it as an omen from God. Luckily we were not accused of sabotage and we moved to a new place, but the constant danger of being sent away to Siberia didn't go away. We continued to live and work, but the fear of being pulled out of bed one night and being sent to the strange land was always there. We didn't know that things could be much worse.

German Surprise

The arrival of the Germans surprised everyone. The Russians refused to believe that the explosions were not coming from their own planes. They thought everything was foreign propaganda and *sabotaga*. The Jews were also surprised. The Russians, although they had lost every war and battle until then, for some reason were still considered an unbeatable power in the eyes of the Jews and other minorities. In the *Beit Midrash* sat Mr. Nekhemiah Shapiro, Mr. Shimshon Dlugin and my father, discussing the Russian–German matter. Their conclusion was that the Germans would not come. Exactly at that moment I came to fetch my father home, telling them the news that the Germans were in the town. These three smart, honorable, and knowledgeable men turned pale and opened their hands in a helpless gesture.

At that moment the ground was already shaking under the heaviness of German tanks; the streets were empty. Everyone who was still in the streets on their way home, waved with a white kerchief as a peaceful harmless citizen.

The German headquarters were set in the house of Yehoshua Grodzenchik. They immediately hired 20 girls for house-cleaning and I was among them. Rivke Shmerkovitsh was constantly preoccupied with thoughts. A German officer noticed it. Once he asked her why is she always dreamy and she replied:

"You can force us to work but you can't force us not to dream and think!"

Decrees, Orders, and Malicious Joy

The first order was to wear on one's sleeve a yellow Star of David with the word "Jude" inscribed. That Tuesday, the market day for years, was a black day for us. The Gentiles gathered in the center of town to see us humiliated and brought down to the level of 2nd class humans. I didn't want to go out with the patch, to give this great 'joy' of the Gentiles, but what could one do. One needs water and the well was on the other side of the marketplace. I went out and they sent mocking glances at me. Tears welled in my eyes, but I was not ready to make them even happier, so I didn't cry.

The second decree was enforced labor. We were taken to clear for the railway, 15km from town. When we came back after a long day of working and walking we were exhausted, and tired of life. Later, the murders started with small and big. They went from house to house, dragged the Jews out, and took them to be killed in the outskirts of town. At one such moment Binyamin Levy pleaded for mercy, telling them he was a father of 10. One of the murderers replied:

"You deserve a double punishment. You brought 10 Jews to this world and now [we] have to waste 10 bullets."

The next time they went for the old and sick. They went from house to house with a list of names and killed those listed in their beds. 17 Jews were killed this way. On the next day they announced and explained their act:

"We did it for your own sake. So they wouldn't infect you with their illnesses. And for the elders we did them a personal favor. We saved them from unnecessary suffering. The day will come when you'll understand that."

Witnessing the Slaughter of the Vilners

The Vilners who escaped from Vilne ghetto and came to us were hungry and exhausted. The people of Voronova took them into their homes and did everything to improve their situation. One day, I and Khayke Gol decided to go to the estate and dairy–plant owner to ask for milk and dairy for the refugees. We went to him with big jugs. We had to walk for several kilometers. Halfway we saw Meir Meirovitsh running towards us from his wagon: 'climb the wagon quickly, we'll move away from the town, it's all surrounded by Germans'.

Khayke jumped on the wagon. I decided to go back to town, to be with my parents. When I approached the Christian cemetery, I saw policemen. I asked one of them, a family acquaintance, to let me through. He looked at me as if I was crazy:

"Be happy that you are outside, run and hide," – he pointed to the direction of the forest – but I insisted, so they let me through.

When I came home I found them sitting on the floor like mourners. I found out that the Germans and their assistants had gone from house to house, taken out all the Vilners and other "strangers", and locked them in the cinema house. We talked to other families and decided to bring food to the prisoners. We divided them in small groups with every family responsible for a group.

Their imprisonment lasted for two weeks, and it's impossible to describe what those miserable people went through every day and every moment. On Saturday morning we were told that the Vilners were to be taken to another location. We thought this might be Vilne. I ran to the house of my friend Bilkeh Levine, which was near the cinema house, to watch, to listen, and to find out what was going to happen.

We saw our poor brothers, taken in long rows from the cinema to the [unknown word[9]]. They walked in an organized manner: first men, behind them women, and at the end several children of about 5 years old. We froze at the sight of this sad procession. We stood without moving for a long while, biting our lips, breaking palms, and pulling our hair out, but we didn't weep— although we understood the tragedy of their fate. Then the door opened. Yakov Kaminetski came in and shouted:

"[Yiddish] Brothers, take shovels, hammers and hoes, and come to [unknown word[10]] to bury our brothers. Don't cry, it's the 15th of Shevat.[11]

I jumped down from the ladder to ask a question. He stopped me, put his hand on my shoulder and said:

"That's how it is!"

Later we were brought to the cinema house to clean up the blood of our brothers. It was an awful sight. The walls and the floors were covered with dry blood and pieces of hair, evidence of the torture and smashed skulls, the desperation and the pulled out hair— indescribable atrocities. We were depressed. From that moment we knew that our end was also near and there would be no escape.

The Big Massacre

We decided to prepare a *"melina"*, a hidden bunker. We picked a small room in the house, covered the door with wallpaper similar to the wallpaper on the rest of the walls. It was meant to hold several neighboring families. We decided not to leave the house, no matter what, even if it was to become our grave.

On the morning of the massacre we found out that the pits had already been prepared for us. All illusions faded, we knew that we were doomed.

From our yard we saw the Gestapo coming in trucks. We shut ourselves in the *melina*. Several minutes passed and then the shooting started. We heard the Gestapo people in our house. They cursed, swore, screamed, knocked on the walls. Now they approached the door of the bunker; we all hold our breath, including the children— even they knew that you had to keep quiet and not cry, not break down, not even to breath. A miracle occurred: a bucket full of excrement that the children used at night spilled at the feet of these 'gentle' German soldiers, and the stench drove them out of the house. They threw a curse, "dirty Jews", and went away.

On that day most of the dear Voronova folk were murdered. We remained alive.

Bound For Slaughter to Lida and Another Bunker

We were relocated to the Lida ghetto. We were placed in the same rooms from which Jews had been taken to mass murder the day before. There were a lot of pillows in the rooms. Those were not the savage murderers that tear up pillows and scatter feathers in the streets, like those collaborating pogromists, the Poles, Ukrainians and Lithuanians. These [Germans] would come back after the slaughter and steal all the pillows and send them to their country, to the State. Russian pogroms were for the benefit of the state, but the spoils belonged to the collaborators. Germans were different: the spoils of even the millionth pogrom would be contributed to the State. The State would know how to clean up the blood of the victims, clean up the national conscience, and to launder the stains.

In Lida we looked for a *melina* again. In "our flat" stayed several families, among them were carpenters. We made a design. The entrance had to be from inside the house, otherwise there'd be no time to get in and stay. It had to be underground and must have an exit outside the yard, outside the camp.

The men did the digging and we the girls took away the soil. It was very hard. During the day we worked on roadways, and at nights we dug and moved the soil as far as possible in order to scatter it in a wide perimeter, so that no one would notice. The construction of the *melina* ruined our bodies and sapped our remaining energy. The tension and the fear weakened our souls and depressed us.

People in the ghetto were well aware of the situation. They knew there was no hope and this depressed them. Some adopted the attitude of 'eat and drink because tomorrow you die'. There were even marriages in the ghetto.

May Werner Be Damned

The hard daily work exhausted us and we almost lost our will to live, but things were still bearable. Much harder to bear was employer abuse–from both the Germans and their collaborators. Abuse kills all life in a person. He becomes a living dead, a state which is hard to describe. The employers were cruel–thirsty animals, and the worst of them was Werner. This German was a cruel sadist who couldn't live without causing suffering to someone else. He had a huge German Shepherd trained, upon a tiny sign, to attack a person and tear him up into pieces, or tear off his skin. Werner also chose Polish guards similar to himself, stupid and miserable sadists. They always found a pretense to take away our free day of week as a punishment for our "crimes".

Once Konopke, a degraded Pole, said:

"You are building a highway but you'll never have the opportunity to use it."

I exploded:

"Yes, we are going to die, but Palestine is in creation and it will be ours forever, while you, stupid Poles will die the death of traitors, and your country will be destroyed and torn like it always has been in history."

He lowered his head. My words penetrated, and he was quiet— to my surprise and the surprise of others. It was the same week the Germans had hanged 18 Polish priests in Krakow, and the Poles got that message.

Next morning everyone went out to work. A rumor had spread in the ghetto: from then on we would not be killed one–by–one shootings, now there would be mass murders by gas.

The good German who told us the news added:

"Gas is a good thing, there is no pain and the death comes quickly."

German stupidity, or the naiveté of a good soul? In either case our situation was made clear to us. People made plans to flee to the forest. Many talked about Tuvye Bielski, his men and actions, but the problem was that partisans accepted only young people who could fight, and only if they came with their own weapons. So, what should we do? We the girls, and our old parents? One of our neighbors suggested he would take along one of our sisters with him, but where could we find money to pay half the price of a gun, as he demanded?

In a short time a solution was found' Near the highway where we worked often passed a nice Pole, whom we knew as an honest man. We told him about our troubles. We agreed to sell him our clothes, and he would bring the money. So Rivke went with the neighbor to the forest hoping to pull us out later. After her went Yaffe, and we waited for our turn. A few days passed; our dream ended when our sisters returned to the ghetto. They told us that there had been a German attack and the whole Bielski squad had scattered towards all directions in the forest. Again, a shred of hope had been smashed. The only remaining hope was the bunker, and who could know whether it would be enough.'

The Bunker was Breached by its Residents

On that night, Mother was the first to notice that the ghetto was surrounded. She woke us up. The ghetto was in turmoil. The Germans ordered everyone to step outside. All Jews were to be moved to Lublin. We knew it was extermination: the end.

The Germans were already standing at our doorstep when we disappeared into the ditch and inside the bunker. We stayed there for a whole week after the ghetto was emptied of Jews. We were 15 people. We, the young girls, had to lie in the ditch. The place was narrow. People lost conscious from time to time. Every day, the Germans came back to check for any remaining witnesses to their crimes. On the eighth day we all were already drenched, we couldn't stand it anymore. One of us broke down the door and went out:

"If we don't go out now, we will all die and rot here" – he screamed.

Others followed, and the *melina* was breached. Suddenly we found ourselves standing in the fresh air, blinded by the light. It was raining. We came close to the ghetto fence. We found an opening in the fence. We went through it, one after another. Father widened the opening for us and we went through. When it was his turn his coat got caught in the iron wire and he couldn't move. Meanwhile people continued forward. Mother, who was sure, that he'd get free in a moment, went with them. My two sisters went with her. I and my sister Mineh stayed with our father. We were already far behind. Father begged us to go back to the bunker, we didn't want to.

When we came to the cemetery, which was close to the ghetto, we lay down between the graves: we couldn't move, for a few meters away a policeman stood and smoked. What to do? Suddenly his cigarette went out. The rain strengthened. He must have gone to his friend for a light. We took the opportunity to run out of the cemetery and leave the guarded area.

On our way we found a pigsty, we got in and stayed for the night. We were wet and frozen, exhausted and tired of life. Early in the morning the farmer came to the pigsty and discovered us, he crossed himself, went back to the house and brought us blankets and hot coffee.

We spent the day in the pigsty. From afar we could hear German sirens activated in the ghetto, they wanted to scare the last remaining Jews hiding in *melinas*. Towards night we were asked by the Gentile to leave. We went to look for the rest of our family, and to the forest.

We will remember this good Gentile forever. How he parted from us and how he escorted us to the exit. It's hard to express the feelings of foreboding that we were heading towards certain death, and that he could do nothing to help us.

After liberation we went to visit him. He almost fainted seeing us alive, as if he were looking at the dead raised from the grave.

Into the Forest and in the Forest

On the way we lost our way and came close to a German post. We hid, survived, and went on. At some point we met a young shepherd. We asked him to show us the way to the forest. We offered him money. He took the money, but then changed his mind out of fear. He told us to go in a certain direction— there lived an estate owner who would let us in and feed us.

The atmosphere in the house was warm and pleasant. The table was loaded with the best food. The whole family was sitting around the table and steam rose from a bowl in the middle of the table. I approached him and told him that my father and sister were waiting outside, hungry for many days now. He took out of the bowl 2 potato latkes[12] soaked and dripping with pork oil. I refused to take them. I said father wouldn't eat them and I preferred to take bread. He became angry, stood up from his chair and shouted:

"Get out of here quickly!"

Before I opened the door, I took courage:

"Sir" – I said, "we too had once a warm home and serene life. Nobody knows what tomorrow will bring."

We went out. Good Gentiles advised us to stay at a distance. After several minutes two Russian partisans appeared, we were happy to see them. They were shocked by Father's appearance: it was a strange sight for them to see a traditional Jew. They greeted us, but immediately started shouting and cursing:

"Until now you spent your time in the ghetto, partying with the Germans, far from danger. Now, when the danger comes close, you ran away."

They put us in their wagon and took us to a park. We thought that they are taking us to Bielski, but they tricked us. They took our father to Bielski and dragged us to their squad. We opposed, cried, and begged, but they threatened to kill us if we didn't come with them. We cried even harder and threatened to scream. They began to hesitate, we clung to each other, and leaned together against a tree. Suddenly we heard a shot. They got scared and left.

We stayed in the park for the night, deciding to continue in the morning. But suddenly the two 'heroes' came back, robbed our boots, and all our possessions, and ordered us to run away.

On the way to the forest a lot of Jews, refugees from Lida ghetto, were wandering around. We joined one of the groups and reached Bielski's squad.

It was *Rosh Hashana* eve. We stretched our coats and sat down, to rest from the road, the stress and the hunger. Here we remembered that our mother and sisters are not with us.

The rumor of our arrival spread throughout the camp, and on the next day we heard someone calling us by names. The rest of our family had preceded us and came to Bielski before we did, now we were united.

Near the Voronova mass grave

Voronova a Town of Graves and a Child's Hand

After the Russian victory over the Nazis we went back to Voronova. We were given jobs, they let us live there, but the sight of our houses occupied by our neighbors was unbearable and prevented us from settling down there.

Father went to see the graves of the martyrs, [to see] if they were well covered. I went with him, and we were joined by several survivors. We started digging. The first layer was hard. I found a pole, knocked hard, and the "cover" opened up. A horrible sight opened to us. Corpses piled one upon another, and clods of dry blood mixed with soil. Suddenly I saw a small hand, a tiny one, poking out between the corpses, stretched up towards the world of orphans: a hand of a Jewish toddler, as if begging to be taken out of this deadly pit. Spontaneously I stretched my arm to him as a mother would stretch her hand to her baby [to take him] for a walk. The bone had already disintegrated and his palm remained in my arm and I was shattered. Suddenly N.K.V.D guards came on horses and drove us away, to prevent the spread of diseases. I succeeded in taking four bullets stained with blood with me, as a horrific souvenir.

These were some of the bullets that exterminated the Voronova Jews, horrible bullets sent toward Jewish eternity hoping it would lie down.[13] But it didn't lie down.

Footnotes

1. Tr. Note: the rabbinical term for the forcefully converted
2. Ed. Note: believed to be the plural of a compound word derived from 'mar' (Aramaic for person) and anus (short for anusim, see footnote 1); the phrase is a reference to the changing terminologies under different regimes for the similar condition of being forced converts away from Judaism.
3. Ed. Note: literally: 'Jewishness', refers to the ability to maintain Jewish traditions
4. Ed. Note: The word 'nest' was used by *Beitar*-ists to refer to

individual town units within the organization.

5. Ed. Note: in this context, meaning non–*Beitar*-ists
6. Ed. Note: see note 5, in this context, meaning the state of being non–*Beitar*-ists
7. Trans. Note: approximate translation of a Hebrew proverb
8. Tr. Note: famous Communist slogan
9. Tr. Note: In the original text the word is spelled: tet–resh–vav–bet–hey.
10. See fn. 9
11. Tr. Note: a Jewish holiday
12. Tr. Note: potato pancakes
13. Tr. Note: a quote from the Book of Samuel: "The Eternity (God) of Israel will not lie down."

[Page 57]

Thanks to Our Child

Moshe Kaplan (with the assistance of Khayeh Kaplan)

Translation by Emma Karabelnik

Ed. Note: This article appears in both Hebrew and Yiddish in the original Yizkor Book. The following is a translation of the Hebrew text. Photos appearing within the Yiddish are included here.

My First Miracle

When the Germans occupied Voronova and its surroundings, I was on my way to the Red Army, but the roads were already blocked. News about German progress was coming from all directions. [Our] commander realized that it would be impossible to get through as a group so he said:

"Let's split up and infiltrate. Those who are from this area can do whatever they decide."

People scattered around the area. I decided to go back to my wife. She was pregnant with her first child, I wanted to be home when the baby was born. I wanted to make my wife's hard days easier.

I came to Voronova in the evening, through the meadow. I found the town in a state of depression. The Germans had already been in town for 2 days. My parents were very confused by my return. Their thinking was that their life would be more comfortable with me around, but maybe it would have been better for me to stay with the Russians.

With my arrival, I found myself in the familiar social order: the *Yudenrat* supplied Jews for forced labor, gold and silver quotas were being forced upon poor Jews, the hard labor of building roads, of chopping wood, of collecting weapons left behind by the Russians in the Berlovits forest, of serving in German households, etc.

The headquarters were in Yehoshua Grodzenchik's house. It was a big house. In there the Germans gathered the painters, among them Pesakh Kuznets, Yehudah Pikovski, Berkovski, and others. We worked for them as painters, painting road signs, boxes, etc. They asked us how much the Russians had paid us, and they paid us the same.

One Saturday, the Germans asked for 10 Jews to load a train with boxes full of goods stolen from Jews. We waited an hour and a half for the train. The Germans arranged as in rows and forced us to do various physical exercises such as run–fall–run, and always ordered us to fall in mud puddles. If someone didn't want to stretch fully, they would push him down and trample him with their feet, and force him into the mud.

When the train arrived, we loaded the 'merchandise'. They held us inside the wagons and wouldn't let us out, under the pretense of looking for communists among us. We sat on the floor and a German announced names, each one whose name was called had to stand up and move to a designated location. When he came to my name, there were 3 people by the name Moshe Kaplan among us. Besides me stood Lutski Arshulki's, a Pole who worked as a junior policeman. He didn't let me respond. My name was called 3 times. I wanted to stand up as ordered, but he stepped on my foot and nailed me to the floor and said in spoken Yiddish:

"Don't be stupid"

It's possible that thanks to this incident I survived.

From the whole group, the Germans arrested: my brother–in–law Yitzakh Volpianski, Sheyke Moshe's, Zerakh Shelovski, his brother David and his sister Esther. Since then their trails have been lost forever.

A curious thing is that [the person] who informed on us was Arshule, the mother of Lutski, the one who saved me.

For some reason we were not enclosed in the ghetto. Movement was still allowed, except that Jews were not allowed to walk on the sidewalks, and they had to take off their hats and bow each time they passed by a German, and various other humiliations.

The Vilners Arrive, the Vilners are Exterminated

At the same time, some refugees from Vilne and its suburbs arrived and told about the atrocities of mass murders and exterminations of Jews, about the bloody massacre in Vilne, and about horrific incidents involving women and children. They believed that in a small town [like ours] that wouldn't happen.

The Germans found out about them. They began searching every house and arresting them. Everyone who was sick at that moment was shot on the spot. Everyone who was healthy was taken to the cinema house, which was built by the Russians on Railway Street. They were held there for several days. They awaited an order from Vilna; one day suddenly they took everyone to a forest near the railway station and shot them one-by-one in small groups. At that time I was staying at my sister Mineh's house on the outskirts. I watched through the window. I saw those groups of Jews and heard the shots that killed them group-by-group.

They were buried in a mass grave near the forest. It was in March 1942.

At the time of the search for Vilners, I was working in Bastuni, 8km from town. The Gentiles told us about the search. Since they also thought that all the Jews were being gathered, they advised us not to go back home. That same night, Zalmen Dukshtulski came to Bastuni, escaping from Voronova frightened. He told us all the details: his first wife who was from Vilne had been killed. On the memorial for the Vilners in Lida the name Zalmen Dukshtulsky is also carved.

After few days we returned to Voronova, and Zalmen, haunted by horrors of those days, went his own way, far from the town.

The German atrocities continued for approximately 2 months. On the 9th of May, a Friday, we woke up and saw Polish and White Russian guards all around town. Our close neighbors stood with axes, pitchforks, and rods, and besieged the town. The night was sleepless, nobody closed an eye that night. On the next day, Saturday morning, the Germans called the *Yudenrat* and ordered them to go house-to-house and calm everybody down, saying that nothing bad would happen to them, and that their only purpose was to look for communists.

Beginning of Extermination

The Jews calmed down and felt relieved. On the same day a Gentile came to Mordechai Pikovski and told him to warn all the Jews to escape, because a huge pit was already dug out in the Bialorovski Forest at the end of Lida Street, and they also had chlorine and whitewash for body disinfection. But, Mordechai got angry with his longtime friend and drove him out of the house, poor guy. Mordechai wanted to believe that this Gentile was only looking to upset him or extort money for saving his life.

On Sunday, May 10, 1942, the *Yudenrat* was called and told that on the next day, Monday, all the Jews would have to gather in Market Square in the center of town, across from the church, for a document-check in order to detect communists.

On May 11, 1942, the Germans, with their Lithuanian and Polish collaborators, went into all the houses and drove out Jews from small to old, and drove them with beatings to Market Square. Whoever tried to escape was beaten to death with axes and iron rods. They chased him and caught him.

When everyone were assembled, Vindish, the Chief of Headquarters, appeared and made a speech in which he explained that in 1938 there was a summit in at the Reichstag in Berlin, and it was proven that the Jews were responsible for all the troubles of the German people and of all humanity. The verdict was the death penalty for all Jews, and now he was here to carry it out in our area. So his request was that order be kept: that every head-of-family called should take his family members, and all related to them, and start walking towards Lida. Whoever tried to resist or escape would be treated with well-deserved brutality.

He was a short man with blond hair, in a neat brown SS uniform, and he spoke with a satanic smile on his face. Later he himself stood at the crossroads of Lida Railway Street and Hermenishki Street and performed the selection – who was to live and who would die. Those who were directed towards Lida went to death. They were instantly attacked, the wild animals, our neighbors, beat them to death even before they came close to the grave.

Apparently the Gentile has spoken the truth. A huge pit was ready, and beside it were piles of chlorine and whitewash. Jews approached group–by–group, undressed nearby, and entered the pit naked, where they were shot. While they breathed their last air they were piled into layers, and between layers they spilled chlorine and whitewash for disinfection. Among those brutally buried there were persons only wounded, who were covered by the bodies of others and choked underneath them.

In this manner all the Jews of Voronova and its surrounding were murdered— approximately 2,300 people.

We craftsmen, and the 'still needed', stood and watched everything and even saw the piles of clothes taken back to town, and other horrible sights that are hard to forget. The brutality of our Gentile neighbors is indescribable. How blood–thirsty they were, and eager to perform any violent act requested of them. Only cannibals are capable of such bloody celebration. They attacked their prey, they beat to death anyone who was weak or resisted, they broke into houses to rob and loot, but most of all they were thirsty for blood.

I specifically remember the violent incident with Shapkona Eliahu and Khayeh (Berkovski). When we were ordered to the Market Place, they left their baby in the cradle, hoping that at least he would survive. Eventually Vindish left them with the 'needed', and when they came back home they found their baby's body chopped into pieces in the cradle. This was done by none other than our good neighbors, who had taken the opportunity to loot houses. Who can imagine such human degradation? Who is capable of taking revenge by chopping the body of a baby?

Of all our Jews, only 700 were left. They didn't allow us back to our homes— they were already confiscated by the Germans. We stayed on Lida Street, which they called the ghetto. After several days we were taken to Lida, to a real ghetto. Before we left, Vindish made another speech and told us that we are still alive because the military needed us, but our fate would soon be the same.

Lida Ghetto and How I was Saved

On Saturday, the first day of Succoth, we were driven out of the houses, and we knew that we were being exiled from them forever. Each one took with him a sack of food and as many clothes as we could carry, and thus we left the town.

Outside town, the Germans and their aides dragged our sacks away from us and threw them to the side of the road while beating us hard. If someone became tired and stayed behind, he was beaten to death.

We walked like this for 9 km to Bastuni. There, we were loaded into cargo wagons and taken to Lida Ghetto.

The *Yudenrat* put us into packed and crowded houses, and then began all the working details, etc. I and Pikovski, who used to work for Vindish as painters, were now assigned to his workshops. By his order, everyone who worked for him now, or had been in his workshops before, was automatically assigned to his workshops here, and that was some luck which others envied.

I worked as a painter in German houses. I also worked in the house of Warner, who was known for his extreme brutality. All the Jews that worked for him had to stand in a 'payment line'. He would walk along the line with his huge dog and from time to time, order the dog to 'pay', and the dog ripped pieces of skin and flesh. I knew about that so I used to run away in the evening [after work], and that saved me.

My brother–in–law Volpianski was hiding at a Gentile's house, his friend and buddy. One evening two Germans came to the house and wanted to take Moshe with them. They were angry with the Gentile for hiding a Jew at his home and threatened him. The Gentile attacked them, they both grabbed the guns from the Germans, and my brother–in–law was saved, but he had to leave the house and hide in the woods. In the afternoon, while he was taking a nap in the warmth of the sun, a beautiful Polish young woman came up to him and said that she had been watching him sleep for an hour now and that she had fallen in love with him, and her love is growing from moment to moment, and she couldn't help herself. She took him to her home. Her family accepted him as a son and she – as a husband.

And thus he disappeared from us and we didn't know, neither us nor his friend, what ever happened to him. We were cut off from him in the ghetto, not knowing his fate.

One day in the end of March 1943 a Gentile woman's mother came to us, told us that he was alive, and offered to take us out from the ghetto. We didn't want to leave without our baby Avraham'le, so after that she used to come from time to time, bringing us food packages but never mentioning the matter of our escape. After a while she again tried to talk about saving us, but again we mentioned our baby. This time she agreed and we all left the ghetto.

According to our agreement we had to prepare some things before leaving.

I told our secret to Mula Khayot (today a movie theater manager in Herzliya). At night the two of us left the ghetto and went to my brother-in-law's house. According to the plan we were each supposed to fetch our families in the morning. Mula started mingling with the Gentiles while my in-law and I confiscated a horse with a winter wagon from one of the Gentiles. I went back to Lida alone.

I arrived at the Lida ghetto early in the morning. Near the gate stood Leibke Azovski, a nice Lida guy, who served as a policeman in the *Yudenrat*. I called him in Yiddish by his name and he opened the gate. I went inside with my wagon.

I rested for several hours after the long trip and so did my horse. In the afternoon I went out through the same gate with the help of the same Leibke. I left the ghetto legally and as soon as I was out of town I stopped and waited.

My wife took Avraham'le and snuck out through a hole in the fence behind the ghetto.

We decided that she would take with her 80 rifle bullets, which I had in my possession, in order to be permitted to join the partisans later. It took a while to make way to my wagon, and on the way her bra opened, letting all the bullets scatter on the ground at the same moment she was encountering some Germans and Ukrainians. Her situation was dire, but thanks to her resourcefulness she placed the baby on the snow over the bullets and pretended to change his diapers. They passed her without paying attention.

Several long hours passed before she reached me. I saw a few German policemen pass by and approach me. From time to time my heart almost exploded, but I pretended to be repairing the harness and the sleigh, or I took the horse to drink water–also, I was dressed in Polish military garb. All this calmed their suspicions and I was saved.

Towards evening I saw her approaching from a distance and towards her were approaching some German policemen. My heart almost leaped out of my chest, but somehow they didn't notice her and we rode away. On the way a Polish policeman stopped us and climbed on to the wagon. We had aroused his suspicion. He began questioning us about where we were from and where we were going. My wife told him:

"The baby is sick with typhus and we are taking him to a doctor."

This made him step away from the wagon. At that time the fear of epidemics was such that he simply ran away. We got rid of him and reached the house of my in–law.

My brother–in–law prepared a bunker for us in the dairy barn of his caretakers, the Tsikovskies, and we hid there for 8 months.

During this time another 15 Jews arrived and were hidden by the brothers of this Gentile, Joseph Tsikovski.

Among them were Dovid Eliahu and Yosef Gershonovitsh, Sarah Rivke Arkov, Yosl Shprintse's, Yoshka Korvo, Mula Khayot, his wife and daughter. These righteous people endangered their property and their lives by hiding all of us.

We Are Separated From Our Baby

One day, Germans attacked the farmhouses in the area, burnt down houses, and executed people as revenge for the 2 Germans killed the day before.

We fled to the forest. We didn't want to go back to that village any more— not only because of the danger to us, but also because we didn't want to bring disaster to our saviors. In the forest we realized that in the fear of escape we had forgotten the baby in the bunker. I went back. The old woman was standing on the porch crying, holding the baby in her arms. I took my baby and left.

In the forest the roads were covered with mud and snow. It was very hard to walk and went on forever. We walked, frightened and silent, and the baby was crying and wailing. Other Jews were afraid that he'd expose all of us, and it was proposed by several of them that we get rid of the baby. One of them, a man from Soletchnik, pointed his gun to the baby's head and asked – kill or not.

I didn't allow him, although the dilemma had gone through my head too. Could I endanger the souls of so many Jews because of one little, innocent baby? I took the baby in my arms. I stroked him. I wanted to comfort him, to silence him, and also to calm down the others. But he was suffering from cold and hunger, his stomach ached, and his whole body was convulsing, legs and fists. He looked at me and continued crying. Then David Gershonovitsh came up and said that he knew a Gentile farmer in the nearby village we could leave the baby with, in exchange for a piece of clothing and bread, until we could come back for him. In spite of all the heartache of separation, we knew that we had to do it.

The Gentile agreed. He had a small house. Eight people slept in one room with one bed, among them an old grandma. They placed Avraham'le as the ninth in the common bed, and he stayed there.

When the situation became calmer, we went to visit him from time to time, to hold him for a while, and to bring a bribe to the Gentile. He was dirty, his head full of lice, but he was lying with other children and enjoying it.

From time to time we took him with us, but it was too dangerous. The baby wanted to talk, to learn to walk, to play around, and we constantly silenced him and denied all his aspirations. Later we built a bunker at the Ulanovski's and came to spend time with the baby for several days at a time, then go back to Tsikovski, who didn't want to take the baby back in. He was too afraid after managing to get rid of him once already.

There were times when we were cut off from him for a while. Once, after one such long separation, I came to visit him in the middle of the day. I heard his ringing voice from afar. I proceeded towards the voice. I found him in the doghouse. The dog wasn't there so he had taken the opportunity to enjoy some space. He lay on his stomach, looking at his own hands, murmuring "wound", "aches", "mommy", "daddy". I hid so he wouldn't notice me. My heart was torn but I couldn't let him see me.

Once I snuck up and saw him crawling into the big family pot in which the housewife prepared the casserole, but it was empty. He whispered "hungry". Then he crawled under the cow and tried to suck her nipples, and said to himself in disappointment "no milk". My heart exploded. He went back to the doghouse, stretched out like a street dog desperate for food, care and warmth, and I went back home with a broken heart.

One night some "white" Poles came to Ulanovski and threatened him so he would say the names of the Jews that he had hidden. Somebody had snitched on him. But that person didn't know the age of this 'dangerous' Jew hiding from them, nor the number of Jews. They picked on him and threatened him, but he didn't talk.

The next day he demanded that we come and take the baby. We couldn't do it. During the day we wandered in the woods, and during nights we looked for shelter and robbed local farmers at gunpoint. This was our life: stealing another day by stealing food. All the miserable parents were organized into small groups. We couldn't take him. There was nowhere to take him. Once we took him with us to the forest. He was already 13 months old, but couldn't walk yet. We knew that he couldn't walk and we were glad of this. Suddenly in the middle of the woods he stood up and started marching on his small feet. He was so enthusiastic that he became hysterical and began laughing, shouting and crying at the same time. We saw some Germans approaching on the road and we got scared. We grabbed him and forcefully shut his mouth so he wouldn't expose us. We had to return him to Ulanovski.

After then it became harder for them to watch him because his playing area had expanded.

On one of our visits, the old woman told us in tears that the day before she had noticed that the baby was gone. She got scared and ran out to look for him in the fields, and found him between the beds of potato plants, which grew as high as his small white head sticking up between the lines.

She called him:

"Where to, Antush?"

He said:

"I'm going to daddy."

Since then he started wandering in the room from corner to corner as if looking for something, always holding an old blanket in his hands, a small pot, and a piece of bread. This was a habit he developed.

We Lived Like Forest Robbers or Forest Animals

We felt that we had to go join the Partisans. Mula was already with them and we were looking for a way to join him. One day Ruvke Arkin, and the engineer from Lodz who was with us, went to the forest. They met some Polish Partisans who promised to take them to the Jewish Partisans. They came back to us to fetch their wives and both left again, with Mula's wife and baby, the engineer's wife and his female cousin. We waited for the sign to follow them. After a few hours Ruvke came back, in shock and fear, and told us that the Polish Partisans had let them come close but then as soon as they approached, attacked them brutally.

They had beaten the engineer to death. Ruvke had managed to escape, but the women stayed behind and who knew what would happen to them. We already had weapons so we ran to attack the Poles and save the wives of Mula and the engineer. The engineer's female relative was already dead.

The Poles couldn't forgive us for such chutzpa. They were wandering the forest, just like us, looking for an opportunity for revenge. We had no choice but to move from Pepeshni Forest to Petrokani Forest.

On one occasion we were took a nap in the forest. I woke up and stood up to straighten my clothes, and to shake off the lice from my body. It was very quiet. I couldn't hear anything. Suddenly I raised my head and saw some Germans approaching in front of me. I jumped and ran and shouted "Germans are coming". Hinde'chka, daughter of Shtumak, ran out with me. We saw Germans in front of us surrounding the houses and we had no choice and no options. I said goodbye to her and broke into the human chain that the Germans had created. They were startled for a moment so I ran straight through them. One of them quickly recovered and ran after me, throwing a grenade in my direction. I fell on the ground, then stood up and fired at him. He ran back and all the Germans took supine positions on the ground. Hinde'chka took this opportunity to run through to one of the backyards, to hide. But a White Pole noticed her and killed her right there in the backyard. From my hiding place I could hear her begging for her life, but he didn't listen and shot her. My wife and a Jew from Ivia whose nickname was *polzhid* [half–Jew], his wife and daughter, got supine in the barley field, putting their life in the hands of destiny, and they survived. My brother–in–law didn't wake up to my warnings and they killed him. Together with him were also killed Yosko and Yosef Pupko.

I lay alone in a high area and waited for darkness. I licked the stones in order to wet my mouth, which was dry from fear and tension, and to recover my breath. When I saw the moon high up in the sky, I presumed it was midnight, and I went out to the nearest village to look for shelter, for brother Jews in sorrow, and for my wife. A hard feeling of loneliness fell upon me. I felt that I had made my last effort to survive and I had failed. It was time to accept death as the conclusion.

I came to Joseph Tsikovski and found my wife there. We burst into tears. We were simply surprised that the other one was alive. The truth is that both of us believed that the other one had been killed. We stood and sobbed like babies, but the Gentiles were not impressed by this shocking scene. They demanded that we leave and release them from the burden we imposed. They were in fear for their lives.

We knew that this time we would not be able to convince them, or bribe them with any goods. We waited until evening and left for the woods, the whole group, the last survivors.

We Are Considering Giving Ourselves Up to the Germans

The woods were filled with groups of the White Polish underground, the Polish Partisans, and other groups of Gentiles. We were afraid of all of them. We wandered from forest to forest like hunted animals, and the autumn was near. The cold and the dampness consumed our remaining energy and exhausted all of our willpower. Every day brought with it atrocities and disaster.

We made an effort to stay alive for the sake of our baby. We tried to stay close to his safekeepers. One day we came to Ulanovski, the poor farmer, and he demanded that we take the baby with us. He told us that the White Poles had been coming to him nights, demanding that he hands over "the Jews". He told us that the last time they had thrown him in a deep pit, an unfinished well, and had fired above his head in order to frighten him, but that he had sworn he wasn't hiding any Jews and they had left him alone for a while. Now he was demanding that we take the baby away.

Meanwhile our entire group dismantled. Each one took his own close family and tried to look for shelter with neighboring Gentiles. We also found out that Dovid Gershonovitsh, his son Yosef, and Sarah Rivke Arkov had been caught by the Poles and murdered.

Ulanovski continued to cry and complain, and demanded that we take the baby, but the frost had begun to attack the world, and above all the homeless. When we slept in the forest we woke up covered with frost in the mornings. We had no food. We were helpless and in despair. To take the baby to the forest meant to take him to a slow death and to major suffering. We began to form thoughts of giving ourselves up to the Germans, for a quick and certain death.

We answered Ulanovski:

"Do with the baby whatever you want, we can't take him to the forest to frost and hunger. In addition we intend to give in to the Germans."

We were sure that this would convince him, because he was a good Gentile. We also thought that the fact that he'd be raising the kid for himself, without the need to return him one day, would change his decision.

The next day we went to the Germans. We wanted to shorten our suffering. We couldn't go on like this anymore.

We went to the forest. We walked upright, without hiding, ready to get caught. We were already close to a German [field] headquarters. My wife saw the German policemen and started crying. She said:

"Why must we give in, let's take another direction and try our luck. Maybe we'll be lucky to find partisans who'll accept us."

It was very difficult. We had to cross the railroad that led to German-occupied areas.

We went back to the forest. We walked at night and hid during the day. The walk was hard. I didn't know the way so I crawled on my knees, groping and scouting, while my wife held on to my coat and followed me. I forgot to mention that Nekhama Katz and her daughter Mashenka were together with us on this terrible march, and they also followed us in this groping chain. We slept with our clothes on, and with time we were covered by lice which prospered and fattened themselves sucking on our exhausted bodies. The clothes got wet and then dried on our bodies. We used to take off our shoes, tie them together by the laces, and put them around our necks in order not to lose them. We knew that we'd need them for many escapes in the future. One can't run without shoes.

[Pages 70-73]

Final Days of Our Town
(Brief Memories)

Keileh Grodzenchik (Shamir)

Translation by Meir Bulman

Ed. Note: This article appears in both Hebrew and Yiddish in the original Yizkor Book. The following is a translation of the Hebrew text. Photos appearing within the Yiddish version are included here.

Saturday, 8/May/1942

We awaken from our sleep and slowly open the blinds. The air this time around looks too dense, irritating and suffocating. Someone remarks: "Today something will happen."

We look out to the street through the window cracks and unwittingly utter : "We are in prison."

Our Polish neighbors stand around, armed with various and varied weapons: hoes, pitchforks, shovels, rakes. It is depressing and sometimes it seems that if those were guns or other firearms things would be more respectable. This is much more depressing, when they come with sticks and pitchforks and choose a strange death that is inappropriate for the 20th century— like dogs, a jungle.

We look at who comes to kill us. They are not strangers: they are the Poles— your close neighbors— your acquaintances. There is Eyseltchok, there is Bibik, Burshu and others that you went to school with and with whom you built a friendship, and here they are. Seeking to do you harm. It is painful, suffocating, and you have trouble breathing, a deep unease lingers in your heart: "So, what? Is this the end?"

Jews sigh. There are moans of helplessness. We know the end is near and there is no escape. We are shut in, enclosed, surrounded by Polish predatory beasts and by German soldiers.

About thirty tenants are cramped into my parents' house, all alone yet unified. Each expresses his anxiety in a different manner. One is steeped in a thundering silence. The second is twitting his fingers or biting his fingernails. The third is squeezing his coat. And the eyes: all the eyes are deep wells of horror. The pressures in the heart and the senses are too heavy, and each person silently prays that the end will come, the troubles be over— for who can stand this horror?

The hours stretch and all are waiting, even those outside, and no one knows why the matter is being delayed.

In the end, after long nightmarish hours, the siege is lifted. The murderers disperse.

Not yet. Not today

This day probably might return with equal horror, but it has been delayed temporarily and nobody knows why and what for.

The following day, the good neighbors, now without pitchforks in hand, explain that it was just a coincidence; they just wanted to search for something— just an experiment.

Sunday, 9/May/42

We are fed up. We want to get away. The thought of an "experiment" like that being repeated is terrifying. The young folks look for a way to escape, each one expresses an opinion of what to expect and the escape route. My husband Meir also proposes we escape, and I know he is right. But when we enter home and see our 4-month-old toddler daughter resting and trusting us to care for her and not abandon her, our conscience does not allow us to escape, and with her it is impossible.

We stay and wait like everyone else.

Tema Dlugin comes from the other side of town, calms the parents, and confirms that from a source credible to her it was just an experimental search that was not conducted, and they believe her, naively.

Monday, 10/May/42

A large force surrounds us. This time we observe them from a distance, entering homes and bringing Jews to the marketplace. Our turn will surely come as well.

We were among the last ones. We are told to go to the marketplace square. We feel like the end is here and we will not return to our homes. We want to leave, but Yosef the Barber comes and says, "You will not leave until you cover me in my bunker and put a bucket of water on the entrance." What the water was for we did not know. But we fulfilled his request/command. He enters the bunker with his wife and four children and indeed he remains alive. He perished later, but this time his luck and the trick work for him.

At the market intersection we remain— the last ones observing the events.

A table stands in the center with the two commanders. Jews approached and were directed to turn either to the right, to die, or else to the left, to expect death. Artshik Weiner and his brother-in-law Dlugin approach. The *ubermeister*, when he sees such a large family, asks Artshik who belongs to his family. The Nazi's eyes twinkle and he commands, "Run straight ahead," but Artshik begs to at least spare his wife and him, to no avail.

Khaikeh Mansfeld was married since the 1920s to a German who converted. As the Russians arrived he disappeared, his whereabouts unknown. Khaikeh thought naively that her German documents would stand her a chance. She approached the table with the stack of papers of insured hope, she was joined by her sister and the sister's husband and children— to extend her German rights to them. She was also joined by Keizeh Gurvits, Reiskke Konikhovski and her daughter. The German tells her to stand aside while he examines her documents. She stood, confident in her redemption and the redemption of those who joined in her fate. He then asked her, "Who are these people with you?"

She hands him her documents and adds an explanation: "My husband was a Germans and the Russians – "

He got angry— "And you dared live with a German!"— as if accusing her of a heinous crime. He immediately sent her to stand among those sentenced to die."

We remained alone. In the last half hour we sat alone without our close friends – the Voronova residents. Berl Levine of the *Yudenrat*[1] sat next to me. He ripped off the *Yudenrat* armband and told me to bury it. That very moment the *Gbitzcomisser*[2] approached and wanted to execute him immediately, but his friend the Voronova *ubermeister*[3] fought and argued with him, "I'm staying with the dumb Jews. I will have nobody to talk to. Leave him and the rest of the *Yudenrat* men to me." Thus they remained alive for a while.

We stayed in Voronova for two more weeks, thirteen miserable families with broken spirits and broken minds, flickering sparks. Nonetheless we wanted to live.

The fateful intersection

After everyone was sent to Lida, Meir went to part with his parents at the edge of town. I then witnessed a scene that is tough to describe: the Poles, even the young ones, stormed the deserted homes and plundered everything. And what was even left there? Nevertheless, they found it all exhilarating, and most exhilarating of all— the absence of people.

I sat in a home on Yinakonski alone with my daughter in my arms and thought: "Dear God, there it is, the positive neighborly relationships, the Polish culture, their aristocracy. It all dissipates and vanishes when you can obtain an object, a broken and abandoned vessel." And then, a group of robbery–crazed youths entered the home, and one of them, a former classmate of mine asked, surprised, "Mrs. Grodzenchik, what are you doing here?" I did not reply. I stormed out and sat with my daughter, my hope, in the middle of the street, for I knew death awaited me in the house.

The Germans felt these friends and neighbors of mine would lynch me, and so they led me to Iytl Olkenitski's house, where they were residing, and kept me there until Meir returned.

They still needed Meir, and so I too was rescued from the 'noble' Poles.

Editor's Footnotes

1. These were Jews forced by the Nazis to supervise and govern the Jewish populations under Nazi control

2. District commander

3. A local mayor

[Pages 74-107]

Ghettos and the Forest

M[eir] Shamir (Shmerkovitsh)

Translation by Emma Karabelnik

The First Pursuit

In the afternoon the Nazi Army appeared on vehicles, tanks, and cannons. The town was hiding behind doors and blinds, afraid to stick its head out.

In the evening we heard strong slaps on our doors. We were frightened, but then we heard a voice in Polish and it calmed us:

"Yakov" – it said – "open up. It's me the *sultis* (village headman)."

We asked what he wanted and didn't open the door.

"First open" – he said – "and don't worry."

We opened.

He explained that the German Mayor (Commandant) had called for me. He wanted to put me in charge of the power station, because he had gotten good recommendations from the station employees about my being a professional and a hard–working man.

I dressed up and went with the headman. In town I was taken to the Commandant's office, passing all the guards. I knocked on his door, went in, and announced:

"You called for me sir, and I am ready for your command." He read a list of things which had to be repaired at the station, and then went to his secretary and dictated a personal pass for me. In the end he said:

"The electrician Shmerkovitsh Meir is appointed as the head electrician and nobody is allowed to employ him at any other job. He is permitted to walk around Voronova during day and night, and nobody may stop him."

He personally signed and sealed.

Before I left he said that if required I may get assistance from workers sent by the *Yudenrat*.

In town everybody was eager to get some kind of permit or certificate in order to get work in town and not to be sent away. Believe me, in general a permit is the "safer" [of the two].

When I came to the *Yudenrat* and asked for workers to help me repair the tolls thrown down by the tanks, people started following me, offering money to hire them. Most of them were people that never did physical work before. It made me sick. Isn't it funny that even in such a difficult hour, the privileged sought to get an advantage by using their money? I took 15 workers who used to work at the mill during the Soviet regime. They worked with me until we put up all the tolls and repaired the power lines. After that some of them continued as steam boilers, harvesters, and general workers at the station.

There was a Pole who was in charge of me. My salary was about 80% of the usual salary [in my position] because I was a Jew. It was 800 rubles per month. It was usually paid to me in groceries, groats, flour, etc. There is always plenty of work for an electrician – at the power station and private jobs. I also repaired telephones. All the Germans used me as the exclusive institution for all [their requirements]. Later they all wanted me to install tape recorders in homes, and they all nagged me.

One day, a group of "snatchers" came to town. One of them, a policeman with a tin helmet on his head, asked us if we were Jews. We didn't deny this. He ordered us, when we are back in town, to assemble in the marketplace, women and men separately. Both I and my father-in-law understood that if they are separating men and women, the situation was getting worse. We decided not to go to the marketplace. We left our working tools with the women and jumped over the fence into the nearby cemetery. We stayed together for a while and then separated because I wanted to check what was happening in my parents' house. I ran through the streets and came in the back door. We had a big cowshed, old and in miserable state. High under the roof was a pile of old straw. It was hard to climb there. I urged my father and my brother, and the three of us climbed up there to hide.

From time to time mother would come to the stall and update us on events in the marketplace, although we knew well before she told us. The whining, the noise, the cries brought to our ears, described the situation well. We even heard screeching orders given by Polish policemen looking for every hiding place and ordering [people] to move to the marketplace. We heard the sounds of beatings on those who were discovered, and the cries of those who were beaten. From time to time we had the opportunity to look out and see these depressing scenes. We also saw how our good longtime neighbors pounced on our property, grabbed everything they could, and robbed the Jewish houses.

They didn't by-pass our house. One of them even tried to climb the crumbling ladder. He changed his mind, retreated, and began shouting at us, without seeing us:

"Come down bastards, or I'll shoot you as dogs, bloody Jews."

We lay close together, terrified, but we didn't reply, we didn't expose ourselves. Finally he went away.

After a while, when the marketplace disaster was over, we learned what was the objective had been, and why it had been organized. Apparently, eight trucks with Gestapo men had been brought in to organize a hunt, and let our Christian neighbors get some satisfaction from [Jewish] blood. They asked our neighbors to tell them which Jews who had collaborated with the Soviets, and then every neighbor pointed at someone with whom he wanted to get even, or at someone whose property he wanted for himself. Those Jews were dragged out of their houses. Among them were two sons of Shmuel Shelovski, David and Zerahke, Yitzach Volpianski and others. They were beaten to death with rubber sticks, loaded on the trucks, and taken to an unknown destination from which nobody returned.

After this horrible, cruel hunt, the Poles began vengeful activities against Jews. The Polish youth, and even children, enlisted into the police, even those who had been devoted communists or worked for the Soviets. There were also some Soviets who had stayed in town, remnants of the previous regime. They were all united in their cruelty against Jews. This police used to patrol the Jewish neighborhood, performing terrible acts. One time, they came to our street and ordered all the women to come outside. Each woman who didn't act as ordered was beaten with a haft. I happened to be home at that time. I didn't allow my pregnant wife and my mother to go out. For some reason the local policemen didn't go in, instead they sent in a policeman from outside the area. He went in and found my wife in the last room. He grabbed her and pushed her to go outside. I wanted to attack him, but my father-in-law Yakov Grodzenchik caught my hand and stopped me. Outside, the policemen stood in a line with sticks and whips in their hands. The women had to march before the line several times with slaps and blows falling on their heads. The "reason" was that the street was dirty, and this was the women's responsibility.

Meanwhile, law and order were more or less stabilized, and the Germans arrived to establish a civilian order.

The arrival of German civilians had a calming effect on the Jews in town. They hoped the Poles would now become restrained. Immediately, an order was given that Poles were not allowed to enter Jewish homes without a German order. The *Yudenrat* people and bribers eased the situation a bit. The *Yudenrat* supplied them [the Germans] with all their needs for one purpose alone – so they wouldn't let Poles rule, racket, and bully us. Much of this was done by Pinkhas Grodzenchik—whatever the Germans needed he supplied. And the Jews gave him everything he asked for, but mostly he collected from his own rich relatives so as to avoid scandals when a Jew wouldn't let go of something [that was later confiscated].

The Germans also requested workers for road work, work at the railway station, or in the forests, where the work consisted mostly of loading wagons. The Germans used to bully workers. Jews returned from work beaten and bleeding. People were afraid to work in the forests and started to look for work in town, even as servants for Germans and Poles. Some paid their last money, jewelry, and gold just to be accepted as "needed".

My mother was approached by her old friend Rachel Weiner who asked to take her Moshe as my assistant. She brought valuables with her as a heart-opening present. My mother became angry at her offer. She promised to help without any bribes. Moshe was then about 45 years old, he had graduated the Vilne Technion [technical school] in electricity but he never worked at it. All his life Moshe had been a shop owner and earned good money. I went to the Mayor and requested him to allow me Moshe as an assistant. I did this to please my mother, because he couldn't be a real assistant to me. The Mayor approved my request. This not only provided Moshe with an easy job including full freedom of movement approved by the police, but also saved his and his family's lives.

The days flew by and there was no ghetto in Voronova. Horrible rumors had come from other towns about ghettos and terrible actions that were taking place there. Especially horrible were the rumors from Ponar and Vilne. We couldn't believe that Jews were being killed wholesale, group by group, and community after community. But one day after an action in the Vilna ghetto, 250 Jews from Vilne came looking for shelter. The authorities took notice and began looking for them. We were ordered not to let anyone from Vilna in, God forbid. Regretfully we followed the orders and didn't let in even a brother, as it happened to Alitovitsh Yitzach's family who couldn't take in their brother Moshe from Vilne. He had to hide in the cemetery, where he was caught.

The hunt for Vilne Jews continued for a week. Everybody was caught, arrested, kept in the cinema building, and later shot. The mass grave of Vilne Jews in Voronova is situated in the field near the Smuk Forest.

Only then did I realize that all the rumors about the German, and their collaborators', cruelty, were true. The town was struck by mortal panic. People avoided going outside. From one day to another the orders of the new regime became more and more severe. People were ordered to wear the yellow star. Borders and lines were drawn to indicate areas where we were allowed, and also curfew hours were imposed – even for those streets where we were allowed to walk.

One Sunday evening while we were busy repairing a power line not far from Gestapo headquarters, we suddenly heard a shower of shots that went on and on like hail. We looked outside through the windows and saw people running and falling near the fence, one after another. I clearly saw Khanne Dukshtulski fall dead before my eyes close to where we were working. Her head was stuck in the snow and her blood colored [the snow] and our hearts. Later we found out that those had been Jews named by Poles as collaborators with communists and enemies of the regime, and also Jews from nearby towns who had been looking for shelter in our town. The organizer of this hunt and execution was a German policeman who bragged of having high morals and not being a Nazi.

The cinema house where Vilne Jews were kept and tortured

Preparations for Slaughter

At the same time an order was issued by which Christians were not allowed to visit Jewish homes, meaning Jews would not be able to buy provisions.

The Poles strictly followed this order. The Jews then offered them their most expensive valuables, furniture, and clothes in return for their help during those hard days. These acts brought some Christians to the idea that it would be better to kill all the Jews and get their property for free. My father-in-law realized this and forbade us from offering bribes. The Jews started digging holes as hiding places for the fruits of their hard work. Everything was hidden: clothes and grain, legumes and gold, goods and money. All was hidden in various places: the walls, the yards, the floors, the stalls and in fields under trees.

After everything was hidden, rumors spread about slaughter of Voronova Jews, so we started to dig hiding places for ourselves. We built bunkers with secret tunnels, or double walls in the houses. And indeed many survived thanks to these preparations.

Some made plans with Christian friends to hide with them when the hour would come and they would have to sneak away from their slaughterers. There were some Christians who dug bunkers in their stalls to save Jews. But others informed on Jews to the Gestapo, after taking all their belongings.

Finally, the news of an action arrived; we received it with despair. One morning, it was on July 15, 1941, we woke up to find ourselves surrounded by Polish Police and the Gestapo. A ring of predators closed around us who were in fear and panic. Jews ran around, going from one to another with outspread arms and hands clapping in helplessness and despair. What to do? We saw the death standing just near us, crawling and approaching. What can we do?

Some sneaked out and managed to get to the house of their Christian saviors. Not all succeeded for the guard was tight. In those days we were trapped, with no loopholes. Meanwhile one of the Gentiles turned it into a business. He had connections with the police. For 20 golden rubles per head he smuggled Jews out. Some managed to be saved this way. Others were shot by their saviors as soon as they paid and were taken outside. It happened mostly to those who were considered rich, because after their death all their property could be confiscated and the house, the land, and the property taken over. That's what happened to Binyamin Kaplan, Nakhum Grodzenchik, Khanneh Dlugin, Leyzer Katzenellenbogen – and others.

The first line of guards let them through, but close to the forest the second line of Polish guards killed them and robbed all their possessions.

On the next day Jews went there and buried them near the new market. When it became known, Jews stopped trying this sort of activity.

Meanwhile the siege continued. One day a few youngsters came to me and invited me to flee to the forest. One of them had a gun. We met behind houses and discussed our big secret. I couldn't decide. I really wanted to leave. I wanted to fight instead of being led to slaughter like sheep, but I was tied to my family by special circumstances. Just several months earlier my wife had given birth to our first daughter. That confused me. I had difficulty deciding. Some people tried to convince me to stay, saying men with a profession would not be endangered, they would be needed, so their families would be spared too. Or – on the contrary – if we were to leave we'd be condemning our families to death.

Finally I decided to flee to the forest. There were several others like me so we decided to leave as a fighting group, not individually.

On the designated day in late afternoon a hail of bullets was fired in the enclosed ghetto. Several Jews were killed while innocently passing the guard line. So, we had to stay. In addition, on the next day I was called in to the power station to repair some problem. I returned from there late at night. On my way I was stopped at one of the checkpoints, but my permit helped me to get through. When I arrived home the whole family was deathly worried. I was upset with myself, that I hadn't run straight from the station to the forest. During the day the rumor had spread that this day would be fatal. Again panic, again helplessness.

At noon the Governor arrived from Lida. He calmed the *Yudenrat* and promised them that nothing bad would happen to the local Jews. "They only want to check papers". We didn't believe him. The police informed him that many Jews are fleeing, so his intentions were already clear.

During that night all checkpoints and police forces were reinforced.

Next morning I met Ugerman, the SS man. He called me aside and said:

"People are fleeing. It's not good. At least don't you flee. They will not touch you. They need you. You are the only senior electrician in the area."

He added:

"I promise you I'll be at my office at 6. I'll talk to my commander about you and then update you. And if there'll be a reason, I myself will urge you to leave. Some Jews saw me talking to him. When I came back home many came to hear what we had talked about."

Impatiently we waited for 6 o'clock.

At that hour a neighbor came to tell me that the German policeman was waiting for me at the corner.

I went over to him with all the neighbors watching us from their windows. He took me to a side street and began a long speech in which he assured me that the commander specifically mentioned that I would not be touched because "electrician is a big deficit" and I should be spared because I am very valued professionally. Besides, he advised me not to abandon my family, and said that he also had a high opinion of me as a professional.

Silently, with my head down, I listened to him. We parted with handclap: I wouldn't flee.

But my confidence left me. I did believe him somewhat. He liked me only because of my punctuality and good service. I installed a tape recorder in his room so he could listen to any conversation, and he was very satisfied. There were also rumors in town that after anyone left, their family would be immediately executed. This was the main factor that stopped me. My head exploded from thoughts for and against. In my situation it seemed reasonable to stay and save myself and my family.

I stayed.

On the next day I was thrown out of my home together with my 2 families, including my parents. We were gathered in the marketplace. The deportation started in its full strength. The Germans recruited local Christians for this job who came to the marketplace armed with pitchforks and axes. They went from house to house and dragged all the Jews to the marketplace, they did it with exceptional eagerness.

I and my families were the last to get out from the house. At the marketplace we saw all the Jews of the town seated on the ground while a lot of motorcycles and policemen swarmed around them. I had to go around the square so the Nazis wouldn't notice me. But the commander's eyesight was sharp. He noticed me and shouted:

"Electrician, hey you! Come here!"

It was a shouted order.

Everybody turned their heads to me. I was scared. I started to push myself between the miserable crowd, squeezing together with my family and their babies in their arms. I walked straight to the commander who, with his giant height and his huge bat, could scare to death any hero and brave man. He asked:

"Who are the people with you?"

I replied: "This is my family and this is my wife's family."

He ordered us to sit aside. I understood his intention. Everybody understood that he intended to save us, me and those related to me. Instantly people turned to him with different requests. People asked to be attached to me, but he didn't react. He walked around loftily above everyone, tapping his high boots with his whip. Pinkhas Grodzenchik begged most of all, who did so much for his people and was literally begging for his life. But the commander didn't even bother to answer him, and when he wouldn't let go, he raised his voice and shouted nervously:

"Don't' prattle too much ([Tr. Note: repeated in Yiddish])." Everybody became quiet, it filled them with fear.

We continued sitting while the German decided on the methods of the 'action'.

Meanwhile we were approached by the Governor of Lida district. He asked why we were separated from others, why we were sitting on the side. When we told him it was the commander's orders, he took us to the others and mixed us with the crowd that was already standing in line for selection. So it happened that I and my family were the last in line. I was holding our baby and my wife was holding her mother's baby.

She told us:

"If we are going to die, at least our baby will survive."

My parents and brother were behind us.

When we approached the selection we already knew what was going on, who was going to death and who to life, it all depended on type and age. Meanwhile one could already hear the sounds of the shots from afar. The commander of the police came to me and said:

"When you approach the table, show them your diploma and permit."

And he disappeared.

Suddenly all my hopes for survival deteriorated. I saw that they were tired of selecting and were just sending everybody to die. We accepted our destiny. Still I had some hope that at the critical moment the local commander would be on my side. I searched for him with my eyes, but he couldn't be seen. When it was my turn, he suddenly appeared. The governor asked:

"What is your profession?"

I replied – electrician.

He took my papers and work permit for inspection, and then the local commander spoke up:

"The man has to stay here."

I was pointed to the left.

"And where are your people?"

He turned us all to the left side and left us with the police.

When I was in Germanishki Street, I suddenly heard lots of shooting. The Germans became confused and I discovered the reason for it. It was because of what Yitzakh Olkenitski had done. When he had felt he couldn't take anymore, he had raised his arm and punched one of the Germans. His friends reacted immediately and fired bullets at him. He was killed right in front of my eyes. He was standing just several meters from me. This scene shocked us strongly. It was a demonstration of what would happen when a person didn't go like a sheep, but also it was a demonstration of resistance, and an example for all of us.

I went to the group that had been sent to the left. They were seated on the ground. We sat down too. Somebody called to me in German from the nearby house of Itteh Olkenitski:

"Electrician, don't be scared. Those are sentenced to live!"

At that moment I didn't appreciate his comforting words. He didn't make me happy. I felt dizzy even though I realized that this time I and my family had been spared.

My dear father Yosef buried his face in the ground; his heart wouldn't let him see how his town people were being driven to death, his friends and comrades for long years and through generations. My mother also covered her face and murmured:

"My God where are you?"

We saw people watching their relatives march to death. They were punching themselves in the heads. How could they watch it? How could we watch the people of our town, dear Jews, old friends and relatives, old and young, taken to a cruel death, in a cruel way.

Driven like animals to slaughter: here is Yehoshua Grodzenchik and his family, here is Shimshon Dlugin and his children, and with him Pinkhas Grodzenchik and his wife Yehudit and their innocent child. And more innocent children, some less than a year of age, some who were walking holding hands, united together to die together on their last day. I hated my life: at that moment I just wanted to die. I knew that my survival would also not last forever: they'd keep us as only as long as they needed us.

At some moment a tall German approached us and began a long speech. We had to realize that we had survived and that it was a great privilege, an act of grace. While speaking he spread a blanket on the ground and ordered us to put all our money there, gold and everything that we had on us. Later he said everyone would be searched, and if something were to be found, the person would be executed. Obviously, everybody put their valuables on the blanket, but some hid items under pavement stones, without knowing that they were being watched from the Dvilianski house balcony by policemen peeking through the windows and watching our every movement. Later, after we were taken from there, they came back and took everything. The blanket was full of stuff. They wrapped it by folding the corners, put it in a car, and took it away.

Then we were joined by some of those who had been pointed to the right. They were probably being required for work in nearby towns, plans had changed. When the selection was over we were all assembled in the marketplace again. There we listened to a speech that we should be the happiest people to have survived. From then on we would live in a special Jewish quarter, etc.

The Clothes of the Victims Returned to the Town

After the speech we were all called to come to the table and we were registered. Meanwhile all those who were hiding stepped out of the bunkers, and [also those who] were not present at the action [in the marketplace]. Among them was the Konopke family and others. There were families whose babies had exposed them by crying, and they were murdered. Others tried to silence and choked their babies with their own hands.

Leah, Moshe Olkenitski's wife, chose another way – when her baby started crying she took him out into the street and was taken to die, but she didn't expose her husband, and eventually he survived.

During the registration terrible scenes occurred. People were crying, sobbing, and whining like children. Some fainted and couldn't regain consciousness. Some of them remained without parents, others without children or wives, and the shootings still continued to exterminate all the Jews of Voronova.

But the most awful scene occurred when the wagons with the clothes of the murdered arrived. The victims had been forced to undress before their deaths. Everyone recognized the clothing of their relatives, as if they were still standing before their eyes. Nobody could remain calm looking at those clothes: it was a total breakdown. And then one Pole approached a wagon and started searching the clothes for gold and money. This was too much even for the German. He approached the Pole, pushed him away, and beat him up. He was a telephonist [telephone operator]. It's important to pause and mention the last German telephonists. They were different from their predecessors. They were less eager to abuse, to swoop on booty, to participate in violent acts. They quietly did their job, while those before them had befriended corrupt Poles and their wives–prostitutes, and participated in the brutal murders of Jews. These last ones dismissed the [Polish] women and preferred Jewish or elderly women instead. When we used to come to them to fix electrical problems, they always tipped us with something, cigarettes or food. We never left empty–handed. Especially outstanding was their driver. I'll tell about him later.

After the registration we were allowed to leave to the designated quarter. The clothes were taken to the municipality building and we followed them as if were following human corpses [as at a funeral] with damp eyes and broken hearts. We were forbidden to go to our own houses by the Poles and the Mayor, but with the mediation of Germans, we were able to go to our houses for a couple of minutes just to take a few things. I asked a German policeman to escort me to my house, allegedly to take my toll climbing equipment and other working tools. The house was almost completely ruined. The Poles had taken advantage while we were at the marketplace, robbing and destroying our homes. Even the German [with me] was shocked by the level of vandalism. He shrugged and said:

"Damned are these Poles."

He let me take everything I could find.

From Swine Street in Voronova to Lida ghetto

The quarter designated for Jews was in Lida Street. We were crammed 8–10 people in one house. It was very narrow and tight.

On the next day I went out with to work my "climbers" over my shoulder. I continued so [every morning] for a week, until an order arrived to relocate all the Voronova Jews to Lida [town], where all the Jews in the surrounding area were to be concentrated. The order mentioned that every Jew not able to be replaced by a Christian should stay until further notice.

The deportation had to be performed in 2 days, and again turmoil began. Who would be allowed to stay? Jews started offering money, clothes, and gold to policemen, to let them remain in town. Everyone declared a profession. Meanwhile, the Poles filled their hands with gold and treasures. They were the ones responsible for this operation, so by spreading sweet promises they milked everyone's valuables.

I was almost sure that I'd be staying because they needed me, and so I didn't throw my money to the winds. I didn't ask or bribe anyone. My boss was a Pole. He also wanted to grab at the opportunity so he told all the employees at the mill and power station that he'd keep them. He also promised my job to someone else. I was informed of this by friends. I didn't want to believe them. After all, I was the only head electrician in the area and no one could dare to replace me. But still I became concerned. I went to the municipality, but I couldn't get anything out of them. Even my boss dismissed me, saying nothing. Later I found out about the whole story.

The boss's brother told me that the former station manager had bribed his brother to put him at the station in my place. I decided no to talk about it to my "rivals", but to try and save my position in another way.

In the evening I took my climbers and went to see the Nazi commander. For hours I walked up and down in the street waiting for him to come out. The street was already dark by the time I saw him walking. I pretended to be walking home from work and "ran" into him. I greeted him. He asked what's new at work. How is the electricity? I replied that it was my last day at work because the boss had hired someone else in my place.

When he heard this he was furious and shouted:

"What? Who is the other one? Who made the decision?"

I said:

"I have no idea, that's what I was told at the municipality."

He declared:

"It won't happen! I need a professional, a person with skills!" – and went away.

I continued home in a bad mood: the municipality in putting together a list of vital persons had chosen my rival instead of me, and I believed nobody could change that.

On the next day everybody was ordered to prepare to leave the town. No one knew if we'd be going by car or by foot, or where we are going.

Everybody was making preparations, making packages, packing everything that they might need on the way. It was hard to part from our belongings, used for years, passed from generation to generation: those were life's souvenirs. People knew that the moment after their departure they'd be robbed of everything. Their hearts didn't want to let them leave their stuff to the robbers.

I prepared the crib and diapers for the baby, put together several packages, and we were ready to leave.

One by one, our Jewish brothers went out from their houses. I went out, pushing the crib in front of me. When I was already on the pavement, the commander approached me with a piece of paper. He asked me:

"Where are you going?"

I replied:

"I got an order to go out to the street."

He ordered me to go back and stay in the house. From our whole neighborhood only I and my wife were permitted to remain.

The quarter was empty. The houses were standing with open windows and doors. There was not a single resident from the street. The Christians walked around from house to house, searching, picking and taking whatever they wanted. Many poor Christians became rich in this manner. They walked around with iron skewers and discovered every item in every hiding place – under the floors, in the walls, and the other hiding places. When they came to my house and found me there they were very surprised and withdrawn. The three of us were seated on a coiled blanket in the middle of the room, as if convicts awaiting execution of a verdict.

Our parents were out "there" with all the Jews. I was heartbroken that I couldn't do anything for them.

Voronova of 13 Families

After half an hour, 13 Jewish families began the return to their homes. This was the group that wasn't being deported yet. All the others were being sent by foot to the railway station at Bastuni, and from there to Lida by train.

After an hour we were again assembled in the marketplace. The commandant called out names one by one from a list. We were assigned to a narrow street that was called Street of Pigs, and used to be the residence of poor Christians in the town. At the end he gave an encouraging speech, telling us we'd be taken care of and that he wouldn't let anyone harm us.

We had to live several families to one room. I chose [Tr. Note: unknown word: kuf–resh–resh] of police, Chaim Maulkenik,[1] and we occupied the house of Kudliansky.

Our neighborhood wasn't surrounded by a fence and nobody guarded us. Every one continued to do his work and sent food packages to their families in Lida through Chaim Solts Maulkenik. We bought the food from local Gentiles and the shipments were done secretly.

This continued for four weeks. We lived and worked, a handful of Jews in emotional stress, until we were informed that we'd also be deported to Lida.

Luckily the information was given to us a week before its implementation. During that week we managed to sell all our belongings. The narrow street turned overnight into a lively "market". Peasants from the area bought everything they could put their hands on. The Polish policemen tried to stop them by informing the Germans, but the Germans didn't mind and the trade continued.

Towards the end of the week the final order arrived, to leave the town... to Lida.

The truth is that we managed to sell everything. Our only worry was what if the Germans performed body searches and took away all our money and valuables. We thought this was their intention when they had let us continue the commerce: they simply wanted to lay hands on all our profits. We didn't know how to save the last of our money, and how to smuggle it into Lida.

On the day [of deportation] the German who worked as a driver for the telephonists came over and took me and Chaim Solts aside, and told us:

"You must know that you'll be ripped of everything you have. You better leave the money with me and I'll bring it to you in Lida."

We knew the man. We trusted him as a decent and humane person. We passed him 75 thousand marks.

On the next day 26 wagons were brought, two for each family. We loaded everything, especially flour, potatoes and other groceries, and all that we had bought from the Gentiles with the money earned from [selling] our belongings. We went to the German quarter, everything was thoroughly checked, and we went off to Lida.

On our way to Lida we began to talk about escaping to the forests and joining the partisans. The peasants told us that in the forest new Russian and Jewish partisan groups are forming. Before we arrived to Lida, we had decided to leave Lida.

In Zhyrmun it became dark and we had to stop and give the horses some rest. The peasants took advantage of the opportunity and robbed everything they could, our groceries and vital items. Those Poles were born with no conscience. A German soldier did what he did because he has been ordered to do so, but they robbed and murdered at every opportunity, they murdered for plunder.

Lida Ghetto

At 9PM we entered Lida ghetto. The wire fence had a depressing effect on us. We unloaded the wagons, each at his families' house.

We barely had time to rest from the road, which we had partly made by foot, when some terrified Jews came running and told us that a German was looking for us and calling our names from a list. We decided to be careful. Me and Chaim decided to go first, and what a surprise! We saw at the fence our German driver looking for us.

This Righteous of the Nations man didn't spare his time and energy to ride on his bike for 35 km. He handed us all our money. He didn't want any reward. He said goodbye and returned on his bike to Voronova.

We found the Jews in Lida ghetto depressed and horrified. A few days before our arrival the Germans had gathered all the "foreign" Jews, especially those from Vilne, who had entered the ghetto illegally and had been living under false identities as locals. They were killed in one day. The act had a horrifying impact on the ghetto for a long time. In conversations with old ghetto residents we found out that they had a negative opinion of the *Yudenrat*.

The next day, when we were sent to work, each one of us was asked his profession in order to assign us to the German workshops. We saw Jewish workers coming to work holding professional diplomas. But we were enlightened that in order to be accepted in a workshop, which was easy work and ensured comfortable life, one needn't be a professional. Everything could be arranged by the *Yudenrat* with gold.

Good that we were warned in advance. We decided to oppose the *Yudenrat* if they tried to make similar demands from us [for gold].

Meanwhile I was sent with several others to dig a basin in the commandant's yard. I did this work for a few days. I made friends with the commandant's driver, a Polish guy, a radio technician. After a few conversations he offered me work with him in the garage. He obtained the permission of the commandant, and I began working as his assistant.

The work was not too pleasant because the commandant used to stand over my head and rush me to hurry up and repair flat tire, or something else. However, it had its advantages: it was close to the ghetto, and I came back home clean.

At some point the *Yudenrat* wanted to push me out of this job in order to put in one of their own, but I resisted. At the request of the *Yudenrat* the police intervened, they tried to arrest me without trial, and to force me into the cellar of the Jewish police building. The incident ended with beatings, as 5 Jewish policemen confronted me together with their infamous commander. Luckily I managed to overcome them by hitting the commander in the chin. They had no choice but to release me, but I was like a malignant thorn to them and they put an eye on me. I continued to work in the garage against their will.

One day the *Yudenrat* received an order to assign 1,000 Jews for railway works near Krasnei. I was one of them. They separated me from my wife and child. We did hard work, and all we had to eat was half a kilo of bread and a bit of soup. The discipline was like in the military, everything was managed by a whistle, with formations and roll calls. We worked from darkness to darkness, with German guards watching and speeding us with curses and beatings. At night, when we returned back to the barracks, we fell on wooden benches and couldn't move a muscle.

At night we were locked up and tightly guarded. The hours were long with talk about the forest. We would have to flee. The Germans might kill all those who had worked for them at the last moment, before leaving. It was almost certain. They always did this. So we had to flee to the forest.

On the next day our watch was doubled at work, and in the camp: somebody had probably babbled and informed on us.

I wasn't planning to flee from Krasnei. I didn't want to leave my wife, daughter and parents behind. I decided to go back to Lida, whatever it would take, and from there escape to the forest. This was arranged by paying 50 golden rubles to the commandant's Jewish assistant. I had no money, so Yosef Gurvits gave me a loan. After two days, we left for

Lida, escorted by an armed convoy. Our guards told us that their orders were to bring us back to Krasnei in 3 days.

I made plans how not to return, to leave Lida for the forests with my entire family. I knew that nobody would help me and the *Yudenrat* would only interfere.

I found out accidentally that a German team had arrived in order to repair the Lida power station, the engine shipyard, and the main warehouse, and they needed electricians. I went over to their camp. The Russian workers told me that the commander was a cruel man who liked to beat up everyone who seemed not to be working hard enough. I decided to apply for the job anyway, because it was the only way to stay in Lida with my wife and child.

I came in and showed my diplomas. I was ordered to stretch and connect a thick wire. After I succeeded in this test the camp commander went to the district commander and arranged a work permit for me.

Thus, I stayed in Lida.

When the time came for me to go back to Krasnei, the *Yudenrat* saw this as a good opportunity to get rid of me, but again this didn't work out for them.

Later I found out that Mendel Benyakonski was taken back to Krasnei, he took his family with him in order to stay together, and they were all killed when the Germans eliminated the camp.

I prepared an escape plan. I used to discuss it with Zerah Arluk, who at my request worked as my assistant. After some time Zerah disappeared: he had joined the partisans. My commander said to me:

"You are a good worker, but if you even only think about the partisans, we'll kill you like a dog."

From that day on he always picked on me. Suddenly, I became personally responsible for all malfunctions and problems, even when it was obvious that someone else was to blame. One day a water leveler disappeared, he ordered me, as the team leader and in charge of the equipment, to return the leveler by 2pm. I ran to town to buy a similar leveler with my own money, but it took time to find one and I returned to the camp at 2.30pm. For being late, he punched my face with the leveler. My face was covered with blood. He then attacked me with all of his huge body, threw me on the ground, and kicked me with his heavy boots. Then he rolled me into the nearest trench and left.

When he met me later, he asked me why I had been beaten by him. I had no choice but to say that I was an hour late contrary to his orders.

How I Produced Weapons

Our conditions, and my condition, became worse every day. This forced me to be thinking of a solution, to hurry up and do something. It was known that in the forest you had to bring a gun in order to be accepted. But how does one obtain a gun?

Sitting across from me in the German kitchen was a pile of old weaponry. It winked at me. The biggest problem was to how to carry the barrel. The other parts were not a problem: they were small. For a barrel they would murder. One day I took courage to approach the Jews that were sorting the pile and asked if I could choose a gun barrel. They were scared. The Germans watched them from the window from time to time. Eventually they agreed. They went away for a couple of minutes and I found what I was looking for. I tied the barrel with a wire to my neck, hid it under my coat, and returned to the ghetto in mortal danger, while my heart pounded – did they notice something? Did the barrel peek out of my coat and had somebody noticed?

The handle was made for me by my brother Meshulam. The rest I brought piece by piece. I lived through dangerous days while building the gun. I polished the parts and built my precious weapon.

Meanwhile there were rumors in the ghetto about groups of Jews preparing to leave for the forest. People obtained pistols and rifles. The youth escaped and their numbers lessened. Married couples still stayed. There was an atmosphere of a double underground, [Tr. Note: against Nazis and] against the *Yudenrat*. Asher was afraid of the consequences "if they find out", because people had vanished. The partisans from the forests who came to ghetto from time to time to smuggle people out, were opposed by the *Yudenrat*. I waited anxiously for a good opportunity. I didn't want to leave without my family.

There were more and more rumors of partisan actions. One morning we came to work and found the shipyard totally blown up by a worker during the night. He had left a mine and fled to the forest. Everyone at work whispered around, but the secret was out – the town was in partisan hands.

Each day the lack of workers grew. The Germans were terrified. Someone spread a rumor that there would be a hunt, the ghetto would be surrounded, and only the workshop workers would remain after all the rest had been deported. Immediately, I with two other Jews, ran to the nearest grove, my brother took my wife and child to hide in the workshop behind an airplane that he was working on.

While in hiding I was making plans to return to the ghetto on the next day, so as to leave as soon as possible alone and to come back for them later. I didn't believe that I would be staying alive for long in the forest. I only knew that I would somehow take revenge on the Nazis. On the next day we sent one of ours to check out what had happened in the ghetto, when he came back telling us that nothing had changed, we went back there that same day.

With Bielski's Squad

Out to the Forest

After a discussion with my wife, we decided that I would leave alone first, and later I'd come back when I could to take the family. At 11pm, 45 people left, led by Manski, a partisan who came to collect people.

On our way we passed a streaming river. When we approached Raselki[2] the dogs in the village started to bark. The whole village was settled by Nazi Germans. The situation became dangerous. We had to hurry up so we continued walking until 2am when we came to a grove: we laid down on the ground and fell asleep exhausted.

Towards evening we renewed our walk and approached the Neman River in the dark. There, a Christian coordinator waited for us and led us across the river where we approached our goal.

The forest was so well camouflaged that you couldn't tell that the headquarters were in that place. On our way we came across a Jewish horseback rider and we knew we had arrived. We approached the place carefully, alongside the road, in order not to leave trails. Over the hill we discovered the partisan camp. It was a dense settlement, a real city, and we were amazed how everything was disguised under the ground.

There were numerous huts arranged in carefully planned rows, a kitchen, weaponry workshops, trenches.

Our arrival made some of the residents happy, but most of them showed signs of unwillingness. We heard various remarks:

"We don't need more people!"

"The new arrivals will bring trouble on us!"

In a couple of hours I had already realized what was going on here.

This group was mostly people from Navaradok, their wives raised their hands as if sensing a coming disaster. It was obvious that they were not interested in revenge. All they wanted was to outlive the Holocaust, not to stand out, to stay in hiding with as little noise and relocation as possible.

Luckily, the Bielski brothers took charge. The greatest of the brothers was the oldest – Tuvye– who never stopped trying to pull people out of the ghettos, with a thought in his heart to save as many Jews as possible from certain death. At that time rescuing Jews was his main purpose in life. In this matter he didn't listen to anyone, not even to his family. This made a great impression on us.

In the end we all stood in line and Tuvye inspected us and our weapons personally. Then we were assigned to different divisions. In the following days we trained a lot and went out to actions.

I Go to Bring My Wife

Weeks passed and I started thinking of ways to bring my family. I discussed it with my commander, and he encouraged me, but he didn't allow me to bring the baby. It would be undesirable to put the group in danger because of a crying baby. I decided to bring over my wife, and baby save the baby only later. I didn't want to leave her with Christians for money, like many others did. At first the commander wouldn't let me leave at all, not even to bring my wife. He told me to wait, but when he saw I persisted he agreed that someone else from the squad would go to Lida and bring her back with him. The man made me a promise. I waited impatiently for the escort person. A week passed and he didn't appear, and the rumors coming from Lida ghetto were horrible. I decided to go myself whatever the outcome. Assael, the commander's brother, helped me with this and eventually I was allowed to go.

As darkness fell we, three guys, left for Lida ghetto. On our way we passed thick groves, proceeded carefully, and suddenly heard human voices in one of the groves. We hid and waited to see who was talking. An hour passed. Then we heard that the approaching voices were speaking Yiddish. We went out to meet them. They were happy to see us and told me that my wife was with them. Our reunion was tinged with sadness. My wife told me about the terrible things happening in the ghetto, and the thought of our baby left behind there was hard.

We were so busy talking that we didn't notice that we had been separated from the group. As the two of us continued, I lost the way and we found ourselves heading towards the Germans. I tried not to hide my fear from my wife as I continued and she followed. Suddenly from afar I saw a man with a gun standing at a checkpoint. I realized we were in mortal danger. I grabbed my wife with one hand, the gun with the other hand, and took to the opposite direction. We jumped into a trench along the Lida–Navaradok road and proceeded further from there.

The trip was hard. We were so tired and tense. At any moment another obstacle could appear. We had to crouch, lie, and wait. On the way, when we were already close to the camp, we came across some people and we heard the gun being made ready to shoot. Somehow we recognized each other as Jews and we were saved from death.

[Ed. Note: Tuvya Bielski]

Apparently, a Jew with his child, because of exhaustion, had stayed behind the group on the way to our camp, and now they too were saved from a terrible mistake. I took them along with us and brought them to our camp.

Activities at the Camp – the Baby

With my wife now in the camp, I was able to dedicate time to important camp activities.

First I was appointed a rider–guard. I began to explore the surrounding road network, the paths, and the trails in the forest. Later

I was ordered to take charge of four watch posts. I was in charge of watch shifts and of obtaining information from surrounding farmers. I had to check on matters in the nearby town of Navaradok, to see whether the Germans were planning to hunt for us Jews who had dared to escape their claws. I used to send Christians to town to check the situation in the ghetto: the Jews there were in urgent need of rescue.

With every arrival of new people to the camp, their entry had to be secured to ensure that the Germans hadn't followed.

One time, on such tour with my people we heard machine guns and sounds of explosions. I left them behind and proceeded to check it out. As I saw that our positions were not harmed, I went back and reported to command. During the short duration of these shootings, the commanders had spread out and hidden all the camp's residents: the camp was completely deserted. I found only Tuvye, with a few of his people, walking around the headquarters. They were worried and sent me out to bring more accurate information. The shooting had lasted for too long.

I went in the direction of the shootings. From farmers I learnt that the Germans were nervous when passing by the forest and would shoot at and explode everything, to scare away the partisans. I decided to continue, and in Ostrovlya I was told the same thing. Only then did we return to the camp and did matters cool down. The camp people were returned to their places and life continued.

My wife didn't stop bothering me about the baby. She almost accused me of forgetting about the baby in favor of my work. The truth is that I couldn't bring her to the camp. The high command wouldn't allow it, and rightfully so. I also couldn't find any Christians who would agree to take her in, even for a large sum of money. It was too early to bring her from the ghetto: the Germans we planning a major attack on us, and the situation was dangerous.

Anyhow, we had to move our camp because too many Christians knew about its position. We moved to a grove near Zurvelnik,[3] where we found neglected partisan trenches, and we stayed there. On the next day our exploration unit had a face–to–face encounter with the Germans near the village. They opened fire on us. We barely escaped from them, went back to the camp, and had to leave there as soon as possible. The Germans stayed behind in Zurvelnik searching for us, and burned several houses along with their residents for having cooperated with the partisans.

Our new camp was in a young birch forest, and from there we continued our raids, watch shifts, etc.

I Go to Lida Ghetto

The rumors from the ghetto were horrific. It was obvious that the end was near. Many people from the camp went to the ghetto to try and save their relatives. Now I also decided to go to the ghetto to bring our girl and members of our families. When I went for Tuvye's permission to go, a huge argument started. People said the Germans would discover us, that children would endanger the camp, that new people would be a liability, and that we didn't have provisions for additional people. Here Tuvyeh displayed his character to the full extent: he clapped his fist on the table and said furiously:

"We are here to create a place for Jews fleeing from ghettos. We came here not to save our skins but to save Jews, to make possible for them to live later on. I don't want to hear a word. Meir, go and bring your girl, and bring as many Jews as you can. You hear, Shmerkovitsh! Bring, bring as many as possible."

I took Leybke with me, a great fellow, and we went away equipped with pistols.

In a village near Lida we found several of our men who hadn't succeeded in entering Lida and who had come back here to wait. One of them, Yakov, even got killed trying to enter the ghetto. We decided to try anyway. We took the way around behind the airport. We noticed a German patrol coming across our way. We hid on an upper floor and waited till darkness, then approached the ghetto via the Raselki[4] Farm.

Near the stream behind the bushes we saw German police and the well-guarded ghetto. Horses were grazing, probably belonging to the commandant. The horse groom was a Jew. He cursed one of the horses in Yiddish. We approached him with our pistols pointed at him. He got a bit scared. We called him from behind the bushes to tell us what was going on in the ghetto and to help us go inside. He was very afraid to stay with us and even to talk to us, but we calmed him down.

He was a barber. Leybke knew him. He said his mind wasn't clear. I saw it when he walked beside the horses murmuring a song as if nothing horrible were going on around him.

He wouldn't even listen of helping us into the ghetto. We tried to do it ourselves, but German guards were constantly patrolling around the ghetto, the gates were tightly guarded.

The day was coming to an end, and we thought about grabbing two horses and going back to the forest, but we didn't do it.

On second thought we decided to spend the night in the field, and in the morning when Jews went out to labor, to try and enter mixed into the crowd. When morning came the horses were going to the stream to drink water. We asked the groom to let us stay as grooms, to approach the stream with them, and then cross the bridge and go into the ghetto.

I Enter the Ghetto and Take Jews to the Forest

The ghetto was empty. I knocked on one of the windows and a woman peeked out to say that by the orders of the *Yudenrat* she wouldn't let any forest man in. I was appalled, but I didn't want to argue with her. I pretended to be someone from the ghetto and made my way straight to my mother's house. In a minute the news of my arrival spread through the ghetto. Friends and relatives came to see me, the *Yudenrat* men came to tell me that they'd help me go out of the ghetto as long as I promised not to take any people with me. I promised them, but I sent my brother-in-law Chaim Eli to tell 40 people to prepare to leave at 12pm.

During the day I tried to persuade my families to go with me, with no success. My brother Meshulam said that he, as a worker in the workshops would be able to save them. He also had a gun and at the last moment he'd escape and join us. My father wandered around the room with the baby in his arms, tears flowing from his eyes. It was his first grandchild, and who knew how long the separation might last— maybe forever.

My wife's parents agreed to let me take their son Chaim–Elya with me.

The day went by, filled with farewells and the most terrible decision-making. It was hard for me to leave my dear parents behind, but my dear father made it easier for me and said:

"My only request is that you avenge them in full, as much as they deserve!"

Towards evening a messenger came to tell me that everything was ready. Between 11pm and 1am the Germans would be partying, the gate would be unwatched, and we could leave— the people were ready.

When the hour came, I tied my little girl with a peasant's scarf to my back and we went out. As agreed, the people were waiting at the stables near the gate. At that same moment Jewish policemen appeared, headed by the Jewish commandant. He declared that he would not let the people go out. In the end they agreed to 20 people, because I insisted and threatened them:

"Jews want to save themselves from mortal danger and you are standing in their way. We won't accept you in the forest when you decide to come. Let people defend themselves instead of dying like fettered sheep."

It had its effect and we went out.

We walked fast during the entire night. People took turns in carrying the babies. The patrol lead us. We had 14 guns and several pistols with us.

Early in the morning we reached Shtsigli,[5] a friendly village and partisan area. We met a partisan squad there from the "Iskra" Regiment. They told us the Germans had conducted a raid on our camp, there were casualties, and the whole battalion had broken into groups.

That shocked me. Who may have been killed? Who knew where to look for them? Anyway we had to make an enquiry. I sent five people out to look for members of the camp— they found some.

We learnt that Bielski's people retreated to Naliboki Fields, that my wife was alive and she was with Assael Bielski. With no trouble we reached a safe place to rest. We fell to the ground and fell asleep, my daughter sleeping beside me the sleep of persecuted partisans.

In the morning we started our walk again. In the afternoon we came across Tuvye's people. The police were after us. Danger was following us. We went deeper into the forest. The sun was burning. From time to time the baby got thirsty and cried, adding to the confusion. While waiting for others, I crated shade from the scarf for her, but she wouldn't calm down. She crawled out to the sun and cried, and tore our hearts. She screamed: Mommy, Mommy, Mommy. It was the only time in my life that I cried from my heart. I was washed with tears – What should I do with my daughter? How could I be a mother to her?

And the doubts crawled in:

"Maybe her mother is not among the living anymore?"

I Gave Away my Daughter to Strangers

Some women tried to calm her down with no result. The general depression was having its effect on the baby, and on all the babies.

There were two more babies in the squad and we were worried about what to do with them. We can't bring them to the forest, but where to leave them?

The parents of two other babies had money and belongings, so they'd probably find Christians. I had nothing so I doubted that I would find a solution for my little baby.

I had one small hope. In the "Iskra" squad there were people I knew, one of them being Zerah Arluk. They had connections with the neighbors, the local peasants, and I hoped they'd find me some peasant.

We went there, the children in the wagon, and us walking along. We reached a river. The water was deep so we put wooden boards on ladders and put the babies high up so they wouldn't get wet. The water covered the wheels. We walked close to the wheels in the deep water. We couldn't see what was awaiting us on the other bank. Suddenly we heard human voices. Shortly after we saw people in the water with their clothes tied to their heads [to keep them dry]. I recognized them. These were our people. They burst out in joy:

"Meir, your wife is alive and she is with us!"

When Carmela approached and saw her daughter and brother she burst out in tears. She handed me my rifle, which I had left with her before leaving for the ghetto. She had saved it during flight. Well, we had one more rifle.

Later on we parted ways. The babies' parents found adoptive families in the villages. I continued. I reached "Iskra" at sunrise, but no one could help me so I went back.

On my way I visited every remote farm looking for saviors for my daughter, but with no results. Meanwhile it became dark and the time was pressing us to hurry up and catch up with our squad. I was exhausted by the disappointing enquiries at every farm, but I thought of the fields, of the possible chases, the dangers awaiting the baby. I decided to make a last attempt, because I couldn't take care of the baby and also participate in the fighting.

My father's provision to "have revenge" burnt my soul. I wouldn't rest until finding a safe place for the baby.

We stayed for another day in Petri[6] village and I continued to search.

In one of the backyards I saw a woman chopping wood, and that she wasn't experienced at this–at any moment she could hurt herself with the axe. I stopped to watch and she became embarrassed. I approached and told her about myself, and what I was looking for. I asked why there was no man to do this job.

I learned from her that her husband, ill for a long time, had passed away. She was very poor and helpless. I asked whether she could take care of my girl, for money. She stopped chopping. We entered the house. She said:

"I can't, dear. Because of poverty I gave my daughter to my mother. I'll give you a letter to her in the nearby village, she'll take her in. I am even ready to take my girl back, so the neighbors will think that yours is mine."

She sat down to write the letter which took her too long, and I began to lose my patience.

The letter was long and begging, as if she was asking for her own daughter. It finished like this:

"Please make an effort, Mother. God will reward you and we'll survive the war."

When Carmela read the letter with no mention of money, she couldn't believe our good luck.

And again we traveled, and again there were deep waters. When we reached one of the farms it was already evening. I entered one of the houses and said that I would like to stay overnight and we were very hungry.

In less than an hour a bowl with hot potatoes was on the table and also sour cream and pudding. The girl was given milk. The peasant spread straw on the floor and we lay down to sleep, keeping watching shifts.

In the morning I tried to find out where the woman that I was looking for lived. I left Carmela with the baby and the rest of the group, and I went alone to look for the woman. The houses were scattered far one from another. I had to pass a grove and a stream. I also lost my way and wandered for a while. When I saw the house and recognized it by description, I slowed down. I didn't want to go in and frighten the people. I hid in the grove and waited. A boy came out with sheep. He passed near me but didn't notice me. After him his father came out with a little boy. I went out from my hiding place. The Gentile got scared, but I calmed him down and gave him his daughter's letter. We sat down on a tree trunk. He read slowly. When he finished reading he asked me to wait while he went to ask his wife and daughter.

I waited for a long time. I won't forget that. Life and death decisions had to be made and who knew whether I would succeed. The waiting seemed endless. When he returned my heart beat like crazy: what if he said no. He said to bring the girl.

I ran as fast as I could to our people. I asked our host to take us with the wagon because it was a long way. He brought us to within 1 km from the savior. I let him go back with gratitude, took my people to the grove to wait for us, and the two of us with our baby went to the Gentile.

The house was poor. Our daughter fell asleep on the way, and the Gentile's wife took her and put her to bed. I took out from my pocket ten golden rubles and gave them to the peasant together with a suit that I had with me. I said:

"Believe me, this is all I possess. I'll bring more if I can." She took the money from his hand and gave it back to me and said:

"Your trip will take long, you'll need it."

Only after a long persuasion did they agree to take the money. Then my wife went to the sleeping baby, bent over her, and wept.

We said goodbye to our sleeping daughter. Who knew whether we'd see each other again.

Partisan Economy – Purpose and Means

The Naliboki situated near our camp area was totally razed: German revenge. As we found out, 400 Jews had been killed there in a battle against the Nazis. Who knows if this act of Jewish heroism is commonly known?

Our squad grew bigger every day. Our armed forces got bigger and stronger, and we became a force in the wide valley area. Jewish partisans used to go out in groups for sabotage missions, combat, raids on German patrols, and railway undermining.

The whole area of Navaredok and Ivia was full with our action groups. We were noticeable everywhere.

We were joined by partisans fleeing from Russian partisan groups, because of the anti–Semitism among the Russians.

Most of them were from the Lubchenka[7] area and survivors from ghettos.

We reached 800 in number and were expecting to grow more, causing a financial problem. Where would we find provisions for such numbers of people? We felt that the mere existence of those hundreds of people was equal in value to all the battles, and that both missions were mutually dependant. Meanwhile all the villages that had fed us had been destroyed: the Germans scorched them down to ash. The commander appointed me in charge of supplies and provision storage. I was relieved of combat service, but I was appointed a mission demanding frequent hard battles, and I experienced much difficulty and travail. The roads in the valleys were long and difficult, with wide swamps spread between villages. Movement was hard and slow and sometimes a village would not cooperate so we had to take it by force in order to obtain their provisions. It was a tough role, but the knowledge that the work would permit so many fighters to be revenged and lash back at the Germans made me feel better.

Near us passed the road to the frontline. We prevented Germans any possibility of bringing enforcement or supplies to soldiers on the front line. The movement of German forces in the area gradually decreased and the few remaining were heavily guarded.

More and more we felt that Germans closing in on us. They surrounded the villages supplying us with provisions, and tried different methods of search and siege.

Our situation was getting worse every day. My task became a real combat role. I had to sapper my path in order to get the required food. I was expected to fight any battle. My commander saw the supply mission as the most crucial one because it kept us alive and because it drew new forces to us and encouraged those who might otherwise be hesitant to flee to the woods. He also sent his brother out on supply missions. My scout was Yosef Kagan, resident of the area who knew all the surrounding roads and paths. I picked a farm near Berezhno.[8] This would be our resting place and storage place for obtained goods. In the evening we loaded everything on the wagons and took it via different roads to the camp.

Search and Siege

There was one occasion when I allowed myself to bring something to my daughter and her saviors. I was about 15km from them in Mishkovitsh.[9] I chose a strong horse. I packed provisions of pork and salt, veal, and leather, and departed. The road was very dangerous, but being so close to my baby I had to see and check on her.

We proceeded with great caution. We waited for nightfall to travel. When we approached Mishkovitsh we heard sounds of shooting. We waited in hiding, determined to enter the farm no matter what.

When it became quiet we continued, but the road was covered with stones and the sounds of horseshoes knocking on stone broke the silence. We were soon discovered and found ourselves under a rain of machine gun bullets. The horse got excited and burst into a gallop. Then we heard fire behind us and we knew that we had fallen into ambush.

When we managed to sneak out we went into the nearest farm and heard that the attack was part of a huge hunt – a plan to search the whole valley. I gave up the idea of seeing my daughter and ordered the Gentile to take us by side roads going in our direction. At half-way I let him go and warned him to keep his mouth shut. We reached our base farm, uploaded all the goods, and started for the camp.

I led a convoy of 12 wagons, filled with crops, sheep, cows and pigs. At the camp we found out that they had moved deeper into the swamp area.

The fear of the approaching hunt was mixed with joy at the sight of the quantity of goods we had brought with us, but it was still frightening. The latest rumors told of thousands of soldiers that the Germans had pulled from the frontline in order to eliminate us, and they were getting close.

We made hasty preparations. We divided into groups equipped with food rations. We didn't intend to fight a face-to-face battle. We decided to go deep into the impassable swamps and hang on there. The situation was tense. People became quiet and there was a depressing silence surrounding us. From time to time patrollers arrived on horses, whispered something to the commanders, and disappeared again. Those were hard hours of self-observation and character testing. The rumors were frightening and it was easy to fall into despair.

A day went by and we were staying on spot, alert and awake. When it became dark we fell asleep, tired and exhausted. In the middle of the night, cannon thunder exploded on us and bullets directed at us whistled by our ears. The commander ordered us to stay still and not to react until further order. Those were horrible unforgettable hours. We had elders and women with us, children and the sick. One's every thought was blurred with their desperate moans. A frightening sound of despair surrounded us, until one lost all hope. From time to time Russian and Jewish partisan groups arrived, their commanders held discussions with our commanders.

At night the artillery fire stopped and it seemed that the hunt was over. But in the morning the fire renewed as if pointed straight at us, as if they knew our exact location.

We had no choice but to move to another place. With us were two Jews from Naliboki, who were well acquainted with the grove and knew every path.

They led us by a winding road along flowing streams and hidden trenches. It was hard to watch the people who were carrying their exhausted children, with provision bags on their backs which were sometimes soaked with moisture and heavy. Those visions are carved in my memory forever: how the Jews walked to their way to salvation, carrying on their backs the future of our nation. I won't forget one widower especially, whose wife had been killed on a previous raid. He walked while carrying his two children – one on his back and one on his chest. We all moaned looking at him but couldn't help him. And he didn't ask for help, he didn't complain— he wanted to bear his contribution to the nation alone.

We walked in water up to our chests, one behind another, in order not to leave a trail in aquatic vegetation. The chain of people was over 1km long and we walked for a whole day until reaching some dry land on which to lay down our exhausted bodies.

First we explored the surroundings to check out the place and ensure that it was well hidden. Meanwhile the shooting stopped and it became quiet.

We stretched out on the ground to have some rest when suddenly we heard urgent German voices. We realized they were in our previous camp and had collected the cows that we kept for the worst days, and now they belonged to the Germans.

We had to make a quick escape, our strength went out, and our despair grew. Even the commander was exhausted. Nevertheless we continued. We wanted to live; we wanted to save each other.

Towards evening we reached the 'red hill'. It was covered with trees swept away by water, but we were so tired that we couldn't even feel on what we were sleeping.

In the morning after we ate only seeds, which had swelled up because they were soaked in the water together with us. The hunger and its consequences began to trouble us. We knew that we were under German siege and the only way to break it was to break through at any price.

We divided into groups of 50. The first to try and break through was Asael Bielski. I was next. I went out leading 55 men. We took extreme caution and reached a place not far from Lubtsch, where we ran into other partisans that made a temporary camp. We decided to take a rest there and to clean up in the nearby lake.

On our way we saw smoldering campfires, food leftovers, and cigarette butts. Those were signs of Germans being there before, and we assumed that we'd be left alone since the Germans were going in the opposite way.

Regretfully, the people felt free to rob the nearest village and take sheep and other provisions. While we were swimming naked in the lake we heard firing and the watch called us to take the defense. We were surrounded by the Polish police that protected the village. Under heavy fire we retreated, breaking in two groups, left that place and again found ourselves in terrible conditions. At least there were no casualties this time.

Our Russian Friends Rob Their Friends – I am Cut Off and in Command Against my Will

We continued our heavy pace for a day and a night until we found a safe place near a village called Chernovitsh.[10] We planned to make contact with the rest of our squad from and felt we would be safe there.

At 12pm we had a visit from Russian partisans, among them people armed with machine guns. We were glad to see them. We saw immediately that they were forest people like us. But we were surprised to see that from a distance they were pointing their guns at us. Several of them approached and demanded clothes and stuff. We refused to do that. I couldn't accept as fact that after all of our suffering from Germans we'd now become the victims of a robbery at the hands of partisans like us. I knew that there is no point in talking to Russian Gentile. I ordered my men to take battle positions, camp against camp.

It worked: they folded their guns and left.

It's important to mention, shamefully, that during the hunt, when we were divided into small groups, discipline was down and some groups effected robberies on others. Stronger groups took advantage of weaker ones and robbed them from head to toe. Especially active were the Russians groups, they lived from what they could rob from other ethnic groups.

We moved to another location and built a camp there. Our goal was to wait until our squad could reunite. Days went by and we started to take care of ourselves. We dug wells for common use. We dug underground shelter–huts, each for himself. We settled and looked for food, each in his own way.

This continued for a rather long time. As much as we were ready to use our force to fight the enemy and live, we were also ready to hang on and live.

On one quiet day we suddenly heard sounds of fire. We took distance from our small camp and hid in the bushes. When the fire stopped we sent our people to find out what had happened and they came back to tell that the Polish police had attacked a nearby village on pretense of its having collaborated with the partisans. They burnt it down and killed everyone with the only purpose of robbery and looting.

As commander of this camp I had to endure huge difficulties and take responsibility for those miserable Jewish souls and their safety. Among my people was a guy from Baksht, a professional engraver. He prepared for me a headquarters' stamp, and I was then able to send people to actions with "official" stamped papers. This was crucial at that time so as not to fall into the hands of other partisan groups. Everybody was suspicious. I made some orders in the group and we waited, preparing for the day when we might reunite with the rest of the squad.

A Painful Split in the Camp

In time people began to express discontent. Some thought that we shouldn't reunite— better to live separately. I had information that the squad was situated in the Yasinov Forest and received orders to bring my people there, in order to renew the ambushes, the attacks against Germans, and the supply cut-offs. But people were exhausted, tired of battles and wandering. They wanted to settle down and build a life without danger and suffering.

One Shmuel Levine from Soletchnik suggested that it would be better for us to stay in the surroundings of his town, to hide with the help of good neighbors, and to lead an easier existence. He succeeded in convincing some young men from Lithuania. He also tried to convince me.

I was immunized against such arguments. First of all, my daughter was in the Ivia area; second, I never saw a purpose in life without battle. Also I didn't believe that we'd survive by just biding our time. In the short time left I wanted to fight the Germans, to help Jews survive and live. In my humble position, with my poor means, I wanted to do all I could to save Jews until my last day. My father's legacy was always with me.

After a month, we left our temporary home in the camp under darkness. Silence fell all around— nobody spoke. We walked with heavy thoughts in our minds: perseverance, willingness to fight, our existence as humans against the Nazi beasts.

We arrived in Chernovitsh. Here Levine began his propaganda again. I tried to stop him and said:

"Remember the slaughter that our neighbors performed against us in Voronova and Soletchnik?"

He wouldn't listen. He succeeded in convincing several men. We came to a crossroad where we had to separate. We went left and they turned right. The separation had a depressing effect.

With him also went Berke and Gotlieb Levine from Voronova. The night was dark with only sounds of barking dogs. Somebody said:

"Lucky dogs, they have a home, we don't."

On our way we passed near Mishkovitsh, the place where my daughter was staying. I couldn't help it— I had to visit her. We went, 5 people and Carmela with us. We walked very cautiously and when we approached the door we heard a baby's voice. We recognized it immediately. When Carmela opened the door the girl was startled. She didn't see her as her ma. She ran away from her to the old peasant woman:

"Mama—" as if looking for protection from the strange woman.

Carmela wept. After some hours Carmela succeeded with tricks known only to mothers in persuading the girl to come to her arms, and I also had a chance to touch her. The girl was covered with wounds, had roughly cut hair, and was as wild as all Gentile children. We knew and felt that the woman was taking care of the girl as well as she could, but we were also sad to see the girl being so Gentile–ish. Carmela cried all the way back.

Back at the camp I gave a full report of what we had gone through. On the same day all the commanders were called to the head commander. He informed us that the situation required that we split up again, and continue to conduct ourselves separately until middle of next month.

This time I led a company of 40 men. I took the road to the Khapinva[11] Forests. Our base took in some Jews from Russian partisan groups who had fled because of anti–Semitism. They spoke of their Russian friends as being enormous anti–Semites.

I invited them to stay with us and later to reunite with our squad.

On the next day they brought with them some more guys from Vasilishok, experienced partisans. We formed a strong unit of 60 fighters, ready and organized.

The Russian Press to Leave the Elders Behind

On the 15th we returned to the squad base situated in the forests of Zhuravelniki. During our absence the group had grown to 1,000 people or more, joined by survivors of other squads tired of being pursued. It appeared that our squad had succeeded in escaping pursuit without casualties. Also joining us were fighters who had escaped from their brothers–in–arms, the Russians, who hated Jews more than they hated Germans. The Russians didn't like it that our squad had become so big, that it had attracted people, that it consisted of a mixed population of young and old, single and married, that it was always prepared for battle and for life according to Holy Jewish Law. All of that upset them.

The headquarters of various partisan groups kept constant communication and open flow of information. Under orders of the Russian command, pressure was put on Bielski to divide his squad between fighters and non–fighters, to break into groups, and to attach to other squads.

Bielski didn't give in to the pressure. All he cared about were Jewish lives. He wanted to save and prolong the lives of the old and the weak at any price, only because they were Jews. Maybe he also had a personal ego motive, like some have thought, but in any event he stood by his principles with great perseverance and thus became the savior and guardian of unprotected Jews.

The decision was then given to Platonov, the highest Russian partisan commander in Belarus.

He decided to separate fighters from dependents. All fighters were taken under the command of Platonov, all the families were left under the command of Tuvya Bielski, at his base in the Naliboki valley.

Then began the arguments on names. Here too the Russian made the decision. He made a detailed list of names by which the people were divided.

According to this list, I and Carmela were assigned to the fighters. I was pleased. I wanted to fight and to have revenge, my blood boiled, I was eager to fight. But Carmela declared:

"The girl!"

I decided to stay with Bielski. There I'd be able to see the girl, to help her guardian, to ensure her safety. I stayed with Bielski, and there were other fighters who stayed with him rather than join the Russians.

Tuvye appointed me in charge of food and supplies. The relocation to Naliboki demanded new supplies. Tuvya gave me 15 young fighters and a list of villages that had collaborated with the Germans during their big pursuit and gave me permission to take "everything we need by any means".

I concentrated everything my attention on the place where the squad was supposed to stop on the way to Naliboki. In the evening I and Joseph went to several villages near Ivia but they had already been robbed by the Russian partisans, and we returned empty-handed.

We didn't want to go back to the base empty-handed. This had never happened to me before. We stopped for rest in a nearby forest and talked it over. The only option was Lazduny. It was a rich village, but of uncertain loyalty, and extremely dangerous. Lazduny was full of German police and the battle would be very hard. But we decided to go.

We parked the wagons in a grove, about 1km from Lazduny, and waited for darkness. We went out after 2 hours. As we passed a tar factory we saw a great fire that lit up the sky in a frightening way. We noticed that it was at a distance so we continued on our way. The entrance road was carved with stones and the wagons made a loud noise in the silence of the night. We proceeded slowly.

We approached the first house. It was covered with darkness and silent. Suddenly the dog began barking wildly. We were afraid of some reaction, but there was no time to waste – we surrounded the house and knocked on the window. Nobody replied, but we knew that people were inside because earlier we had seen a dim light. We persisted. Finally the owner came out, scared. We asked him about the situation in the village. He said that there was a stationary force of Polish police there, and in the afternoon Germans were there.

I had no time to waste. I ordered him to give me his son to guide us in the village between the houses. It was his first encounter with a partisan. He fell to my feet, kissed my boots, and said he'd give me all his cows and possessions if only I would leave him his son. I noticed that he was against partisans, which is why he was so afraid, thinking we had came to kill him.

His son went with us. We left a guide near his house to ensure against intrusions. We went in the direction of the center of the village. The plan was to start from the other end and come back to the wagons full. I divided people into two groups and we began the operation.

At that same moment I saw a movement of people, about 20 of them. We fell on the ground. I waited for them to come close and called in Russian:

"Who are you?"

They didn't reply. They instantly fell into a nearby trench. I demanded that one of them come over and identify himself, otherwise I'd open fire. I saw one of them walking on shaking feet. We stood up and came to talk to him. He told us they were part of a partisan group named after Stalin. To my question what they were doing in the village and where the rest were, he replied:

"They are robbing the village."

This aroused my suspicion: partisans never talked like that. I approached him. He didn't wear a hat. He looked like a military man pointing a machine gun at me. I wanted to grab his gun but I was afraid that his friends would start to shoot, and they held machine guns against our miserable rifles.

I ordered him to turn around and walk to the nearest farm. I was planning to shoot him there. My group stayed in place. I took with me only Volf'ke and Shlom'ke Boyarski. He approached the house and opened the door. A bright light came out through the opening. We saw that the house was filled with policemen. He turned around immediately and opened fire. One of us was hurt and fell down. In a moment I recovered and retreated to the fence. I fired back and escaped, and ran further away between jumps and falls while we were followed by heavy fire.

I thought that Shlomo Boyarski was running along with me and the one to fall was Velf'ke. I continued running when it became obvious it wasn't Shlom'ke, but it was one of ours, someone else. I found myself without a guide, without connection to my people. The burning fire lit my way and led me to the starting point. At the tar factory we confiscated a horse and a wagon and forced the owner to take us to the next village, Chernovitsh.[12] When dawn came up on the next day we let the peasant go.

At 12 we all met at the rendezvous point. Only Shlomo Boyarski was missing. I sent a peasant to find out what had happened. He came back to tell that there were about 100 policemen in the village, and that Shlomo was the one who had fallen from the Polish bullet.

We were devastated. Shlom'ke had joined us after deserting from the Russians. He was a nice guy, a good friend, and a bold fighter.

We found our squad near Berezhno. Tuvye wasn't there and there was no one to report to. I dropped on an empty wagon and fell asleep.

We Fight and Wreak Revenge

In the morning several guys went out to Lida to visit the ghetto. They planned to retrieve clothes because they had lost everything during the pursuit.

We continued walking and came to the camp of Kessler and his people from Naliboki. They were well provisioned. The nearest village,

Kaltsitsh,[13] had been burnt down by the Germans, all its people murdered, while all the crops were still in the fields.

Tuvye received orders to take the squad into the valley and he himself was to report to the regional headquarters near Navaredok. He didn't go alone. He took several fighters with him. He was determined to bring more Jews to the camp, especially fighters.

I was appointed as Kessler's deputy and was given orders to collect potatoes, as many as possible, then to dig pits in the forest and bury the potatoes for winter. I was in charge of the work. I organized the family men, assisted them, and we buried thousands of pounds of potatoes. Tuvye returned with a large number of Jewish fighters, expanding our squad. Our military actions became larger and more frequent. Now we sabotaged trains, destroyed bridges, and mined roads. I was attached to the fighting knights under the command of Asael Bielski. My life became meaningful; it was nice to join in actions with these guys.

Later on we went out for actions far–off in the Lida–Navaredok area.

Once, we found out that a convoy of 30 German trucks was on its way to Lida to fetch supplies. We went out the night before and mined the road in three different places, one of them under a small bridge close to the town.

With dawn, the first car went up in the air with all its passengers. They were gone without a trace. The Germans presumed that the first mine was also the last time and continued on their way. Very soon more cars exploded together with the Nazis in them.

It was a great day for me. About 120 beasts were wiped from the earth on that day, and the feelings of revenge raised our spirits.

Sometimes we would place mines without success. The commander sent me and Yehuda to find out why. At 12 we carefully approached the mined area. There were no German movements here so we felt safe. When we approached a drainage trench we suddenly saw Germans running around us and we had no possibility of retreat. They looked as if they were trying to catch us alive with only 50 meters between us. I raised my pick and broke from my hiding. They sent a rain of bullets after me. It was a miracle that I was not hurt, that my friend wasn't hurt, and also our horses. We escaped through the farm to the forest. The horses were pulling us forward with their bellies almost touching the ground. We were saved.

On the next day we passed the same place. The peasants saw us and crossed themselves: they began to believe in resurrection.

We heard from them that the Germans had discovered all our mines, dismantled them, and prepared an ambush for us.

From then on we began an ambush and counter–ambush game. We concentrated on undermining trains, though the Germans would dig bunkers along the railways and guard them. We acted at nights, improving from bunker to bunker. We disguised the mines in such way that they walked on them without noticing while a single nail on the rail could trigger the mine to explode at the lightest touch of a wheel.

In September 1943 the Lida Ghetto Was Liquidated

Information arrived that the Germans were taking the Jews of the Lida ghetto to an unknown destination. Some dug bunkers and trenches leading to outside the ghetto and fled, some jumped out of moving trains and came to us. From Voronova there came only one family, cantor Konopke's. Nobody came from our families. My heart was broken, mostly for my younger brother Meshulam who didn't come although he had a rifle and had promised to run away when the moment arrived. Did he decide to stay with our parents? Maybe he tried to help them by sacrificing himself... and he was only twenty?

Later we found out that all of them were taken to Majdenek.

We were also joined by Jews from Navaredok— they too had prepared a trench in advance. They turned out to be the only survivors from the Navaredok ghetto. Our squad had several workshops serving us and the other partisans in the area. We also had a hospital.

Our camp looked like a town, with streets, a hospital, defense trenches, a carpentry shop, a shoemaking workshop, a large bakery for baking bread, a leather factory and a bath house.

My greatest pride, then and today, is that our camp accepted elders too, who were saved thanks to the shelter they found in our camp. We far exceeded 1000 people, and even exceeded the first hundred of the second thousand. We took it upon ourselves to care for those who were unable to fight or work. They were useful for us in workshops and they could continue to live with the feeling of being needed.

The fact that we were a town, that we were well organized, that we appreciated life and the rescuing, made the Russians angry. Our neighbors, and brothers-in-arms in a battle of life or death, looked for every way to divide us, to use us for their needs, while we wanted only two things, which were actually three things: revenge by destroying and weakening our enemies, but more importantly to save as many Jewish lives as possible so they could live and defeat the enemy, increase the nation, and win the eternity of Israel.

We stood against three enemies – the Germans, the Polish nationalists and the Russian partisans, and the last ones knew where to find us. In the forest they were our most dangerous enemy. I remember their rifles pointed at my face many times, each time they had coveted something in my possession: my horse, my weapon, or my clothes. This was the main difference between us and the Gentiles. Their national conscience was so shallow that on certain days it disappeared completely, while ours was constantly growing and continuous.

They used to steal our food on its way to us. I remember numerous fights with them when they tried to steal our supplies as I made my way to the camp.

They were afraid to travel to dangerous locations, to steal from deserted places, or to collect left-over crops. They waited for us to do the job and then tried their courage on us. More than once they smashed my head for a piece of bread, but the rescue missions strengthened me, and they didn't prevail.

Once, during the big pursuit, I and my friends were traveling in search of a new location for our camp. We were near Lugomovitsh [Tr. Note: Lugomovichi] when we came upon a group of Russian partisans. We were armed with our best weapons, Thank God— a machine gun, several rifles and revolvers. At that time those were our greatest treasure, and they wanted to take them away. They outnumbered us by far. They surrounded us. They picked on me and a huge fight started. Finally they took out the bolt from the machine gun, threw me on the ground, and beat me with the gunstock. They stunned me... and then they got what they had come for, and they took my old watch from my back pocket.

They also took our squad's seals and later used them to forge facts in our names. They robbed, boycotted, and stained us with blood. They took my shirt and belt, but I didn't let go of my weapon. When they left my friends took me to the nearest spring, cleaned me up, and the river became red from my blood, spilled for a good cause. My head was swollen and heavy, my eyes narrow, and my whole body looked like one huge blueish bruise.

After a month, a commission arrived to allegedly investigate the incident; all its members were Russians. I don't know whose initiative this was. I was sleeping in the wagon at that moment, tired after the last mission. They woke me up. I came over and recognized the one who had attacked. I wanted to avenge but Tuvye held me back. The commission sat on a tree stump. They made a good impression, but when they asked to tell what had happened, I said:

"Ask him, he knows all the details."

And I left demonstratively.

Only then did I tell Tuvye the details of the incident. Who initiated that investigation, and what was its outcome, I don't know till this day.

Jewish partisans serving in Russian squads deserted from them in increasing numbers. Their stories about active anti-Semitism frightened us. Each day our numbers grew, and each day I thought and said:

"Who knows what would be the fate of the Jews who had escaped from Nazis. Probably they would be the victims of other Christian barbarians of different kinds, their brothers-in-arms.

And my thoughts were right: our squad and our actions for the sake of rescuing Jews, then became a shelter for those victims as well.

There were many cases where Jews who managed to escape from the Germans were then killed by their brothers-in-arms. There were many cases where Jewish partisans were robbed and left behind to die from hunger and scarcity. There were many cases where Jews were murdered by their neighbors or by Russian partisans.

Those thoughts and memories increase my appreciation for Tuvye Bielski. He was a man opposed by many of his friends, when he decided to save all those who came looking for shelter. They thought that a large group would make our movement slower and endanger the whole squad.

Tuvye didn't give in to pressure. His warm Jewish heart was eager to save as many Jewish lives as possible. Tuvye also initiated the rescue of Jews by smuggling them out of ghettos, and this is his greatest achievement.

Exodus from the Forests

A new day arrived. Russian marines and wireless devices announced the defeat of the Nazis, and hope returned. I received a letter from my daughter's rescuer stating that his situation was becoming worse, that neighbors had found out that the girl was Jewish, and that we must come as quickly as possible to take her.

I took a strong horse, a wagon, and several men, and I hit the road. I took some food for my rescuer in order to help him with his bad situation. As we approached we stopped at the nearest forest, and my wife and I went to the farmer's house. When we entered and approached her, our girl was frightened of us and took a distance. We tried to coax her with different stuff we had brought with us, but it didn't help. It took a long time before she agreed to come with us.

It was time for separation. Our rescuers burst into tears. It was hard for them. The mother followed the wagon by foot for several kilometers and cried all the way.

"The house will be empty; how shall we continue without her?"

Meanwhile the retreat of the German army continued. There came orders from Moscow to undermine all their retreat routes. We were ordered to act in the Navaredok area. It took us a whole day to prepare the mines via self-production. All the electrical parts were prepared by me, together with Leybke Federman.

We traveled under darkness. We were 11 people led by Asael Bielski. After a 24-hour ride we came near Stankevitsh, Tuvye's birthplace. We laid mines all the way and now climbed a hill to look at our work site.

In the morning we watched the explosions. We saw the Germans crashing and our hearts we full with joy of revenge. But immediately we were surrounded by Germans and had no choice but to retreat to the swampy area. Asael was familiar with the area so we hid in the swamps for two days, and then sneaked out.

In the camp we found out about a new danger. The Germans, on the way of retreat, were attacking partisan camps and villages, and robbing food and clothes. On one occasion they attacked our camp at a moment when there were not enough fighters on site— there were victims. It was extremely sorrowful for those who died so near to salvation. Our consolation was that we had managed to catch some of the Nazi killers alive. We conducted a trial before some of the victims and we let some of the elders, like Shmuel Pupko, carry out the verdict and feel the sweet taste of revenge.

The Russians were approaching and we were ordered to leave the forest. The forests were full of fleeing Germans. There were about 1,200 surviving Jews among us on these last days. We prepared for the journey. I happened to be amongst the last to leave. The journey was for only 1km, but it was very dangerous. The forest was full of enemies. Our moving–camp proceeded slowly. All along the way were scattered bodies of dead German soldiers. We had to step on them in order to get through. The journey proceeded in full silence. Mourning and sadness overwhelmed us. We knew that we had been saved, but we didn't know why or what for. We didn't know where to go, nor where our home would be now.

After several days we arrived at Navaredok. The site of the ghost town made us shiver.

The partisan commanders were ordered to give away their young fighters to the Red Army, who would send them to the frontier to continue in bitter battle. There was an undercurrent of anti–Semitism in this order: we knew that some wanted to disguise the part played by Jews in this war and the victory, and the way to disguise this would be to send them out to their deaths in the battlefield.

Here Tuvye showed his utmost Jewish spirit. He gathered us together, and at his own risk told us what was being planned, and at the end he said:

"Guys, if you want to live, split and run in any direction."

Tuvye Bielski created opportunities to save many Jews in the forests, but his last act of rescue was uttering this one sentence. It should never be forgotten that if his Russian friends had known about this, he would have paid with his life.

Editor's Footnotes

1. In the original text, the surname is spelled: mem–aleph–vov–lamed–kuf–nun–yud–kuf.

2. This town has not yet been identified. In the original text the spelling is: resh–samekh–lamed–kuf–yud.

3. Possibly the town know today as Survilishki. In the original text the spelling is: zayen–vov–resh–beyz (or veyz)–lamed–nun–yud–kof.

4. In the original text the spelling is: resh–samekh–lamed–kuf–yud.

5. This town has not yet been identified. In the original text the spelling is: shin–tsadek–yud–gimel–lamed–yud.

6. Possibly the town know today as Petrovichi. In the original text the spelling is: pey (or fey)–tes–resh–yud.

7. Probably the town known today as Lubcha. In the original text the spelling is: lamed–vov–beyz–yud–tsadek–geresh–nun–kuf–hey.

8. This town has not yet been identified. In the original text the spelling is: beys–resh–zayen–nun–hey.

9. This town has not yet been identified. In the original text the spelling is: mem–yud–shin–kuf–vov–veyz (or beyz)–yud–langer tsadek.

10. This town has not yet been identified, possibly Chernevichi. In the original text the spelling is: tsadek–geresh–resh–nun–vov–beyz (or veyz)–yud–langer tsadek.

11. This forest has not yet been identified. In the original text the spelling is: khes–aleph–pey (or fey)–yud–nun–tsvey vov–hey.

12. See note 10.

13. This town has not yet been identified. In the original text the spelling is: kuf–lamed–tsadek–yud–samekh–tsadek–geresh.

A Child's Gift During the Holocaust

K. Lisorski

Ed. Note: This article appears in both Hebrew and Yiddish in the original Yizkor Book; only the Yiddish version has been translated and published in this book. The title of the Yiddish version is "Our Child Saved Us" and may be found at page 363 of this book.

A Son of Voronova's Heroism and Revenge

Zalmen Dukshtulski

Ed. Note: This article appears in both Hebrew and Yiddish in the original Yizkor Book; only the Yiddish version has been translated and published in this book. The title of the Yiddish version is "An Involuntary Hero" and may be found at page 347 of this book.

Story of an Avenging Youth

Yekuthiel (Kushke) Boyarski

Ed. Note: This article appears in both Hebrew and Yiddish in the original Yizkor Book; only the Yiddish version has been translated and published in this book. The title of the Yiddish version is "A Chid Partisan" and may be found at page 379 of this book.

[Pages 123-126]

I Left for the Forest at Age 15

Ze'ev Kaplan

Translation by Meir Bulman

22/June/42[1]

The Germans entered Voronova on that day. I was out of town. The Russians sent me and Motl Daikhovski (the Cobbler) to guard the railroad tracks so Ukrainians and others would not sabotage them. In actuality they sent father, but I went in his place; I wanted father to rest.

Mother worked at the beer shop. It was a time of large–scale enlistment, the guys busied themselves with drinking and she had much work on her hands.

When the two of us approached the tracks we witnessed something odd. From an unknown direction, a few motorcycle riders appeared and one showed the other the riding direction while gesturing with his thumb, "Onward! Onward!" And the area peasants stood in groups and cheered.

I recognized each of the Gentiles. They were the farmers from Kltkin, Alsorishok and other villages. They greeted us gleefully and happily, "Now your end will come, damned Jews. The Germans will finish you along with the damned Russians— we will no longer see the two of you around, thank God."

The Germans, who at the time could not differentiate between a Jew and a Gentile, paid no attention to us and so we returned to town in peace and no one harmed us.

On the way back we heard gunshots from all sides. Those were planned shots, I think there were already German marines undercover and they responded in signals.

As we neared the town, Stshisko the Pole greeted us by yelling, "Your end is now, Communist Jews!"

The word of the German arrival spread quickly. Those enlisted [Tr. Note: local Jews in the Russian military] dispersed, and each went home. My parents returned from the shop at dusk. We entered Netta-Alia's home and sat there all night, waiting for the morning.

In the morning large German military forces came in from different directions. We saw Russian prisoners led with their hands raised. Jews stayed home. Gentiles appeared and began looting stores. We heard them yell, "Your time has come, blood-sucking Jews, communist Jews, now you'll burn along with the communists who favored you."

Meanwhile, the German commanders were replaced, and the harassment of Jews began. We heard the Kletzk Rabbi was arrested on the claim he threw a grenade on the military. Jews immediately gathered a ransom and had him released.

Several weeks passed and we became acquainted with the methods of the Nazi regime. In the beginning of August, a Gentile woman, Tklle Bworonov, wanted to summon the *Gestapo* in order to tell them who had supposedly collaborated with the Russians. The Germans allowed the Gentiles to gather all the Jews in the market place. They went into each home and commanded us to gather in the square. Selebrita, who worked at Goldstein's tar workshop, led a group of Gentiles, our neighbors, and they struck us with death blows, with batons; our lives were made expendable to them.

At the marketplace, all the Jews were instructed to stand in a line, from which they took out Yitzhak Volpianski, Yitzhak Kaplan, Zerakh Shelovski and his siblings, Esther and David, and then sat them on the ground and told them to wait. The rest of those gathered were dispersed and sent home with blows and blood-curdling beratement.

The fate of these five youths remains unknown to us.

That week they also enacted, by decree, the wearing of patches on both the back and chest to highlight Jewish identity. Jews were also forbidden from walking on the sidewalks.

In December of 1941, all Jews were taken for forced labor, cleaning the occupiers' bikes, homes, and more. We were a group of youths who cleared the snow from the roads. For a long while I worked with Yekutiel 'Kushke' Boyarski, Barukh Garbatski, Zerakh Pupko, Yakov Dvilianski, Arke Dvilianski, Gutko Eishishki, and some young women, Rokhl Dukshtulski and others. We worked on Benakani–Vilne streets. Then on the Saturday before *Hannukah* the Vilne folks were murdered.

9/May/1942

We woke up in the morning and saw the town swarming with people armed with weapons. In the distance, Gentiles prepared large pits and we did not know. Many families gathered in our home. There was Moshe Gershonovitsh, his wife and two children, Sarah Gershonovitsh, his cousin, with her daughter Khasye and her sons Avraham and Zalmen. Nevankhe Grodzenchik, and Leyzerke Katzenellenbogen, and my father Binyamin, my mother Riva, my sister Zelda, and my cousins Avraham and Ze'ev Kaplan.

We gathered because Gtzvitz, the kind Gentile from Dutchshiyok,[2] wanted to rescue us from the enclosed town and transfer us to his village. He returned after working out with the guards to allow us to leave. We followed him, reaching the horse market without incident. All was in order. Near the fence stood Bentovits, a Polish neighbor on guard duty. Gtzvitz went to "work it out" with another guard. Suddenly gunshots rained down on us. I heard him nervously saying, "Oh Jezus kochany jestem Poliak" (Oh dear Jesus I am Polish).

We spread out in all directions. At first I ran with my parents, but I lost them on the way. Running nervously, I reached Berlovits the pharmacist's terrain in the Zamuk Forest (Tr. Note: Polish word for citadel; see town map). A policeman stood there. I knew him— he was the town shepherd's son. He began shooting at us but stopped. We gave him money and he allowed us to continue. We reached the rail tracks, where an armed guard came out and threatened to turn us over to the

Germans. I recognized his gurgling voice. He used to work near us as a guard. I called his name and he accommodated us. We paid him a hundred dollars and he allowed us to continue.

We reached Dutchshiyok and did not know who was killed and who remained alive. We were very hungry. I entered a peasant's home, took some bread, and we made our way to the woods.

Zalmenke Gershonovitsh woke up Moshe In the morning and they went to ask the peasants what was going on, and to get some food. The Gentiles said that kind Gtzvitz was killed along with my dear parents at the horse market. Sarah Gershonovitz, her daughter Khasya, Nevankke Grodzenchik, Leyzer Katzenellenbogen and his girlfriend Khanke Dlugin were killed later.

Yitzhak Dvilianski buried them at the marketplace square when the gunfire stopped.

We heard from the villagers that my sister Zelda, and Shoshke Gershonovitsh were saved, but we could not know where to search for them.

We spent that day in the woods with the intention of leaving at dark and continuing on to a safer place. In the evening, our gurgling guard showed up with several Gentiles armed with guns. They surrounded us and opened fire. We managed to escape and reached a small village where we were sheltered by a Gentile named Khadrovich for two days, Sunday and Monday. That Monday, the massacre of the Voronova Jews took place.

Most of the Jews were massacred. The *Yudenrat*[0] had made a list of survivors to be transferred to the Lida ghetto.

A kind Gentile brought this news to us from town.

What could we have done? We were trapped and so decided to return home.

We returned to Voronova on Tuesday. I found my sister and Shoshke

Gershonovitsh, as well as part of our family. There were also Leybke Kaplan, his sister Libka and her husband, Avraham Kaplan, and my cousin Ze'ev. The houses were boarded up. The survivors were concentrated in the New Plan.[4]

At the start of 1943, the remnants of our town reached the Lida ghetto. The Germans took Kushke and I to work construction. We were young men who still looked human and ready for work.

Rumors of partisans in the nearby woods then began to spread. We eventually learned that Meir Shmerkovitsh (Shamir), his family, and Altshik Blyakher had joined the partisans. Yekutiel escaped to the woods immediately, and I remained without guidance. One day I heard that Meir Shamir and Leybke Katsev[5] from Lida were in the ghetto and about to rescue people by taking them to the woods. I made up my mind to join them and sneak out.

I was a child and so I knew they would not want to take me, but from the rumors I knew they were leaving that night. I walked ahead of them then lay by the designated exit point and waited. They did not leave that night. It was postponed to the next night. I returned to work, labored all day, and at dusk I again left to wait for them near the gate. I heard them say: "Guys, everyone is drunk, get ready, we are leaving soon." They passed near me. I heard their footsteps. Meir was the last one to pass. When I saw him I rose and joined those walking. When Meir noticed me he did not say a word and instead hugged me happily. My exit was granted. Eighty people were rescued that night, among them Lida residents, a family from Seltshnik,[6] and Altshik Blyakher from Divenishok.

In the Woods with Bielski

We spent a day in the woods, and at night we left to join Bielski's battalion. As luck would have it, the Germans were conducting a raid on the partisans and we were in the line of fire. We were miraculously saved because the Germans liked staying in trenches to fire, so as not to fall prey to ambushes set up by the partisans. Our guides knew this and so we reached the target unharmed. When we arrived we were directed towards the Naliboki Plains where we set up for prolonged stay.

Each person dug a shed in the ground to live in. I dug near Meir Shamir. I stuck to them like the parents that I missed, and in my vast loneliness they served as a good replacement.

When the big siege began where the Germans wanted to permanently rid themselves of Bielski's "wasp nest", we split into different groups that traveled in different directions. I did not belong to any group and was in a dire state, but Meir Shamir who commanded fifty people took me with him and I was rescued. I worked as a shepherd, served in the squad kitchen, and grew up near the Shmerkovitsh and Konopke families. Once I was ill with typhus and people were careful not to come near me. I was very miserable in my loneliness and the quarantine that I suffered due to my illness, but Karmela Shamir and Beyleh Olkenitski cared for me at risk to themselves, and they saved me. The Konopke girls that lived in our neighborhood also took a risk and cared for me, washed my loused clothes, and paid no mind to the danger.

When I think of those days of holocaust and hopelessness, and think of the horrors I endured, and of my life that was saved thanks to a humanity that was not damaged. I can only conclude and say that I owe my life to Meir Shamir. May my words serve him as a medal of honor during days of crisis.

Footnotes

1. Tr. Note: Although the text says 1942, this is a misprint. From the context of the article, the correct year is noted as being 1941.

2. Ed. Note: this town has not yet been located

3. Ed. Note: these were Jews forced by the Nazis to supervise and govern the Jewish populations under Nazi control

4. Ed. Note: 'New Plan' is the name given to a new neighborhood in Voronova created on lands recently purchased from Count Shvanbakh.

5. Ed. Note: 'Katsev' is the approximate transliteration of the name given in the text.

6. Ed. Note: the exact location of this town is not yet known

[Pages 137-142]

Unjust Regimes

Yitzach Ben-Ami

Ed. Note: This article appears in both Hebrew and Yiddish in the original Yizkor Book; only the Yiddish version has been translated and published in this book. The title of the Yiddish version is "Under Gentile Regimes" and may be found at page 387 of this book.

A Fifteen Year Old Boy in Fate's Hands

Yakov Olkenitski

Translation by Miriam Olkenitski z"l

Edited by Yocheved Klausner

During the Russian regime I worked in a bakery. I was young, only about 15 years old. I had not yet established any kind of relationship toward one regime or the other, but one thing was clear to me: there was no threat to life in this regime. You may end up your life in prison or in Siberia but no one was going to come and kill you because of your national origins, unlike under the Nazis where being a Jew was a crime and you were sentenced to death and torture before death.

This I have understood and when the war broke out between Germany and Russia, I arranged to get a truck with Hershel Sokolick and drove toward Soviet territory. As we passed Dzwanishik I wanted to say good bye to my sister there. In the market I ran into my brother-in-law and he said to me: "Boy, where are you running to? The family and we are here. Your place is with us. Stay here and don't rush into anything!" I stayed with them that day and then I went back to Voronova to my parents' house and to my only brother. My other brother had been sent to Siberia and was still there. The Germans were already controlling Voronova, but life had not yet ceased. I went on working in the bakery like nothing had happened but in my soul I had a feeling of disaster and I wanted to escape by all means.

When the Germans assembled the entire Jewish population of the town in the market square, it was the first and last time that I obeyed them. I went there, I saw the torture, I saw how they selected seven

Jews and killed them without a trial and I said to myself that I have to escape no matter what happens. When we were called out to go to the market square for the second time, I did not go. I escaped with my brother Meyer to the nearby forest and we returned to town when the horrible show of execution was over. We delayed our escape for a more suitable time. At the third time, when the Nazis gathered the Jews in the market square and murdered hundreds of them so that half of the Jews of our town had been killed, we escaped to the forest together with a few more youngsters and students. We stayed there for five days. We were looking for a way to escape the Holocaust that had been prepared for us but when we heard that the Nazis had established a Ghetto and had collected everybody into the Ghetto, we also returned. From there we were transported to the Lida Ghetto with my sister and my brother-in-law from Dzwanishik. My mother and my other sisters were not alive anymore, may God avenge their blood.

One day they demanded us to give them 250 Jews for work out of town. Everybody knew that this was a death sentence for the Jews. They would never return. I was working at that time for the Gabitz Commissar and I did not have to go, but when I heard that my brother-in-law, Eliahu Blyakher was among the people chosen for death, I tried to think of what would happen to my sisters and the children. I volunteered to go instead of him. We appeared at the meeting place, the name roll was read and everybody answered. When the name Blyakher was called, I answered instead and we marched toward the train. There we were supposed to get on the cars and be shipped away. As soon as we got outside the Jewish settlement, I jumped from the row and escaped. Until this day I don't remember how it was, if they ever noticed and how they responded. I was really fast then and did not stop running toward the forest. I ran for six hours straight and did not turn left or right. At the end of the sixth hour, tired and worn out to the edge of unconsciousness, I found myself again at the gates of the Ghetto. I was shocked and could not understand how I got there, but I could not think of another escape. I was too tired and too depressed and I sneaked in and mingled with other people. I remained in the Ghetto, but now I was there illegally. When I rested a bit and gathered my strength and realized that my life was again in great danger, I decided to escape again and fight for my life. I never abandoned the idea of escape.

In the meantime, rumors about partisans operating in the forests near Lida got to the Ghetto. We wanted to join them but the rumors said that without arms no one would be accepted and we did not have any weapons. By chance, we found a treasure in the house we were staying in, a treasure of gold coins, chains and watches. The owners of this treasure were no longer alive. We took the treasure to one of the Poles. We bought a rifle from him and ammunition and we went – me and my brother-in-law – to the forest near Lida with the idea of coming back and saving the rest of our family.

After two weeks, Meir Shamir went out to bring some people from the Lida ghetto. My brother-in-law joined him and among the Jews they saved was my sister from Dzwanishik and Meir Shamir's wife. We stayed in the forest for four months and managed to provide supplies for ourselves and our Brigade. We were thinking about ways of saving Jews and planning how to get the Jews out of the Lida ghetto. The place we were staying was dangerous because we were too close to Lida, which was full of Germans and their Polish collaborators. But the idea of being able to save the Jews made us forget the danger and stay in the same place. In the meantime, we were discovered by the Germans and in the big hunt they organized in the forest we were forced to break up into smaller groups and hide or sneak out towards the Naliboki fields. Our group consisted of about fifteen people. We lived off food we stole during the night and we hid during the day – like animals separated from our command post without any knowledge of what was going on around us and what was happening in our Brigade. But we could never let go of the idea of escape and liberation.

We decided that we would save from the Ghetto everyone we could. I wanted to go to the Ghetto to save my sister. Our people agreed and I went. That night I went to the Ghetto but found my sister ill with typhoid, unable to walk or to be moved. I took with me seven Jews, among them Isaac and Jacob Dovilinsky and returned to the forest with them. I promised my sister that in 10 days I would be back to take her and I told her to do her best to get well. In the evening when I tried to get out I was discovered by a Ghetto policeman. He walked toward me and tried to stop me from getting out. He said that it would cause a catastrophe for the Jews in the Ghetto. When he could not convince me he slapped me in the face. We delayed our escape for a few hours and under the cover of night we left and got to the forest in the morning.

*

Ten days after this mission, the Brigade organized again. We were going to return to Naliboki. I decided on my own to return to Lida before we left the area and to save my sister. When I got close to the ghetto I heard shots. I knew that this meant the end of the Jews in there but I sneaked in anyway. I entered the first section of the Ghetto; I couldn't reach the second section, where my sister was, since it was separated from the first section by barbed wire. I went to the house of some friends and fell asleep. At 5 in the morning, my friend woke me and said: "You got here exactly in time for the wedding. What did you do? Why did you come back?" With those words he pulled me toward the window. I looked out and saw that the Ghetto was surrounded by armed men and there was no way of escaping death. From my place of safety, I had entered the Ghetto exactly on the day of its liquidation.

At 7 o'clock the Germans started leading groups of 50 to the killing ground. During the chaos, I managed to sneak to the other part of the Ghetto where my sister was staying. She was waiting for her turn. When she saw me she screamed: "What did you do Yankele? "Run if you value your life! Run, I'm begging you!" I started inquiring who among the people had any kind of a weapon. Three people joined me. One of them remembered a bunker that he had seen some time ago and he led us there. We hid there until 9 o'clock in he morning. Suddenly a woman walked in and started screaming "What are you doing here? Because of you they will "murder all of us! Get out!" So we got out. We joined the last group of Jews that were awaiting their certain death. While we were waiting, six of us got out of the group. We walked to the Ghetto's fence. It was a wooden fence, ten feet high and we knew that behind that fence was Lida's lumber yard. We wanted to cross the fence and hide in the yard but the fence was made of solid boards without a crack or a hole. Only between two walls we found a small crack. We wanted to push ourselves through it but suddenly we noticed an armed German looking at us. We got scared but he told us: "Escape, I don't see you." We crossed the fence and hid between blocks of lumber. In fact, we were exposed to the laborers who were working in the yard. They saw us clearly but we couldn't help it. We were waiting for four o'clock when they were to go home and we could have a real hiding place.

At four o'clock, the bell sounded and the workers started leaving. Only two of them stayed behind, and when the rest of the workers had left, they walked over to us and said: "We saw you. We know that you are Jews escaping from death. We will not report you if you will tell us where you left your gold and treasures. If you keep your promise, we'll come at night with buggies and will take you to the forest."

There was one among us who had a gold watch which he had inherited from his father. He gave it to the workers. We also promised them everything and begged them to come in the evening. We waited for the darkness and worried about the promises of the goyim. We got out when darkness fell. Behind the lumberyard there was a foundry and we saw the guard. He saw us, too. We got up our courage and approached him and said to him: Tell us at once if there is an escape route where there are no Germans." He showed us a way to get out and we left. We hid behind residential houses so that we couldn't be seen when suddenly someone shouted, in Yiddish: "Jews, where are you going?" It was a Jewish young man who was hiding behind some bushes. He warned us not to go on because every 50 meters there were two armed Germans and there was no way to escape from them. We joined them and waited 24 hours. It was a dangerous hiding place, but we had no other choice. At dawn we began to worry since we were entirely exposed and we knew that at full daylight we would be discovered and lost. At six in the morning we saw a group of Christian workers going to work so we joined them silently, trying to mingle with them by groups of two, at safe distances. The first few pairs passed safely, the last pair was discovered and the Christians began pursuing them. One of them, a young man from Lida was shot and killed.

Somehow we managed to go out of there. Twelve kilometers from Lida there was a thick forest. We made it to the forest to hide and waited for the Partisans that we were certain were there. We simply did not know where to go without taking a chance.

We stayed there for a week. At night we went to steal food and during the day we slept in our hiding place. On the seventh day we met the Partisans. They told us that the Ghetto was completely liquidated and there was no one alive in that area. They also told us that Bielski and his unit were in that area and that one Jewish family was hiding at a goy's place in the nearest village. At night we went out to free the Jewish family and were surprised to learn that there were only women and two old people, and who knows what would have happened to them if we hadn't come. We learned from them that there was another Jewish family hiding there and Tuvia Bielski had promised to come and get them out.

We waited for Bielski. The goy was one of us, helping the Partisans. We told him where we were hiding and asked him to let Bielski know where we were. The next day, Bielski arrived and within two weeks we got to our camp. These two weeks were nerve racking for all of us. No one really believed that we were alive. How was it possible to be out in the forest for two weeks and stay alive in an area full of murderous Nazis? The only people who believed were my brother and sister. She knew that I was a survivor.

From that time on we stayed in the forest and lived a Partisan's life. When I recall this kind of life, I don't know whether or not the things we did were heroic; the whole existence of the Camp Bielski was heroic as well as dangerous – all in order to save the remnants of the Holocaust.

We were 1,200 people in the camp and we were all helping each other to survive and each of us did the right thing at that time and in those conditions. But there were indeed also acts of real heroism, acts that involved danger and revenge. I myself took part in many ambushes against the Germans, I mined their convoys, I looked for them everywhere and I also guarded our forest against German troops. The most dangerous act that I remember was confiscating food for the members of our unit. I also remember our commander Meir Shamir; it was reassuring to be under his serious and responsible command.

Before we left the forest, our lives changed to a happier phase. German deserters were trying to escape and it was a pleasure for us to ambush them. For us it was sweet vengeance. Once we caught ten Germans. The Russian Commander declared himself Judge and a Jew from Meliboki was the translator in the trial. According to his translation, all the Germans admitted that they murdered and demolished and robbed and the Russian Commander sentenced them to death. I was appointed to carry out the death sentence. I carried it out with a sacred feeling and I knew it would teach the generations to come a good lesson. They fell, one by one, and I had the pleasure of seeing them helpless and frightened and miserable and knowing that they wouldn't dare to talk anymore about their heroic and unbeatable nation.

Of course, this was not the reason of collecting and writing my memories as a Partisan. My main reason was to note the big part of those who established the Brigade and those who gave it a heroic agenda of keeping the Jewish survivors alive, month after month despite fear and hunger. Their heroism should be told over and over again and it should not be forgotten.

My Miserable Russian Days

Bat Sheba Podesiuk (Kalmanovitsh)

Ed. Note: This article appears in both Hebrew and Yiddish in the original Yizkor Book; only the Yiddish version has been translated in this book. The title of the Yiddish version is "My Miserable Russian Days" and may be found at page 414 of this book.

Long is the Road to Zion

Yitzach Olkenitski

Translation by Miriam Olkenitski z"l

Edited by Yocheved Klausner

Back to Voronova

The train slowed down. From the platform I'm standing on, I can see the wooden buildings of the Voronova train station. I know that this train will not stop at the town of my birth but when I got on the train at the station of Binyaconi, the train engineer surrendered to my pleadings and promised to slow down the train while passing near Voronova so I can jump home...

I jumped from the train into the grave of brothers. Large groups of Jews from Vilna left in 1942 and got to Voronova to find shelter from German bestiality there. They believed that the Germans would not find them in small towns but they did. They were arrested and ordered to dig a grave for themselves. They were thrown in alive and shot. Even before that I have heard about this common grave. I gave my last respects to the victims of the "Lithuanian Jerusalem" who were the first victims of the Holocaust, even before the official "aktzia" in Voronova.

At the train station nothing has changed. The same manager Petchikowski, the Pole that stayed on his job during all the regimes, the Polish, the Soviet, the German, and back to the Soviet. There is peace and quiet here and my heart is pounding. How could it be that nothing has changed? How could this old terminal still stand here after all that happened to our town, after the destruction of our Jewry? For a moment I stood like stricken but I shook myself away from these thoughts and walked toward the town. My head felt heavy. I'm walking and feeling like a Holocaust survivor who is coming back to a home that does not exist anymore. When I got close to town, I suddenly observed a young woman walking toward the train station. It was my sister Beila, still living in Voronova and waiting for me. I sent her some telegrams about my coming home and now she was here to greet me.

It was the spring season and the fields on both sides of the road were covered with wild flowers, the cherry trees were blooming and I breathed their delicate smell. I breathed the Polish Spring or maybe the Lithuanian – those places that are described by the great poet Mickewitz in "Pan Tadeusz". It was the spring of 1946 after the great slaughter of the Jewish Nation. And there were four other springs, springs like those described by the poet [Bialik] "And God called for spring and slaughter together; the sun was shining, the tree was blooming and the butcher was slaughtering."

[Page 147]

I go back six years, not Spring but the winter of 1940, not day but night. Bitter cold was sneaking through my warm clothes and leather boots. Then too I was walking the same road but not from the station but toward it. My mother walked with me all shaking and crying. She was walking with her second son, the same way she walked with my oldest brother when he was drafted into the Polish Army to fight the German hoards that had invaded Poland in September 1939 – and he was taken prisoner. She held my hand strongly and I begged her: "Please go back, Mother, go back home, it's so cold outside. Those few hundred yards you walk with me won't help. We'll still see each other. I'm walking the road I walked in my youth. And this is the road to Zion – that is how you brought me up in our warm, Jewish home. You, my dear mother, the daughter of R' Leyzer, the head of the Yeshivah of Szczuchin near Novogrodki and my dear father who worked hard as a tailor to keep us together. He even found time to work for the Community. Go back, Mother we'll still see each other."

So mother went back; she is still standing in front of me waving her hand, and as she gets further away it looked as if she were blessing me. "Dear Son, go in Peace from Voronova and come in Peace to Zion."

Six years have passed since then and I'm still on my way to Zion. Difficult was the road, full of tortures and full of suffering. It was the road of a Prisoner of Zion, whose only crime was that he belonged to the Youth Organization, BEITAR, sentenced to spend long years in the jails of the Soviet Union – concentration camps that for some reason are called in their language "Camps of Labor and Education."

I came back to you, Voronova, to the grave of my ancestors, to the grave of my father who died in 1936. Now my sister Beila brings me to the common grave of my Jewish brothers of Voronova, the grave my mother is buried in. This grave is located in an area on the outskirts of town. It was hard to go through this terrible test. Twice in the same day to stand in front of common graves: one near the train station and the other on the other side of town in a place that in the past served as a range for the Polish riflemen. The Germans knew how to use it for their purpose: "the final solution of the Jewish problem." I stood there; I gave my respects to the Saints of Voronova who were led like sheep to be slaughtered – choking with tears. My dear Mother, I didn't succeed in seeing you alive and I wanted to see you so much, to hug you and to tell you all the things I went through, to take you with me, to leave this horrible place and to go together to our country.

My sister Beila stood beside me. She was trying to cheer me up. Soon we will be on our way – she said – to Meir and Jacob, your brothers. They were already in "independent" Poland. From there, the road is open to Zion. It won't be long and your dream will come true. Beila tells me about the heroic acts of my two brothers, my two partisan brothers who were together with her husband, Eliahu, and many of our townspeople in Bielski's partisan brigade. This Brigade that is remembered for its heroic acts in the Jewish Resistance in the Holocaust, the Brigade that fought and took revenge on the Germans and their collaborators. Our brother Jacob was among the bravest of the partisans. He had a big share in the attacks performed by the Brigade, and he saved the lives of many people from Voronova that he led out of the Leda Ghetto. After he escaped to the forest he came back to the Leda Ghetto many times and each time he led out people and brought them to Bielski's Brigade. Sadly, he could not get our sister Esther out. He found her sick and a few days later the Ghetto was liquidated.

[Page 148]

Beila and went back to town. Beila kept telling me about the horrors that happened to the people of our town and about the fate of some of them. No miracles happened for the Jews, but something amazing did happen, the most significant is what happened to my aunt.

Aunt Musia was the wife of Isaac Olkenitski, may God avenge his blood, Starosta of Voronova during the Czar's regime and I am the carrier of his name. He was murdered on Passover of 1919 when the Poles captured Voronova. They murdered him because one of his sons was a Commandant of the Red Police. The son succeeded in escaping with the Red Army into the Soviet Union. My Aunt suffered a stroke on that day and she was bound to her bed for the rest of her life. Her children, Esther, Rachel, Moshe and Yesheyahu took care of her during all of those years and showed her unusual dedication and respect. They summoned the best doctors for her and nothing seemed to work. It was impossible to get her out of her sick bed. On the day of the "aktzia", all of the Jews were ordered to get out into the Market Place. Those that couldn't get out were shot in their houses. When the Germans arrived at her house and found her in bed they pointed their weapons at her; she got up and said: "I am going to die together with everybody else. After 20 year of paralysis she got up and walked half a mile toward the common grave.

At the End of the Road

We went on the road to Poland and from there to refugee camps. In Germany we taught the "children of Israel," the survivors of the Holocaust, the use of weapons. We purchased weapons and ammunition to bring them to Israel to help the settlements struggling for their survival. These weapons were part of the weapons that were hidden on the *Etzel* [*Irgun Tzeva'i Le'umi*] ship Altalena. On the same ship my brother Jacob and I arrived at the shores of Israel.

Sometimes I am overtaken with the feelings of nostalgia for the place I was born in and grew up, for the place I spent my childhood and my youth. I do not miss the cursed land soaked in the blood of the saints of Israel, but I miss you, my father, mother, brothers and sisters and Jews of Voronova who are lost to us forever. My heart aches for you that you have never succeeded in arriving at the end of the road to Zion.

[Page 155]

A Little More Revenge

Shmuel Kopelovitsh

Ed. Note: This article appears in both Hebrew and Yiddish in the original Yizkor Book; only the Yiddish version has been translated in this book. The title of the Yiddish version is "Taking Some More Revenge" and may be found at page 407 of this book.

My Revenge Against the Liquidator of Jews in Our Region

Moshe Kaplan

Translation by Emma Karabelnik

In December 1947 I was called by the German government and the Department of Criminal Prosecution for our region to go to Germany in order to testify against *Shtabsleiter* Vindish.

Everyone whose fate had made them suffer the atrocities of the Lida ghetto and experience the death torments in the open ghetto of our town knew who Vindish was. Vindish was in charge *de facto* of the liquidation of Voronova Jews and Jews from all the environs, but Vindish didn't miss any opportunity to kill a Jew by his own hands.

I knew him well. I worked for him and also as a painter in Lida for a whole month before the liquidation of our dear Jewish community. When the horrible day came and our community was liquidated, and two mass graves were dug, it was Vindish himself who decided who would live and who would die. I was left alive by him as a person useful to him and that's why he also let my family live.

Those days spent close to him made me a natural witness in this trial.

The trial was held in Mainz, in Hebrew *Magentza*. It is a town known for its pogroms in the Middle Ages. When I entered the courtroom Vindish stood up, saluted, and cried out:

"Herr Kaplan, ich liebe Isroel (Mr. Kaplan I love and admire Israel)

I replied:

"Israel doesn't need praises from a dog like you."

He sat down. This affected the whole atmosphere of the trial, clarifying that his tricks wouldn't work and that he would have to change his attitude for this trial.

The judge began the procedures and I was asked in what language I would prefer to testify. Near me was sitting an Israeli Police officer who had prepared the case and he also served as a translator. I didn't wait for his translation and replied in German:

"I now have a state of my own, a homeland with its own language in which I want to testify."

I told everything I knew against him and against Verner, the famous murderer whose atrocities in Voronova could freeze your blood simply by listening to them.

The trial was cancelled in the middle of the procedures because it was discovered that Vindish's lawyers had placed listening devices, and they asked for a delay.

It was a pre-calculated trick to gain time and wait for a more favorable judge.

*

During my stay in Germany I lived with a German anti-Nazi family. They did everything they could to make me feel comfortable and pleasant in their country. It was the teacher Vickry, a well-known educator in the Mainz professional school – he, his wife and his wife's parents.

In the evening they brought me to a priest's house. When we came in we found about ten people were invited to the meeting. They asked me to tell them something from my bitter experience. I told them things as they were. They wept while listening to me and [kept crying] for a long hour after I finished.

When I finished, a heavy silence fell. The priest was the first to recover and said:

"You see, those acts are in total contradiction to Christianity, how could they do it."

I couldn't resist a reply:

"Honorable gentlemen, but this conduct in Christianity has gone on for centuries, Spanish Inquisition, Blood libel, etc."

They kept silent, the priest said:

"I invite you to come to my Church tomorrow and see something which will be an answer for you in this matter."

On the next day I went to Church with him. He showed me paintings depicting the celebrations of the Christians at the sites of pogroms performed by local Christians during the time of Baruch of Mainz.[1] They were covered with sheets.

He explained:

"I am ashamed of it, that's why I covered the paintings with sheets. Now I am going to pass a decision to uncover them."

*

In May 1969 the trial against Vindish was reopened. This time Verner was not charged with him. He had severe diabetes, he was confined to bed.

At the start of the trial the judges asked for my permission to record my testimony. I complied.

I testified in Hebrew.

The judge asked me to describe everything I went through. I was allowed to cross the boundaries of pure facts and to add my personal feelings. He also offered me tranquilizers, ready to take the risk on my emotional state.

I took his advice and elaborated in my descriptions, incidents, and feelings, and I stayed calm the whole time. According to local laws of Mainz, judges may ask the witness questions during his testimony. I calmly replied to all their questions, even those that seemed provocative or tendentious. I didn't lose my temper until Vindish interfered.

The judge requested that I tell what was before Vindish and his last actions. I told all, including the fact that he had spared my life during the liquidation, and how he had ordered who was to live and who was to die. I didn't see him murder with his own hands— I myself didn't see it, but I heard it from many reliable people who saw it with their own eyes. Here Vindish burst out:

"Herr Kaplan, if it wasn't for me saving you, you wouldn't be standing here with your fancy tie."

I replied:

"You didn't save me, you just kept 700 slaves for your own needs, and I happened to be one of them."

I felt myself losing control, my emotions went high. He asked me where was I after the war, on my way to Israel:

"Have you been to Austria by any chance?"

I responded – "Why do you ask?"

He replied:

"Because in Austria there were gangs of dog hunters."

To my question what gangs and what dogs, he replied:

"Gangs of Jews looking for Nazi officers and handing them over to the police."

I said:

"If so, I feel sorry deep in my heart that I and my children didn't have the privilege to participate in this sacred dog hunt."

The prosecutor winked at me with sparkling eyes, he agreed with me fully.

From then on he became more and more impudent, asking frequent and arrogant questions. I couldn't take it anymore. My eyes were filled with tears, my throat was choked. I couldn't stop the tears from dripping and washing my face, I had to drink water frequently, but I couldn't calm down my emotions.

He asked:

"And what are you doing to poor Arabs in Israel?"

I replied:

"If you would treat us the way we treat Arabs, 6 million Jews could still be alive and living peaceful and prosperous lives."

In the end he took a practical direction:

"How many Jews were murdered in Voronova?"

I replied:

"I couldn't know exactly, I think approximately three thousand Jews." He burst out:

"You are a liar! In your previous testimony you spoke about two thousand five hundred and now you add 500 more!"

I had to respond and I burst out:

"Murderer, don't you know that murder of one person or one baby is a serious crime, and you bargain with me about 500? You are and have always been a murderer with sick mentality."

After saying it, I took the glass full with water and threw it straight in his face.

Then something very common to all murderers happened, to most of them. As soon as he was injured by the glass and his nose started to bleed, he became hysterical and screamed like a pig.

The chairman of the court stopped the discussion and all the judges left the room. I was taken out of court by a policeman but I wasn't arrested.

The trial reopened after 10 minutes. I burst out again and shouted:

"You want to save your own dog skin but you'll never understand the price of a human life. You were and always will be a murderer."

The judge ordered me to leave and declared to the audience that my testimony was complete. When I went out, the prosecutor said to me:

"It's good that you agreed to be recorded. The tape keeps the intonation of your sincere outbursts and this will add to the arguments against him."

My host told me later that pupils from his school had attended the trial for both sessions, one time with him and the second time with the principal himself, Monk, who allowed all of them to skip school twice for two hours. He also told me that the two of them had performed public trials against Nazis in order to educate future citizens and to show them the depth of the crimes forced on their people by one psychopath. They invited me to come to a senior class and tell my story. And again, I simply told my story in simple words and they all cried and shed endless tears.

I knew the importance of sharing and spreading the lesson of those days to all humanity, and our mission is this: to remember, to remind and not to allow forgetting.

Editor's Footnote

1. One of the most prominent rabbis of Germany. Died in Mainz in 1221. (Public Domain: Louis Ginzberg (1901–1906). "Baruch ben Samuel". In Singer, Isidore; et al. (eds.). The Jewish Encyclopedia. New York: Funk & Wagnalls.)

[Page 160]

After the Underground

Y. Dvilianski

Translation by Meir Bulman

After WWII ended, the few Jews who stayed in Europe began departing from their dispersed locations with the purpose of reaching Eretz Israel. They encountered many difficulties: shuttered borders in Eastern Europe, gangs of robbers that still operated in those countries, and lack of organizational guidance for the refugees. Despite that, all means and all ways were justified in reaching the goal and overcoming obstacles. It overtook the war–remnants like an electric current. The idea of *Aliyah* overtook everyone. Rumors spread quickly that the time had indeed come and that there was an avenue by which to reach the destination where they, their children, and generations to come would not have to endure the perils of exile and the horrors of the holocaust they had endured.

Ironically, passage to the final and safe harbor was through Germany, the very same country from which the destructive toxins had been released and which had started the war. In West Germany, war–remnants gathered in camps for displaced persons from all over Eastern Europe: from the ghettos, the death camps, the labor camps, soldiers released from various militaries, partisans who took their liberation into their own hands, and Jews who had simply survived.

One day just before evening, a truck stopped on Ornenburg Street in Berlin, and out of it jumped two young men who had made their way to a house which served as a sleeping spot and halfway–house to the Shlekhtensa boarder camp in West Berlin. The next day they had a meeting with their wives, who had waited for them impatiently because such a trip entailed the risk of life, or life imprisonment in a best case scenario. They had a meeting no less exciting with the brigade man who operated in the aforementioned camp and prepared young folks and Jews for the future and its events, which would lead to the establishment of Israel. The brigade man was very dynamic and affable. We bonded with him at first sight and began thinking of two matters: organizing the youth and preparing them for *Aliyah*, and searching for and rescuing children and young folks who had remained deserted and orphaned in most Eastern–European countries so as to unite them, transfer them to Germany, and from there to Israel. Organizations dedicated to escape and *Aliyah* were on the ground guiding the process.

After some fact–finding it was decided to avoid dividing the youth, and to unite them under the banner of a unified pioneering banner. That is how *Nokham* came to be, an organization which included all youth groups, from *Agudat Israel* to *HaShomer HaTzair*. *Nokham* officials were sent from Berlin to the American–controlled parts of Germany where they placed youth on ranches as well as in child and youth camps which we established.

I had the good fortune to be among those who were active and cared for the youth brought from Romania, Hungary, and some from Poland. It is difficult to describe the conditions facing children in those countries at the time, and also what conditions they faced while being transferred to Germany. The children were afraid, insecure, suspicious, and lacked faith in humanity; they with disheveled in appearance, almost naked, and mentally unkempt. In a hotel in the German Alps, near Bad Reichenhall, one of the most beautiful spots in Germany, such a group of children was settled for care and preparation towards a new life.

At first, they had to be fed to satiation to extract from them the fear of hunger, and obtain their trust.

On the first festive night, the tables were set, the children sat by them, the dining hall large and pretty, and a nice filling meal is served, anticipating a signal to start eating. Suddenly, we look and see that all the food is gone, but did not see the children eating. It turns out that fear conditioned them to hoard food for a dark day, and indeed the food was found in the children's pockets. Explanations that they would be getting food the next day, and also in days to come, did not help. That evening the meal was hampered. Only after several days passed and our assurances were confirmed to them did we begin gaining their trust. After the food incident came the education as to hygiene and clothing habits, such as a having a clean bed with a white sheet. More than once we had to remove children form bed so that they would wash their hands and feet before bed. After they got accustomed to a normal social life which depended on keeping hygiene and order, we overcame the obstacles of physicality, and began their mental care. Groups were organized to teach the Hebrew language, some general knowledge of Israel, and national history, as well as some occupational instruction. Mental care for the children was among the most difficult, as most of them were from the town of Yas,[1] from the *Green Bridge*, a famous bridge known as an underworld, rife with trafficking, prostitution, and theft, which the children absorbed into their blood. They know that "the intent of man's heart is evil," etc. and must not be trusted. When we told them of Israel, of the abundance, of a place where everyone is Jewish, they did not want to believe it, they simply persisted in their defensiveness against any influence.

Preparations for the Hanukkah ball saved the day. For two months, they learned Hebrew songs and dances, and an indescribable enthusiasm overtook the children. With unusual interest, they began listening to our stories about the land and the people who inhabited it, and with even more enthusiasm they studied self-defense and fighting which the *Shurah* guide taught them.

Each evening, groups would venture out into the Alps and conduct preliminary training in fighting, field navigation, etc. We were all surprised by the change that took place in the children we cared for. They leaped from fear and insecurity to confidence, sticking to goals, and willingness for self-sacrifice. No obstacle or hesitation existed to them, and every task they were put to was completed with remarkable thoroughness.

It seems to me that the play they put on for Hanukkah under the guidance of instructor Litman was what transferred them to another world and instilled in them the confidence and the ambition to change their lives within the framework of changes occurring in the life of the nation.

On the day the UN agreed on the establishment of a state they erupted with cries of freedom, happiness and crying were entangled in an inseparable combination. They danced the *hora* accompanied by hysterical shrieking, kissing, and hugging. Their celebration and wild behavior continued all night until the morning; we knew then that all the efforts in caring for them had been worthwhile: the seed that was planted grew nicely. We the counselors, including emissaries from Israel, were also influenced and the children's happiness infected us too.

On one of those days while traveling by bus in Israel, M. Z. suddenly arose, a handsome young man wearing glasses, called me by my first name and offering me his seat. I did not recognize him at first, but then it became clear that he was one of the young men from that hotel in Germany. I heard a bit from him about the rest of the young folks that were with us in that German hotel. Some of the youngsters had fallen in the Kastel offensive, some had fought and fallen in the Old City of Jerusalem. Only a few remain alive and reside in various places in Israel.

Editor's Footnote

1. Believed to be Iasi in present day Romania.

[Page 163]

My Father is Summoning Me

Shlomo Aviel (Shmerkovitsh)

Translation by Emma Karabelnik

At night I see my father in my dreams
At the big table in *Beth Hamidrash* in my town
Across a large bookcase full with books
Sitting alone absorbed in a *Gemarah* page
By the dim light of a single candle
He is murmuring a sad melody, how awful
A melody of pain, of the injustice of the universe
And a tear on his cheek
Rolls down in silence and grief.

Quiet and depressed, I am all in a shiver
Terrified and shocked,
I am trying to look at him
To move and walk in his direction,
But somehow my feet can't move
But somehow they don't obey me,
Father! My father! My God!
Have mercy! It's me!
Why are you hiding your face from me?
Why are you turning your head to the wall?
But he didn't reply, he slipped away and was gone
Took his feet and went away.
Look he is quickening his pace
Jumping and hopping with surprising energy,

Between bushes and thorns, graves and gravestones
And at the cemetery near the grave
Are scattered wounded and dead
Burnt corpses in all directions,
And Yom Kippur candles are burning all around

Suddenly the corpses arouse like angels
Up in the sky, up high,
And fly, and fly, and fly...

*

Suddenly the picture changes:
I am again in the prayer house,
Reb Yudel, the *chazan* is covered with his *talith*
He is weeping in a high gentle sound
Spilling his heart to the Almighty
Asking and begging for mercy:
God Almighty! Whoever you forgive will be saved
Whoever you pity will be pardoned
Eyes are turned up to the sky
Hearts are pleading to you
God, have mercy on your people!
You are the savior in each generation!
And the whole crowd, covered in *talith*
Answers him in prayer and weeping,
Reb Yosef goes up to the stage with his *shofar*
Holding his *shofar* and *siddur*, begging, murmuring with sadness and grief:
"From the depths I am calling, Adonai, answer me, Adonai,"[1]
"You heard my voice, don't shut your ears."
And the sound of *shofar* bursts out
Tears up the sky, calls for mercy

Tekya, Truah, Shvarim,[2]

And a scream emerges from *Ezrat Nashim,*[3]

My mother Z"L[4] is also there

Sheds a tear over the *siddur*...
Suddenly there is no praying crowd
No chazzan and no prayer.

*

Across the large bookcase filled with books,
Near the big table in *Beth Hamidrash*
Jews study, argue and fight.

My father Reb Yosef against Chaim Fleig,[5]

None of them is ready to concede

They are discussing *Pirkei Avot*, arguing

My father joined in [*in Aramaic*: reference to a page of *Talmud*],[6]

His opponent [*in Hebrew*: reference to a page of *Talmud*],[7]

He doesn't agree, that's why they are arguing.

*

Jews finished their prayer
Folded their *talith* and *Tefilin* and left
And they were still arguing
Proving by examples and quotes
That they are right?
Only God can explain this dream.

*

My dream ends and I wake up.
This dream keeps coming back
Coming back again and again
And I know that my father sends me a sign and orders
To avenge him, not to rest
Until I build a gravestone, to my father, to fathers
And mothers of Voronova, to brothers and sisters.
May this gravestone be a substitute for revenge
Like a bundle of life, a bundle of souls.

Footnotes

1. Trans. Note: This is a verse from a biblical Psalm.

2. Trans. Note: These are the prayer words accompanying successive soundings of the *Shofar*.

3. Trans. Note: The womens' area of the synagogue

4. Ed. Note: Of blessed memory

5. Ed. Note: In the original text the surname is spelled: fey–lamed–yud–gimel

6. Ed. Note: The reference consists of three Aramaic words spelled: mem–alef–yud // dalet–kuf–alef–mem–resh–yud // resh–bet–nun–langer nun

7. Ed. Note: The reference consists of four Aramaic words spelled: mem–ayen–dalet–nun ayen–dalet–nun resh–bet het–yud–yud–mem

Our Town – Memoirs, Images, Short Stories

[Pages 169-172]

Voronova: A Town of Blue and White

Yekhezkel Poz-Puziriski

Translation by Meir Bulman

Today, in the Jewish State that stretches from Shlomo Bay to the Golan, the blue-and-white *Keren Kayemet* collection box has lost its initial meaning. Zionism, the central focus of which was fundraising to redeem the Holy land, also has lost the glow that illuminated the Jews during their exile in the towns of Poland and Lithuania. However, before WWI, things were different. Our town, Voronova, was relatively small and was home to 220 Jewish families of ultra-Orthodox Jewish culture, where Zionism was almost unneeded and unwanted. The Torah was the residents' nearly sole focus of study and nationalism. Teacher Miller's was the only house of study to teach Hebrew, and that too was without a defined goal. I was 16 at the time and cannot recall any Zionist organization in town, although there was already the Bund, and other leftist organizations.

I traveled to Russia during WWI. When I returned after the war's end in 1918, I sensed a change of atmosphere. The scent of Zionism began spreading through the air, and with it, hope. A longing for a Jewish life was evident, a life connected to the awakening Jewish world. We founded our first community committee, which I joined. There was a need and desire for a genuine Hebrew-Jewish school, which I had the honor of taking an active role in establishing. A general communal awakening began. Our school was not part of the *Tarbut* network, as the town rabbi, Rabbi Luski, objected to a non-religious school. Parents and the community council joined in their desire for a religious Hebrew school. Since by that time the Rabbi was a fully-fledged Zionist, the school was founded as compromise between Hebrew and Religion. At the same time, a drama club reconvened and I too took part in its activities. The club contributed much to the Jewish atmosphere and culture.

One day, a letter arrived from the regional office of *Keren Kayemet* in Vilna, addressed to Nekhemiah Shapira. Nekhemiah was one of the first Zionists in the town who had encouraged the town to establish local chapters of the Zionist Organization and *Keren Kayemet*. Nekhemiah invited a few people to his home including me. He told us about the letter and its content, and the mitzvah of founding a chapter. He told us an envoy from the Zionist Organization in Vilna would arrive in town. Our souls were ignited and we sensed that we were on the verge of joining the organized Zionist movement. Suddenly there was a purpose to our lives and a goal to achieve.

HaKhaluts - Zionist Youth

The envoy from Vilna was spoken about in every Jewish home. His arrival was anticipated like he was the messenger of *Geula*[1], and many preparations were made for his arrival. When he finally arrived I was proud to be among those who greeted him. In his first meeting with the organized committee, the representative spoke of Zionist activity and *Keren Kayemet's* goal to redeem the Holy Land to house on it those who would return to Zion to establish the Jewish state.

Such ideas took hold of us and filled our minds to capacity. We approached the holy mission enthusiastically. We set a high goal of putting a *Keren Kayemet* box in every Jewish home, which was accomplished. A committee for *KK* was established, including as its members Esther Olkenitski as secretary and Avraham Eliahu Dvilianski as treasurer. Meetings were held at Avraham Yitzach Poditvianski's home. Additional members included Yosef Shmerkovitsh who was an educated Zionist, Gottlieb Trotski, Yaakov Trotski, Shmuel Berkovski, and me.

A short time later the shipment of boxes arrived. Few days passed before a box was honorably displayed in every Jewish home in the town. There were many families who lacked the means to contribute and we did not approach them. However, when they became aware of their exclusion they were deeply offended and insisted they too receive a *KK* box, so they could, as they insisted, fulfill their national obligation of redeeming the Holy Land. Their request was happily granted. The town rabbi also insisted that a box be placed in his home. There was not a home in Voronova lacking a *KK* box. Members of the youth groups *HaHalutz HaMizrachi* and *HaHalutz General* emptied the boxes. We did not make do with collection boxes alone, and would also fundraise at every celebration and gathering. If there was a wedding in town, we arrived with our box, as we did for a *bris* or any other occasion like 15 *Shvat* and 20 *Tamuz*. We fulfilled the fundraising obligation even on *Erev Yom Kippur* by placing a *KK* collection plate in the synagogue. Even the drama club set aside a percentage of ticket sales to *KK*.

On 20 *Tamuz*, we would hold a ceremony in the synagogue commemorating Dr. Theodore Herzl. I recall that one year 20 *Tamuz* was on a Tuesday, the town's market day. Since on market day all town residents were busy, we prepared the synagogue for the celebration the day before. We placed Dr. Herzl's portrait on the eastern wall and decorated the synagogue. The next day, at the height of business, Treasurer A.E. Dvilianski and I were urgently called to the rabbi. *Nu*, when the rabbi calls, you go - even on market day. We approached the rabbi, wondering, and slightly angry. "The portrait," said the rabbi, "the portrait- and on top of that he's bare-headed. 'Thou shalt not make unto thee any graven image, or any likeness,' I ask that you remove the image from the synagogue wall." "Is this why his honor had bothered us on market day, our day of income?" we asked: "Rabbi, your honor, you prayed here yesterday afternoon and evening, and this morning, and said nothing, why now?" We concluded categorically, "We will not remove the portrait. We will not dishonor Dr. Herzl." We began deliberating and eventually reached a compromise. We promised to cover the portrait in thin, transparent, black cloth so Dr. Herzl could look at us during the gathering. We suspected the rabbi's demand was due to external pressure.

The town gained new character: Zionism was now at the center of communal activity. Slowly but surely Zionism allowed for a practical consideration of fulfilling the dreams and desires of so many generations: to emigrate to Eretz Israel, to build a home, and hold the land. At that time the youth movements were strong. Their central activity and goal were *aliyah*. Occasionally, one Jew, and then another, disappeared from the town's horizon and left to enrich the horizon of *Eretz Israel*.

Before I made *aliyah*, we received a letter from *KK* headquarters in Vilna with news that we had received a commendation for our devoted, productive activities. *KK* found that our town had raised more money *per capita* than the larger towns. Later, when I announced my decision to make *aliyah*, some attempted to dissuade me so that I could continue my activity for *KK*. To this day I am proud of the gold medal I received from *KK* headquarters in Warsaw. I feel that without that pure devotion my friends and I had towards the blue collection box, we would not have gotten so far. I am proud of my blue-and-white clad Voronova.

Grove of Voronova martyrs in the forest of martyrs
Pictured: Nekhama Shur-Shapira and Yehoshua Gol

Translator's Footnote

1. The beginning of the period of redemption promised in the Old Testament.

[Pages 173-176]

A Town with a Marketplace and Neighborhoods

Shimon Levine

Translation by Meir Bulman

Herem[1] on the Neighborhood

Our neighborhood stood at the bottom of the hill, on the road to the river and bridge. Though we realized it only after some time had passed, our neighborhood was quite picturesque, as it extended down the hill, dipping its feet in the river. The neighborhood was a part of Voronova the town, yet different.

The town was surrounded by woods and immersed in various evergreen flora. Straight ahead continued the Belrovski Forest grove, where we would walk at summer's end and harvest various berries. Separated between our neighborhood and the forests were large plots of land that surrounded it on all sides and gave it a pristine panoramic look of greenery. Those fields belonged to a Polish landowner, Count Shvanbakh. Voronova was built on those lands, including its homes and public buildings. For years the town residents paid the Count land royalties and rent, until one day it was decided to purchase the land: with assistance from the *Joint*[2] and ICA[3] those fields became their permanent property.

On some of that land a new neighborhood was established, dubbed "The New Plan", and the remainder of the purchased land served as grazing land for cattle. It should be remembered that every household in Voronova owned a cow.

The new neighborhood was not planned by an urban engineer, so the two house–rows were built far apart; in between them, in the Fall and Spring, large puddles formed, leading to endless mud and swamps.

The residents of the new neighborhood wanted to transfer the marketplace to their area so it would contribute to its growth and success. On that matter, their activists showed much initiative in dealing with the authorities, and their efforts reached the district and region officials in Lida and Navaradok. However, the [Jewish] town institutions rigidly opposed that plan, and when methods of persistent dissuasion did not pan out, the community and the rabbi decided to enact a boycott, so that they would be dissuaded from further activism on the matter and not cause the authorities to transfer the marketplace.

On an evening just before Passover the town erupted. Arguments and shouting matches intensified with each passing moment. Occasionally a fight broke out accompanied by insults and cursing. Once the boycott verdict arrived, all neighborhood residents joined together and marched to attempt and put a stop to it. They started a shouting choir, made noise, pretended to fight amongst themselves, all to disrupt the initiators of the boycott. But their efforts were futile, the boycott would take place. But when the rabbi began announcing the actual verdict they began yelling, "Fire! The town is on fire, everything is in flames!" The rabbi had to pause. The offensive boycotters were close to despair and the boycott was near to being called off. But when the crowd wanted to disperse, the rabbi took advantage of the situation, and when they exhausted themselves and the shouting stopped, he read the ceremonial text and the censure became a reality.

In fact, the marketplace was transferred anyway, but not to the neighborhood and not all of it, meaning only the horse marketplace.

The plot that was designated to become the marketplace in the new neighborhood later became a mass-grave for both the boycotters and the boycotted.

The Marketplace

It spanned across the town center and was the source of income for many residents. We children did not like it. On market days, the church at its center was crowded with prayer attendees, and its bells struck fear in our hearts. They reminded us of the pogroms and the [Spanish] Inquisition. They tolled three times on market day; their notes seemed to us like a call for blood and murder. On market days, hatred of Jews rose up through the air. It originated at that house of impurity, its sole purpose being to remind the Gentiles of their God's murder, and point a finger at the murderers, supposedly the Jews.

The farmers in the area were in fact not the worst of the lot, because they too hated the government. They got close to the Jews regarding strategy. We still feared every gathering of Gentiles, and detested that area on market days. By contrast, our parents awaited that day like the day of salvation and income, from which they sustained themselves for half a week or longer. This pattern continued for generations.

The peasants would gather and come here twice a week, bring their products, and sell them to various Jews, especially to the Vilne travelers – the commissary merchants. It functioned as a middle ground in transferring village products to the Vilne metropolitan area. There were some Jews who owed that marketplace their position, respect, and wealth. It was the root of their existence and the source of their pride, week after week, month after month. But it reminded us children of Torquemada; it seemed like at any moment we would see a murder procession decked with colorful statuettes, walking delicately from the house of impurity to a large arena, as dust would rise along with cries of agony, and as dirt would mix with red Jewish blood.

On the other weekdays we were attracted to the marketplace, where we would play soccer and other games. The large field compensated us for the perils of our childhoods with its spaciousness and light, childhoods of *Cheder* in cramped rooms during dark daytime hours.

We would be especially entertained in the marketplace when firefighters would train there. That happened with regular frequency; with each fire that flamed in town, the firemen felt they were lacking training, and would go and supplement their "education". The entire town was in the state of glee that accompanies such pronounced masculinity. It was a day devoted to the body, contrasting the qualities of mind, faith, Judaism, and body-torment that usually pervaded in the Jewish community. Everyone had a personal reason to be proud of someone out there on the field, to enjoy the beauty of speed and physical talents, but we children and youths were the most engaged. We enjoyed that the adults too were playing and expressing lightheartedness and absentmindedness, as we always did. Childhood ruled that day and, concurrently, victory belonged to us. We would release and go wild around the trainees, a short distance from them. An undeclared holiday took place and the pleasure was ours.

Market day in town

When market day returned the curtain came down once more, and heavyheartedness overtook the children.

The Dangerous Neighborhood

Our town was free of Gentiles and not one resided on their streets. It knew of Gentiles only from afar, from the surrounding villages which functioned as the home front. Those peasants were agreeable and kind in their dealings with Jews. It is difficult to define these farmers' nationality. They themselves could not answer that question when asked, and would reply, "We are *Ktulim Vadi*," which was a sort of underground of White Russians and Lithuanians who loathed the Poles with a passion, and that is what brought them closer to the Jews. Farmers would joke around with their Jewish friends, call them antichrist, God killer, etc. but that was done in good spirit and always jokingly. The bond between the area Jews and their lands, as cattle milk farmers and from working gardens near their homes, also created a sort of understanding bridge between the two populations.

And so it seemed that "it would not happen to us, our Gentiles [are better], etc." And so what they later did to us and their murderous collaborations with the Germans came as a surprise.

There was only one neighborhood where ten or so Gentile families lived among the Jews. We called that neighborhood *Das Khasirishe Gessel*, Swine Street.[4] Among those Gentiles were those who depended on the Jews and ate from their bread, but with every misfortune that took place in Voronova when regimes and governments were changed, they were the first to volunteer and participate in inflicting harm and to grease the wheels of the machinations.

That was the case in 1919 when the Poles arrived as the new masters and violence was unleashed, shedding Jewish blood was permissible as became the case during the Holocaust. Evil acts directed at Voronovan Jews originated in that mixed neighborhood and its crimes expanded to the rest of the town.

The homes of the Novokovski brothers were at the root of incitement. The doctrinal, burning hatred towards Jews came from them. Ranked after them in malice and lust for murder and looting was the Orshulka family. They would eat of their Jewish neighbors' bread and grind their teeth while doing so. When the Holocaust arrived they fulfilled their wishes by collaborating with the Russians in pointing out "typical anti-revolutionary" Jews. They also collaborated with the Germans closely and diligently, at first pointing towards "Communist revolutionaries" and then assisting them in murdering, torturing, looting and destroying. Like them were Yashka Vashavitz the priest's butler, and

Yan Borisha the cobbler and his wicked wife Helenka. Yan, Helenka, and their sons volunteered with the German police to maximize the murder of Jews on behalf of the regime.

The Jews were never comfortable with that minority of Gentiles. We had this feeling that no good would come of them, but the dimensions of the horror far exceeded what we felt.

May they be damned for eternity.

Editor's Footnotes

1. Exclusion of a person, or persons, from the community. In this case the term means 'boycott'.

2. 'Joint' (aka JDC) refers to The Joint Distribution Committee of the American Funds for Jewish War Sufferers, founded in 1914.

3. The ICA (aka JCA) was founded in 1891 by Maurice de Hirsch to assist Jews facing depressed economic circumstances and/or persecution. (https://www.jewishvirtuallibrary.org/jewish-colonization-association-ica)

4. The street's name is due to the fact that pork might be consumed there by the Gentiles.

[Pages 177-178]

A Town of Unsettled Youth

Aharon Konikhovski (Krani)

Translation by Meir Bulman

Voronova was very small, yet filled with uncertainty, problems, path-searching, and solutions more than any other comparable town.

Due to its proximity, Voronova benefited from the treasures of Vilna, where Voronovan broadened their horizons, touched the sky, but then returned, clipped of their wings, to the reality of troubles and limitations.

Voronova was alert, responsive, and full of traditional values and progressive culture. Voronova was in the throes of redemption along with preservation of what once was: traditions inherited from forefathers intersected with the paving of a new path towards national freedom and the redemption represented by Israel. All this caused an inner turmoil in the generation before the Holocaust.

Voronova was also a backwards town without sources of income nor opportunities for expansion. Most Voronova residents worked as craftspeople. Almost everyone groaned in the discouraging battle for existence. The youth were raised in an atmosphere of desperation, forced to see that same situation becoming its own. The troubles of their beloved ancestors were also their troubles; their youthful souls were rooted in the local past.

Spiritual and social matters were addressed at the synagogue, but only in reaction to external facts. The synagogue's answers did not replace [external facts] or continue [an alternative way of life], but merely provided a consolation for aching hearts as a remedy for helplessness.

The youth remained in an empty space, uprooted from the source of their upbringing, and detached from horizons of development. No spark of hope could be seen in the town and its reality. The love of parents and the familial environment burdened the youth who were caught between the weakness of family sentiments and their preparations for personal heroism. The youth were called to action on the barricades of struggle in a newly formed world. The youth were attracted to *Aliyah*. The center of the youth's interests were concentrated now at the movement clubhouses, where one suppressed personal uncertainties, was consoled by the collective struggle, and quieted his cries for redemption with *hora* dancing and songs of Israel.

Together we began to reorient in the dark. We searched for the 'something' in the 'nothing' of our surroundings. We searched for release, a way to exit to a wider space.

The first two who made Aliyah:
Shabtai Grodzenchik–Goren and Shlomo Aviel

When the envoy came from Vilne and organized *HaShomer HaTsair* we did not examine the values, outlook, or solutions offered within that movement. We entered as if entering a youth temple to sanctify our sacrifices. There we found a continuation of the striving awakened in our childhood. "*Tehezakna*," "*Hatikva*,"[1] gatherings, conferences, sailing, and summer colonies opened our heavy young hearts and showed us the general exit to the open space. There we learned to turn general hardship into a crane with an immense power–lift, able to break down fences and build safety walls. Romanticism, dreams, the waking nightmares, all became desired assets. Here, in this youthful company, weaknesses were mended into affirmations which created paths towards the redemption of the individual and the masses.

Everything combined into a single stream towards Eretz Israel. *Hakhshara*[2] and *Aliyah* changed values and renewed life patterns.

Later, other youth movements were formed in the town. There were splits and debates about trivial issues, but we were all unified in our desire for *Aliyah*. We all knocked on Zion's locked gates, and together we encouraged soldiers to stand guard, faithful of our rightful path. All the youth were happy when the first two pioneers departed Voronova for Eretz Israel, and it was then made clear we had found a pathway shared by both parents and offspring and the various factions of the younger generation.

As we look back we see our town Voronova as joining in the creation of a national solution which the youth reached by its own right and liveliness. The heart aches when we remember the Voronova which is no longer and the youth who were cut down whilst forming their dream of leaving Voronova forever. They were unfortunate to not leave Voronova and their desires are buried in mass–graves with the skeletons of their young bodies. We will never forget and will forever mourn the youth severed in their prime.

Editor's Footnotes

1. These are the names of popular Zionist songs from the period. Hatikva eventually became the national anthem of the State of Israel.

2. Hebrew word meaning 'preparation'. Applies here to describe the training programs for migration to Israel.

[Page 179]

"Chayei Adam" Society and "Mishniyot" Society

S. Levine

Translation by Emma Karabelnik

There were no religious institutions in Voronova during all the years of its existence as a respectful community seeking light and Judaism. It was blessed with many Rabbis and a vibrant community, but not one of its members thought to build a yeshiva or a religious school, though there was a great thirst for knowledge which was felt in all socio-economical groups.

So what did Jews do? They established their own Torah study groups, if not to expand and glorify the Torah, at least to not let it be forgotten.

The first such society was "Mishniyot". Its members were Jews who thought themselves scholars and Torah experts, and conducted themselves with great self-importance. Each night between *minha* and *maariv*, and also on Sabbath and holidays, they used to gather in the synagogue, to the right of the entrance, sit around a long table, and listen to Torah by Reb Shlomo Goldberg, bible teacher in the Tarbut, Torah, and Knowledge school.

The second society was "Chevrat Chayei Adam" – who used to sit to the left of the entrance, behind the stage, opposite from the "Mishniyot" society. They were also seated around a long table, at the head of which a *maggid*[1] taught lessons from Torah. Those were simple folk, "amcha,"[2] looking for something beyond there apprehension, knowing that something beyond did exist but not quite comprehending it.

These simple people, strong in their belief and strong in their action, were also strong in their hearts. They knew the limitations of their knowledge and of their poor understanding of Torah, so they were ready to become pupils of someone more knowledgeable; the first group considered themselves scholars, commensurate with their social status. They'd have been better off putting their status aside and opening their minds to absorb some knowledge.

Actually, all were graduates of the same schools in town as were their friends across the stage, but the privileged ones couldn't exist without the Torah crown, as if something troubled their souls. And how can you gain a crown if not by crowning yourself, so they announced themselves scholars. For example, an interesting explanation by a grumpy Jew about himself to himself:

"My father, of blessed memory, was a scholar, and I, may I live a long and good life,[3] I am also a scholar and a *talmid chokhem*. I don't have proof of my being a scholar, but I do have proof about my predecessor, and I am his follower."

Among them was Reuven the *Mohel*. For 50 years there wasn't one person in town who was circumcised without Reuben's *mila*.[4] There was also Itze Shelovski, Feyvl Pupko and other rich[5] Jews. The whole lesson was taught in a dry, precise manner. The topics chosen were important for a Jew to know, but didn't touch the heart. It is a fact that many Rabbis, Shohets and other religious worshippers make an effort to live their lives strictly, according to duty and mitzvah.

It was different in "Chayei Adam", where the lesson was taught by Reb Avraml the tinsmith, an honest and naïve Jew, a religious believer who followed his fate day and night, when he went to sleep and when he woke up. His friends and co–scholars were all men of labor, craftsmen, shoemakers, tailors, carpenters and tinsmiths. They crossed their tired, calloused hands on the table, and listened attentively to his every word. Reb Avraml read from the book, emphasized every word, and commented according to his grasp. For the sake of variety he read from the book "*Menorat haMaor*"[6], accompanied by examples and short stories, and this was Torah *Shebealpeh*[7] in its greatness. As soon as he came to a segment not written in the book – then he rose to the level of a talented story teller who fascinated his audience. He always found an allegory or legend to make his argument spicier. Usually he did so when coming upon an "obstacle" in the book, something beyond his knowledge. Oh, then he used to take his audience to other worlds and ascended together with them to the highest levels of beauty and fantasy, to the deeds and the wisdom of the sages, to heaven and hell, he exposed them to the dilemma of reward and punishment,[8] and shared with them all his thoughts that went "beyond his comprehension". In his stories he spoke so vividly about The End of The Days[9] and the arrival of the Savior that his audience could hear the bells of the Messiah. When he described the torments awaiting the evil ones in Hell, these good Jews were terrified and decided for the thousandth time that it would not be wise to challenge the Almighty and risk ending up in the horrors of Hell. On the contrary, in Heaven a person is happy, after long life of labor, to study Torah day and night, to enrich one's soul with tales of the wild bull and the whale, and for desert the Persimmon River.

Reb Avraml was a very religious man and didn't want any of his friends to fail in their good measures and thus lose their way to Heaven. There were some who challenged him with difficult questions and doubts about the laws, or about "honesty" and loyalty, and about their reward, and other contradictions for which they requested explanations. In these cases, Avraml listened to their doubts and questions, and replied in his classic manner:

"*Nu*, you doubt Him, the Almighty? With him everything is possible and everything can happen, you can't doubt him."

There were huge social differences between those two groups. The "Mishniyot" crowd was united during the lesson and dispersed outside. Their connection in Synagogue was like a love that depends on something else, and when this something ended, in this particular case it was the lesson, the love and friendship also ended. For those in the "Chayei Adam" society, the meeting around the table was only an alibi, the real reason was their interest in people and people's lives. They were united in love, comradeship and mutual support, both during the lesson and after. If somebody missed a lesson, immediately everybody wanted to know the reason, they went to his home to find out the reason and to assist him if he needed any help. They operated as a support group in sorrow and in joy, in suffering and in pleasure. If somebody got sick, the whole group came to visit, sat with him for long hours to diminish his pain and study at his bedside to ensure health to the body and soul.

Such were our parents and our ancestors and such was their spiritual activity.

Footnotes

1. Trans. Note: Teacher

2. Ed. Note: 'Everyday' people

3. Trans. Note: A traditional Jewish expression said when mentioning a living person directly after mentioning a person who has died

4. Trans. Note: Prayer, blessing

5. Trans. Note: The phrase used means, literally: house owners

6. Ed. Note: The Menorah of Light by Isaac Aboab, a book from circa 1300CE, which according to the Jewish Encyclopedia "...has contributed probably more than any other medieval book to the popularization of rabbinical lore and to the religious edification and elevation of the masses." Originally written for the Sephardic, Arabic speaking community, the book was translated into Yiddish in Vilna in 1880. (*Aboab*, Jewish Encyclopedia, http://www.jewishencyclopedia.com/articles/344–aboab)

7. Trans. Note: Oral law

8. Trans. Note: This phrase is written in the original text as "tzadik vera lo"

9. Trans. Note: This phrase is written in the original text as "aharit hayamim"

[Page 182]

The Boulevards of Voronova

Shlomo Aviel-Shmerkovitsh

Translation by Emma Karabelnik

Ancient trees with wide strong branches
Stand in a long boulevard.
Under each tree a naked rock
Lonely, bleeding, and sad.

These trees live for generations,
Whisper and tell the chain of legends,
Tell stories and secrets
In their language – the language of trees.

The rocks are sad,
They never knew life.
They are lonely and silent
But they keep deep secrets.

I have good memories of you, boulevard,
From my young years, the nights
I found shelter in the shade of the trees and the rocks
While dreaming dreams of a youth.

Days and nights of grief and joy,
Gaiety, happiness and heavy breath,
Disappointment and pain, moments of forgiveness
And that girl in the light of the moon.

That girl, most beautiful of all,
With her black penetrating eyes,
Sometimes sad or tired,
But usually happy and laughing.

Her braids fall on her shoulders
And her body smells like fruit,
Her pulse sounds like a calling,
And she is all so sweet and precious.

We sit together hugging,
Above us the moon with shining stars.
The trees are asleep, the rocks are silent
Only she and I are awake and in love.

The night was covered with silence,
We were both quiet, not to disturb it,
Silent and quiet in the shade,
Not to desecrate the purity of youth.

The trees and boulevards kept the secret
And never told anyone.
They live and feel
The loving friendly hearts.

Year 40, days of war,
The sword kills outside, terror at home.
Polish legions retreat on the roads
Jewish children hungry at homes.

The granaries are empty, the shops burglarized
No comers or goers, no visitors.
The travelers look for alternative paths.
All the roads are deadly dangerous.

A Jew wakes up early
To visit his friend Ivan in the village.
To obtain some grain for his home.
He leaves alone.

He sneaks between trees and bushes.
Got up early, came to the village,
Quickly entered the farmer's house,

But the host hastily said:

Quick! Come Yosel! Be quick!
I'll take you to the granary, hide there.
Look, from afar, on the horizon
Two armed horsemen are approaching.

Yosel declined and didn't hide.
The goy was begging, crying.
Meanwhile the two came to the yard
Tied their horses to the well.

Jew! Zhid! Here is a traitor!
Jewish blood flows in your veins.
Quickly! Pray! If you have a God!
To the forest! Quickly, to shoot him.

They also ordered the farmer:
Quickly prepare a meal.
Fry eggs and meat in butter
And oat for the horses in stable.

The two eat and drink till they get drunk.
Reb Yosel came up with a thought.
He sneaked and jumped into the bushes,
And from there crawled towards the boulevard.

The trees and boulevards kept the secret
And never told anyone.
They live and feel
The hearts of the miserable

Excuse me my motherland,
Please don't be jealous of my song.
There were trees and rocks in my town
Their loyalty is still in my memory.

Now we are back here, motherland,
We found you empty and dry.

For long time, a plow didn't cut your earth
And the spirit deserted your highlands.

We returned to you to save you from your disgrace,
Disgrace of emptiness in your lands.
Look around and see,
Begin dancing and drumming.

Felds and vineyards are growing.
Combines and tractors working joyfully in the fields,
Hundreds of settlements in the desert.
Yesterday almost gone, revived today.

Between the rocks, in the mountains,
The number of trees is growing, new seedlings are planted.
In the dry fields a plow is stuck,
A new railway is paved between roads and fields.

Forgive me my motherland,
Don't be jealous of my song.
There were trees and rocks in my town
And their memory is still with me.

My father and mother stayed behind in *Galuth*,[1]
My brother, relatives, and family members.
This song is devoted only to them.
Their memory will always stay with me.

Editor's Footnote

1. exile

[Pages 186-187]

The Rabbis and The Rabbinical Dispute

S. Levine

Translation by Meir Bulman

For many years Voronova knew rabbis of greater stature than the town's size and the number of its Torah scholars would justify. Things began with a single rabbi, each one serving in successive periods, and then, later, two became necessary. The two rabbis came due to a dispute in our town, a dispute which further intensified because of the differences and scholarly disagreements between the two rabbis.

The grandeur of our rabbis was very pronounced. They were men who were satisfied with very little and avoided luxury. Whatever the community designated for them as a living ration was enough for them, and their sole interests were Torah and the guidance of the community in the Torah's ways and commands.

I heard many tales about our rabbis from aged men, but I will tell only of those I knew. At the end of the first war Rabbi Nafatali David sat on the rabbinate throne. He was a man of great manners, a devoted scholar, sharp and knowledgeable, a scholar by merit, and an excellent conveyor of his knowledge to the residents of his city.

After him, Rabbi Zalman Sorotzkin filled the position. A wise scholar, a clear public personality, and a great lecturer, Rabbi Zalman was well loved by the community, as he was a peace–maker, a lover of peace, and devoted to it in every situation.

The Jews of Voronova felt that he was too great for their town, especially as his reputation spread far and wide, and large communities laid eyes him.

Eventually the Lutsk community, which followed him for many years, was fortunate to receive him. He was greeted there like royalty, and quickly gained the admiration of many in Lutsk and its surrounding area. In a relatively short time, Rabbi Sorotzkin became famous throughout Poland, and was appointed chairman of the national *Agudath Israel*.[1] He later made Aliyah as a representative of *Agudath Israel*, after representing it at gatherings and conventions. Eventually he was appointed chairman of *Moetzes Gedolei HaTorah*[2] in Jerusalem, a position he kept until old age.

After that, our town greeted Rabbi Mishkuvski, a Jerusalem native, descendent of an extensive rabbinical dynasty. He too was a respectable Agudath man, a public activist with an appearance that was quite impressive. His family acclimated well to the town, each with his own age group. His sons Chaim–Leyb, and Avraham, currently rabbis in Israel, were members of the Zionist youth groups as were his daughters. They returned to their home country near the eruption the Holocaust. When he left Voronova, a large town accepted him, where he served honorably until he returned to Israel.

Following this, our town greeted Rabbi Moshe Aharon Luski. He was a young man when he arrived in our town, having recently completed his studies at the Volozhin Yeshiva. He was sharp and well–versed, witty in his speeches, and an innovative lecturer. His rabbinic role was different form that of his predecessors. He was more involved in community matters and representation, serving also as a respected and top leader of the community. His activism brought him to the district and regional capitols, to lobby for the residents of his town with various ministers and officials. It was said about him that at times he prayed without a *minyan*[3] due to the abundance of public troubles and matters. His three brothers were seminary graduates and certified teachers. They befriended the youth of Voronova and were similar to them in every aspect. The family troubles that befell him broke the spirits of the energetic Rabbi Luski; he was sadden by the death at a young age of his two sons, Pinya'li and Yosef. He was taken to serve as a rabbi in Zhtel, but his light had dimmed, and he decayed there until he died, depressed after many trials and tribulations. The town remembered his fiery speeches many years after he left us.

*

With Rabbi Luski's departure from Voronova, the golden age of the Voronova rabbinate concluded. After him, the community became divided beyond unification, and each sect brought its own rabbi. Thus the grand town of Voronova perished, divided into factions, and its two rabbis sank to the depths along with it.

That development was rooted in the various pretensions that overtook the community leaders, who saw themselves as experts in examining the extent of scholarly capabilities possessed by the many rabbinical candidates that blessed our town. Our activists were willing to concede many things, but they did not have the strength to remove their scholar hats. There was no other option: the town received two rabbis.

The first was Rabbi Yakov Tsipkovitsh, son in law of the Kletzk Rabbi, thus nicknamed "The Kletzker". The second was Rabbi Tsiplovitsh who came to us from Myadl and was nicknamed "the Myadler."

Rabbi Tsipkovitsh was a scholar and a man of deeply original thoughts, while Rabbi Tsiplovitsh was a majestic figure with a talent for public-speaking who knew how to attract the attention of his listeners.

Both rabbis were respectable, but the 10 years in which they served turned out to be a decade of mutual insults and conflicts in speeches, with every Sabbath destined to affronts and arguments unrelated to the Torah or its *mitzvot*.[4]

It is distressing that this scholarly dispute did not elevate the level of the community and did not increase yeshivot and the study of Torah.[5]

And so when Voronova sank to the depths of hell, it was a community regretful of the years that had passed without a search for common ground and a resolution. At that time all public attention was then drawn to a matter which rouses instincts and numbs the mind: on the edge of the mass grave, it was told, the two rabbis united as brothers— but that was too late.

Editor's Footnotes

1. Literally, the Israelite Union, the *Agudath* was established in the early 20th Century as the political wing of traditional Orthodoxy, being largely religiously oriented and hostile to Zionism as a movement. ("The *'Aguddat Israel'* Movement", http://people.ucalgary.ca/~elsegal/363_Transp/Orthodoxy/Aguddah.html, last accessed 10 October 2017)

2. Council of Torah Sages

3. The required minimum prayer quorum of ten men

4. Religious commandments

5. While other communities in our area flourished and established Torah institutions, Voronova was a community that abandoned the advancement of Torah, and no yeshiva or other study structures were established.

[Pages 188-189]

Yakov "Yankel" Kaminetski

M.S.V.

Translation by Meir Bulman

Yankel was a from a long lineage of Voronova residents. He was tied to this community, even if he made his living elsewhere.

He began by selling pharmaceuticals, but when that was outlawed for those who were unlicensed, Yankel returned to his old trade: he worked as a forestry and tree consultant.

He spent most of his days wandering outside of his home town, but he still maintained a family bond in his own unique manner.

Yankel was notable for three traits: (a) his belief in general education and culture necessary for the Jewish people to go out to the political and social arena, (b) his love for Zion, and (3) the wonderful sense of humor he was blessed with.

Yankel (Yakov) Kaminetski[1]

As a product of those three traits, another trait emerged in his personality: the love for youth— as the subjects of education, Zionist groups, and fearless levity.

His Zionism was rooted both in instinct and logic. He was one of the first Zionists in town. He read *HaTzfira*[2], and did not let go of *Haynt*[3] and *Der Moment*[4], whose content was to his liking and discussed mostly Zionism in their pages. He especially liked Itsheleh – Yaushzon[5] – Yustman, who wrote essays on deep and serious topics in an easy to digest form that did not sadden the reader. As the Zionist movement splintered, he [Yankel] became an admirer of Jabotinsky, who he saw as the fruition of practical Zionism, and whose approach to Zionism was adjusted into a rational and practical form. When the riots against Jewish students in Polish universities began, he told his son, who studied in Vilne, to part with his Polish school and make *Aliyah*.

He wanted to support that expense, despite his financial limitations. His whole life he dreamed of returning to Zion but was not fortunate enough, so his son's *Aliyah* served as a consolation and a symbol of hope. When he was dying in the Holocaust, so they say, he did not cease speaking of Zion and his son who was already there.

He allowed his sons to study in Vilne from a young age, to extract them from the *Cheder* atmosphere and the "cultural mold" which he so feared. When Yankel's wife proposed to relocate to Vilne and build a home so the children could study, he agreed fully.

He loved his work and worked often for many reasons. One of them was his love of the forest. The main motivator was the fulfillment of his dream of educating his children in his spirit. Yankel did not force–feed Zionism to his children, because he thought his children would reach similar conclusions as proud, professionally trained individuals, capable of independent thought, and who would reach their potential only in a country of their own. Thus, his sons were not Zionists, but when he commanded one son to travel to study in Jerusalem, his son did not object. The son made *Aliyah*, and at least one of Yankel's Zionist wishes was fulfilled.

His letters to his son are a continuous stream of fatherly love and Zionism. In those letters, he reached a degree of passionate expression that revealed the man and his Zionist passion.

He spoke often at Zionist gatherings. When he spoke, he was always very excited, bordering on shedding tears. Memorable was his outburst in 1936, when news of the riots in Israel arrived and his son was already there. Yankel wanted to express his happiness that his son was among those defending the security of Eretz Israel. In the middle of his words, he stopped speaking as he choked back tears.

Yankel was a symbol of witty humor. His jokes were famous in Voronova. The youth adhered to Yankel and admired him, preserving the respect of old age. Despite the age differences, the youth saw him as one of their own, yet recognized his greater experience, personal trials, and his manners which encouraged respect.

Yankel loved reading serious books and took an interest in everything that happened around him. Because he was more knowledgeable than others on world events, he was always surrounded by people who listened carefully to his opinions and varied knowledge.

The looming Holocaust and the sadness of the Zionist leadership harmed his health. The Russian occupation, which seemed to him would last long, extinguished any hope of fulfilling his Zionist dream. As the Germans arrived, he was afflicted by an illness from which he never recovered. The cantor of the town of Konopki, who was fortunate to make *Aliyah* in old age, told that Kaminetski died still speaking of the homeland.

He was 64 when he died.

Yankel spent most of his time outside of Voronova, but he drew from it all his doubts, dreams, and hopes, and so his name will be commemorated in the last ledger of our town.

Editorial Footnotes

1. Inferred to be photo of subject of article

2. The first Hebrew–language newspaper in Poland.

3. A Yiddish–language daily newspaper published in Warsaw.

4. A Yiddish–language daily newspaper published in Warsaw.

5. The name 'Yaushzon' is spelled yud–aleph–vov–shin–zayen–vov–langer nun in the original text.

[Pages 190-193]

Illustrative Curiosities

Khaye Levine (Rothbart)

Translation by Meir Bulman

Friendly Strumille

Father owned a department store for food, beverages and agriculture. He much loved agriculture and was quite knowledgeable in that field, so may Gentiles would come to him and buy their materials, consult him, and listen to his advice.

Shombakh the castle owner was also in correspondence with us, and his farm custodian was a customer. The friendship between him and father flourished: we gained a close friend of the family.

Once, father came to him to compare transactions, which Strumille viewed as an honor and went out of his way to entertain him. Among other things, he gave father a slice of meat, summoned his large dog, and told father, "try and give him the meat." Father tried. The dog approached, and when he was about to take the meat in his mouth, Strumille said, "to od Żyda (that's from the Jew)." The dog folded its tail and turned away. He then told the dog, "od Poliaka." The dog ate. Father got up, slammed the door, and walked away.

When he returned home he was pale and agitated. We could not calm him, nor would he tell us what had happened,

Then Strumille himself arrived and began begging father for forgiveness, asking him to understand that he did not mean it as an insult. With my own eyes I witnessed his degradation, how he kneeled and kissed father's boots, but father was not willing to forgive. We persuaded him and only then did he accept the apology.

But he did not forgive him until Strumille swore that his intention was not to mock Jews, but simply that the Jews who visited his property were afraid of the dog and he was told that they were planning to poison him— so he had trained the dog to not accept any food without his permission.

Since that incident he regarded father with great respect and said, "I respect you because you are not a 'Moshk'e'[1] who allows himself to be humiliated."

My takeaway from this was: "If this is Polish friendship, it must be avoided, and if the respect for Jews is determined by the trials they must pass, then what point is there to stay in their country?"

Antushke our Housemaid

Antushke served with us for ten years, understood Yiddish like one of us and was bound to our customs, loved her employers, and enjoyed full freedom in her work.

Antushke was pleasant to us all year, except for Easter, when she would travel to Vilne, to their *Kalwaria.* That spot in Vilne was very famous. It was a site with rows of sanctified statues, spanning dozens of meters, and the Gentiles would pass through while crawling on their knees, and the priests would sprinkle holy water on them, reminding them of the evil the Jews committed by crucifying the Savior.

After a visit like that, the maid would return to us with distorted senses, and for two days one could not return her to her former life and work routine, after which she would sober up and return to normal and relax, and once more she would do her work in silence, with devotion and homeliness.

After one such visit, during the days leading up to our Passover, she returned immersed in delusions, and at night while sleeping she began yelling, "Help!"

When we asked what had happened to her, she said that my brother Arke approached her with a plucking knife and wanted to slaughter her to use her blood for baking matzah. Father immediately ran to the police inspector, a Gentile who lived on our vodka and father's bribes. He came and slapped her a few times, freed her from her hysteria, and thus we were saved from a pogrom and the blood libel.

We fired her the next day, but I decided that even those eating from our bread are thirsty for our blood, and that even ten years of mutual trust would not help with the way the Gentiles regarded us.

Murder of the Small Gardner

We used to distill liquor in secret and sell it as an extras source of income. Gentiles would come to drink and keep quiet. The police too came and kept quiet.

Once, the small gardener came, drank his fix, and then wanted more. I kicked him out, as I did not want him to leave drunk and endanger us. He went to Pokribke and continued drinking there. Once he was intoxicated, he quarreled with his two drinking companions and he had to escape them. They chased him and he ran towards our house. They caught up near our door. My brother, who had heard him screaming, went out with a flashlight to see what had happened, and the two threatened him, "Arke go back inside, otherwise we will murder you too."

And they indeed murdered the gardener.

The two of them, along with Pokribke, ran off immediately and claimed that the gardener had gotten drunk at our place. Father once more arranged the matter with the inspector. Once more we were saved from the murder–libel, or the accusation of having caused a murder. I knew that was how it was: the Gentiles would murder each other in a friendly brawl and we would be blamed because of their friendship with the murder victim. Truth is that I also grew tired of that underground income.

Are You Getting Off?

On Passover Seder nights, Father would praise the land of Israel and tell of the love of the Jewish people towards it. Once he told of a lessee (I forgot his name), who sat at Passover with his wife, recited the *Hagadah*, stuffed himself with *knaidels*, very much enjoying Judaism. He lived among the Gentiles, but his heart was elsewhere, and when it was towards the end and had reached the part where one prays for "the next year in Jerusalem," he said to his wife, "Shprintze my love, every Jew must see Jerusalem. Next year, God willing, we will harness the wagon and travel to see it."

Shprintze was excited by the idea, but he warned her that, "it is no game, because the road to Jerusalem is long and full of troubles, and when we reach it is also difficult, because Jerusalem is surrounded by mountains, and one of us must get off the wagon and let the horse rest. And so," he concluded, "you, Shprintze, will have to get off the wagon and let the horse rest."

That upset her. "Why me? You get off! How could I schlep near the wagon after such a long and exhausting road? Is it for me to jump and hop off wagons?"

An argument erupted, and the lessee lifted the table, and over the voice of cracking porcelain he shouted, "Shprintze, are you getting off the wagon or not?"

Master of the Universe, how big was the love of ordinary Jews to this foreign mountainous, hilly land!

I too was attached to that love and stuck to it. I loved the land of my mysteries so much that in my dreams I saw it and its non–sloped roofs. When I arrived in Israel I saw that my dreams were accurate and did not know how.

Translator's Footnote

1. This is a generic name that is used in many Jewish folktales about Jews dealing with Polish noblemen; the 'Moshke' is often depicted as an exploited victim.

[Page 194]

Women of Our Town

Aharon Karni (Konikhovski)

Translation by Emma Karabelnik

Reyzl – Ida-Yakhe's was a happy mother sending her daughter Yocheved as a harbinger to *Erets Israel*. She walked around proudly holding letters from the Palestine Government, and told stories of miracles and wonders in the Dream Land.

Soon after, the second in line, Avraham, made *aliyah* to *Erets Israel*. Our mother Reyzl's satisfaction rose even more. Who could compare and compete with her with 2 from the household making *aliyah*? In those days this was a great privilege. And with God's help, Reyzl lived to see her third daughter, Khayeh, make *aliyah*. Well? So much honor to one family was rare to find.

After some time, when the fourth, Yankele, was going to make *aliyah*, on exactly that same day, a tragedy occurred... the horse died, the source of income for his brother Eliezer who provided for the whole family. Reyzl went out with a smile on her face and said: The horse died? We all will die one day. Whatever could, God forbid, happen to Yankele on his way, happened to the horse... *kaparah*[1]...

And Yankele made it safely to *Erets Israel*.

Translator's Footnote

1. Forget about it!

[Page 195]

A Tale About a Telephone

Yekhezkel Poz (Puziriski)

Translation by Meir Bulman

There once was a Jew in our town who was about to marry off his son to a rich man's daughter from a neighboring town.

The engagement was conducted properly when the bride's father arrived. A few days after the engagement, a messenger arrived from the post office – the site of the only telephone in our town – and urgently announced that the bride's father from the neighboring town was calling the groom to the telephone.

The groom was excited, ran to his father, and notified him. The father commanded his son to wear his best clothes: the dark suit, the white shirt, the new tie, and hat. "My dear son," he concluded, "don't forget to shine your shoes!" and the father accompanied his son to the wonder machine – the telephone.

During the conversation the father stood near his son and nodded his head to the beat of his son's words. He stood there, his mouth agape, until the call ended.

In the evening between afternoon and evening prayers, the father sat in the synagogue and spoke to congregants who stood there and interrogated him on the details of the sensational telephone conversation. "Do you understand?" he repeated a second and third time, "The boy stands there and speaks to my future in-law as if face-to-face, deliberates, disagrees, and eventually agrees, all like they were standing next to each other, just like I'm speaking to you now, no distance, no kilometers. It is witchcraft!"

A Tale About a Handshake

Yekhezkel Poz (Puziriski)

Translation by Meir Bulman

There once was a Jew, a fur trader. He traveled to the villages near our town and purchased and sold various animals. He had an indecent habit: he spent nights wasting money playing card games.

While he played cards, his wife and children sat at home and eagerly awaited his arrival, desperate and hungry. After the wife had had enough, she approached the town rabbi and told him of her troubles. The rabbi quickly summoned her husband and severely scolded him. The rabbi preached to the husband on the duties a Jew has towards his wife and children, and the sins of the husband's behavior. The rabbi then demanded that the husband cease playing cards. With no other options, our Jew agreed to not go to any more card games, sealed with a handshake.

One Saturday night, he gave in to temptation and left the house, claiming that he was promised merchandise in a neighboring village. He then boarded his wagon and traveled directly to the card game. The Jewish night guards in the town saw the fur trader's wagon parked near the casino. Since they knew of the promise he had made to the rabbi, they decided to act. They freed the horse to run home. Not long afterwards the fur trader's wife ran out to the street crying, "My husband, My husband! The Gentiles murdered him! The horse returned without its owner and his coat is in the wagon, my husband was murdered, woe is me!"

All the town's Jews left their homes, including the rabbi. The night guards announced that the 'promiser' was in a certain house, absorbed in his card game.

The next day, the rabbi summoned the fur trader. "You broke a promise sealed with a handshake," the rabbi scolded.

"No, rabbi," the Jew passionately replied, "I promised I would not go [on foot] to another card game and kept my promise. I rode: I did not promise not to ride to another game."

[Page 199]

The Route to Redemption – Community, Movements, and Organizations

Hashomer HaTsair Nest in Voronova

Abrashka Moltsadski (Sharid)

Translation by Emma Karabelnik

I wasn't privileged to be among the founders of the nest, I was too young then, but to my recollection this privilege belonged to the late Shabtai Grodzenchik and, may they live, Sheyke Olkenitski and Shloma'le (Berkovitch) Aviel.

The group began to organize in autumn 1929. With their poor savings they hired a club in the house of Shaya (Yehoshua) Grodzenchik and began preparing activities.

We usually gathered in the evenings. We divided into groups by age or seniority. We learned Hebrew songs about *Erets Israel*, we danced *Hora* to the sounds of Hassidic music, which was new in our town due to its having belonged to the Mitnagdim–Litaim,[1] and we conducted discussions. Most of the talks were about the new community life formed in Israel and about life in *kibbutzim*.

The elders saw our activity as a game of youngsters. They couldn't decide – should they ignore this phenomenon or take it seriously.

We were not the first in town to start Zionist activity. Before us there were experienced activists who collected money for *Keren Kayemet*, spread Zionist newspapers etc. We were also not the first to make *Aliyah* in 1924/25. Some of those returned to Voronova to tell us about *HaAretz*.[2]

Our achievement was innovation in our activities. We added young spirit to the Zionist movement and were prepared to act and live the [dream] through its weakest moments.

At that time communist propaganda was increasing. They organized textile workers unions and it looked like a pragmatic action. Our activity was considered "utopian", not connected to reality. We were mocked, called "detached", and given "convincing" arguments from the communist lexicon— which was very popular with the revolutionary youth.

Gradually the nest became more attractive to the youth, and more youngsters came to join it.

What was its secret? First of all, the personal approach to every girl and boy, and a committed interest in their issues; second, a warm embrace offered to reserved or shy kids who were looking for attention and affection.

We went hiking outside the town. We called it "sailing". These escapes to nature and nighttime walks brought a romantic atmosphere and calmness to the soul, which couldn't be found elsewhere.

During our first activity, a political argument broke out, and we split in two factions. Several friends resigned and joined *Betar*. Until 1939, the two factions acted separately. As a result, the whole town divided into 2 factions. Every parent joined the camp of his son or daughter.

In 1930, Shlomo Aviel and Shabtai Grodzenchik departed for *Hachshara*.[3] This started a new phase in our life. No more youthful tricks and actions; now we were concerned with vital matters of destiny. The short training course those two took before their *Aliyah* was a turning point for us. We absorbed passionately all their stories about kibbutz life, all seemed so new, unusual and inspiring. They were escorted to the train station by old and young, with excitement, singing and dancing– "*Hatikva*", "*Vetehazekna*".[4] This was to the amazement of the Polish passengers who didn't understand what could be so exciting about a couple of *zhidaki*[5] traveling to Palestine. They wondered how that could be so joyful.

The nest was strong. The departure of 2 of its heads didn't cause a negative impact. Every evening we met for our activities. With our poor savings and with hard work (such as "wood–carving", etc.) we maintained our club— which was our escape from boredom and emptiness in a town so slow in development and growth.

Hashomer HaTsair alumni before departing for training

Friends kept departing for *Hachshara*. An *Aliyah* action by one of us always turned into a big event and celebration for the whole town.

We were taken to the railway station embraced by love and blessings, with a clear sense of the unity between the individual and the community.

The first Hashomer HaTsair chapter

In our memories, the years spent in the *Hashomer HaTsair* nest in Voronova are the most beautiful years of our lives.

Since 1933, the year I went to *Hachshara*, I never went back to our town. But I know that the nest continued to be active until 1939, and in this crucial year many youngsters from other places found shelter there, help and assistance, and a place to stay. Members of the nest smuggled them across the Lithuanian border while risking their own lives, just as they had been trained.

They succeeded in helping many, but were not able to help themselves. In 1942 their lives were taken together with all the Nazi victims in Voronova.

The dear youth, dozens of young boys who represented future dreamers and fulfillers, were lost. With their loss our nation lost future generations of creativity and devotion. We, the Voronovers, remained brothers in our hearts and connected with our souls and minds.

May we be worthy to say: in our lives we shall fulfill your dreams and aspirations.

Translator's Footnotes:

1. Lithuanian Jewish faction considered more conservative and strict and non–Hassidic

2. i.e., Israel

3. Literally training, temporary living and training in a *Kibbutz*

4. The Israeli national anthem and a popular song

5. Polish slang for Jews

[Pages 202-204]

The Zionist and HeKhaluts Movement in Voronova

M. Kuznets, Of Blessed Memory

Translation by Emma Karabelnik

In the beginning of 1925, I was among the founders of the "HeKhaluts–HaTsair–HaMizrahi" union. At that time in Voronova 2 Khaluts unions coexisted: "HeKhaluts–HaMizrahi" and "HeKhalutz–HaKlali". "HeKhaluts–HaMizrahi" was considered a strong force in Voronova, with many members making *Aliyah*. Yocheved Bloch (Yachka) the first pioneer to make *Aliyah* from our town, did it as a member of "HeKhaluts–HaMizrahi". But for some reason there was no continuity in "HeKhaluts–HaMizrahi" and only few of us were left – about 12 members[1]. The members of the committee were Shimon Levine, Avraham Levine (rest in peace), Moshe Volpianski (rest in peace) and me. And also there was a representative of the seniors' "HeKhaluts–HaMizrahi": first Yakov Konikhovski, then later Yakov Konopke. Our club was in the house of Avraham–Eli and Mettla Dvilianski on Eshishuk Street. This was near my parents' house and so that's why I could dedicate myself to the "HeKhaluts–HaTsair–HaMizrahi" activities, but this didn't last for long. In the beginning of 1926, with the breakout of an economic crisis in *Erets–Israel*, some of the pioneers from both organizations returned to Voronova, and things fell apart.

In 1927 there was no Zionist activity in Voronova, and one could see influence of the communists who had bought the trust of the youth by organizing a professional union. They even took charge of the Y.L. Perets library.

In 1928 a unified, non–political Zionist movement was founded in Voronova. Its leader was then Nekhemia Shapiro with a couple of other senior Zionist activists. All of the youth with Zionist beliefs joined this movement. I remember the arguments we had with other youngsters. We didn't know which Zionist movement to choose. Finally we decided to join the "HaShomer HaTsair", which at that time was more of a scout–movement than a political movement. We made contact with the district leadership of the movement, situated in Grodne, and with the leadership of the whole region in Lida. The first committee members were Ysroel Berkovski, Abba Lipniski (of blessed memory), Aharon Kalmanovitsh, Shabtai Grodzenchik (of blessed memory), Yesheyahu Olkenitski, Shlomo Shmerkovitsh, Avraham Levine (of blessed memory), and me.

Our activity went smoothly for several months, until we went to a regional convention in Lida. We went there with patches on our shoulders symbolizing the movement as a scout–movement. But as soon as we returned, there was a split because many members felt that the "Hashomer–HaTsair" movement was becoming too left–winged. A large group of members, with Ysroel Berkovski and Aharon Kalmanovitsh at the head, then established "Betar".

Thus there were two strong organizations in Voronova. In the month of Av Tarpa"t (1929), while the violent events of Hebron–Zefat took place in *Erets Israel*, we participated in a convention of commanders of the

HaShomer movement in Yeshtsenko[2] near Grodne. I didn't like the discussions there and I left the movement disappointed. I joined the activity of "HeKhaluts". Incidentally, the graduates of HaShomer–HaTsair now belonged to "HeKhaluts", so this made my transition easier.

The clubhouse of "HeKhaluts" was then in the home of Meirovitsh on Vilne street, down the hill,[3] and the leaders were Shabtai Dlugin (of blessed memory), Yehoshua Shmerkovitsh, Abrashka Moltsadski, Katriel Kaplan (of blessed memory), Yakov Bloch, and me. During the period of our activity we sent Daniel Grodzenchik, Leyb Abramiski and Pesyeh Piskovski (the miller's daughter) to *hakhshara*.[4] At the end of their *hakhshara* they made *Aliyah* to *Erets Israel*. We got help from some of our supporters, especially from Peysakh Itskovitsh and Aharon Lefkovitsh.

The HeKhaluts Union in Voronova

One day a "Gordonya" group from Vilne came to Voronova. They asked us to help them with their work and accommodations in the neighborhood. I took them to Herminishok estate. The estate owner Kulvitsky agreed to give them part–time jobs in his estate and accommodation in one of his buildings. During their spare time they did educational activities. We, the members of "HeKaluts", used to visit them every evening. They had a great influence on our town.

When we returned to Voronova from *hakhshara*, I found "HeKhaluts" almost paralyzed. In order to bring some renewal of spirit we decided to organize a regional convention of "HeKhaluts" in Voronova. Katriel Kaplan (of blessed memory) and I went on foot to Divenishok, Eshishuk, Olkenik, Ivia, Lipnishok, and Lida. We met members of the "HeKhaluts" committees and persuaded them to take part in the convention. The HeKhaluts convention in Voronova turned out to be an impressive event. After the convention the Voronova branch became very active.

Sometimes small, haphazard connect into one long chain of narrative, and one sees them as logical links of a chain leading to revolution and the struggle to change reality. Such were our *hakhshara* and *Aliyah* activities— pity we managed to save so few.

Translator's and Editor's Footnotes:

1. Trans. Note: Both boys and girls

2. Ed. Note: In the original text this name is spelled: yud–shin–tzadek–nun–kuf–vov.

3. Trans. Note: This phrase is written in Yiddish in the original text: arop–barg.

4. Ed. Note: Hebrew word meaning 'preparation'. These were training programs to ready participants for the challenges of making *Aliyah*.

[Pages 205-206]

From the Memories of an Emissary

Yosef Bankover (of *Ramat Hakovesh*)

Translation by Emma Karabelnik

For me Voronova is connected to something special and has kept a special place of honor in my memory.

I was an emissary from Israel. I come to recruit people for *Aliyah*, but I received much more in Voronova. I received encouragement and high spirit. This small town made me a believer in the Jewish folk of the *Gola*.[1] I'll try to recreate the circumstances and factors that bonded my soul to Voronova. It was in 1923–24.

Erets Israel was experiencing a huge crisis. Part of the *Olim* had departed.[2]

The unemployment in the cities – and especially in the settlements – was a result of the farmers' neglect of the national need for Hebrew employment and absorption of *Aliyah*. The farmers flooded the settlements with cheap Arab labor. There was a strong need of an organized, pioneer *Aliyah*, conscious of its needs and mission, aware of the reality of having to deal with, and fight for work positions with, the Arabs who had expanded everywhere, and with Jewish farmers who supported the Arabs.

The *HeKhaluts* movement – in Poland – stood before a challenging trial. Its fast and unnatural growth (from 2,000 to 10,000 members) endangered the whole movement and could have lead to paths totally unwelcome by us. Acute intuition would be required to control the situation, and to turn the *HeKhaluts* into a union of the masses, without compromising its ideological principles. While the movement expanded there would be a need for stronger implementation of its values, for organized training, and for management of the difficult situation.³

We, the emissaries, had to put a special effort into our triple mission: to prepare a new generation for leadership of *HeKhaluts*, to organize and enforce the union [Trans. Note: the *Histadrut*] in Poland, and to fix the situation in *Erets Israel* by means of a steady flow of people of shared ideology and eagerness, consciousness and readiness. The news from the *Histadrut* in Israel was that the pioneers weren't up to the challenge and were relocating to the cities and other places where they would not face any immediate danger from hostile elements, and from the authorities who supported these elements.

The district committee of *HeKhaluts* in Vilne took upon itself to perform this most urgent mission, and decided to establish a Kibbuts by the name "*Hakovesh*", populated by *HeKhaluts* members from the Vilne district, who would make *Aliyah* as a group, and would lead the Workers' Union⁴ in *Erets Israel* in the fight for settlement and labor. Approximately 200 people were approved by the Center for immediate *Aliyah*.

The establishment of "*Hakovesh*" inspired the whole Vilne district: hundreds of pioneers scattered around various small, far–off towns, united for an immediate *Aliyah* and fulfillment. It was not only about shaking off the chains of the *Gola* and apathy, but even more it was about a readiness to offer a supporting shoulder, to join a big Zionist organization, and to try building a life together in *Erets Israel* through labor, occupation, and settlement. This spark spread electrically through the ranks of the *HeKhaluts*.

In this aspect, Voronova stood out and excelled, with its vibrant and sparkling youth.

The youth of Voronova's surroundings excelled as well. In every town there was a *HeKhaluts* branch, an incipient *HeKhaluts–HaTsair*, and a wide chain of Hachshara groups doing their initial steps. It was an ideological and personal pleasure to visit those *HeKhaluts* branches, to meet the vibrant youth, to see the education system with Yiddish and

Hebrew schools, the drama circles for the youngsters— to be swept away in the flow of their excitement and to enjoy the freshness and beauty of the surroundings.

The people of Voronova didn't disappoint. They were among the first to join "*Hakovesh*" at its first convention in Vilne, and were among the first groups to make *Aliyah* – in big numbers. After repatriation they took hard labor upon themselves, as well as activities for the movement.

During these days of preparation for the book of Voronova and its surroundings, we approach the 45th anniversary of "*Hakovesh's*" establishment in Israel. Today we can be proud of Voronova's young pioneers. They played an important role in this historical transfer and brought a major change to the formation of the state and to the understanding of its needs.

During these days, descendants of the Voronova district can look at their past with pride and satisfaction.

For me as an emissary from Israel, Voronova will always be the source of encouragement, and when I remind myself of this period, I feel that I am a part of Voronova and that together we wrote beautiful pages in the history of *Aliyah*, "*Ramat Hakovesh*" being the outstanding symbol.

Translator's and Editor's Footnotes:

1. Tr. Note: i.e., Galuth, or the community of Jewish exiles

2. Ed. Note: i.e., People who had made *Aliyah* to Israel

3. Trans. Note: Refers to the situation in *Erets Israel*

4. Trans. Note: *Histradut*

[Pages 207-209]

Betar in Voronova

As Told by A.A. Olkenitski, Khenyeh Konopke and Khaye Levine (Rothbart)

Translation by Emma Karabelnik

The founders of *Betar* in Voronova were mostly members of *HaShomer–HaTsair*. At first it was considered a scout movement, with no political status, but in 1928 at the first convention in Lida, a leftwing tendency became obvious, which was strange to us. So 9 of the delegates that returned from the convention then connected to *Betar*.

The first nest consisted of 30–40 members under the leadership of *Betar's* founders in Voronova: Ysroel Berkovski, Arkeh Kalmanovitsh, Avkeh Lipniski, Khaye Levine (Rothbart), Leyzkeh Katzenellenbogen, Khayeh Mineh Konopke, Dlugin, Avramkeh Levine, Arkeh Levine, and others.

We were divided by age into *Kfirim*[1], middle–agers, and elders. We invited instructors from Vilne to establish the ideological foundation of the nest, and *Betar* in Voronova became a fact.

In 1928, at the first *Betar* convention in Vilne, presided over by Aharon Profos,[2] decisions were made to start *hachshara* and *aliyah*, and we began to implement.

We conducted numerous cultural events. We gathered every evening to have conversations on literature, Zionist movements, to exchange opinions on social structure in *Erets Israel* and other topics. We used our youngsters to pursue Zionist financial activities.[3] We participated with others in money raising campaigns for National Funds. We also raised money for the *Tel–Chai* Fund. We arranged dance balls, organized bazaars on Khanukeh and Purim; and also academic events on 11th of Adar and 20th of Tamuz. After a bitter fight, some of our members were accepted to the library committee. From inside, we fought for inclusion of nationalistic literature and reading material reflecting our views on national and personal matters.

Alongside our propaganda activity, we also worked on our physical fitness. We were involved in sports, purchased tents and sports equipment, and went out hiking and sailing during summer camps in the region, in order to strengthen our ideological and physical foundations.

Gradually, we began military training. Under the initiative and instruction of Yermyahu Halperin, military training commander of Global *Betar*, we performed this activity with enthusiasm and devotion.

In July 1939, a regional training course for military instructors was conducted by the Etzel organization. We rented a backyard from a Polish farmer in Mikelkuni near Oshmene. We obtained weapons from the Polish Army. We also obtained a Polish low-rank command for smaller units. The high command and instructors were emissaries from *Erets Israel*. The commander of the camp was Shraga Chaikin, his deputy was Michael Ashbal who was killed during the raid attempt on Akko prison.

It was a military regime like in a rookie camp. We arranged beds in a hayloft, which was also a compound for all personal matters. There was a tight military schedule; we trained for the use of cold weapons, for performing diversions, and for street combat. We prepared for a military underground future in *Erets Israel*.

The first group that went out, in 1929, for *Betar hachshara* in Klisov[4] and Nadvorna, included Tsve Sokolik, Arkeh Levine, Avkeh Lipniski, Menachem Olkenitski, and Hirshkeh Arkin.

With the establishment of the nest, there was an atmosphere of the concrete realization of Zionism in town, and the nest kept growing. One could say that along the way the movement was a magnet for "lost" youth. We were joined by simple folk who otherwise spent their time playing cards to forget their troubles. Tis a pity that because of various reasons we were deprived distributions of *aliyah* visas, and that our salvation window was short, otherwise we could save a lot of the youth from misery.

Voronova Betar – 1930

The *"Tsoar"* movement also prospered in Voronova. Our parents, influenced by our enthusiasm, felt that they have to join a movement with a similar ideology.

We used to demonstrate our achievements by performing military exercises and participating in military parades, marching in long rows, fully dressed in our uniforms— this had a great impact on the surrounding region.

Our serious attitude towards military training was well demonstrated and persuasive. Such were our parades held on our holidays or Polish holiday vacations, i.e. May 3 and November 11.

During *hachshara* we experienced suffering and hunger. We bore the suffering knowing that our turn to make *aliyah* would take time. We experienced frustrations that prepared us for *HaApala*[5] because we couldn't see a chance for legal *aliyah*.

But despite organizational, ideological and official difficulties, the *hachshara* groups maintained friendly relationships with other *hachshara* groups, and this brought brotherhood and cooperation even with *HaShomer–HaTsair*.

There was one occasion when our group in Nadvorna went for a hike— only three girls and one boy stayed back to protect the house from hostile Ukrainians who treated us as invaders in their work territory. Some Ukrainians who idle, noticed there were only few of us, and decided to liquidate us— as simple as that. In a few moments our house was surrounded by mean "*hutzuls*",[6] and we were in immediate danger. Khayeh Levine showed extraordinary courage. When she saw that they were slowly approaching the house, she jumped out of a window straight into the crowd, determined to fight instead of wait for miracles.

They were startled and let her through. In a short while, in the middle of the night, she managed to fetch friends from *Hashomer HatSair* and Gordonya, who attacked these Ukrainian "heroes" with axes and sticks. The "*hutzuls*" ran away. The next day we saw them at the public medical clinic, injured and beaten–up, embarrassed and miserable.

It's important to tell this story because it demonstrates the primal hatred of the Gentiles towards Jews, and the brotherhood of all the movements which was simple and concrete.

After Ysroel Berkovski, Aharon Kalmanovitsh was appointed the next commander of the nest, and he was tragically privileged to be the last one. Together with all the dear youth of Voronova, our friends from *Betar* also perished. When we mourn for our Voronova youth, we also mourn for our *Betar* friends with whom we shared a dream of a national home, but who didn't survive.

Translator's and Editor's Footnotes:

1. Trans. Note: Young lions

2. Ed. Note: In the original text the name is spelled: pey (or fey) – resh – vov – pey (or fey) – vov – samekh.

3. Trans. Note: i.e., collect money

4. Ed. Note: In the original text the name is spelled: kuf – lamed – vov – samekh – vov – veyz.

5. Trans. Note: Illegal immigration

6. Trans. Note: Ukrainian peasants

[Pages 210-212]

'Supplement' to the Image of *Betar*

Shlomo Pikovski

Translation by Emma Karabelnik

The youth that resigned from HaShomer HaTsair were mostly from traditional families, who held radical views on the revival of Judaism. They opposed HaShomer HaTsair activities because of the Marxist elements in its ideology, and also because of the sports activities, which were mostly of a scouting nature, rather than defensive, and in their eyes this didn't match the seriousness of the situation.

Our first foundational meeting took place in Khayeh Levine's backyard. There, in their dairy barn, we read Jabotinsky's essay, we decided on fundamental principles and united in common goals. First we used the name "Shomer–Hashchar"[1] and later *Betar*.

We Voronova people also joined the cause after taking an oath of allegiance to the people, the homeland, and the movement. After a trial period, a boy had to go through a test, and if he passed, he was given the "*Betar* Oath" insignia. As proof of the special importance to us of this insignia is the fact that I kept mine through all the hardships of my illegal Aliyah and I brought it with me to Israel.

Our cultural and educational activity was well planned and directed towards training civilians to settle, work, and defend *Erets Israel*. We were assisted by frequent guests from *Erets Israel*, all *Betar* emissaries, who helped us form an image of the future citizens of Israel. They also helped us analyze the essays of *Betar* leaders. The "Di Welt"[2] newspaper became our impeachable source for developing solutions to Zionist problems, and for forming opinions on world and Israeli policy. We distributed the paper devotedly, thus enlarging the number of revisionist movement followers.

According to our founding principles, the so–called transition period during our stay in *Golah*,[3] we used the time for physical and military training, done in compliance with Polish authorities and with the assistance of their military facilities. In the Voronova nest, we put all our efforts into both. Our members participated in military training courses in significant numbers, and also in physical training camps in Klisov, Nadvorna, Baranovitsh, Kaltzeh,[4] Volozhin and with other squads, where they served as commanders and leaders.

A great boost for the whole movement, and for the Voronova nest, was made by the historical "Evacuation" speech by Jabotinsky, in which he suggested that the Jews take advantage of the Gentiles' wish to "get rid" of us and utilize their hatred as a driving force to transfer all the Jews from Poland, and other Diasporas, to a safer shore.

His words were like a sign of an incipient fulfillment of prophesy. We saw ourselves as if floating on a ship headed for wreckage, and realized that we had to act quickly for our own safety, and the safety of others. I heard his speech in the Conservatorium Hall in Vilne. I saw the urgency of the matter so clearly that I couldn't think of anything else. As soon as I was released from the Army, I immediately joined the illegal Aliyah with all its hardships.

For some reason, the "evil waves" described to us in the allegory seemed to me more realistic and dangerous than the waves of a stormy sea. I was ready to board a raft, to sail the dangerous Mediterranean, so as to not remain in the sea of Polish anti–Semitism, with the prospect of German Nazism getting closer every day.

My father, Rest in Peace, discovered my plans and he took me for a mountain hike near the town, trying to dissuade me from my intentions. When he saw he was failing, he tried persuading me to postpone for at least half a year:

"You have just been released from the Polish Army," he pleaded, "please stay at home for a while, with your family, and then no one will stop you."

Voronova Betar – 1929

"Father," I said to him, "I think it would be better if we sold everything we own and made Aliyah. As far as I am concerned, I can't wait. I feel that there is no certainty that ships will continue sailing; the doors of illegal Aliyah may close any time. The sea will be closed for us."

*

It's a pity that we don't take the words of our leaders seriously and don't treat them as a living reality.

We are lucky that some did acted according to their hunch and foresight, and thus many of us became the last remnants available to build the country and prepare for the entire people, and for survivors.

At the same time that the Jews of Europe were being taken to crematoriums and gas chambers in Auschwitz and Birkenau, their sons were fighting here in Israel against English manipulations and against Arabs–the few against the many–both openly and secretly, with a sense of disaster and a strong desire to live, and with the power of faith: because when wanted, we have the capacity to overcome anything, and we succeeded.

Translator's and Editor's Footnotes:

1. Trans. Note: Defender of dawn

2. Trans. Note: The World

3. Ed. Note: Exile

4. Ed. Note: In the original text this name is spelled: kuf–lamed–tzedek–hey

[Pages 213-215]

Restless Youth
(A Guide to Our Perplexed Town)

S. Levine

Translation by Meir Bulman

The times pushed the town's youth into the arms of enlightenment, progress, and freedom. The youth felt uncomfortable in their quiet town and were restless and rebellious. Their restlessness caused them to seek horizons for unwinding and change.

From the 1880s until the Russian Revolution, Voronova knew generational rebellion and father-son opinion wars. Along with the Russian Empire and Central-Eastern Europe, many Voronova residents followed the various 'isms' which cut through the space of idealist rebellion. They did not differentiate between socialism, anarchism, communism, and nihilism. Each ideology spoke to them with novelty and conquered their hearts with change and a rebellious shattering of the consensus. After the disappointment of the 1905 revolution the wrath of the masses was directed towards Jews in the known pogroms, and the restlessness of the Jewish youths in our town was channeled to within the Jewish community. Zion-loving romantic songs echoed through the streets of the town. The yearning Jewish soul was calmed by dreams of *HaMakhresha* [The Plough], and the songs of Alikhum Tsunzer,[1] Sh.I. Imber,[2] Alexander Shapiro, and Abraham Goldfaden.[3] Since then the energy of the youth entered a single path, which had its ups and downs, but was not steep, and led to Zion.

Still, on the margins of the nation there were scattered people who persisted in their loyalty to the revolutionary past. Their revolutionary spirit, however, was expressed solely by hanging a red cloth on May 1 and quietly singing *The Internationale*. This ensured they would not be sent to Siberia.

*

A small movement of underground communists was formed in the 1920s. The group was very small and was limited to a few families, but the anti-Polish stance in its platform caused its members to think they could enlist a few sympathizers from the Zionist movements. The communists began to work amongst the Zionist youth and charmed them with the romanticism of the underground and by appealing to Jewish interests against minority discrimination.

That communist organization operated for 15 years. Although unable to trap Jews using anti-Polish sentiment, the communists still invited the wrath and suspicions of the Polish police. Almost all were sent to jail. To them, jail was a sort-of certification for their empty heroism, which is still heroism. As time passed, many realized the meaninglessness of their corrupt ways and repented. The wrong they committed to themselves and their people was atoned for by ascending and sobering up towards Zionism. There were some who remained loyal to their old ideals and unfortunately paid for their mistakes with their lives.

Among the underground activists were those with solid foundations. There were thinkers, scholars, talented persons, and strong-willed individuals alert to worldly and Jewish events. We all remember Ysroel Virshudski, Alter's son (Dem Stelmakhs), who was active in the underground, and the net of his activity was cast over the whole area. Eventually he was forced to escape to Russia, but instead of reaching his idealistic resting spot, he was accused of betraying Stalin the Father of Nations, and was executed in the dark 30s of wild Stalinism.

Most prominent among the communists were the brothers Yankel and Ben-Zion Trotski. Those men, who acquired their extensive education on their own, managed to maintain a wide underground movement in our area. They were in direct contact with the pseudo-communist empire and were invincible. Until the Holocaust, they were fortunate, their rebellion bore fruit. They disappeared on the eve of the Holocaust and none of us knows what their end was.

A unique figure was Alterk'e Vidlenski, the anarcho-communist. He was an albino man of Slavic features. Alterke saw himself as Russian and identified with the teachings and actions of the *Yevsektsiya*.[4] He saw Voronova as an obstacle to progress and was prepared to sacrifice the town to his idealistic idol. His big dream was to shutter the houses of worship and to jail as a traitor anyone who objected. He wanted to send all the worshipers in the synagogue to Siberia.

Thoughts of *Aliyah*

His faith in communism was blind; he was incapable of successfully explaining himself. It was enough for someone to disagree with him to be considered a traitor to the working class and the working man. Even the craftsmen and laborers in town seemed to him to be obstructing the revolution. He would have executed them all, or exiled them to Siberia, without a trial or explanation. The movement rewarded him with its full support and gave him important underground tasks which he completed responsibly and with talent. Eventually he was captured and jailed at Vronki, a jail and labor camp for political prisoners. He was tortured to death as the secret police interrogated him. He died a short time after he was released. It can be said that until the day he died he worked for Marx, but not once in his life attempted to fully understand Marx. Alter sacrificed his life to an idol he did not comprehend.

*

The modern youth movement in its Zionist form arrived in our town in the 1920s. The first was an organization named *Herut U'Tkhiya*[5] which later joined *HaKhaluts* and *Mizrachi*. The members of *Herut* were the first to fulfill their dreams of *Aliyah*.

Membership of the youth in the Zionist framework brought hope and joy to the parents' homes. It seemed that the persistent misunderstandings among fathers and sons ended. Hebrew was heard in the streets. Songs of Zion were raised by all and *Eretz Israel* became the solution to the problems facing the Jews of Voronova.

In the late 1920s, as the *Aliyah* crisis began, and with tensions in *Eretz Israel*, there was a crisis in Voronova too, but the youth quickly recovered. The youth established additional youth movements which persisted until the great tragedy arrived. These movements were not particularly instrumental in Voronova and so we will not write about them. We will note that the youth's power shined in times of crisis. Our youth withstood the test of seriousness and fitness. The youth responded to the crisis in their world with unusual mental strength and continued to nurture their growth as they journeyed on the path towards the State of Israel.

Footnotes

1. Ed. Note: See http://www.yivoencyclopedia.org/article.aspx/Tsunzer_Elyokem

2. Ed. Note: See http://yleksikon.blogspot.com/2014/06/shmuel-yankev-samuel-jacob-imber.html

3. Ed. Note: See http://www.yivoencyclopedia.org/article.aspx/Goldfadn_Avrom

4. Ed. Note: The Jewish section of the Soviet Communist Party.

5. Trans. Note: Freedom and Rejuvenation

[Pages 216-218]

Impressions of a Teacher in Voronova

Tova Shomroni

Translation by Emma Karabelnik

Rabbi Goldberg, teacher

Before the beginning of the 1933–4 school year I was sent by Dr. Tzemel, Chairman of "Tarbut" education chain, to take a teacher position in the "Tarbut" elementary school in Voronova. The members of the school committee Avraham Eliahu Dvilianski and Shlomo Puziriski came to welcome me in Vilne, in a beautiful gesture and sign of their serious attitude towards education and their respect for those who profess to it.

As a young teacher, just finished with the Seminary, I was full of doubts and fears, and I took my position with great hesitation. But Voronova surprised me and made my first professional steps easier.

I found an enthusiastic parents' committee, dedicated to Hebrew education. All of them were educated people with an elevated national awareness and a deep understanding of educational needs.

The school was a 2-story building, with large spacious rooms, and a hall for dramatics and conventions.

It was an extraordinary school. In the eyes of the authorities it was a religious institution headed by Rabbi Tsipkovitsh "HaMyadler",[1] but inside it was a modern nationalistic school. Most of its pupils were excellent. Almost all were members of Zionist youth movements and not of religious movements. The education program was similar to all "Tarbut" schools, but by common accord, senior classes studied religion and Jewish culture: *Yiddishkeit.*

All the teachers who taught secular studies were sent from the center in Vilne. The two teachers of religious studies were local Voronovers. One, Rabbi Goldberg, the "Wiler" Rabbi,[2] was a man of virtues, full of knowledge and wisdom. The second, R. Yosef Shmerkovitsh, father of Shlomo Aviel and Meir Shamir, was a great Torah and Gemarah scholar and highly educated. His general knowledge covered a wide range of topics. Being a patriot, he added a Zionist spirit to his classes. He exposed his pupils to the eternal problems of the Jewish people, and their implications for the present. He also tried to convince his colleague Rabbi Goldberg to adopt his educational policies; they used to burst into hot arguments which were very interesting and culturally enriching, and for me – fascinating. R. Yosef was a nice man, good-hearted, gentle and fascinating. We always learned something new from him.

The financial status of the school was terrible. The parents who were asked to pay these high fees were common poor folk and couldn't afford such payments. In this regard, committee members rose to their glory: at the end of a market day they would go from door to door collecting money for the teachers' salaries. Dear Jews: R. Eliahu Dvilianski, R. Chaim Olkenitski, R. Shlomo Puziriski and R. Nekhemiah Shapiro, who can measure the heat of your Zionist patriotic enthusiasm, and your sacrifice for its fulfillment? Last and not least was R. Zeidl Boyarski, committee treasurer, who worked hard day and night to ensure the school's maintenance. It was the apple of his eye and his devotion was unprecedented.

Over time, the school turned into a cultural center and a social lighthouse, which spread the light of national patriotism to the whole town and its residents. All Zionist activities were held there, from conventions and committee meetings, to bazaars for the benefit of national funds, to memorial ceremonies and receptions for emissaries from Israel, etc.

*

We experienced many difficulties from the racist and shallow Polish regime. Before visits from the Polish inspector we were all terrified. Teachers and parents lived with the constant threat of closure, of their most precious establishment, and this common emotion created a special bond between them. The inspector came solely with the purpose of finding faults, and to create obstacles in order to close the school. He was always unhappy with sanitary conditions and expressed his pretended surprise:

"Why don't you send your children to a public school? The level of education is international and the children have extra privileges."

His insinuations were clear.

I won't forget his last surprise visit, this enemy of Jews. With his arrival the rumor spread that he was in the school. He appeared with an attitude of openly rude anti Semitism. He burst into classrooms without asking, without listening, without hearing out, bursting out with screaming accusations:

"How is it possible that the portrait of the President of Poland, Moschitski, is hanging under the portraits of Dr. Herzl and Bialik. This is unbearable Jewish *hutzpah*."

After that he turned to Mr. Gindlin, the school principal and called him humiliating names in the presence of teachers and pupils. Then he slammed the door and wouldn't speak to him anymore. Luckily, the town Rabbis and leaders somehow succeeded in calming him down.

Voronova Hebrew School, 1929

We overcame all, as did the dear parents, the children's representatives together with us. Despite all these difficulties we succeeded in keeping the school alive and producing excellent graduates each year, who were devoted to the values bestowed by nationalistic Hebrew education, and prepared to carry the burden of reviving Jewish culture and existence as a nation. Each graduating class created new pioneers, each with a vision of the Jewish state and its social structure.

Special mention should be made of the school housekeeper Libe Zilberman whose nickname was "the bell", not only because she was responsible for ringing the school bell, but also because she tended to talk too much, usually to herself.

She did her job like on a special mission, and performed all her assignments with great devotion and dignity. Sometimes I see Libe as an actress playing a small secondary role on the stage of the nationalistic revival in Voronova, but she played it with absolute conviction of its necessity, certain of its contribution to the narrative. In this breeding ground of the nation's soul, who can tell which part was more important than any other? For me Voronova was a spiritual and emotional second home.

Editor's Footnotes:

1. i.e., From Myadl

2. In the original text the name is spelled: vov–yud–lamed–ayen–resh. Possibly refers to the town of origin of the rabbi.

[Pages 219-221]

Educators, Education, Educational Establishments, Educational Conditions, and *Melameds*[1]

Shimon Levine

Translation by Emma Karabelnik

Reb Tzvi Hirsh Lemelevin: he was called the "*Talmud* Torah Rabbi" and in his *cheder*[2] studied the best members of our youth since the end of 19th century until beginning of 20th century.

He was a strict Jew, punctual, straightforward and he never preferred one pupil over another. He was devoted to his work, put all his effort into teaching *Chomesh*,[3] Rashi, and sections of the Bible to his flock.

He was the one and only acknowledged rabbi for 50 years. Although his pupils didn't get far beyond *Chomesh* and Rashi, parents still wholeheartedly sent their children to study with the old well-known educator.

In 1920 a Polish hooligan pushed him under a train, and thus ended his life in an unexpected and tragic way.

His pupils were mostly members of the same families yet almost all the families in town mourned the death of this irreplaceable educator.

R. Feyvl Weiss and R. Berl haMelamed: both managed *cheders* alongside R. H. Lemelevin, but they were overshadowed by the latter.

R. Yehuda Karczmer: his *cheder* was unique and of high level. His pupils were only boys, and they also studied *Gemarah*.

His wife Keileh, the hump-backed, was a *"melamedet"* aside her husband. She used to teach girls to read the parts of the sacred writings that every kosher Jewish girl should know.

Their *cheder* turned into an academic institution, and with R. Yehuda's death his *Gemarah* and *Mishniyot* pupils became orphans.

Enhanced *cheder* Teachers

At the end of the war in 1914 War, a teacher from Divenishok arrived in our town. He established an enhanced *cheder*, where he himself taught religious topics including the Bible, while his eldest daughter taught Yiddish, Russian, German and even Math; she was his assistant and subordinate to him.

Because of family reasons this institution was closed shortly after its establishment.

After him came the teacher Igolski who continued with an enhanced *cheder* in our neighbor Beile's house on Vilne Street. The whole institution consisted of one big classroom with 40 pupils of mixed age and gender. This teacher taught Yiddish, Hebrew and a little Math, and to him were sent children whose parents could afford the high fees.

I, for example, couldn't afford to pay the fees, so I used to hide in the corner outside the window and absorb his progressive teaching, and the atmosphere in which it was presented, like a breath of fresh air after a gloomy, rainy day.

Most of all I loved the singing on *Shabat* nights. This singing lit a sparkle in me which kept sparkling until it brought me to *Erets Israel*. I think that it had the same effect on everyone.

In the same *cheder* R. Shmuel Olkenitski taught Russian, Polish and German. Later the two parted ways. R. Shmuel remained the principal of this institution, while teacher Igolsky resigned and started a similar class in the house of Yankl Kamiunski. He got lucky: his class was recognized as a public school for the academic year 1921–22, and later as a Hebrew school "Torah veDaat".[4]

According to tradition, for generations, in *cheder* the studies continued 12 hours a day till dark. Our older brothers used to come over with torches to escort us back home. The "Torah veDaat" school brought a revolution in this area. The studies lasted only for 5–6 hours a day. We studied a variety of topics, but mostly languages, math and reading at home – homework.

For several years the school grew constantly in its achievements, education level, educational methods, and clear Zionist tendency. The teachers were seminary graduates from Grodne, Vilne and Bialystok. The curriculum was approved by the center.

The principal, Shimon Dubinski, from Lida, was a true lover of children and a natural born educator. And the same teacher Igolski from Lomzhe, whose position as leader was taken from him, remained a professional and highly educated *Talmud*ic teacher. He was tall, potbellied, and bold, about 50 years old at the time I was his pupil. I saw him as a man of free opinions, but he taught *Talmud* and Torah with great conviction and dignity. More than once we found him alone in Beit *Midrash* struggling over a *Gemarah* page, with the traditional melody.

For a short period the staff was joined by Shmuel Gurvits, a student, a pioneer who deserted from the Red Army and was waiting to make *aliyah*. At first he slept in the synagogue and earned money doing various types of physical work. He dug holes, chopped trees, and did other similar jobs with low wages and at random. His employers felt that there is some hidden positive force there and offered him a position in the school. He taught Russian, Math and Geography and appeared to possess extraordinary didactic skills. His personality had a great impact on us by his personal example. Without words we absorbed his personal charm and adored his frame of mind... until one day he disappeared, and we knew that he was in *Erets Israel*.

And indeed we found him here.[5] He was the principal of a school in one of the cities until he retired.

We have warm memory of a young teacher Gelgort, the daughter of a Rabbi from a town near Vilne. She also enchanted us with her beauty, her entire personality, and her secret dream of *aliyah* to escape from home.

The last to close the list of teachers who had a great influence on us is Shimon Tlopp, a Hebrew High School graduate, for whom our town was a temporary stop on his way to teaching in Israel.

Teacher Gelgort died here several years ago, but Tlopp is still with us and teaching, holding a principal's position in Holon.

As proof of the high level of education in our schools are the names of its teachers: Weksler: today Dr. Weksler is a High School principal in Haifa and the author of textbooks and teachers' guides. I met him in 1947 in Germany when he was an emissary teacher. He instantly recognized me after all these years. And last is Tova Polinski, aka Tova Shomroni, a successful teacher and deputy principal, and here a successful teacher and educator of Zionism and *aliyah*.

We keep a tragic memory of the Math and Geography teacher Chaim Luski, brother of Rabbi Moshe Aryeh Luski, who came to our town after graduating from a Russian Technical School, and of the teacher of

Polish, Mirmelshteyn. Both married in our town and continued teaching in our school until the *Shoah*. Both loved our town, our youth and their parents, and all together they were murdered and buried in a brothers' grave.

*

During their existence, the *cheders* continued to work and to build the foundations of Judaism, to preserve *Yidishkeit* at a time when new trends and influences were tempting and threatening the youth who were always looking for new paths for themselves and the nation.

We will always keep pleasant memories of the *melameds* of Voronova despite our differences in opinions and upbringings.

To be honest fissures opened up in this school from time to time, and the winds of Polish culture managed to waft into the institution. But the town's people kept a vivid memory of the connection between the Polish "culture" people and the murders of Olkenitski and the youngster Moshe Zhabinski, and they declined that culture and language.

One of these experiments was done by Mr. Lichtman who wanted to merge Yiddish, Russian and Polish studies, but it didn't work out. We remember him as one who married one of our compatriots Esther Eishishke, and as one of the leaders of the Yudenrat in the Lida ghetto who endangered his own life on behalf of the Jews of Voronova, and perished together with them. Another person who tried to make us nobler by bringing Polish nobleness was the teacher Paz from Galitsia. But because of his unpleasant character we rejected him and his theories, he soon had to move to Lida and there… he converted to Christianity.

We write this in honor of our admirable teachers, thanks to whom our school was a training ground for youngsters devoted to nation and culture. The nationalistic Hebrew values we obtained in school are preserved, and have accompanied us throughout our lives, serving us like a shield against foreign cultures and directing us on our long road towards safety and a homeland.

Translator's and Editor's Footnotes:

1. Trans. Note: Religious teachers

2. Ed. Note: Jewish elementary school

3. Ed. Note: Old Testament

4. Trans. Note: "Bible and Knowledge"

5. Trans. Note: The writer is in Israel

[Pages 222-221]

The Building and its Contents
(Housing The Spirit)

Shimon Levine

Translation by Emma Karabelnik

The *cheder* and *cheder* "*mesukan*"[1] didn't need a house or a building to spread their spirit and to teach their doctrines. A single room, with a long table and benches around, was enough for Torah to exist.[2] That's the origin of the word *cheder* – one room, a home where Torah can exist. The Rabbi didn't need a podium. He sat at the head of the table and encouraged and pushed his flock to keep repeating after him word by word the text curved in the tablets of stone. The pupils absorbed the sounds into their blood and you got the next generation of *Am Israel*.[3] There was no need for learning equipment or laboratories, writing and drawing accessories, not blackboards, nor visual props. Here was only the voice of Jacob, the sounds and melodies alone did the didactic work, and the Torah was absorbed.

With time the winds of change arrived and the "Tarbut" school was established, but Voronova faced various difficulties. Now, not one room for all ages, but rooms for each grade were needed, with furniture for pupils and teachers, hallways and a school yard, and learning and writing equipment, and all of it in a suitable building. There was no such building in Voronova.

At first the school was in the house of Yankl Kamiunski (Svolik). In this house there were 5–6 rather small rooms with walls made of thin wooden boards with cracks between them. Although each class had its own room and the classrooms were separated, when the studies began, all the voices merged into one chaotic sound, with segments of sentences without beginning or ending. Whatever happened in one classroom was clearly seen by another through the cracks, and all the walls seemed to vanish– again one big room, what to do?

The entrance was through a long dark corridor, with tools scattered along the way. When the children bustled in, running from the playground, they stumbled into things, entered the wrong classrooms – there was too much failure and turmoil, interruption and difficulty.

Despite everything, this period is considered the golden age of Hebrew education in our town. The teachers' enthusiasm infected the pupils, and the pupils, who loved their school, put in every effort and executed all assignments demanded from them, including the self–restraint test which was the hardest of youth challenges.

As the number of pupils drawn to the school grew, the problem of the school building became more relevant and urgent. Everybody in town knew that there is no chance of a new building; the resources are not enough for such a mission. But against all odds that's what happened, and the building was built.

First there were contributions from town's common folk. Each one contributed as much as he could and more. From old to small, women and youngsters, in the name of every one and by everyone, the amount of money accumulated in the building fund. Then came the contributions of Voronovers in America, loyal to their home town and their old homeland, and there were also fundraising activities in town. Soon the construction began.

The architectural design was entrusted into the hands of R. Leyzer the Builder and he was the one to build the first of its kind in town: two stories of heavy wooden beams "that will stand for ages; you build once–you can't build every ten years or even hundred years".

I remember this R. Leyzer. He was at that time the most famous man in the area. He did magic in the construction field like a wizard that no common human could understand or imagine. He used to stand with a spirit level in his hand, and this spirit level was like a magic wand which a magician holds until the end of the show. Nobody understood how this tool assisted him nor why no beam was laid on another without his approval, and without this instrument's touch. Everybody put their trust in R. Leyzer and his reputation rapidly grew in the eyes of Voronova people. There is no need to say more, enough to mention that every *fritz*[4] in the area hired him to build his house–palace and that no Jew ever asked to see his professional diplomas. If a Jew was acknowledged by Gentiles, no other Jew doubted him.

For us, the children, his personality was fascinating. For long days we used to watch him clapping the workers, urging them to work faster, and they obeyed. We also wanted to help. We offered ourselves, our energy and our agility to do deliveries, but he rejected and drove us out of the construction site. He succeeded so well that the Jews asked him to build the synagogue and redecorate the *Beth Midrash*. R. Leyzer was a great man, an outstanding Jew, and a unique character in our eyes. The roof, made of red tiles was laid by two kosher Jews Aizik and Shmerl, the shingle makers.

It was a hard summer for us the pupils. The classrooms were relocated to the synagogue, the *Ezrat Nashim* and *Talmud* Torah room with its broken windows and a view on the cemetery. That used to be a *cheder* full of pupils. Many of us had to study in the hallway and "work" on our knees. Yet, we tolerated these difficulties with no effort because we knew that soon would come the day for us to enter the new school.

The summer ended and we were saved. The new school was ready and it was magnificent and spacious, and we were all proud of it. It was big and bathed in light, strong and fresh, smelling of resin and forest trees, and each class had its own room totally separated from others

The new school and teacher Tovah Shomroni

Along came the winter and frost occupied the spacious building, the ovens built into the rooms without a proper architectural plan burnt too many trees for the town to finance. The more you tried to warm the space, the more the walls dripped steam and the doors and windows dripped water. It was like finding ourselves in hell. Heat and cold alternately caused headaches and fainting, noses leaked, and throats were hoarse. Miraculously nobody complained. We were proud of our large building, of its hallways and its curved staircase, of its separate classrooms and teachers' room, and library and office, and that was enough for us.

In this building we spent our best years. We studied there and enriched our souls. In there we cherished our dreams for change and progress.

Who financed the school? We didn't know the answer for a long time. It seemed a miracle to us – what were its means? Who pays all the teachers and the other employees? Who keeps it clean? And who takes care of its maintenance?

Until finally the parents committee was established, with R. Nekhemia Shapiro as its chairman. The committee was elected by everyone. There was no other more important subject in Voronova than the children's fate and education. R. Nekhemia was an educated man who was once a Hebrew teacher and had turned into a successful businessman in older age. He was rich in material and in spirit, with education and modern youth's problems flowing in his blood. And with him there were other dear enthusiastic Jews who assisted in maintaining the school.

The story of the foundation of the Hebrew school in Voronova and the history of its maintenance is the story of the long struggle of poor communities for better education, which in their opinion was crucial for the future, and they ended up as winners. It's a shame that their victory came too late.

Translator's and Editor's Footnotes:

1. Ed. Note: The meaning of this word is not yet known. In the original text the word is spelled: mem–samekh–vov–kuf–nun.

2. Trans. Note: The word *cheder* in Hebrew means literally 'a room'.

3. Trans. Note: The People of Israel

4. Trans. Note: A rich Gentile

[Page 227]

Persons of Quality

The Zionist Veteran Nekhemye Shapira

Yehoshua Shomroni

Ed. Note: This article appears in both Hebrew and Yiddish in the original Yizkor Book; only the Yiddish version has been translated and published here and may be found at page 314 in this book.

[Page 229]

Mr. Yosef Shmerkovitsh

M.S.V.

Translation by Emma Karabelnik

Mr. Yosef was a person of new–age erudition who never stopped learning and constantly expanding his knowledge, biblical as well as secular. He spent his nights studying all that was written on *halakha*[1] and the general law. That is why his opinions were so progressive. He was way ahead of the town's people. He was known as a pioneer fighting for knowledge, education, and progress. Long before the youth raised the flag of Hebrew education, he spoke fluent Hebrew, and enjoyed its ancient sound and grammar. Its simple poetic words took his imagination to the nation's past, when the people were settled in their homeland with their Lord and Kings. This made him a warm Zionist, and a proud Jew. From there he drew his strength and his manner of dealing with all the hardships and financial difficulties of life. He never complained or was depressed, because his soul was always up–lifted by looking back on his people's past, gaining from there hope and tolerance.

Mr. Yosef had several crises in his life. From rich wood trader he descended to small shopkeeper. Later the shop also went into financial hardship, so he rented it. And yet, nobody ever saw him in a bad mood and you wouldn't see any signs of crisis in him.

His wife Shtisl, a simple and naïve woman, knew her husband well and tried to help him with his ideological aspirations. She took upon herself the management of the small shop, and like every Kosher Bat Israel she raised her children and did performed all duties of a Jewish wife and mother. Thus her husband had the freedom to devote himself to his "hobby": knowledge.

You could see Mr. Yosef at night bent above books by the light of a candle, studying. According to legend, a visitor to town wandering the streets at night discovered that Mr. Yosef was studying the Roman language in order to read the books of Yosefus Flavius in the original.

*

He loved agricultural work, which combined the symbolism and goal of hard work and soil, mutually connected. He saw in agricultural work a path to salvation for the nation that had lost its land and devoted itself to spiritualism and spiritual life. He believed that when a Jew works the land he gives up his pride and gains the modesty that will keep him from exaggerated feelings of intellectual superiority, and wean him from a life of comfort. Only then would salvation come and become an existing fact. Furthermore, he saw agriculture as a symbol of growth and renovation, of a temporary withering giving way to new beginnings. This is why he constantly worked in his private garden. He not only brought provision to his children from the vegetables and the dairy of his milk cow, he also enjoyed watching his garden grow and bloom, and the earth giving way to his hard work. In the blooming flowers he saw national revival and the primary meaning of his own life, the life of his sons, and the young generation.

He tried in different ways to pass on his ideas of rebirth and Hebrew language to his children and to the town's youth. He loved the youth. In their company he felt young and renewed, and he conducted himself as one of them. It was an ideology that said:

'If a person has aspiration for renewal and revival, then renewal and revival already exist in him *de facto*.'

Mr. Yosef's perception of youth was not as a temporary biological period, but as a continuous state of mind which has to be preserved by prolonged spiritual effort, according to each political era and historical developments. This was the reason for his sympathies towards *HaShomer Hatsair* which emphasized the *tsair* ["youth"] as a symbol of renovation and the establishment of a new society. He believed in social education, which was the primary goal of this movement above all other values. He also admired the national labor movement, even the extreme lefties, because he believed that a man of labor brings hope (by his opinion) to the whole nation. He was ready to forgive any deviation from Judaism if it was for the sake of labor, turning a Jewish man into a working man. He saw labor as a tool of education.

*

Yosef Shmerkovitsh was an outstanding father, sensitive to his children's emotional needs, and one who always made space for their desires, and implemented them. Shabbat nights around the table were always emotional and joyful. He used to challenge his children with an unusual idea just for the sake of an argument, and they like a "herd released" came up with their own ideas, shocking existing notions. In the end Mr. Joseph would stand up, calm everyone down, huddle the extremists close, and finish with:

"We need the rebellion of the youth, but only in one field, in *Aliyah*, which involves changes in the family structure, leaving behind parents and towns, and mutiny against father–mother. But in all other fields, honor and respect to parents is the guarantee of a continued existence."

He saw parenting during this era of revival as a mission, like the 'last generation of slavery'. He treated his sons as leaders of the future army who he had to train and nourish. He insisted on speaking Hebrew whenever he had a chance, eager to show how far his knowledge of the language had progressed. On every *Simhat Torah* holiday he was one of the organizers of the Zionist *minyan*.[2] He did it with great enthusiasm, as someone throwing away the troubles of the past year and giving in to the future, when the Temple would be rebuilt and the youth would be happy. At times of anger, he used to fling upon whoever annoyed him:

"May the Temple be built on you!"

To the rebuked it sounded like a Russian curse, but to the youth and to himself it meant:

"We are awaiting the "Reconstruction of the Temple" and you are obstructing."

The biggest punishment he could put on his children was to read 25 times and learn by heart 5 Torah chapters, mostly from the books of Yesheyahu Ben Amotz and Micha HaMorashti.[3] As a reward he would allow them to play with their mates. The idea behind this punishment was to draw a parallel between irresponsibility and perseverance, as expressed in the Prophets and their prophecies, showing that this was their obligation, and that fun is permitted only after following strict laws.

Only three people in town received the *Hatzfira* newspaper – Mr. Nekhemia Shapiro, Mr. Velvl Shelovski and he. But the three of them received one paper, because they signed for it together, so the arrangement was that Mr. Joseph was the last to read it in order to keep it for a longer time, in order to read it slowly and most importantly in order to keep the papers at his home for future reading. Packs of newspapers piled up in his home and he used to look at them from time to time, tasting old wine as if it was new. But his favorites were the pages for kids, attached to the newspapers once a week. He used to browse them from a to z, and at every opportunity would sit with his children and read to them with two explanations for each sentence, in order to connect their world of imagination to the reality of the Hebrew language, and to make them absorb and make Hebrew the language of their dreams and thoughts.

In the summer, on Shabbat mornings, he used to take his children out for a hike in a nearby forest, when everything was lit by dawn's rays. He taught his children folk songs and Zionist songs: "Faraway in the Land of Cedars", "With my Plow", "We are the Macabees". He used to sing, tap with his feet, and urge the children to join in. The combination of human song with the song of nature, of human joy with the joy of Creation, was a product of his educational skills and wild imagination. As a result his children remained forever enchanted with these Shabbat mornings filled with yearning for a homeland, and they were the first candidates to make *Aliyah*.

When his oldest son was among the first Voronovers to make *Aliyah*, he was the happiest of fathers, and he used to read his letters to the other parents with heartfelt feeling. It was a day of celebration when he received every two weeks the *Davar* newspaper from Israel, which literally brought the scent of Israel into his home, and his heart brimmed with happiness. Between the pages his son hid Israeli cigarettes with Hebrew writing such as *Adin*,[4] *Malka*,[5] *Latif*.[6] He used to hide them and bring them to *Beit Midrash* on a Holidays, share with everyone and say in Hebrew:

"Here, take a *papirosa*7 from *Erets Israel* with Hebrew writing and a very, very pleasant taste."

His close relationship with the youth finally paid off for him – when he went totally bankrupt he was accepted as a teacher in the *Tarbut* school, and no one was happier than he. Although he was dependent on the low salary and on donations from parents, his true reward was the love of and thirst for knowledge demonstrated by the children. It filled his heart with joy.

*

Mr. Yosef walked around the streets of Voronova as if floating, as if preparing himself to walk along the flowerbeds of a reborn Israel. He was totally devoted to preparing for the big transition, which would be happening for sure, and he would be there to work the land, be safe, and speak in the language of his people and of his dreams. But this did not come to pass and he had to be satisfied with his role in the National Revival of having sent his son to fulfill his dream. This was a consolation for his aching heart, and it kept him strong and determined in his belief in redemption until, at the verge of death, he cried out to his German murderers:

"You won't destroy me, your hands are too short. I have a son in Israel, and you will never reach him or the deeds of his generation, because by then your evil hands will be cut off."

We will remember him as a man who dreamed of our current glory and who could only feel the glory from afar.

Footnotes

1. Tr. Note: The Jewish law

2. Tr. Note: Most likely this refers to the traditional Simhat Torah celebration

3. Ed. Note: The biblical books of the prophets Isaiah and Micah

4. Tr. Note: Mild (cigarette type)

5. Tr. Note: Queen (cigarette type)

6. Tr. Note: A brand of cigarette

7. Tr. Note: A cigarette

[Page 233]

Reyzl Moltsadski

M.S.V.

Translation by Emma Karabelnik

The pharmacist couple, the Moltsadskis, were considered to be in an economic class of their own–as were all the free professionals in all the towns. Unlike in other towns though they didn't behave like nobility. They were not arrogant and didn't separate themselves from others. They tried to stay involved in community life along other simpler folk.

This was especially true of the pharmacist Reyzl Moltsadski. A smart, dynamic woman, energetic and assertive, Reyzl was the only woman in town who took part in political arguments and public debates, and dared to oppose men involved in politics and win them over in argument.

She had special charisma when she spoke, and endless enthusiasm. For these reasons she had a great influence on her audience. Nobody promised to change his opinion or follow her beliefs, but everyone enjoyed listening to her, hearing her passionate speech, and witnessing the extraordinary show presented by this high class woman trying to be one of the people, and seeking their moral support and approval.

Her tendency among the various Zionist movements was towards *HaShomer HaTsair*. We can't remember if this tendency was caused by the fact that her sons had joined the movement, or whether, conversely, her sons joined the movement because of her tendency. Anyway, it was known in town that Reyzl and *HaShomer HaTsair* were one organic, inseparable unit with no possibility of change. She was the Politruk for the parents. From time to time she addressed certain parents so that they send their children to *HaShomer HaTsair*, and tried to convince them in every possible way.

Her affinity with the movement was ideological, as strange as this may sound. It wasn't her professional–economical status as a rich woman which drew her to a movement gradually turning towards the ideological left, but rather her duty as a parent who despised the religious influences of the *cheder*.[1] She liked the emphasis on social education, the gender equality, and European–style uniform, which became this movement's identifying mark.

Her house became a hostel for all the emissaries who came to visit the local 'nest', and her name was known all over Poland as the patron of the Voronova 'nest' who could solve any accommodation or financial problem related to her guests.

In time she shared *HaShomer*'s friendly or hostile attitude towards the other movements. She used to praise certain movements, and send her force towards others, all according to their relations with *HaShomer HaTsair*.

She used to give special privileges to movement members. The cherries that grew in all the yards in town, also grew in her backyard, and were being constantly protected from little thieves that might sneak into the gardens to pick them. Reyzl guarded her fruits and crops like the apple of her eye, but if she found out that the thief was one a movement scout, she was more forgiving:

"Never mind, children, eat, don't be shy, they are very good."

But when she found out about the murder of Arlozorov[2] and that suspicion had fallen on the movement's ex-members she was the first to react with great anger to her movement's representatives in Israel. At all hours of the day during this sensationally painful month she used to gather a small crowd in the street and spit fire, using expressions like "blacker than black", "dark person", "retarded reaction" and other offensive adjectives.

In any other matter that didn't concern *HaShomer HaTsair*, Reyzl was an enthusiastic Zionist and acted in every possible way to further its course with great energy and organizational skills. She initiated fundraising events for the benefit of national funds, organized bazaars, and made fundraising activities on a daily basis.

Every piece of news from Eretz Israel concerned her, for better or worse, and when her sons were the first from our pioneers to make *Aliyah*, Reyzl felt personally connected to the newborn country, and was mostly proud of its development.

In the human and female panoroma of Voronova, Reyzl stood out like a volcano, always active and sometimes bursting fire. Her personality always provided public attraction, something Voronova badly needed. Her conduct shocked the serenity of the quiet waters of Voronova, made waves, and drowned the stagnation that covered the quiet lake.

A valiant woman, a devoted mother, a brave fighter against her enemies, all in all Reyzl was a model woman living up to vibrant new trends, stepping beyond customary concepts of womanhood and motherhood.

Footnotes

1. Ed. Note: The more traditional schooling system

2. Tr. Note: In Erets Israel

[Page 235]

The New Synagogue
(a memorial candle for Reb Tsvi Yitzakh the gabbai[1])

Shimon Levine

Translation by Emma Karabelnik

The old synagogue that had stood for centuries was falling apart, but survived that way for years. The window frames had collapsed, and it was impossible to open a window for some air. The door at the only entrance was rotten and opened only with great effort. And if it opened, it couldn't be closed. Somebody had installed a pulley with a wire and weight block at the end of it. The pulley made the door heavy and difficult to open. But when the door was opened and left alone, the weight rolled down and pulled the door to slam on the lintel with great annoying noise.

Rabbi Luski, beloved by his pasture, decided to ask his followers to help build a new synagogue. First he consulted Tsvi Yitzach Levine, the gabbai, to ensure that his request would be executed. Some say that if it wasn't for Tsvi Yitzach the new synagogue would never have been built. Furthermore, the decision would never have been made, and if it had been made, it would never have been executed

Reb Tsvi Yitzach was childless so he put all his energy into taking care of religious institutions in town. He was short, and as are all energetic people, smart and resourceful. We, the children, loved him because of his good nature, honesty and affection for us, all of us, all the children in town. He couldn't pass by a Voronova child without tweaking a cheek or stroking a head. The worshippers respected him for his religious knowledge and his good manners. He knew about public relations, never got angry, and never hurt anyone, even those from lower classes.

Reb Tsvi Yitzach also knew how to collect and preserve money for the common good. On Rosh Hashana and Yom Kippur eves, and during the Ten Days of Penitence, he used to send *Shana Tova* and *Hatima Tova* greeting cards to the whole community, and on the back of the card he listed all their debts – for being called to read the Torah, for Haftarah readings, for Friday rolling up [of the Torah], for removal and insertion [of the Torah], and all the other mitzva activities. He wrote the numbers in a curly handwriting with percentage signs, until it was almost illegible. Nobody could understand his writing, so on Yom Kippur before the *maariv* prayer each one paid to Tsvi Yitzach personally according to his vague, curly accounting.

And it went on for years, until he collected a large sum of money.

When the construction of a new synagogue was announced publicly, the gabbai had built enough of a reputation to ask for assistance, and the people consented. Each one promised to donate days and to assist in the removal of the old synagogue, and to help to build the new one.

We'll never forget the day of the opening of the new synagogue and reinstatement of the Torah to its new gorgeous residence.

It was in the 20s', and we were all like children who imagined the synagogue as the reincarnated and improved Temple of Jerusalem. The whole town celebrated the event, and the main conductor was Hirsch Itzye.[2] He led the dancing, excited by the great *mitzva*, with his eyes rolled up to the sky – the place of mitzvot and prayers, brotherhood and peace.

At the end of the celebration, the crowd carried him with songs and dances, thanking him for the enthusiasm he had brought to the celebration. That night, neighbors hugged and kissed, enemies made peace, and everybody experienced a communal happiness, a brotherhood between all Voronovers, near and far.

*

Both synagogues were burnt down by the evil hands of regime representatives. They didn't know that by burning two small temples in

Voronova, they would also be burning down trust in their man and their nation, and were sentencing themselves to the elimination of their faith and independence.

The New Synagogue

Footnotes

1. Trans. Note: manager of the synagogue

2. Ed. Note: Hirsch Itzye is another way of saying Tsvi Yitzach

[Page 237]

Died in Israel

[Page 238]

List of Voronova Residents Who Died in Israel

Transliterated by Judy Petersen

Surname	Given name	Remarks
GOLDBERG	Shlomo	Rabbi
GOLDBERG	Rokhl	
KONOPKE	Yehuda	Cantor
KONOPKE	Rokhl	
KONIKHOVSKI	Gotlieb	
KONIKHOVSKI	Henya-Chava	
KONIKHOVSKI	Eliezer	
LEVINE	Malka	
HERTZ	Taubeh	
GOREN (GRODZENCHIK)	Shabtai	

GOL	Reuven	
GURVITS	Yakov	
PUPKO	Shlomo	
COHEN	Yitzchak	son of Yocheved; fell in defense of the country
DVILIANSKI	Yosef	
POZ	Masha	
KALMANOVITSH	Alta	
SHOMRONI	Yehoshua	
KUZNETZ	Matisyahu	
KAPLAN	Avraham	
MOLTSADSKI	Moshe	
BLOCH	Yehudit	
HERTZ (LEVINE)	Osnat	
DUKSHTULSKI	Binyamin	died outside of Israel on the day the book was printed.

[Page 239]

Eulogies For Those I Lament

S. Aviel

Translation by Emma Karabelnik

Shabtai Goren (Grodzenchik) *Of Blessed Memory*

Shabtai was gone at an early age. His death was a hard blow for all of us, maybe because we loved and admired him so much, or maybe because we were so young and couldn't cope with a friend's death who was of the same age as us, and who was a good friend with us the all the way since early childhood until that time, and whose soul was bound to our souls with unbreakable knots.

Shabtai was a typical Voronova man. This small and lovely town surrounded by forests and springs was a wonderful place settled by Jews and the Spirit of God, the Jewish Bible, and a longing for the Sacred Land and Jerusalem. Shabtai grew up in this fragrant spiritual atmosphere, absorbing the good spirit of a Jewish education –

in *cheder*, in school, in high school and later in *yeshiva*.

In the 20s, with the revival of Zionism, he was also awakened with a special enthusiasm. He founded Zionist institutions and organized all the youth. He agitated, took action, and drew many to Zionist-*Halutz* activities, to training, and to *Aliyah*. He was one of the first founders of *HaShomer HaTsair* in town and stood out as one of the activists devoted to the idea of an Eretz Israel tied to labor. After *Aliyah* he planted roots in socialist organizations in Jerusalem. He was member of *Hagana* and was always ready to respond to any call. During World War II he responded to the call and joined the British army. After the discoveries of the Jewish community's destruction in Europe and the liquidation of all our loved ones, he networked survivors and was always one of the organizers and speakers at Memorial ceremonies.

It was always a pleasure to be around and spend time with him. From early childhood until his last days in exile and in Israel we were always connected by strong ties of love and friendship. We all admired his joyfulness and constant optimism, his radiant face and sparkling eyes, his love of others, his devotion and loyalty to friends. His good spirits infected us with love, hope, faith and magic. Since early youth he had this effect on others.

I remember Shabtai during training, while working in a plywood factory. Nobody could compare to him as a hard worker, rolling beams from the huge pile to the steam cellar. The Ukrainian workers who worked with him called him the "Palestinian Hero". He always worked hard without complaint or comparisons to others, always in a good mood which affected all who worked with him.

He was loved by everyone. We loved him with pure heart and soul. With great pain and sorrow, we escorted him to his eternal rest. He left an open wound in the hearts of many of his friends. His memory will stay with us forever.

Reuven Gol *Of Blessed Memory*

He was a young, joyful, and vibrant youth. When he escaped from Polish police he traveled to Cuba, which at that time had opened its gates to young people from all over the world. Yet, Reuven Gol, who was raised on the Zionist ideal, didn't conform to settling down in another *Galuth* [Ed. Note: Exile], although he did very well in Cuba. Reuven did everything to maintain his ties with the Zionist movement and its vision. He joined the Zionist movement and *HeKhalutz* in Havana. He wrapped up his business in Havana, acquired a certificate, and made *Aliyah*. After *Aliyah* he moved to Jerusalem, found a job, raised a family and found peace for his soul.

Reuven loved Israel with all his soul, Israel and all its residents. He was always joyful, content, hopeful, and energetic, active and devoted to *Hagana*. During the events of 1929 he participated in the defense of Jerusalem, and did so for every cause at any time.

He became a victim to malignant disease. He left us in the middle establishing our organization, and he'll always be a part of it. His loss left a hole in our society. He will always be missed.

Blessed be his memory.

Yakov Gurvits *Of Blessed Memory*

Since an early age he was raised in prosperity and wealth. He never knew want and was always happy, friendly, and in good spirits. In the 20s with the revival of Zionism and activities by the youth, he never joined any faction or movement. He used to say: I love everyone, so how can I choose whom to join? We loved and respected him. We excused his somewhat mischievous attitude and never demanded serious action from him.

In time, he left the prosperous house of his parents and made *Aliyah*. He experienced a drastic change in all aspects of his life. We simply didn't recognize him. He became serious and now devoted himself to work, defense, and creativity. For years he took any job no matter how hard it was. After his marriage he continued to work hard and live in poor conditions (one room) but he never complained. He was happy with what he had and never said that this country was too small for him.

During the dangerous years he enlisted and helped as much as he could, with loyalty and devotion.

After the establishment of the State of Israel he worked in the military industry and was a great success. He was appointed foreman and performed his job with great devotion. He was loved by all, the workers and his superiors. He managed to settle in a residential area of Kiryat-Shalom and later moved to a larger apartment in Givataim.

He loved us, his fellows from the old town, with all his soul. He devoted all his warmth and spare time to us. Saturdays were devoted to visits with landsmen. After he finally reached his peace and prosperity, he got was struck by heart failure, from which he never recovered.

The union and his friends will miss him and his solid friendship. T.N.Ts.B.Kh [Tr. Note: may his soul be bound up in the bond of life]

Yosef Dvilianski *Of Blessed Memory*

Pioneer, laborer, movement member in full heart and devotion. That was dear Yosef, a devoted friend to everyone he knew since childhood. His house was always open, everyone welcomed with joy and warm-heartedness – whether a friend, an acquaintance, or just someone he knew. He was always ready to help out, and when he succeeded in such an effort he was the happiest man. Yosef was known for his hospitality. Most of us will never forget him and his wife Rokhl, *l'chaim.* We will never forget their house and their bountiful table during times of poverty and shortage. He was a man of hard work, never afraid of any job – bricks, blocks, and any other hard labor. For many years he worked in a bakery near the hot oven, always with a big smile on his face. He was always happy with what he had, although he lived a hard and poor life. His miserable shack was always warm and clean, filled with light and the joy of life. Many of us found peace and quiet in his home, always with a hot meal, a glass of tea, and comforting talk. He never complained that his place was too small. That's why people were attracted to him. He never complained, always loved his country, his neighborhood, and his numerous friends. He became happiest when he finally moved to a new spacious neighborhood, surrounded by a fruit and vegetable garden and flowers. When he worked his garden, it was as if the Holy Spirit had settled upon him.

He was a man of culture and he did a lot to implant literature when it was still in abeyance.

Yosef was one of the founders of the Voronova library containing thousands of books, and continued this tradition all his life. In Newe-Kibush in Petah Tikwa he was known for his knowledge and activity in the field of literature.

Lately, when he became exhausted of hard labor, he was hired at the Workers' council in Petah Tikwa. He was given many responsibilities, including being in charge of housing. He performed all his responsibilities with endless devotion and happiness, everybody loved and respected him. Lately he became ill with a malignant disease which put an end to all his hopes and aspirations.

He didn't have the privilege of seeing this book, which was so important to him. He was taken from us while still in full strength and energy, and now he is gone. His death created wide circles of mourning, and his funeral was a presentation of love and respect felt by many. Many people from the town [Tr. Note: Petah Tikwa] and from outside participated in his funeral. The police had to close public transportation in town to let through hundreds of vehicles carrying his friends and relatives. May the memory of the righteous be a blessing

Yehoshua Shomroni *Of Blessed Memory*

The setting for Yehoshua's growth and development was Voronova.

This small town, a piece of beauty surrounded by forests and green fields, grain and wild flowers of all colors, springs flowing into a lake in the middle of a forest like in ancient dreams. This town infused his spirit and enriched his soul with a variety of feelings and emotions.

Yehoshua was a gentle youngster, sensitive to the surrounding world and its people.

His warm heart and enthusiastic soul characterized him from childhood, and he dedicated himself to service of society. He took upon himself public service in any field. He was one of the managers of our famous library, participated in drama studio, was a member of the Zionist union, was active in K.K.L. [Tr. Note. Jewish National Fund], and was one of the founders of the *HaShomer HaTsair* nest. His life and energy were dedicated to this movement. After the first founders of the movement made *Aliyah*, he took upon himself the burden of the nest's existence, dedicating day and night to its activity.

He was tall and handsome, with a black curly mane covering his head and pretty face. He had dreamy, smiling eyes, and he always drew attention. His greatest dream was to learn Hebrew and to make *Aliyah*.

With time he met Doba, a teacher at the Tarbut school in Voronova. Their hearts met and fell in love, and together they fulfilled their dream of making *Aliyah*.

They built a gorgeous house in *Ein Ganim* in *Petah Tikwa*, a house filled with Hebrew culture which inspired the whole surrounding. They created an enviable cultural society. They educated their children to Torah, labor and good deeds, to grace, glory and beauty and they took a lot of pride in them.

As a member of our committee, he was dedicated to his work, especially after the Shoah. He was in charge of all meetings and memorial ceremonies—one cannot imagine them without him. He dedicated time to the writing of this memory book, and despite his illness he was active and ran around organizing and planning. He was impatiently waiting for the book to be published.

One day his medical condition worsened and he was hospitalized. We were very worried and we prayed for his recovery. After some time he was released home, and we were hopeful that he'd get better. But our shock was huge when we suddenly found out that the man was gone.

Matisyahu Kuznets *Of Blessed Memory*

And again we received tragic and awful news that Matisyahu, best and warmest friend, adored and loved by everyone, was gone. Only a few days ago we were so happy that his condition had improved and he'd soon be with us. Matisyahu was an institution in the eyes of our friends, a symbol of friendship, comradeship, loyalty and devotion, an enthusiast and a sensitive man. He was so in his youth, in the movement and HaShomer HaTsair nest, and it didn't change to his last days of life.

We called his home in Haifa: the Masada 48 Hotel [Tr. Note: after the street address] because Matisyahu was a man of unseen hospitality. He lived his social life with all his heart and devotion, happy and grieving with others. Everybody who visited their home knew they'd find a warm and joyful household, arms open wide and a nice talk.

Matisyahu loved Israel with all his heart. After the Liberation War he was the happiest of all. After the 6-Day War his happiness was endless:

'Look what we lived to see' – he said – 'we are the happiest of all recent generations: Jerusalem is ours, Judea and Samaria. Eretz Israel belongs to us, we have everything. It's a pity that our parents, brothers and sisters have perished in Shoah and didn't live to see all this.'

Matisyahu was a member of Voronova community association committee in Israel. He was a constant participant in memorial ceremonies. Lately, when he was severely ill, his family members asked him to spare himself and to skip the long ride to Petah Tikwa, but he never listened. He came despite not feeling well, said goodbye to everyone, and left. And we didn't know that it would be our last goodbye.

His dream was to see the Voronova Book published, but who could know, and who could guess that his picture would appear on one of the pages in a black frame.

With his death, one of the typical folk figures of Voronova was gone, and it's a great pity. Blessed may his memory be.

Malkeh Levine *Of Blessed Memory*

At a very young age, in her best years, she became a widow and was left with 6 children. She gathered the whole family to discuss the future and it was decided that Asnat would move to Israel, son Arke would take over the wagon left by his father, and all the rest will adjust to life as orphans.

In those days there were several sewing workshops in town, which provided men and women clothing and sold wholesale to merchants from big cities. Malkeh sent her sons and daughters to learn the sewing trade in the workshop of Binyamin Levine, and that had an unexpected outcome. The apprentices joined the tailors union and there they were exposed to the new ideas of Marxism and the World of the Future. Malkeh's house shortly became the headquarters and secret meeting place of the Communist Party. With time, two of her sons were arrested. One was sentenced to imprisonment and was tortured; he became sick with tuberculosis. The other escaped to Russia, was arrested there, and sent to Siberia. Since then nobody has ever heard anything more about him.

Asnat, the eldest, who made *Aliyah* to Yavniel [Tr. Note: a town in Israel] immediately became a devoted pioneer. She didn't forget her family. She managed to arrange certificates for her two sisters Taubeh and Masha, who had meanwhile become disappointed with the World of the Future and made *Aliyah*. Taubeh *OBM* also built her home in Yavniel, and after several years they were joined by their mother Malkeh. Here she was finally content, happy with her daughters who had settled in Israel, and established a new generation of healthy and pretty grandchildren and great-grandchildren. She found her peace and quiet, made connections with local residents, and loved them. Here she was happy and joyful. During the dangerous years she volunteered with *Hagana*, smuggling weapons from town to town, and was even in Naharaim [Tr. Note: today's Jordan]. She did it with the assumption:

'They won't look [for weapons] on an old lady.' [Tr. Note: same sentence appears in Yiddish]

One day while she visiting her daughter in Tel Aviv she felt a weakness. She called her daughter and said:

'You know, I think and I feel that I am out of gas. I am going to father. Notify your sisters of my death, do it quietly and without rush, because Taubeh has two little children— don't scare them.'

Then she closed her eyes and died. It was death by kiss.

[Page 249]

In memory of Yehoshua,[1] Of Blessed Memory

Aharon Karni

Translation by Emma Karabelnik

I go back a long way together with Yehoshua: in the nest,[2] during training, and *aliyah*. His maturity and personality led him to be the leader of the nest. We met frequently at various conventions, sail trips through wilderness areas, and meetings with nests from surrounding towns. We always knew that we had a leader. Due to his personality and natural beauty he stood out above other nests. He was an authority and he ruled with wisdom, responsibility, and dedication— mixed with good humor, cheerfulness and enthusiasm. All this had a great impact on his dynamic development and cultural level.

It was the will of fate that Yehoshua didn't join any *kibbutz* group to do his training and *alyah*. All the others had made *aliyah* long earlier and he remained the Last of the Mohicans. Soon the years passed and he wasn't able to join a young *kibbutz*. What did Yehoshua do? He did his training in his home town of residence. He worked tirelessly in all areas and succeeded at every assignment, in the name of the Zionist-Socialist project. His training was never ending, he missed no activity – if there was a bazaar, he'd run around to collect various objects and art items for the KKL lottery. If it was time for the traditional Zionist prayers of *Simchat Torah*, he was the *gabbai*[3] and the *shamash*.[4] On the next day of Shmini Atzeret[5] he went from house to house to collect the "Ata hereta"[6] vows. If there was someone who went through *aliyah* difficulties, there was Yehoshua. Few knew what was happening to him during what was probably the most critical period of his life. After he was disconnected from everything, burnt all the bridges, and the soil slipped under his feet, still he saw no other option or alternative for himself. Yehoshua was very modest when it came to himself, never bothered, asked, or forced others. He was too ashamed. He kept his pain to himself carrying it in his heart. His yearning for *Erets Israel* was so strong that he couldn't think of *aliyah* without desperation and worry. The fact that he didn't receive an *aliyah* permit depressed him. It was too much for him to wait another year of anticipation and inactivity until some more certificates would be granted. I remember we once sat in the room of teacher Tova (his wife) and had an idle chat. As soon as the topic of *aliyah* came up I saw Yehoshua's spirit fall. He had to make *aliyah* or his world would fall apart. We took the initiative and he was saved.

He received his *aliyah* certificate, and when I made *aliyah* we parted with a blessing:

See you soon in the *Erets Israel* of the workers. After seven to eight months we met in Petah–Tikva. Yehoshua looked radiant. He rehabilitated himself in this town and his spirit was high again. Later on, he and his wife Tova built their home in Israel.

With his death, our small company lost heart and mourned our leader, because he was our heart and spirit and we'll always remember him thus.

Translator's and Editor's Footnotes:

1. Ed. Note: This article refers to Yehoshua Shomroni, whose surname is never mentioned in the article.

2. Ed. Note: In this context, nest refers to the local chapter of the HaShomer HaTsair.

3. Ed. Note: Person who assists the rabbi in running the synagogue, often involved with the synagogue's finances

4. Ed. Note: Person who assists the rabbi in running the synagogue

5. Trans. Note: The last day of Sukkot.

6. Trans. Note: Literally: "You showed us" vows

[Page 250]

My Father Matisyahu, Of Blessed Memory
(Born in Voronova to Nachum and Sheine on March 1, 1909, died on August 4, 1970)

Prof. Moshe Kuznets

Translation by Emma Karabelnik

Father was a man of amazing virtues: a proud man with a lot of knowledge, a religious Jew, a devoted and loving husband and father, a generous host, a sensitive artist, a joyful and honest man, a man of labor, books and order.

Love of work, love of books, and love of order are marvelous attributes which we inherited from our father on our independent paths. Above all, his integrity and his good nature made him very popular man. He was loved by his family, popular in his home town Voronova in Poland, and respected by his neighbors and friends at work. His warm personality will remain forever in the hearts of all those who knew him.

Since childhood I have always proud of my father's laboriousness and he taught me to appreciate everything that he gave me through his hard work. Father always tried to do a perfect job.

Father left behind diaries and notes that he wrote to himself. Due to his love to order, many details and documents were preserved which gave us a clear vision of Jewish life, beginning from his hometown, to the elementary school in town, to the "Tarbut" high-school in Lida, training days in *Alkosh* and *Aliyah* to *Erets Israel* on February 20, 1933, and finally through his life in Israel, taking care of his wife Nekhama, may she live long, of my sister Hadassa, and of me and our families. His love and affection towards us aligned him with all parents who know the secret of family unity, and of the children's education, based on affection and encouragement towards a better future, creativity, and hard work.

The notes that my father left behind are in almost perfect order. They tell the story of a meaningful period of time in the town in Poland, about the preparatory events, the training, and *Aliyah*, of the establishment of the Hebrew workers' movement in Israel and its role in the revival of the state of Israel.

In one of father's notes I found the following text: "There is only one holy word in the hearts of Voronovers, *Aliyah*, to our land…our land"

His memory will live forever in our hearts, a memory of love, perfection and devotion to the goals of the era.

[Page 251]

Reb Gottlieb Konikhovski, Of Blessed Memory

S. Aviel

Translation by Emma Karabelnik

Towards the end of 1933 I was surprised to hear that Reb Gottlieb had come to Israel with his wife Khenye–Chava'l. I was surprised because I had known all the Zionists in Voronova and I thought I could predict who'd be brave enough to make *Aliyah* under the hard conditions in Israel at that time. This list would not have included R. Gottlieb in my wildest dreams. He came across the opportunity and he took advantage of it, a brave decision.

He asked me how he to find a job in Israel. I told him to go to *Histadrut*[1] and he replied:

"*Histradrut, zol zein,*[2] *Histadrut*. Where is it, how do I find it? I mean I don't care who gives me work and what it is called. The first smart move is to find work; after work is found everything else will be found. My absorption in *Erets Israel* will be a solid fact. Just let me work."

I was sitting with P. Mishori, who worked in a workers' committee,[3] when suddenly he appeared. When Mishori heard what his professional skills are, he jumped from joy:

"[In Hebrew:] Can you build a railing? [In Yiddish:] A railing? A railing for stairs?"

Reb Gottlieb laughed out:

"[In Yiddish:] A railing? Who? Where? When? [In Hebrew:] Who can't build a railing?"

He didn't know that at that precise moment the construction of the Agricultural Bank building (Agro–Bank) on Allenby street in Tel Aviv had stopped because of the lack of a "reasonable carpenter" who could design the railing for the interior staircase leading to the upper floors.

Mishori was overjoyed. The construction engineer was even happier.

At the end of the conversation between Reb Gottlieb and the engineer it was agreed that he'd be paid 40 agorot per day, exactly twice the average wage of the period.

At the end of the working day, the engineer was satisfied and thanked Reb Gottlieb, to which the latter replied:

"You are satisfied? Very good. But I am not working here anymore, I quit."

He didn't say this in order to bargain for wages. What upset him was the lack of professionalism on the site, the lack of appreciation for talent and skill.

The engineer begged and raised the wage up to 70 agorot, and it seemed that they came to an understanding.

But one day I met Reb Gottlieb walking around Tel Aviv's streets in the middle of the day. I wondered:

"Why is Reb Gottlieb is walking around? Don't you have work?"

"I work, I work. But guess how much they pay me."

I tried to guess. 80? 90?

"[In Yiddish:] Listen to this," he said, "you can't count any higher? 110 piastres." (the money was called agorot, but he still called them piasters)

And thus, with no help of any organization he worked his own way, settled for good in Israel, and set deep and steady roots for a good life.

Reb Gottlieb succeeded in bringing his whole family to Israel, and they are all firmly established here.

During his free hours he used to go out and wander in the streets of little Tel Aviv,[4] which was in his eyes a symbol of big city growth and development. He loved Tel Aviv deeply, and his life there provided for all of his spiritual needs. The city always made him feel content and satisfied— an answer to his loneliness. He enjoyed walking alone the narrow streets with no need for company.

But as much as he was integrated in Israel's life, he didn't succeed in integrating fully into its society since he didn't learn the language. At first he was angry that they had decided to revive a dead language instead of using its living friend. He didn't understand the purpose of this.

"Why Hebrew language, he complained. Yiddish is a language that every Jew understands. It is also respectful, because German is so similar to Yiddish. [In Yiddish:] You see? In Hebrew who, what, when?"

He was upset that he didn't share a language in common with his grandchildren. This made him very annoyed, but with age he understood his mistake and was sorry that he didn't speak the language of his nation. His only consolation was:

"[In Yiddish:] You know, you can get by in Israel with Yiddish. When I address a "strazhnik" (a police officer) in Yiddish, he understands me."

All this didn't affect his joyful and humorous nature. Nothing could destroy his good mood. His pride grew every time he thought about how he had been almost 60 when making *Aliyah*, and till this day he is totally independent. He used to declare:

"[In Yiddish:] I ask you to look. None of your previously rich and powerful made *Aliyah*. They didn't have the courage to come, but I came. Farshteist!"[5]

Then he used to look at his hands, covered with blisters – the source of his subsistence and his future – and it made him happy. To feel young again, he joined a group of young people, and he loved to spend time with them.

When I try to visualize his image, I see a simple Jew, honest, with skillful hands and a wisdom of life, who embraced *Erets Israel* in his own simple manner formed back in his town of Voronova – a town of hard work and a yearning for simple salvation.

Translator's Footnotes:

1. The workers' union
2. Yiddish for 'let it be so'
3. Here the Hebrew initials are given: m.p. for *moetzet poalim*
4. Famous quarter in Northern Tel Aviv
5. 'Understand!'

[Page 258]

Our Shtete'le

[Pages 259-260]

I See You, My Little Town

V. Shomroni, Of Blessed Memory

Translation by Tina Lunson

I see you, my little town, my little Voronove
where I was born and spent my youth.
With you a lovely blossom withered,
with you a blossoming life faded.

> In you, Jews were busy alas,
> but happy and merry-
> laboring Jews –
> shoemakers, leather–cutters,
> carpenters and tailors,
> bakers and shopkeepers,
> tinsmiths and blacksmiths.

There were strong young wagon–drivers,
who rode a life of wandering and gusto;
without their merriment – need I mention –
all was sad, dismal, and empty..

> I see the *beyt–medresh*, I still
> see the shul
> where Shmerl the Elder used
> to kindle the lights.
> Here God's presence made its
> holy display,
> illuminating each Jewish face
> with beams of light.

I see sites of youth and brew
eliciting merry song and noise,
from youth who build a land, a
people and homes
and lighten their heavy sorrow with
profound song.

> I see too workers in unions
> and parties
> who fight for equality of
> Gentile and Jew
> and when the holiday First of
> May arrives
> they hang blood–red banners
> at Velvele the Smith's.

I weep when I recall the library
and the *kheyder*
with their Rokhls, Shleymeles,
Khanneles, and Niomeles.
Where are you now dear Yiddishe
children

Voronove hearts, pure holy little
souls.

[Page 260]

I remember you, Jews of spirit,
soul, heart
from "new town" to the other side of
the bridge.
Summer in jackets, and winter in
fur coats
belting the warmth with a plain
length of rope.

I remember you from songs,
from Vilne Street and the
market,
from houses, from shops,
sacks and with pestle,
in the shul–yard,
Hermanishki, from valley and
hill,
from stream, from forest and
Eishishok Alley..

I remember your acuity, your
driven polemics,
you would debate without stop,
without end,
not about money or pleasure, not
about losses or earnings,
but about the appearance of Ysroel
and over a new rabbi.

I remember you walking
on *shabbes* with long silent steps,
in the alleys, in the forest, by river
and by train
after a heavy–yoked watch, with a
bare–livelihood face,
you'd drive away troubles with
walking and doing.

I see and I long
I weep and I recall
For you Voronove my home
I weep for you in secret.

[Pages 261-263]

Tsimes, Psalms and Medicine

M. Kuznets

Translation by Tina Lunson

I do not need to tell you anything about *tsholent*. Everyone knows that on *shabbes* after returning home from morning prayers at the study house or *shul*, one quickly gets to the *tsholent*, but not everyone knows about eating *tsimes* every *shabbes*; and not everyone fulfills this *mitsveh*. Also, the *Tsimes* is cooked Friday during the day, and placed in the hot tiled oven and only taken out at night a few hours after eating the first feast, coming home from the study house or *shul*, after reciting "Come let us sing" in the evening.

The bath-house in Voronove

On *shabbes* it is a *mitsveh* to eat three large meals, one Friday night, the second as a *shabbes* lunch with *tsholent*, and the third one *shabbes* evening between *minchah* and *maariv*.[1] These are called *shaleshudes*, or the three feasts. When I was a small child I recall I would go to my mother *shabbes* evening and say that I wanted something to eat; she would say to me: "Wait my child, your father will soon be home from *minchah* at the study–house and we will all eat the third feast together." I thought that *shaleshudes* was a certain dish. The *tsimes* had many flavors when we ate it Friday evening still hot, and then drank a hot glass of tea which was poured from the hot pot that stood on the tiled oven in what we used to call the oven niche.

Friday night after eating and singing the *zmiros*[2] some Jews went to the study–house to a group study of *Mishnayos* led by Avreml the Kotler; or a group for *shulkhan Orekh* or *Khay–adom* with the Vilner Rebbi, and there was a group for *Tehilim* and whoever did not go to the study–house found something to study at home. They might look through the *parsha* of the week or recite the entire Song of Songs.

So, then a wonder! Friday night before going to sleep it was a *mitsveh* to eat the *tsimes*. On *shabbes* morning we finished the *tsimes* when it was already cold. And the tea in the niche was also cold. No matter! When there was no tea we drank a cup of cold water. It was the same cold water from the pail that we drank after the *tsholent*, and thank God it never did anyone damage.

After eating the *tsholent* we laid down and slept for a couple of hours. And when we woke up in good health we went to the *beys–medresh* to pray.

But one Friday evening something very tragic happened with the *tsimes*. A good and quiet Jew in Voronove got a little sliver of metal from the cooking pot suddenly stuck in his throat. Many women baked their *tsimes* in round, cast–iron pots, and in trying to get the burned *tsimes* from around the pot someone broke off a little piece of iron from the pot, so that when eating the *tsimes* the shard got stuck in his throat. No one could get it out. They called for the unlicensed doctor from town but he could do nothing to help. He said that the patient should be taken to the hospital in Vilne— there was nothing to be done here. It was late Friday night, there was no automobile or taxi in Voronove, so soon a wagon drawn by a horse was made ready to take him to Vilne, a trip of more than 60 *viorst*,[3] and who knew how long it would be until they dragged into Vilne. Meanwhile there was something that could be done here. In the end, one of our local Jews – who himself would not go to a doctor – said that tea and psalms never hurt anyone and that that could be done right here, they would not have to drive to Vilne, and they should do it soon before it was too late. Rebi Shmerl and Rebi Lipe assembled the regular psalm–reciters and they sat all night in the study house and then in the morning up until time for the morning prayers and they recited the entire "Psalms for Certain Situations" and "Bless, My Soul" and it turned out that their prayers were received in heaven.

When they took the patient to the Vilne Jewish Hospital they found a famous ear–and–throat doctor there and he was successful in extracting the piece of iron from the throat without an operation, and with great joy they brought this popular Voronove Jew home on Saturday night

After that incident everyone was quite careful in eating *tsimes*.

Editor's Footnotes

1. The afternoon and evening prayer services

2. Jewish hymns

3. More than 39 miles

[Pages 264-266]

Little Memories

Yehoshua Shomroni

Translation by Tina Lunson

Pliarke the Gentile made me a Zionist

It was the fifteenth of *Shevet*– a cold, sunny, beautiful winter day. I went out for a while to skate on the pond with several friends from the other shore; I was the only Jew among the gang. My skates were wooden, I had made them myself, and getting them fixed onto my shoes took quite a long time. I had just begun skating when I heard Pliarke Adashke the smithy's son call out to me,

"Shike, your father is calling you!"

In fact, I was waiting that day for my father to return from Vilne, the fifteenth of *Shevet*; I knew that he would be bringing us "*khumeshuser greyts*", "*payers*" from "*Erets–Israel*".

With my half–frozen hands I just managed to untie the snowy laces of the skates and ran as if shot from a gun to the snow–covered sleigh that my father was sitting in and waiting for me. My three curious *shkotsim*[1] ran after me too.

My father handed me a piece of dried fig and a big heap of carob pods, and told me quietly to treat the uncircumcised ones to the fruits. A crack of the whip over the horse and he was off to town to distribute the merchandise that he had brought from Vilne for the shopkeepers.

We all four went into our stable and I gave each of them some figs to try. I gave them the carob on the condition that they would give me back the seeds – the bones of the carob – I wanted to play even–or–odd.

They started gnawing on the hard fruit and I turned aside,

concealing my making a blessing and a *shehekhianu*, and also began eating. Pliarke who was a lot older than Zianke Liamberg's and Viktor Heydul's, started questioning me, "Where does such sweet and delicious fruit grow?"

I explained to him, "They grow in our land, in Palestina, it takes them 70 years until there are blooms on the carob, but there are so many there that goats scramble up the trees and eat them without paying, for free."

Pliarke fixed his two, big blue eyes on me, gave a quick thought and said half questioning and half in wonder, "If this is your land with such fruits then why are you sitting here? Why don't you go there?"

I did not have any answers for him. In order to turn away from that situation I gave them each two more figs and we went back out to the river to skate.

On *shabbes* of that same week, when I went to *shul* with my father I saw a bulletin on the door of the study–house: "Today (tomorrow), *shabbes* after *tsholent*, the messenger from *Erets–Isroel*, Avitkhay, will deliver a living greeting from Palestina. We invite all Voronove youth to come to Alter Trotski's house to hear the messenger."

That same *shabbes* night Ester'ke Musi'e signed me up as a member in the "Freedom and Rebirth" Zionist youth group.

Otherwise[2] the smithy's son was not willing to take me to the *Erets–Isroel* messenger and from him to Zionism.

The Turk, the Well, and the Moon

When they dug a second well in the market square and had to install a winch with a long dunking pole in order to use the well, a sharp disagreement broke out between Itshe Terk and Tsalel the Harness–Maker:

If they installed the pole on the north side it would obstruct Itshe's house and his daughter Leah's shop, but Tsalel maintained that if they installed the pole on the eastern side it would obstruct his Bashele's shop.

It broke out as a war with three fronts: in the market square, in the study house and in the Rov's house. Neither side would give in, and they fought between themselves at every opportunity.

The town regarded the fight passively and felt that Voronove would not be affected: after a little tension–filled time all would come to an end with the well. For now it was an opportunity for various distractions. Each day presented a sensation with its reports from the "front", and there was no authority that could put an end to the unclear situation so as to make a distinction one way or another.

Once on a *shabbes* night, the congregation came out of the study–house into the courtyard looking for a place where they could see the wonder of the new moon and begin to recite the blessing. From all sides came murmuring. Jews were hurrying to one another with commentary and quick recitals of the prayers and blurting out "*sholem–aleykhem*" and "*aleykhem– sholem*" at one another, stepping around to see the moon. Jews bumped into each other and called out 'peace' to one another, and then Itshe the Turk ran at Tsaltsl the Harness–Maker and gave him a slap in the face with a remnant he was holding in his hand and shouted,

"Tsalke you thief, get away from the moon, you scoundrel!"

In the morning the Rov gathered his courage and made his decision:

"Due to the honor of the moon and the trouble to the council they would put a wheel on the well, with chains and a crank, and peace on Isroel."

A Horse with a Rabbinic Act

One rainy day after *sukhes* Chaim Aryeh was driving the *Myadler* Rov[3] and Berl Eliohu's to Eyshishok for a council conference.

The road stretched out before them. Every time a downpour hit their faces, their beards and *peyes*[4] held drops of water like on Friday after the sweat–bath and the *mikveh*. The wheels cut deeply into the softened earth with a monotonous slip–slosh, but as soon as the rain let up a little Chaim Aryeh continued with the story he had begun when they started out. He poured out his heart to the Rov about his neighbor Yudl Dovid–Lipa's, a terrible neighbor, an assassin: "So for example he never ties his horse up, so the horse wanders around all night, goes into my garden and destroys my clover, devastates my *harvania*[5] – what can you do with a neighbor like that? In the end Jews are merciful, how does one come out like this?"

He asked for advice from the Rov and waited for what he would say. A Rov is a son of Torah, where Torah is wisdom, so let us hear. And then his horse stopped and waited too: he stood still and did not move from the spot. He [the Rov] looked at the horse and it seemed that the horse was somewhat correct: there they [both] were in the Tuzginian muds. Who doesn't know about the Tuzginian muds?

Chaim Arye was enraged about Yudl Dovid–Lipe's, and now consumed with this anger, leapt down from the wagon and started to serve the horse with the wooden handle of the whip. But the horse made nothing of it. He stamped his feet, twirled his tail, and did not move.

Now Chaim Aryeh completely lost his mind and screamed, "You vile creature: now you are starting to perform rabbinic tricks too!"

The two respectable Jews could not bear it. The Rov clutched his breast. The mistreatment of the horse so, a kosher animal, poor thing, brought up in him the instinct for kindness to animals. He gave a wink to Berl Eliahu's and both got out of the wagon and went up the hill by foot.

Editor's Footnotes

1. Plural of *shegetz*, a Gentile boy or man

2. That is, 'but for the figs'

3. The Rabbi from Myadl

4. Side–locks

5. Possibly *Rumex thyrsiflorus* (aka 'haraviniets'), a type of sorrel producing usable leaves for soup, or also *Sorbus aucuparia* (aka 'jarzebina'), a type of mountain–ash producing bitter but usable fruit if properly de–bittered.

[Pages 267-269]

To the First *Minyan* with the Cows

M. Kuznets

Translation by Tina Lunson

We – his grandchildren – used to call our grandfather Aba, our Voronove grandfather; people in the town called him Aba the *Midsvedzker*.[1] The Gentiles from the villages around Voronove always used to say about him, "The beer at Aba's is just like sour cream," because for all the years he lived in Voronove he operated a beer business.

I am reminded that as a child of ten, one fine bright early morning in summer I jumped out of bed because I heard someone trumpeting. I quickly got dressed and opened the door to the street. I went outside and I saw from far off on Vilne Street the town shepherd Dovid Leyb the "*bezruk*"[2] coming with several cows and blowing his horn.

My grandfather Aba, who had gotten up long before and milked both of our white cows, opened the stall and let the cows out onto the street, and so did our neighbors who had cows, and then the market and the bridge were full of cows, a whole herd. They disappeared from my eyes through Lida Street, past the New Plan,[3] to the green fields of the new pasture, which the Voronove cow-owners had recently bought from the Voronove prince, Kekhle-Shvanbakh.

Standing there outside I had an opportunity to consider the Jews who always go to the beys-medresh to pray with the first minyan. I see Yankev-Meyshe the shoemaker from the end of Lida Street, with Ayzik the shingle-maker, Itshe-Meyshe the baker, and Neyekh-Eli the carpenter, and Avremele Mashe's the Vilna-Rider; then I see that Yerakhmiel the smith and Itshe the charcoal maker are walking from Hermanishker Lane and Yeshie (Yehoshue) the turner and Shmerlen the shingle-maker from Cantor's Lane. And of those who live on the market square, Avremele the doctor, Neyekh the bar, Groynem the shoemaker, Avremele the butcher, Itshe the Turk, Motl the harness-maker, Nota-Eli the butcher, Dovid Lipe the peddler and Motel Mine-Rive's, who lives near the priest. From Eyshishok Lane come Chaim Zerekh the glazier, and Simkhe the shoemaker. I also see two women as they walk to the first minyan: they are Sore–Mere, Nokhem–Hirsh's wife, and Zelde the harness–maker; each is carrying a thick *Korban–mincha* prayer–book in her hand.[4]

My grandfather Aba takes his *talis* and *t'filin* sack under his armpit and, joined by our neighbor Itshe the *kvash*–maker,[5] they both walk to the *beys–medresh*. I am curious to know who else prays with the first *minyan*. I go after them quietly and I position myself by the Rov's house so I can see who is arriving from the Bath–House Alley: Velvl the *mishandznik*,[6] Efroym the shoemaker, Shepsl the smith (the pancake–maker) and from down the hill come Arye the bath–keeper, Berl the shoemaker, Eliahu the tailor and Yosl Menukhe's. My grandfather tells me that these are the sworn attendees of the first *minyan*.

Then for the second *minyan* – or, as we call it in Voronove the Rov's *minyan* – others come to pray in the beys–medresh: Reuven the circumciser, Avreml the kettle–maker, Hirsh–Itshe the shul trustee, Ayzik the pharmacist, Yosl–Shtisil's, my father Nokhem–Aba's, Betsalel the harness–maker, Yeshaye Nokhem's, Leyzer–Hirsh the tailor, Feivel–Borukh–Aharon's the restaurateur, Nekhemye the shopkeeper and cantor, and other Jews who live near the Rov and of course Efroim the beadle prays in both *minyonim*... For my grandfather, when he returns from praying, his first task is to sweep up the dust and collect the manure. Afterwards he goes into the house, washes his hands and busies himself with organizing the milk. He carries the fresh milk down to the cellar and brings up yesterday's milk – the already–fermented jugs – and makes milk–products from it.

This was his daily work. My grandfather did all the housework in our house. He was a carpenter, a painter, a shoemaker and a tailor. He was healthy all his years and he was famous for never getting sick. Until one time he went to bed sick and never got up again.

May the memory of all these Jews remain dear to us.

Editor's Footnotes

1. The meaning of this word is not yet known.

2. The meaning of this word is not yet known.

3. The 'New Plan' refers to a newer section of the town.

4. This is a prayer book prepared specifically for women.

5. *Kvash* is believed to be either a sour–dough bread or a sour beverage made of rye–bread and malt.

6. This meaning of this word has not yet been found.

[Page 270]

Voronove, Concept of Hospitalty
(in memory of the dear Shelovskis)

Avraham Ginsburg

Translation by Tina Lunson

I am not a Voronover. I first visited Voronove in 1929 and spent several years there and then grew up there.

This was a town of hard–working Jews with an unusual approach to work. In their free time after a hard pursuit of their livelihoods, they worked in their gardens near home, raising vegetables and potatoes to calm their minds.

The young people in Voronove were dynamic, intelligent, and full of the urge for renewal and creativity. They were also known for their hospitality to visitors. When someone came to visit Voronove the youth took him in with warmth and sincerity, and thus there were always visitors in Voronove, both summer and winter. There were always some who needed a warm home and they found it in Voronove, and amidst its youth. Each one lent a hand in whatever way they could.

I must mention a few families to whom I owe a moral debt and record a few words about the families: Meytshik and Yehoshue Shmerkovitsh, Khenekh and Libe Grodzenchik and especially the dear family of Velvl and Sarah Shelovski. Velvl the carpenter was a fine Jew – a hard worker who lived exclusively from his work. Sarah was a very lovely woman who worked and ran the business along with her daughter, a garden and fields, like many of the families in the town did. The four daughters – each more lovely than the next – were productive, creative, and social. Their home was open to all. There were always groups of friends, guests, relatives or acquaintances. The family was noted for the special flavor of their friendliness. And so people were always drawn there. Velvl Shelovski's home was unforgettable, because this was an operational concept.

May the warmth and friendship of that home go from generation to generation, and may we find consolation in everything and in all those who remain from the shtetl Voronove. I will never forget the family Shelovski.

[Page 271]

Let Us Recall

Ahuva Konopke

Translation by Tina Lunson

On the roads between Lida and
Vilne
there are fields and forests of
green;
among them, as though sprung
from the dew
are little towns of Jews full of
sacred beauty.

Little towns of Jews, alive with cheer,
with joys and sorrows as God has ordained.
There by the river, near to the wood,
our town stood for generations long.

Streets and lanes crossed and branched,
a *shul*, a *beys–medresh*, a cemetery on the side,
a one–story house, a porch on the ground,
and alongside, a path to the garden and stall.

In the market square a church with ringing bells.
Down the lanes, the palace, the *shabbes* stroll,
a little train station by the forest, by the wood;
maybe it will bring news... we await its arrival...

A wedding in town is a wedding for all.
Everyone comes, making bride and groom happy.

No invitation needed, who asks the in–laws,
we are one here, no fools among us.

> Once the couple is paired there'll be children,
> Jews who will share in our joy and pain.
> So was Voronove a shtetl – one – family
> here each shared a fate, for better or worse.

Suddenly winds blazed around her,
uprooting the shtetl, like leveling a field,
we were emptied, hearts rent
lonely ever after, driven from conscience.[1]

> But once a year we are together
> with our dear people, martyrs of Jewish torment,
> asking forgiveness from them,
> our hearts weep a little;
> may we always remember
> each and every one together.

At the common grave of our dear ones

Editor's Footnote

1. The word used is 'gevisn'; in the original text the word is spelled: gimel–ayin–tsvey vovn–yud–samekh–langer nun.

[Pages 273-274]

The Zionist Veteran Nekhemye Shapira

Yehoshua Shomroni, Of Blessed Memory

Translation by Tina Lunson

Ed. Note: This article appears in both Hebrew and Yiddish in the original Yizkor Book. The following is a translation of the Yiddish text. Photos appearing within the Hebrew version are included here.

I met him when the news about the Balfour Declaration reached our town.

I was a *kheyder–yingl*[1] and on a rainy day after *sukkes*, as I was walking through the muddy market place, I saw that near Mr. Nekhemye's house, by the porch, there was a "wheel" of people, old, young and children, a lot of children. On a banner up high on the steeple of the church, where Nekhemye's room was, there was an image that made an impression: Mr. Nekhemye stood at the top on the balcony – in one hand he held a *Telegram* newspaper that Benyamin Levine had brought to him straight from Vilne – and he read in a declamatory voice:

"The English government will support and help to build a national home for the Jewish people in *Erets–Isroel.*"

In his other hand he held Nakhum Sokolov's picture and gesticulated with it to underscore what should be emphasized as he read, "The English government", etc., the greatest power in the world, the dominators of Asia, would support, would help. Nu!

With that he turned to us children and said, "Go home and say "*shehecheyanu*".[2] It is your celebration, because this miracle has happened in your generation. The "dawn of Redemption" is beginning in your time.

At the time I was studying *khumesh mit rashe*[3] with the Eyshishok Rov[4] and I knew about the departure from Egypt. Looking at Reb Nekhemye as he spoke down from the heights of the balcony I imagined *Meyshe Rabeynu.*[5] The *Meyshe Rabeynu* of our time gave his people to comprehend the greatness of the moment. In my childish heart something that was not yet completely clear to me began to develop.

Later when Zionism began to grow wide and deep in our town, with all its currents and levels, Reb Nekhemye Shapira was the chief representative for the General Zionists Organization, he presided at the top of the Hebrew Torah as patriarch of the Pioneer organizations and chaired all the meetings which dealt with organizational and financial questions.

He himself belonged to the radical Zionists in Poland and had great sympathy for the working–wing in Israel and for the '*Zionizmus*', as he called it, with a special passion and magnificence. And that gave a progressive quality to his personality.

He was proud of the fact that Sokolov led a '*tsvisnshrift*'.[6] His home was set up to serve the Zioinist movement and with special satisfaction he reported the actions of the bank – which Dr. Hertzl had founded – and thus he knew where to invest his own money.

Despite his age he was always ready to step up with a speech in the *beys–medresh* or with a talk in a salon, and to go door–to–door collecting money for every Zionist cause, and on *erev yom–kippur* he used to dress in his holiday clothes and sit by the donation plate for *Keren Hayesod* and *Keren Kayemes l'Isroel*.[7]

When Zionism suffered defeats in the 1920s and all the enemies of Isroel rejoiced about it, he was the only brave soul who consoled and encouraged everyone: "These are the sufferings before the redemption," he used to say, "but good for us, we have the merit, that after the suffering will come the redemption."

And we were consoled.

Reb Nekhemye was so certain of the idea of redemption that in the very worst times in the land, when Arab bands were rebelling against the support of "their" [the Jews'] England, he sent his youngest daughter to *Erets Isroel*.

His belief in Zionism comprised the long view also: the elements of prophecy and vision. Without such visionaries as Nekhemye Shapira, Zionism would never have survived its set–backs and perhaps not have come to fruition.

In any case, Zionism would not have existed in Voronove without Reb Nekhemye.

We have much to thank him for.

Editor's Footnotes

1. A school boy.

2. A prayer to commemorate special occasions.

3. The Pentateuch with Rashi's commentaries.

4. The Rabbi from Eyshishok.

5. Moses, our Rabbi

6. The precise meaning of this word is not yet known. It appears to be a compound word made up of the words 'visn' (knowledge) and shrift (writing), suggesting a type of informative text or briefing.

7. United Israel Appeal and Jewish National Fund

[Pages 275-278]

Memories, Types, and Victims

R. Gol, Of Blessed Memory

Translation by Tina Lunson

My father, a criminal expert

In 1918, when the Germans left Voronove, they created a situation without a regime in the town and we had to create a regime in the town ourselves. We organized a self-defense group of Jews and non-Jews.

The self-help group consisted of the Jews Aryeh Gurvits, Nokhem Kuznets, Avrom Elye Dvilianski, and Yekhezkel Puziriski; and of the Gentiles the priest Novakanski, also a kind of Jew. "Chaim Tcharny" conducted the militaristic part.

We set as a goal the protection of the shtetl from bands, thieves, and robbers, so members had to be armed and each had to present his arms. I for example had two pistols and thousands of bullets.

I remember one winter night a band of Gentiles attacked Shmuel-Hirsh at the end of the town and took some possessions from him. There was a tumult early in the morning; soon experts were investigating and found the thieves. Among them [the investigators] was my father. He knew all the Gentiles in the area, so while the experts talked, he bent down and pondered. He studied the snow and said, "According to the footprints there was a lame Gentile among them; that must be Fiferke from *Trikele Dayneve*.[1] We should go to him."

They quickly assembled 40 armed men and went off for Fiferke in *Trikele Dayneve*. The group encircled the village. Someone went in to the lame Fifirke's house and he was sleeping; when they woke him up he tried to run away but could not get out. Through Fifirke they found all the stolen goods and his collaborators.

Polish Nazism is Older than the German One

(In memory of Yitzach Olkenitski and Moshe Zhabinski)

The times that I remember he was known as Ayzik "*der Staroste*". He was the *Staroste* of the town for Tsar Nikolay, a kind of nominal mayor. During the German occupation they also relied on him as the town manager. So he was the eternal candidate for post of mayor of the town.

He was a tall man, with broad shoulders, a beautiful big beard, always with a big smile on his face, and the impression of a clever *Talmud* expert shone out from his broad forehead. He was always wise and was also "stuffed" with education.

"Der staroste" – A. Olkenitski,
may God avenge his blood

It was a rarity in those days to have such a smart Jew to defend the Jewish interests with wisdom both for private Jewish matters and for the Jewish council and the town.

He dealt with the local officer of the tsarist regime – whose habit was to find ways to torment the Jews – with his sharp mind and wisdom, so that he [the tsarist officer] was satisfied with him and had full respect for him and the Jews were never harmed. He rescued Jewish lads from *priziv*, from decades–long military service and he did not spare any effort or money when he had to deal with Jewish discrimination, and so on.

In 1914 under German occupation he was concerned that the town not suffer from hunger even during times when bread was scarce. Thanks to him the distribution was honest, without differentiation between rich and poor, Gentile and Jew.

When the World War ended and Poland was in rebellion, in 1919, the [Polish] general called him to the priest's house, started an investigation into crimes that he had not committed and sentenced him to death. Meyshe'ke the brazier was also sentenced to death along with him.

The Polish vandals and ordinary blood–suckers led them all over the town, not far from Vigodke,[2] and brutally murdered them. Polish horse–riders hacked at them with their swords and beheaded them while they were still alive.

Nazism in Poland is older than the German one.

The Jerusalemite

So they called him in our town, perhaps because Rov Mishkuvski also stemmed from Jerusalem.

I do not remember his proper name. He lived with Zisl, down the hill near Shimsl Borekh Aharon's. His wife was called Khenke the braider, because she had an illness and she was always braiding.

This was in 1917, when a new German Commandant name Fliger arrived in the town. Upon his arrival one could see that all the Jews would have to go out to the market square, and the Jerusalemite also had to go. He was very weak and so a very slow walker. When Fliger saw him walking so slowly, he went up behind him and killed him; that happened near the inn at the beginning of the market.

The death march of Jews to the market square began again in 1917.

Hirsh Itsye

The most popular figure in town was Tsvi Levine, which is what we called Hirsh Itsye the trustee. He was the eternal trustee and the town had him to thank for many achievements in the communal religious life for the Voronove Jews.

We young people loved him because of his sincerity and love for us children. He himself was childless, and was drawn to every child in town with love, patience and attention. He always greeted us with a smile and with a pinch on the cheek. But we especially loved him for his sweet, heart–felt singing while he was praying. On the Days of Awe when he prayed at the cantor's desk, his sweet, ringing voice penetrated our souls and permeated our hearts, and even non–religious Jews were touched by his heart–felt praying, his devotions and his *shmone-esres*[3] attracted people to come to the *beys–medresh*; his Lamentations on *tishebov*[4] broke your heart and bound the long days and years to the beys–medresh and to the land and the people. This was his craft. He was not an official, active Zionist, but he planted the bond to Zion with sound and voice and strengthened the sense of belonging to ancient Zion.

In his everyday conduct he could draw people and enchant old and young, observant and free; he was simply loved for his own simplicity, despite the fact that he was deeply educated in Torah, *Talmud* and knowledge, and because of his willingness to serve despite his belonging to a high class in our town hierarchy.

When he became trustee everything was renewed in the life of the town. He had a new *shul* built, he revived the *beys–medresh* so Jews could congregate and have an appropriate place with their Creator; he enlarged the poorhouse so that the poor would have a humane place to spend the night; in his term it was always warm and light in the schools. Where he got money from no one ever knew.

In giving out *aliyes* and honors he did not differentiate between poor and rich and it felt like a democracy with equal attention for every prayerful Voronover.

Who knows how much bad–blood and disputes about honors Reb Hirsh Itshe spared Voronove.

He was a great, attractive personality who drew and inspired people by his own example.

Editor's Footnotes

1. The location of this place has not yet been found.

2. The meaning of this proper noun is yet unknown.

3. Synonym for the Amidah prayer.

4. The 9th of Av: fast–day in memory of the destruction of the ancient temples.

[Pages 279-283]

Direct and Indirect Paths to Zionism

Reuven Gol, Of Blessed Memory

Translation by Tina Lunson

On the road between Vilne and Lida, by the line between the green meadow and the sky-high pine forests, lay my shtetl Voronove.

The entire town was stretched out along one long street, with the market square and the church in the middle, so, we called the length of street on the Vilne side, up to the market, the Vilner Street, and the opposite on the other end toward Lida – Lider Street.

Voronove was considered a cultural town more than any of the other towns around. Already before the First World War there was a drama club, a kind of voluntary troupe that presented plays, and a rich library, which in those days was a rare phenomenon.

In 1910 to 1914 there were already Zionists who had ties to the Russian General Zionists movement; in tsarist Russia, Zionism was covert, but that did not weaken the devoted Zionists like Nekhemye Shapira, Yosef Shmerkovitsh (Shtisl's) and Zev Shelovski (the Turk's). When they despaired of the older folks they sought inroads to press the youth, to revive a spark in them, an impulse for improvement. They were successful with small measures and limited opportunities in fanning a flame in us and a passion for all that is connected to *Erets-Yisroel*. They infiltrated the teacher Miller's *kheyder*, brought us Hebrew books, Hebrew songs, and we swallowed the songs like a sweet drink. Miller himself was a Zionist and we spent hours with him, singing songs like: 'If I Forget You, Jerusalem'[1], 'To Zion Carry Flags and Banners'Hebrew songs, and we swallowed the songs like a sweet drink. Miller himself was a Zionist and we spent hours with him, singing songs like: 'If I Forget You, Jerusalem'[2], 'The Zionist Oath'Hebrew songs, and we swallowed the songs like a sweet drink. Miller himself was a Zionist and we spent hours with him, singing songs like: 'If I Forget You, Jerusalem'[3], 'We Raise our Hands to the East and Swear'Hebrew songs, and we swallowed the songs like a sweet drink. Miller himself was a Zionist and we spent hours with him, singing songs like: 'If I Forget You, Jerusalem'[4], 'In the Plow is Happiness and Blessing'Hebrew songs, and we swallowed the songs like a sweet drink. Miller himself was a Zionist and we spent hours with him, singing songs like: 'If I Forget You, Jerusalem'[5], and other songs.

Kherut v'tkhiya – 1924

Everything was disrupted during the First World War. People fled from the town. With the rise of the Polish government all the Zionist leaders were soon seeking support in the periphery and vice versa. That was especially so for those who stood at the apex of Zionist activity. This was the beginning of political and material Zionism on the one side and financial activity on the other, in search of ways out to the larger world.

Then came the Balfour Declaration. We understood that the time had come to create a new Zionist organization.

We got in contact with Vilne, and speakers came. We organized ourselves, we revived the dramatic circle, we played theater, and the money furthered the *Keren-kayemet* and the library. We also created a youth organization *"Kherut v'tkhiya"*. We had gatherings and speeches, and created evening courses. Evenings became full of activity and study.

One hot summer day in 1920, there arrived from Vilne a young man in a white hat with a blue ribbon who was seeking ways to reach young people between 13 and 18 years of age. It appeared that he was himself from Eyshishok and knew half the town. He had studied in Vilne, and I think his name was Shaul Kalika, the later famous Hebrew researcher and lexicographer. He spoke with Esther'ke Olkenitski (Mushe's), with Khanneke Weiner, and Yenkele Trotski, and then they came to me. Everything was ready but there was one difficulty: Where could we meet where the parents would not disturb us? They thought it would not be easy because Zionism was something untouchable for the elders and we had to work illegally. The task was given to me, Ruvke, Alter the butcher's son.

I called for Chaim Meyshe'ke Kaplan (son of Yankl the Pipe Maker) and Leyb'ke Kaplan (of the Alekuts). We went off to the women's shul, broke open the door, and the news spread secretly by word of mouth. Some 30 people gathered there. The speaker explained our assignment, everything was clear, but off to the side a sharp discussion had broken out over the unfortunate question, Hebrew or Yiddish. The chief opponents of Hebrew totaled three members: Yosef Dvilianski, Frum'ke Bykhvit (Alte Rede's) and Lea'ke Rubinovitsh (Neyekh Eliye the carpenter's). It was a miracle that the majority won and we decided to speak Hebrew.

Taken onto the council were Gitl Mishkuvski (the Rov's daughter), Ester'ke Olkenitski, Khenke Weiner, Rueven Gol, Yankl Trotski, Yisroel Virshudski and Shuel Gurvits.

We took a room at Alter Trotski's for a site. In order to attract the youth in its majority we decided to create a recreational and sport place. We began with a swing and someone asked where to hang the swing – that is, where will the recreational place be? Suddenly I was at the center of the creation of the sport-direction and [finding] a location was placed on me. The point was where to get a place?

And then the point of our secrecy was raised, and [our] illegality. The search was on for roundabout ways to Zionism and for Zionism.

I went off to the Voronove court of the prince and let him know that I was the son of Alter the butcher, and the prince allowed me to choose a place. It was at the end of town, near the Christian cemetery. He even allowed me to use some trees for the sports equipment. In two days Chiam Meyshe'ki Kaplan and I had prepared everything. Then the council arrived and approved the work.

The youth began to stream to us. We gathered members from the movement for the dramas and that was effective. Youths signed up, the movement's members increased, and we woke Voronove up. Our sports place became the youth center in town and... in the town it caused a hue and cry:

"The youth are being mislead. God help us!" "They are dragging them to the devil knows where!" "What's this all of a sudden with *erets-yisroel* and other foolishness."

The chief opponents were Ayzik Berman and Itshe the Turk, and things simmered and fermented. They were against an *"ikhuv hakriah"* in the *beys-medresh*. Two fronts developed on a day that we thought victory would belong to our followers. We had become large, strong, and were growing. We had collected money, played theater, bought books, but the fire of the opponents flamed up more and more. They had a strong complaint:

"It is shabes!"

And the second strong complaint:

"It is boys and girls together! And Jews a silent?"

My father was summoned to the Rov:

"Your son is the chief cause of all this to-do, God help us, and you must take him away, and the thing will fall apart."

They pressed him so long he went to the place with an axe and chopped up and broke everything.

No one stood up against this, certainly not I. If it had been some other Jew who had dared he would not even have come close to the place, but this was my father.

It did not work, though: the structure was built. We could already exist without the sports place. We had 200 books, the newest, most modern, and we had time and youth to read with us and live with us.

The Library Committee– 1924

We were the foundation of the dramatic department and received a large percentage of the sales. The elders tried every time to trick us, but we were too strong. However much money we had coming to us, we got. It happened once that they did not want to honor our agreement. We taught them such a lesson that they promised never to do it again. It was during *sukkot*. We were playing in the town's inn. We ourselves had set up benches of plain board, and the second day of *sukkot*, at night, we were supposed to present the play. In the middle of the holiday we went in and smeared all the benches with pitch. They came in the afternoon to the last rehearsal and saw that, and they gave in completely.

By night we had made it right. We had brought in a Gentile wheelwright. It cost money, but he cleaned up all the benches.

In time we melded with the General Zionist movement and with the elder Zionists of our town. We joined our library with theirs and gave our money to the *Keren-ha'kayemet,* and Zionism generally became a factor in the town.

That is how we had to organize the youth by direct and indirect paths, to set them on the road to *aliyah,* freedom and life assurance.

Our dear, naïve parents: who knows how many more youth from Voronove, your children, might have been saved if not for your naïve belief in miracles.

Editor's Footnotes

1. "Im ashkahech Yerushalaim"

2. "Seu tziona nes vadegel"

3. "Di tzionistishe shvueh"

4. "Mir hoibn di hent to mizrah and shvern"

5. "In der sokkeh iz mazl and broche"

[Pages 284-288]

The Society of Voronove in America
Isidore Dikson

(From the Society's Bulletin)

Translation by Tina Lunson

Sixty-seven years ago a group of Voronover *landslayt* gathered and decided to found a society.

Since the number of Voronover *landslayt* was few, the task was very difficult. They enjoyed meeting with their *landslayt* and did not want to lose that homey comradeship and friendship.

The first meeting was called on October 22, 1904, by Willie Rosenshteyn at 198 Henry Street, New York.

Those who participated in the first meeting and were considered organizers are as follows:

Avram Bernshteyn, Avram Trotski, Max Movelitski, Max Ostrinski, Harry Ostrinski, Harris Dayem, Louis Levine, Phillip Olken, Morris Levine, Sam Zhabinski, Meyer Levine, Avram Drozhets, Sam Volpianski, Ysroel Bhykvit, Jacob Gold, Eli Tsirinski, Hyman Kaminetski.

It is worthwhile to mention that our first chairman was Phillip Dlugin.

Some of them left the state and to our sorrow some of them are no longer among the living, honor their memories.

Years and years hurried by. People went different ways. It was impossible to exist, but we did not want to give up our struggle.

In 1498 [sic] when Israel declared its independence, and we realized that many Voronovers were arriving in Israel and that they waited for our help, we promptly established an "emergency relief" with the help of the Voronover Ladies' Auxiliary and Dikson, as always, served as financial secretary, and threw himself energetically into the work, and helped them with packages, money, clothing. We even managed to bring over a few *landslayt* from Israel and other parts of Europe, concerning ourselves with their clothing and various other things, and now they are established and making a good living.

A party for the Diksons in Israel

Now a Few Words About Isidore Dikson:

Isidore Dikson first joined the Society on August 11, 1914, at the outbreak of the First World War. He was very active in helping *landslayt* on the other side of the ocean. He attempted to found a relief committee and was the Secretary of Relief for many years. He helped send a messenger to Voronove with 22,000 dollars, which went through his hands. A folks-school was organized there, as well as a loan bureau, medical help, and so on. He tried to collect clothing and foodstuffs to send them to Voronove. And here we must give credit to our brother Isidore Dikson for the good and noble work he did for years and years.

On April 28th, 1925, he was elected Protocol Secretary and held that office until 1927.

In 1927 he was elected as Finance Secretary. He held that office for 18 years. He wrote the constitution on February 15, 1930.

He participated in all the activities of the Society.

In the Second World War, when our boys were sent off, the Society decided to ship various packages to them, overseas and in the States. Dikson laid out a world of work to pack the packages and ship them off. Nothing was too hard.

We provide here the picture of our brother Isidore Dikson (Dukshtulski), who is tied heart and soul to everything that has a relationship to our Voronover brothers.

In the span of his 56 years in America Dikson managed to remain connected with Voronovers and solicit help on [their behalf on] many occasions.

We express our appreciation to Isodore Dikson for his monetary support of this *Yisker-Bukh* and his collecting money for that goal.

My Life's Song

Isidore Dikson

Translation by Tina Lunson

> I long for a comfort that once I had.
> In hunger and pain I was sated.
> Solitary in the world I remain,
> an orphan from the age of seven.

I recall like a dream my Mama's singing
the tune still sounds in my ears.
I cannot forget that dearest of tunes,
the lullaby she rocked me to.

"Sleep, my child, my dear little love,
may the Eternal give you long years,
may you rise in the morning in health,
your father and mother will care for you."

Where is the vow you spoke to me,
you have broken your promise completely.
Why are you silent, why don't you answer me now!
You still owe me an answer, your only son!

[Pages 307-318]

Heroism and Destruction

Thanks to Our Child

Moshe Kaplan (with the assistance of Khayeh Kaplan)

Ed. Note: This article appears in both Hebrew and Yiddish in the original Yizkor Book; only the Hebrew version has been translated and published here and may be found at page 79 in this book.

Final Days of Our Town

Keileh Grodzenchik (Shamir)

Ed. Note: This article appears in both Hebrew and Yiddish in the original Yizkor Book; only the Hebrew version has been translated and published here and may be found at page 94 in this book.

In My Own "Partizanka"[1]

Y. Konikhovski

Translation by Emma Karabelnik

Kissing Russian Tanks

In the last years before Nazi occupation, Voronove Jewish [community] suffered from Polish regime, not only religious persecution but also simple hooligan acts and economic restrictions. With the call of "svoy do svege",[2] [new] Polish stores were built, and Poles were forbidden to buy at Jewish shops. The youth was left without a future and looked around for opportunities – which some found in Zionism and some in Communism.

In 1939, when the Russians came to Voronove, the Jews welcomed them as long-awaited relief, the youth kissed the dusty tanks and danced for joy.

I was instantly appointed as leader of a temporary order. I appointed a commandant and organized a mixed Jewish–Lithuanian–Belarussian police. Life changed and took on new organized forms.

Later I was elected representative to the People's Assembly in Bialystok, which was supposed to decide the destiny of occupied Western Belarus. Not surprisingly, after several days of discussions it was decided to unite Western with Eastern Belarus, which belonged to Soviet Russia.

On the next morning, immediately after the vote, the party leaders of Soviet Belarus took over the assembly.

Most of the youth of Voronove were nominated to different managerial posts. Estherke Olkenitski and Yakov Trotski worked at the post office. Tsvi Sokolik, Berke Peysah's, Olkenitski and Konopke worked at the shop co-operative, Konopke in the savings bank, Tsvi Krashanski at the police, Yitzakh Olkenitski in the restaurant, and others in different positions. I became the director of District Social Security (RSB). I had to take care of all the old Polish pensions and determine the new work- and war-pensions. I wanted to avoid such a post, but when I said that I am too weak for such a responsibility, the reply was "ne znayesh nautchim, ne xotchesh zastavim" (if you don't know how we'll teach you, if you don't want we'll force you). So I started a job which I didn't know anything about.

After I hired an inspector and an accountant, I placed an advertisement for several days in the newspaper defining who would be entitled to a pension. I took a course and took care of the needs of the elderly and the veterans. After a while I was criticized at every turn, and I realized that under the Soviet regime you don't have to do a job right, you just need to present good reports in order to protect yourself from the spears of critics. You were evaluated according to your reports. I learned the profession and my reports were so good that I received bonuses and was praised in the newspapers.

First Soviet Pride and Soon Thereafter a Spy

In 1941, with the breakout of the Russian-German war, I was appointed as an assistant for recruiting men to the Red Army. We worked in the palace. After a few hours of work we were already told that the Germans were already in the town. We walked out through doors and the windows and ran to the nearest forest. From there we went on heading East by foot. On the way we ran into a Soviet military unit. After long negotiations we were attached to a military squad, and were equipped with grenades, and were ordered to hide near the forest road so as to throw grenades when the German tanks passed by.

We heard the noise of the tanks. The earth was trembling under their heavy pace. The commander ordered:

"Ready! Wait for the "fire" command!"

Meanwhile the tanks are approaching. They go by me— the first, the second. I lie alone and don't know what to do. Then comes the order:

"Ogon" (fire)

I threw my grenade and the shooting starts— a war. We managed to stop them. They ran away and left behind several burning tanks. The commander was proud of us. He ordered an assembly, congratulated us, and said:

"That's how we'll chase them to Berlin. I am proud of you. We'll teach them how to fight."

But shortly after, a big enforcement of German tanks arrived and they taught us "how to fight".

We ran away as mice, everyone in a different direction. I, along with others from the Voronove Military Office, among them I think was Tsvi Krashanski, ran on the road to Lipnishok. There we met the Russian military. They thought we were spies and arrested us immediately. Our guard was severe, with guns pointed at us. We were forbidden to exchange a word. In the end they took us deep into the forest where we were kept for long hours until the order came: "to prosecutor".

We imagined different scenarios of Russian "processes" and we felt frost in our veins. Who knew what they would do to us here? Meanwhile, someone came to take me to the prosecutor. I went under a real investigation. He asked me different questions as if were a spy. I explained to him that we are escaping from the Germans. I showed him my round stamp and he didn't believe me:

"My vas znayem;" (we know you); you are gifted in everything (he means Jews).

And throws this to another one there:

"Otpravit!" (send away)

Who knows where? Maybe Siberia, maybe Moscow, and open a trial. But I was sure that during wartime they would finish us off without "process".

After making long various inquiries the prosecutor proclaims an order:

"Osvobodit!" (release)

And he says to us: Immediately report to nearest enlistment office.

My Ideological Friends – Bandits [and] Murderers

We decided to go to Ivia and look there for an enlistment office. But the Germans were already there. We continued to Lubtsch. There we discovered an awful scene. The town was settled with Gentiles from surrounding villages, and they were destroying and ripping off everything on their way; before them, others had packed and shipped away Jewish possessions and goods. This was awful for me because I recognized among the robbers some of my ideological comrades, with whom not long ago I had collaborated and strived for a common better future. Here is comrade Leikavitsh, a Gentile with whom I was in the same cell. And here is Abramchik, the quiet philosopher, and others. I thought it was a dark dream, but it wasn't a dream, it was a dark reality.

Jews were powerless, locked in their houses, and there was no one from whom to ask for a drop of water.

We went on further. The roads were crowded. Thousands of Jew walking, running, no one knew where. My legs refused to serve me. I had seen with my own eyes what had happened in Lubtsch and I didn't know where to run.

Thus we ended up in Minsk, but the Germans had arrived there before us so we had to go back. We had to pass through the Koidenav (Dzerzhinski) railway station, and this was impossible because it was covered with human bones and torn bodies. On the telephone cables were hanging human body parts; bodies that were still alive were laying about calling for help. Some [were] exhausted and asked for a bit of water. From under the ruins, crushed bodies cried for help. Those who were still alive were so helpless that the Germans came and captured us all.

I Escape from the German Horror

They took us to a field at a distance, put us in pits, and guarded us hard. We asked each other with our eyes: what will they do with us. The fear was great, we were hungry and exhausted. Suddenly one German asks who among us speaks German. Nobody replied so he asked:

"Who is a Jew here?"

They pointed at me. He called me. I go. When I approached him he asked who I am. I replied, a Jew. He kicked me with his foot several times and said:

"A dirty Jew."

Thus [it happened] several times. When I didn't want to answer, he would beat me with his whip until I fell down into the pit, powerless, and then he would leave me alone.

He conducted himself like this with other victims until nightfall.

Then I came up with the thought of running away as soon as possible. There was anyway nothing to lose. I talked with several guys and also with Tsvi Krashansky from down the road, and we ran away.

But not everybody succeeded. The Germans noticed and I was

suddenly alone.

I ran by myself through the big night until tired and dehydrated I fell down and fell asleep somewhere in a field.

They found me asleep and took me to Shtolptse.[3] All those arrested were kept in a mill where they organized a camp. Man on top of man without food. After three days I managed to reach the pot, but I didn't have a dish for the thin soup so I took it in a hat and drank whatever was left.

A Month of Shivering in a Voronove Attic

I decided again to escape. I walked away through the fields, far from the roads, and came to Ivia. I met acquaintances. I heard what the German murderers were doing to the Jews...but strangely I felt compelled to go back home to see how my wife and child were.

I entered Voronove when nobody would notice me. I asked my aunt Peyshe–Reikhl to take a message to my wife Reishke that I was there. My daughter Biene'le came over. She told me that Shaykeh Olkenitski, Yitzakh Volpianski, Shelovski, Zocharkin,[4] and others, had been arrested yesterday, and that I was also on the list.

I hid in my aunt's attic and stayed there for three months. I used to look out at the street through a crack and see horrible things. Once I saw how they dragged Klareh Mansfeld, beating her all the way. They pushed down Velvl Rothman on the bridge and trampled him with their feet and didn't stop. Yitzakh Olkenitski and other Jews were [forced to] sweep the street near Aunt's house. I was informed of the mass murders in Eshishuk. I realised that the War would not be over for a while, so I decided to leave the attic and the shtetl.

On a dark night, my dearest Reishke and Biene'le came to say goodbye to me and I walked away to Radin. The nights were frightening with various explosions. The thought of leaving my closest ones behind was tearing up my heart. I walked away, couldn't help them, and who knew when we'd see each other again.

The nights were endless. I only wanted to see the light of the day and to know where I was, though the day brought with it perils. Finally after several days I saw the pinpoint of the Radin church. I went first to a home of an acquaintance, but he met me with horror on his face, and told me that he had his own aunt there, and didn't even invite me to sit down. I went to her, she welcomed me warmly, and then I went to the *Yudenrat*[5] to register myself under a false name. I wanted to rest here a bit. Towards the end of the War I received a letter from my Reishke, thru Itskovitsh: they were looking for me in Radin because a Gentile had recognized me. I had to run again.

I Made Myself a "Partizanka"

From Radin, Jews were taken to forced labor in the forest for the whole week and on Fridays were taken back home. I volunteered for this work, but on Friday I would stay in the woods instead of going back. I worked as a forest guard.

Once, the *politzei* came in the middle of the week to take Jews back to Radin. I decided not to go back. I convinced several other Jews; we spent the night in the forest. That night Radin was surrounded by armed beastial–men, the Germans picked out 70+ young Jewish guys, gave them shovels, and drove them to the cemetery outside the town. The guys understood what was going to happen so they decided to attack the Germans with the shovels and stones; they beat them up and fled. Some were killed by the murderers, but most of them were saved. They knew that I was hiding in the woods so they turned to me and proposed to organize a partisan squad.

The first mission was to get armaments. Meanwhile some Radin Jews had joined us with their belongings. We sold them and I managed to buy the first French rifle with several bullets. The Polish policeman who sold us the rifle told us where to obtain more rifles. The new rifles had already been taken by force. In a short time we had several guns and we decided to begin partisan activity against the murderers of our dear wives, children, brothers and parents.

First we went to the Lida–Grodno road and exploded the bridges. Then we blew up and ruined their dairies in the town of Zavlats[6] and in the village of Natsie,[7] which had provided the murderers with butter, cheese and other dairy products.

We had to choose "missions" that would prevent us from encountering heavily armed murderer–Germans, but we didn't want to limit our activities. Thus we took over 120 cows from German shepherds leading them to German battalions in Grodno, which cows had been stolen from Gentiles.

In Vashilishok and Radin we burnt down German food stores that worked for those rulers.

While still few in number and with primitive means, we blew up a train in which according to reports traveled mostly German victims.

I Killed the Murderer of Radin Jews

We were already 27 guys. Not all were armed, but were energetic and strong, and our lives strove for revenge against the murderers. We actually sought out confrontations with small German groups. Once, a released Polish officer informed us that in a village not far away 4 policemen are staying and preparing return. So we decided to attack them and take their arms. We gathered together. We gave each an advance. Not everyone was trained for combat. I was appointed to lead. According to my sign, Yehuda Bonk, a Lithuanian Jew and an ex–military man, had to run out to the road and stop the wagon.

We chose a suitable spot, got close crawling on our bellies, and waited impatiently for our victims, and even more for their guns.

I was shocked when I saw instead of one wagon – several, instead of 4 men – 28–30 Germans, armed from head to toe, and with them *politzei*.[8] They stopped just by us, got off the wagons, and walked straight in our direction with pointed guns. I didn't know what to do. It was clear that we were betrayed and they had seen us. It would have been impossible to attack them; it was too close to run away; it was too stupid to let them through. Momentarily, there was a German standing near me pointing a machine gun at me. It was Obermeister Fried from the Radin ghetto, who was the leader of murderous acts against Radin Jews. I drew the trigger of my rifle and he fell down dead.

But it was also Yehuda Bonk's death verdict. He thought that it was my sign for him and he ran out to the road. He went out and never came back. To our luck, the Germans got frightened and fell flat on the road, so we ran away.

The next morning, Gentiles told that they [the Germans] had laid there for a long time. The German cowards didn't try to go further.

Shlomo Sodovsky's Revenge a Minute Before His Death

Our relationship with the Russian partisans was very bad. They constantly made trouble for their Jewish co–fighters. Later we found out that they were criminals the Russians had brought from Siberian prisons to build barracks, stretch railways, and work fields. When the Russians retreated, they[9] decided to stay in the Polish–Lithuanian forests. They earned their living by robbing and murdering under the disguise of [being] partisans.

But there were also Russian partisans with whom we collaborated closely. Once, looking for a bigger organization in order to join forces, we met a Russian group of ex–Russian officers. They had been imprisoned in an [unknown word][10] of the so–called Third Reich. In their midst were 3 Jews from Vashilishok. We united and a Russian officer became the commander of both groups. Both groups were poor on ammunition, but we managed to execute. One time I had the chance of blowing up a train with a shell, at other time with more primitive means. Not a minute passed without our making plans for revenge and death to the German murderers.

Meanwhile, a large portion of criminals broke off from their groups and formed a partisan squad not far from us in the same forest. We wanted to unite, but a war for leadership broke out and we had to retreat.

Before retreating, one snowy day the Germans captured a brother of one of the partisans. They tortured him to reveal the partisan locations. He brought them close to us and told them to fire a shot— the partisans would go out from their 'zemianki'[11] and the Germans could capture them. But the partisans replied with fire and scattered [them?]. So did the brother [scatter]. We went out to the road again to see what was going on. Some local drivers for the Germans told us everything and also how many Germans were there.

We lay not far from their quarters and when they came near we opened a crossfire and took down 8 corpses with guns. Among us only one was killed, but not from their bullets. He suddenly started running after an escaping German, shot his rifle and screamed:

"This is for you for your murders! What did you have against my brothers and sisters?"

And thus running and screaming, he fell down without breath and died. It was Shlomo Sodovsky from Subotnik.

According to partisan ethics and code it was a very honorable death when a man returns his soul while viewing falling and escaping fearful murderers of his folks and family.

1943 – We are Expanding, I am Decorated

We moved to another forest. There we connected with a pioneer group from the Headquarters of All Partisan Units and organized into one squad, by the name "Kotovski".

The criminal groups were executed the Soviet way and we began our new life. We were sent on big operations. In my eyes those days were the most fulfilling in my entire miserable life. I became a group leader. Everybody praised me. Everybody wanted to go to battle and on "missions" under my leadership, because I was a self–confident and front-line commander. But most important I never lost a man in combat, I didn't allow drinking, and I always knew where my men were. In most difficult situations I always knew where to find each one of them and brought them back to the squad.

But about this on another occasion.

Once, my group was sent to the Drosknik–Aran line to off a train containing German officers traveling back from leave. We were delighted to hear that more than 100 of them were dead and dozens more wounded. On our way back a few guys decided to take some more revenge on a Polish forest guard who had murdered and handed over Jews for profit. He lived not far from the railway station in Aran. We meted out justice to him, but on our way back we received heavy fire. We had to retreat, but I didn't leave one man behind. We carried them on our backs and brought them back to the squad.

Almost that same month I participated in an operation on the Martsishants–Zubrove railway line. We had to blow up a narrow line on which they carried wood from the forests. Heavy combat took place there. The Germans left behind 7 dead and 3 wounded who didn't survive. Among us there was one wounded, Shlomo Kurliantsik, from Aran. At the camp he managed to ask how many of the enemy had died. When we told him – 10, he exclaimed:

"Now it will be easier for me"...and died.

At the end of '43, I was sent to blow up a telephone cable line and telephone posts on the Vilne–Grodne line. I executed the ask with few explosives and with no casualties.

At the same time I blew up a train carrying ammunitions, together with its passengers.

When I came back the commander called me in and decorated me with a high medal, on the order from high command in Moscow (copy of the medal order – see page 331).

We Pick Off the German Murderers

That year our Jewish squad got a special assignment.

There were several Lithuanian villages around Vilne where the Germans had organized groups of locals, armed, and trained them to fight against the partisans. They were mostly after the guns, but even more was the wish to exterminate Jewish partisans. Naturally, for such a mission, they [Russians] sent Jews, and we accepted with joy the mission of picking them off.

I fought in the murderous Lithuanian village of Masteikiai. We surrounded them, captured all their fighters, the so-called "samo-chava" —murderers for money— we killed them all to the last. During this action I met Moshe Kaganovitsh from Ivia.

1943 was for me a year of action and fighting. There were times when we had to move back and forth from Third Reich [territory] to Belarus almost every day. The border patrol was guarding the borders very tightly, according to Hitler's orders, and guarded closely the territory which he wanted to annex to the Third Reich. So each time we had to cross it was with fighting and bravery. Both sides became tired and in one of [those] bloody confrontations we eliminated the patrol. We even obtained official control of the border passage and surrounding area.

Provisions were a complicated issue [and for that] we had a family unit, most of them Jews. Not all [civilian Jews] could bear camp conditions where supplies are so poor and dangerous to obtain. We [partisan] Jews understood and had to act. Thus in addition to all the fighting alongside the Christians we had an additional task: to get food and supplies for the families so they wouldn't die so near to liberation and victory. In one of such combats we lost a good partisan and friend, Tentser, and his blood stained my clothes.

Antisemitism of the Partisans

We expanded day by day. Our Kotovsksi squad grew to be a whole brigade under the name "Leninsky Komsomol", so we received gun supplies from Russia by different ways and means, even from airplanes.

We even started recruiting people from the civil population, but then a bitter anti-semitism broke out among the fighters and later also between the commanders. They were fed up with us. They didn't need us anymore. The orders became anti-Jewish: "To deport part of the Jewish population to the east", etc.

In the forest there were more and more White-Polish partisans-killers which used to attack our groups. They conducted negotiations with Russian partisans to betray Jewish fighters so they [the White-Polish partisans] would stop attacking Russian squads. Once they captured a couple of Russians and demanded for them an exchange of several Jewish guys. Luckily, such decisions had to be made in the [communist] party, and there [in the party] my reputation was very strong due to my clean past and my name as a fighter, a fighter with two official decorations and a list of dozens of Germans killed by me personally. Along with me were several more similar Jewish heroes. Thanks to us they didn't succeed in their latest attempts to destroy the last Jewish survivors. Towards the end, three of us Jews were appointed to official posts wherein we had direct connections with Moscow, and thanks to this miracle we managed to survive until the end.

Again I Saved Myself From Voronove

After the War we came back from the woods. I was appointed chairman of District Social Aid in the town of Ostrin. I did everything to be relocated to Voronove for the same job. Voronove was empty of Jews. From every Jewish window looked out local robbers— Gentiles who ripped off all the Jewish property without opposition.

On one occasion I was traveling with five other friends to Poletskishki, a village 11 km from us, to collect a "zaym", a "folk loan". We stayed for the night in the house of a Gentile, a loyal friend. That night someone clapped the door for me to go out. I understood that those were White–Polish partisans. Our host told me that we were surrounded. I knew that it would be my certain death. I grabbed my revolver, told my friends to take care of themselves, stepped out through a window shooting, and escaped. Together with me escaped a high ranking Gentile and this saved me again. If not, my friends would have said that I was connected to the Poles and I would have had a close meeting with my killed friends.[12]

It became clear to me for the 100th time that there is no life possibility for a Jew among Gentiles. I issued myself a job–trip to Grodne. From there I took a train to Lodz. There I got help from Meir Shamir and I left the cursed Poland forever.

*

After the destruction of Nazism, the grab for all Jewish property and goods, under the cover of a new [world order], was no less a crime.

In Voronove I went thru another kind of tragedy.

Footnotes

1. Ed. Note: Another word for a partisan group.

2. Ed, Note: In the original this phrase is spelled: samekh–tsvey vovn–aleph–yud//daled–aleph//samekh–tsvey vovn–ayen–gimel–ayen. This is a nationalistic slogan which means something like 'every man for himself'.

3. Ed. Note: This place has not yet been positively identified. The spelling in the original text is: shin–tes–aleph–lamed–pey (or fey)–tsadek–ayen.

4. Ed. Note: In the original text the name is spelled: zayen–aleph–khof–aleph–reysh–kuf–yud–nun.

5. Ed. Note: The Jewish administrators for the town.

6. Ed. Note: This place has not yet been positively identified. The spelling in the original text is: zayen–aleph–beyz (or veyz)–lamed–

aleph–langer tsadek.

7. This place has not yet been positively identified. The spelling in the original text is: nun–aleph–tsadek–yud–ayin.

8. Tr. Note: The *politzei* were local collaborators.

9. Ed. Note: That is, the 'criminals' brought by the Russians.

10. Ed. Note: In the original text the word is spelled: pey–reysh–shin–tes–shin–ayen.

11. Ed. Note: Trenches

12. Tr. Note: The meaning of this sentence is unclear.

[Pages 319-331]

An Involuntary Hero

Zalmen Dukshtulski

Translation by Emma Karabelnik

Ed. Note: This article appears in both Hebrew and Yiddish in the original Yizkor Book. The following is a translation of the Yiddish text. Photos appearing within the Hebrew version are included here.

From Vilne to Voronove on a Thorny Road

When the war between Russia and the Nazis started in June 1941, I was in Vilne. The Lithuanians knew that war was near. They took advantage of the negligence of the Russians, their aggressors, and slaughtered all of them until the last. The Lithuanian army had a significant part in it.

The Germans entered Vilne on June 26, 1941. I sensed the bitter taste of their regime and immediately started to arrange my escape. On the day they arrived I was not there anymore. I traveled to Biale Voki[1] and from there to Voronove.

In Biale Voki they were digging peat for the Polish regime. The Germans exploited the Jews to dig heating–materials but didn't keep them locked up in ghetto. It was quite a nice feeling, and I decided to stay there. But the Germans themselves spread the rumor that in Voronove the Jews lived better than anywhere else, because it was in Polish district and the government was more liberal. I left behind Biale Voki and together with my family went to Voronove.

Near the town I was stopped by the Polish police. They were looking for my brother who was a longtime communist. They took me for my brother and arrested me.

In prison I met Yitzach Dvilianski and several other youngsters. The Poles had tortured us to death; they pushed and packed us into tiny rooms— one could only stand. Even our natural needs we had to do standing.

On Yom Kippur night the Poles, some of them our school friends, decided to "settle the account with us". They surrounded the prison and opened fire through the windows. We bent down, literally fell one on another, and somehow miraculously survived.

Luckily the Mayor showed up, a Pole who had escaped from Russians and for some time had lived in Vilne. He was handicapped and I had helped him there, as one would help a compatriot. I talked to his conscience and he released me.

So again I lived in Voronove, in a house of a Jew in the outskirts. Suddenly they arrested his wife. When he found out about it, being himself a bandit, he caught the Polish policemen and broke their bones. At night they came back with a bigger group and arrested all the men. Meanwhile the guy escaped and disappeared. They brought us to the "Telephonists house", ordered us to strip naked, took us into a room one by one, put on the gramophone, and to the sounds of music beat us up to death, until the loss of consciousness. When a beaten man lost consciousness, they threw him out in the street. Once in the street, I regained my strength and crawled on all fours to the house of an acquaintance where I was taken care of.

In the morning I met a Polish policeman whom I had known before. He was surprised that I was still alive, that I was still walking around in his world. He promised me that one way or another I'd soon be dead, even if I had been saved this time.

I ran to Moshe Kaplan's brother. Moshe was also there. I wanted to go to my family as soon as possible. I was totally black and blue from the beating. I felt lonely and unprotected like a child.

I dragged myself home, walking and falling. It was February 1942. The authorities went after all Vilne Jews in Voronove. They gathered everyone in the cinema theater and murdered them to the last one. Among them was my wife who was also from Vilne. I didn't know that. On my way back home I met a Vilner from Avraham Marevski's troupe. He had miraculously survived and had fled the town disguised as a Gentile. He pretended not to know me and approached me as a Gentile. He strongly advised me not to go back to Voronove. He took me to Zhyrmun, 16 km from Lida. From there we continued to Lida. From him I learned about my wife's death. In Lida, Jews were still living in some peace, they were treated more liberally. The Head of the *Yudenrat*, Mr. Lichtman, had studied for years together with the Head Commissar so now they had friendly relationship. The town's priest was also friendly to Jews. Thanks to him the Germans were made to show some humanity, they eased conditions in the ghetto and provided necessities. There was no sign of Gestapo. Once, thieves sneaked into the priest's house and robbed him. In the morning the priest found a jacket with a yellow star. He demanded from the Jews that they give away the thieves and return what was stolen. The thieves were Jews, professionals. They wanted to turn suspicion away from them so they invented this:

"It turned out that nonnative Jews from Vilne had done it, because local Jews wouldn't do such a thing to the good priest. Vilne Jews pretending to be ghetto Jews had performed the robbery. They also added that the robbers had bribed the Head of *Yudenrat* and the Head Commissar not to search them."

This was a typical underworld trick. The Gestapo took advantage and immediately arrested all the town elders. They collected all the Jews in the town square while the criminals walked around between the lines and pointed out every non–local. The Gestapo arrested all of these on the spot. I also was among them.

We spent 10 days in prison. We were about 60 men, and Lichtman was one of them. On the tenth day they took us out to shoot us. Luckily my "bullet" just scratched me. I was bleeding. I fell down in horrible shock. Those who had been shot after me fell on top of me, covering me, and I survived. Later, after several hours, at night, I woke up and was sorry that I was still alive. I was tired of my life. My bitter loneliness depressed and tormented me. I sat up, then stood up, and then noticed two other survivors. I recognized the two from Vilne, Konski and Perlshteyn, my acquaintances. We instinctively started running, crossed the fence, and ran away. I ran into the house of Slomnitski. I burned my bloodstained clothes and put on others.

Next morning I went out into the street and went to look for some work. I went to the painters. They had better conditions because they were useful to the Germans, who used them for their private works. There I met our Moshe Kaplan.

The Jews soon found out that I had survived. My relative spoke about me to some Gentile, so he said to find me and bring me immediately over. I took Perlshteyn with me and went away. First I wanted to go to Biale Voki. The winter was harsh. I knew that my mother had left some clothes with Christian friends. I let my mother know that I needed some clothing, so she had gone to the Christians to bring some warm clothing for her big miserable baby. The Christians handed her over to the murderers and she was murdered. My solitude grew even worse. I was disgusted with my life. I was disgusted to be a hunted animal. But I was alive, and with every day in which I managed to survive, my will to do everything to survive became stronger.

In Biale Voki Jews continued to work digging turf and were free to move around. I decided to run away and join the partisans, so we ran away.

When we were close to the forest, we asked some Gentiles to take us to the other side, because we had heard there were partisans there. The Gentiles wanted money from us. They also demanded wheat and corn. We had to make our way on our own. In the village Soroki Tatarov we met a Tatar, a talker. He told us that at nights "bandits" would come to steal food and meat. We understood who the bandits were. It was clear to me that in the Radin–Eshishuk surroundings their "bands" were hiding. I organized a group of 12 people (among them Grisha Gurvits who later became a substitute to Yitzach Sadeh in Palmah,[2] and Lyuba Katz who now works in the university, and others). With great risk and time loss we got some weapons and went to Natscher Forest near Radin.

May 1942

With trouble, hunger and hunted by Gentiles we finally arrived in the forest. We made our way with the help of our weapons and with being ready to fight for our lives.

We asked a Gentile in a field if there were partisans in the area. He was very frightened [of the Germans], but being afraid of us too he answered with typical Gentile diplomacy:

"If you stay here for the night, you'll find out something."

We believed him.

We took to hiding and slept in two shifts. In the morning we heard the noise of wagons. When we went out of hiding we saw on the road slowly moving wagons filled with provisions. Obviously those were partisans. We approached them and asked them to take us with them. We told them we were friends of Yankele Konikhovski from Voronove. They believed we are "kosher". Among them he was an important person so they took us along, but wouldn't let us into the camp. They wanted to wait for their commander, Stashevitsh, to return.

He came at night. He was a brave Russian paratrooper, and with him was his deputy. When they came close to us the deputy almost fell from his horse. It was Lyuba's brother Liova Katz. The meeting of the siblings was very dramatic. We were instantly attached to the partisans.

We immediately became involved in the partisans' activity. We lived in the moment. We got back our human dignity. The thoughts of revenge took over our minds and overcame all thoughts of danger in confronting the Germans.

From time to time, I and Grishka were sent to keep communications with Naliboker Forest – which was our sector.

On our way we once found that in Eshishuk there were Jews hidden by Christians. When they ran out of money their hosts began picking on them and murdering them. We decided on our own initiative to do Jewish work. At night we went into a Gentile's who had murdered a Jew. We murdered him and left a note:

"This Christian was murdered because of his crimes against Jews who were hiding at his place. And the same will be done to every one of you who decide to murder Jews or hand them over to Germans."

We were three who did this. Later we were joined by Niamke Zogovski (now a member of Egged Haifa[3]). It had its effect: murders of Jews had stopped.

December 1942

A delegation from Vilne ghetto came to us. They said that in Vilne there were Jews ready to take chances and flee to the forests. We arranged a meeting between them and Stashevitsh. He asked us who was ready to go into the ghetto to save people. I offered myself. I asked for 12 men, and together we went to Vilne.

We stopped in Biale Voki. Six of us went out in the direction of the ghetto, six others stayed behind in case the first six were caught by the Germans.

We entered the ghetto secretly so the Germans wouldn't notice us. The Jewish ghetto leaders did know about us. We were immediately fetched by Gants, the chairman of the *Yudenrat* and Dessler, the Jewish Police Commandant. Before we had time to think about our actions, Dessler took out a revolver and shouted and demanded for us to leave. Gants was ready to hear us out and agreed that we stay in the ghetto, but only if we promise not to take any Jews with us, "This can bring great trouble upon us". We understood his fear. The man was decent in his own way; we promised him not to take anyone out of the ghetto.

We stayed in ghetto for a few days and then we left.with forty people, most of them young and patriotic. On our way we encountered a German ambush. A battle broke, and some of the 40 rescued were killed— poor fellows didn't live to see the forest.

In Natsche, in the "Leninsky Komsomol" squad, the situation was very difficult. During the time we were gone, several raids and battles had taken place. The new men had no arms so we had to move them to Naliboki.

Our partisans retreated from the Polish partisans; we retreated to Rudnik where we found Russian paratroopers. At the same time partisans from the Vilne ghetto headed by Aba Kovner joined [us]. We had to assist them. Our purpose now was to help every Jew that had fled to save himself in the forest, and to continue actions to save more Jews. We again went to Vilne ghetto and took out groups to the partisans. Once, while leading such a group, we got caught into a battle with Poles. Chaim Laze, now the Chairman of Leumit Health Care in Israel, had lost his arm there. Several times we found Jews wandering in the forest.

They were usually hiding in some distant corner, cut off from all roads, from hope and security. They ran away from the Poles who, after they had managed to escape Hitler, persecuted and murdered them. They wanted to finish off the extermination of Jews. We took them in; we protected them until they were fit for fighting squads. One of such survivors was Lizka Weinshteyn, today a member of the Labor Committee in Histadrut.

With the *Chapayevtzi*[4]

Here in this area we had bitter battles with the White Poles. While seeking to reconquer their homeland, on the way, they also sought to murder all remaining Jews. From time to time we had to retreat from our camp to prevent casualties.

During one such march, we came across Naratscher partisans, from the *Chapayevtzi*, who were fighting in Vilne area. Their commander, Lunka, took us in to lay landmines.

We began to lay mines under German military trains; hundreds and hundreds of German soldiers paid with their lives. Two weeks passed laying mines, sabotaging, and fighting. Then we went back to our base with trophies. I came back with an RKM Polish machine gun and Tuvye Shirs with a German automatic gun. Then our combat brothers offended us brutally and forced us to give away our dangerously-earned automatic weapons. That was pure anti-Semitism. Our Russian brothers didn't take into consideration our needs: our dangerous tasks required these weapons more than others. They just couldn't stand that Jews would be better armed than they. Luckily for us, our common commander, Makov, was friends with a Jewish guy. We told him about what had happened and expressed our fear and suspicion towards our brothers-in-arms.

He understood us well. He called the commissar for a clarification talk and ordered him to do everything to return the weapons to us. Obviously it caused a strong anti-Semitic tumult. They tried to resist but he called them in and told them:

Well take a look: the Jews don't want to hide in pits, they want to fight. They are 'boytsy'[5] fighters like us, and they are our brothers, so why do you bother them?"

Then they assigned us to a special squad and our missions became interesting.

The Great Victory and the Great Danger

A striking thing occurred in Petratshi,[6] which was described by Sutzkever and Kaczerginski after they asked us for details of this incident.

The post was supposed to come from Vileyka, Postov, and Narach[7] but didn't arrive. The German post-train was afraid to pass close to the forests. They were afraid to take a long trip so it was divided in two: one half the distance was traveled from one direction, the other from the opposite direction. They met in the middle and handed over the post to each other.

Our espionage squad found out about this and we went out to ambush the Germans. We waited for several hours and when the German *Miadzshuler* police appeared we let them through and then attacked them from behind and liquidated them to the last one.

Those were Belarusians and Poles under the command of a German. Our joy was enormous. We were happy with our great victory. We went into the nearest village, got drunk, and overdid it a little. Luckily for us the vodka was not so strong so we were not totally drunk, otherwise who knows what might have happened. Meanwhile the Postov garrison came in [to the village] and they bumped into us. The battle lasted 6 hours. Partisans from the area came to help us, but they came too late. Meanwhile we, alone, managed to kill them and take 20 prisoners.

The prisoners were from surrounding villages. The partisans knew them well and asked the commander to hand them over to them for trial. Vengeance filled everyone's hearts. The commander conducted a trial by the book. The verdict was clear; we treated them in their own way. They had to dig their own pits and we did the rest. We didn't waste bullets on them. We used knives. We inhaled the taste of revenge in all its ugliness.

And Another Battle, also Neat and Justified

We were on our way to occupy a hostile Lithuanian camp. There we lost a good friend of ours, a famous hero who received the highest decoration after his death. His name was Itzke Blatt, from Glubok. Itzke used to cross German lines and perform the most outrageous tasks. When we were close to occupying the camp, in perfect Lithuanian he decided to convince them to defect, to surrender by their own free will, and to spare needless suffering: they shot him at close range. It was a low cowardly act befitting cowardly murderers. After surviving for years in the partizanka he fell from a cowardly bullet. We paid them back with all our strength. We have had many battles, but this one, I think, was the neatest and the most interesting.

As '*chapayevtsy*' we had to live up to the name, meaning to wipe out every track of Germans and their collaborators wherever we could find them. We did as we were ordered. A lot of Germans fell into our hands and didn't see the world anymore. There were Germans who we kept alive according to orders from Moscow; later they collaborated with us against their own folks. When we demobilized we left them alive [because] they were really loyal to us and deserved to live. They probably became important founders of East Germany. It was a time of Russian imperialism, and that was always more important than the simple human and Jewish need for revenge.

In Narach Jews Are in Charge

Here we built up a strong partisan unit. We had to continue fighting, paid for with expensive casualties. Frequent German blockades forced us to fight for our lives and sometimes to hide in bunkers. The German terror continued to bother us and we had no peace and quiet, but those encounters added more meaning. We were fighting against a death threat which was around us all the time. Of course it affected the Jewish squads more than others. The most extraordinary was the unit of Podpolnien,[8] a Jewish guy, brave like a leopard, he spread fear and terror in the surroundings. This all came to the point where the whole forest up to Baranovitsh–Naliboki, tens of kilometers in width and in depth, became partisan territory. People could get through only with our passes, while all around was the German regime.

The truth is that the Germans burnt their [local population] houses in order not to give them away to partisan hands, while we demanded various food–contributions and took everything from them by force.

Jewish Contribution to the Russian Victory over the Nazis

On the 1st of May, 1944 the central command in Moscow ordered us to blow up all the railway lines from Vilne to the Neman frontline. This was meant to be a holiday present for Mother–Russia.

We performed our mission completely. By June 22 of the same year all the lines were blown up and destroyed.

Then began the Russian counter–attack from Stalingrad, and our work helped them a lot. The Germans who were cut off from their transportation lines remained stuck in small weak positions, isolated from their command points, and their defeat was coming closer and closer.

We accomplished this on our own, without anyone's help. We wanted to emphasize our special contribution to the Nazi fall. Among us were young fighters, strong and brave. I remember Tevke Shirs, Magid, Kutcher and others. Later we had to take over Myadl, a city surrounded by lakes which was totally a German island, heavily settled by them and heavily protected by their murderous guns. We occupied and took many of them into captivity. Among them was also a Russian partisan who had earlier betrayed us. We made justice with them all, like it should be.

Finally we encountered the Russian Army. Among them I noticed a Jew, an officer. He also recognized me. Like Joseph and Benjamin in the Bible, we wept on each other's shoulder. He told me:

"Until I came to here, I didn't find any sign of Jews, and all the evidence of their extermination was covered up. I didn't believe that I'd be seeing any living Jews."

They continued and we were left again in the forests, spending many long months full of danger, fighting, and revenge.

Out of the Forest

We lived with the hope that all of this would end and we could go home, bringing consolation to our remaining most beloved, but there was nobody left, unfortunately.

Mr. Yona the Feltsher

Vilne was partly destroyed, but most of Jewish houses were still standing intact and untouched. They were occupied by Gentiles— the "good" neighbors. Tevke Shirs did find his father and his brother alive.

The Russians treated me with great honor. They took me for my brother, the long time communist from the Polish regime. I was appointed to an important position. I was nominated for police commandant in Turgal. I started to organize local police there. There I met with a Jewish youngster, Weitzman, with whom I had worked digging peat before I left Voronove. He is now in Netanya. He told me:

"Run away from here, as soon as possible. As soon as they find out that you are a Jew, they'll kill you at night and nobody will even notice."

I escaped to Voronove again.

It was mid–August of 1944. There I met Yitzach Dvilianski. Meir Shamir had been there before me and had left. Moshe Kaplan was in the Russian Army. There were several others, mostly women, with the same tragedies. Jewish houses stood untouched and Gentiles lives in them. They would walk around Voronove and behave as if they were in their own backyard, without a bit of shame. I was appointed Head of the Fire Department. I found amidst the firemen all the murderers of our parents. They had been prison guards over us in the German prisons. When I informed on them to the higher authorities, they replied:

"We know, we know!"

I couldn't stay in Voronove anymore. Gentiles continued to murder the remaining Jews whenever they had an opportunity. I was together with Dvilianski; we both had a bad feeling. The fact that one could walk around in one's own town, see doors opening up, and instead of seeing the expected familiar bunch of people so dear to you, one sees Gentile faces, Amalek's grandchildren. This alone killed any desire to stay in the town. Meanwhile Moshe Kaplan arrived. He also thought we should leave there. The Russian Army was short of *friziern*,[10] so I joined him. Obviously I deserted, but I had no other choice.

I felt a certain responsibility for Dvilianski. I was afraid he would have trouble because of me. We both went to our commander, who was looking for meat for his soldiers, and we offered him to go to Voronove to confiscate a cow from every house. In that way we pulled out Dvilianski with us.

Here a remarkable incident happened.

Our unit served with the "Normandy–Neman" division. These were French air forces that assisted the Russian Army. The command was in Russian hands. The battles on the frontline were still quite strong, many casualties were still falling. Only we were not sent to the frontline. When we wanted to understand the reason, one of the [officers] in the headquarters explained:

"We will not send you to be killed. There are so few survivors among you. Not even one of you should be endangered. Just a small number of Jews remained in the world. You have suffered enough killing, enough is enough."

In Gerda,[11] Germany we were paid a visit by General Volfianov from the *Tschelushkin* expedition. The situation there was critical, the famous hero Tscherniachovsky has fallen. Volfianov had come to collect all the [scattered] formations and bring them together closer to the frontline. He was about to give us an order to come with him but Major Cohen, Head of the local N.K.V.D. introduced me and Dvilianski as representatives of the partisans who had fought the enemy for all those long war years. Volfianov stood up in front of us, saluted, and said:

My fullest acknowledgement, such people should be protected, don't send them to the frontline!"

*

I never thought of myself as a fighter, a person with military skills, a sabotage doer and a terrorist, but there are no inexplicable surprises in life: the Nazi satan awoke in me such powers. And I was not the only one. All my friends, partisans from Voronove, were like me. In such a manner, Nazism had planted the seeds of its own death.

This should be a lesson for the future generations. One should not look at a person from the outside only; one should look at a person as an endless source of abilities and skills. As soon as one is ordered or forced to unveil and use them, one unveils and uses them.

This is an important conclusion for us, for our children, for our children's children, for the small Jewish folk.

Mass grave of folks from Vilne – where the author's wife is buried

Thanks to Yankele Konikhovski we all became kosher,
Y. Konikhovski partisan medal[12]

Footnotes

1. Ed. Note: The name Biale Voki is spelled: beyz–yud–alpeh–lamed–ayen [space] tsvey vovn–aleph–kuf–yud in the original text.

2. Ed. Note: An elite Jewish fighting force within the Haganah during the British Mandate period in Palestine.

3. Ed. Note: A bus drivers' cooperative in Haifa.

4. Trans. Note: Partisan squads: Chapayev was a Russian Red Army hero

5. Ed. Note: Unknown Russian language word.

6. Ed. Note: The name is spelled pey (or fey)–ayen–tes–reysh–aleph–

tes–shin–yud in the original text.

7. Ed. Note: The town was known as Kobylnik in earlier times.

8. Ed. Note: The name is spelled: pey (or fey)–aleph–daled–pey (or fey)–aleph–lamed–nun–yud–ayen–langer nun in the original text.

9. Ed. Note: a feltsher is a medical professional with authority less than a physician and more than a nurse

10. Ed. Note: This word is as of yet unknown. The word is spelled: fey (or pey)–resh–yud–zayen–yud–ayen–resh–langer nun in the original text.

11. Ed. Note: This name is spelled: gimel–ayen–resh–daled–aleph in the original text.

12. Trans. Note: The document, in Russian, is a certificate and letter of honor for Konikhovski Yakov Gotliebovich, for his service as a partisan.

[Pages 332-336]

Our Child Saved Us

Kay Lisorski

Translation by Emma Karabelnik

Ed. Note: This article appears in both Hebrew and Yiddish in the original Yizkor Book. The following is a translation of the Yiddish text.

When the German–Russian war broke out, my husband was [serving] in the Russian military and I was staying with my tiny baby in Lida.

The baby was then 1 year and 22 days old.

On that day they set fire all around the ghetto. On my chest, tied with the hem of my dress, I carried my little bird. I was escaping to my hometown Voronove.

On the way I became tired so I stopped to spend the night in Bastuni, about 10km from Voronove. Together with me stayed Mrs. Levine, Yoshke Levine's mother. In the morning a pair arrived from Voronove to take us home. My father, my devoted [father] had thought about his daughter. I invited her [Mrs. Levine] to come with us, but she didn't want to; the driver had told us that Germans had occupied Voronove and that he was not very eager to go near their [the Levine] residence. The same night Bastuni was bombarded and Mrs. Levine was killed.

On May 5, 1942, shabbat, they surrounded the ghetto. After 3 days of organizing their camps they started shooting straight into the ghetto.

Before that the Germans had brought to our ghetto all the Jews from Soletchnik, Divenishok, and Bastuni. It became very crowded, impossible to live. The shootings were unbearable, the whistling sound of the bullets spread fear. The bullets were flying from all directions. Jews hid; they wanted to live just a bit more. They knew that all this firing and siege meant death and destruction, but they wanted to live a little more.

We had a bunker under the floor in our house. All the Jews hid there, but we stayed out of the bunker. We were afraid that the baby would cry and reveal the hiding place. Nevertheless, my little one didn't cry, as if he understood the situation and kept quiet for us.

On Sunday the *Yudenrat* people ran around and shouted:

"Jews come out of the bunkers, nothing [bad] will be done to you."

But the Jews didn't come out and stayed in the bunkers.

On Monday, the Germans and their henchmen increased the siege around the ghetto. They went from house to house, dragging out all Jews.

1,800 Jews were taken to the market place. They were ordered to lie on the ground. Photographers with cameras ran around and took pictures of them lying down.

The son of the Soletchnik Rabbi, a cripple without feet, also lay down. When the Head Commissar noticed him from a distance, he came over to him and asked him where he had lost his feet. The fellow told him. The German expressed his condolences. You could see on his face an expression of genuine regret and compassion, but all this didn't stop him from murdering him shortly after. Only moments before the slaughter, the mega–murderer had felt pity for his victim without feet.

Round and round stood our good neighbors with sticks and hacks, with shovels and pitchforks, guarding us so we couldn't escape from death.

The order was given:

"Stand up! March!"

Before us walked my parents and my sister. My husband was terrified about our son's destiny. I looked at my baby and he looked back with his little eyes at me, at my husband, at me, at my husband, suddenly he exclaimed:

"They will not kill us, they'll let us go home."

He knew that we needed compassion and he decided to comfort us.

The Head Commissar stood on the crossroad and divided the Jews to life or to death. He instantly sent my parents [to death], and we clinged on to them, wanting to be with them in any situation. But the nice murderer pushed us to the right, tore us away from father and mother and sent us …to live. We could still be useful to him. We both had a profession, and he still needed professional people.

We remained seated; we heard the shootings that finished away all our dearest ones. When all the shooting ended a Polish policeman approached us and said:

"Don't worry, you will live."

As if it was our only concern at that moment.

In the evening they gathered the surviving Jews at the market place again. A photographer took pictures of us again. As it turned out, the purpose was to show how many Jews were exterminated on that day— for statistical purposes.

They took off all our jewelry, piled up all the valuable things in huge shawls spread out on the ground, and we were told to go back to our homes.

When I stood up, I immediately ran to the mass graves. They were already covered with soil, but the soil was moving, went up and down at the edges, like a huge chest breathing and catching air.

*

Ten days later we were sent to Lida ghetto.

We were allowed to take with us only what we could carry. We were driven by foot to Bastuni. There they pushed us into cargo wagons and took us to Lida.

We arrived in Lida ghetto on May 23, 1942.

The Goyim came every day to warn us that in a few days we'd all be shot and dead.

My husband worked in a workshop outside town. When we felt that the last day of extermination was coming close, we went to him. He hid me and my baby in a closet.

Inside the closet I told the baby:

"Now you will be safe, don't talk."

He put his little finger to his lips and replied:

"Shh, no talking."

And he didn't talk. He cried silently, crying that you couldn't hear.

After a couple of days we were discovered and sent back into the ghetto.

*

On the last day of Pesach my husband went into the forest. I stayed in the Ghetto with my baby. He was ill with diphtheria and I wanted to cure him from this fatal illness though the chances were low. All diphtheria patients didn't survive in the Ghetto because of the lack of medical supplies and food, and the minimal services. Luckily for me there was a young Jewish doctor in the Ghetto (oh my, I forgot his name), and he took upon himself to cure my little bird. By his orders I ran around the ghetto from place to place, despite the mortal danger, and I managed to obtain injections against diphtheria. The pharmacists just couldn't cope with my sorrow and gave me all the bottles they had. My baby recovered. The doctor didn't leave his bed until he saw him healthy.

When my husband came back for a second time to take us to the forest, we wanted to take the young doctor with us. He refused. He didn't want to desert the ghetto people and leave them without his devoted care. Now you tell me, who is the person who looks for Jewish heroism in the Nazi ghettos and doesn't find any?

*

While walking in the forest we encountered great hardships. It was a very hot Iyar[1] day, a month after Pesach. It was hard walking in the heat. In addition, we lost our way and wandered around. After a hard day we entered a house of a Gentile woman. Her son was a policeman with the Germans in the Lida Ghetto, a murderous youngster. She served a table full of food for us, and delighted our souls.

The baby didn't eat. He took all the pieces of bread with his small hands and built a pile out of them. The woman told us to ask him why he wouldn't eat, he replied:

"Mommy, later I'll be hungry again."

In the forest Keileh Grodzenchik (Shamir) gave us a piece of bread. I broke it in two and kept the second piece for later. But he [the baby] wanted both halves. When I wouldn't let him and I told him:

"Later you'll be hungry again."

He replied:

"Mommy, why do you worry? When you have no bread, do I nag? Am I hungry on purpose?"

*

The raids in the forest became more and more frequent. In the forest he was carefree. Sometimes I was afraid for him not being careful enough, forgetting what he had learned in the ghetto, the terrible lessons of horrible days. But as soon as an order was given to leave, [or] to hide, [or] to move to another place in the forest, he would immediately jump on the shoulders of my husband, ready to confront all the dangers of the dark roads in the thick woods. When running – escaping from a raid – he would again close himself in, never crying, or talking or requesting food.

On the dark wandering roads during the days of Nazi horror we suffered a lot of hunger, dampness, and cold that broke our souls and spirit. But he, the tiny little man, suffered all those things with the patience and spirit of a grownup man, and even better.

In the days of severe hunger, day after day, it was hard for me to see my baby eager for food. But he had a special instinct for such hours: to comfort and lighten us up. His comforting words and good talking gave us motivation to live and hope.

And so because of him and thanks to him we survived.

Footnote

1. Tr. Note: Jewish month, usually occurring in May.

[Pages 337-345]

Exactly When It Rained

Mineh Konopke (Mutshnik)

Translation by Emma Karabelnik

On the day the Germans occupied our region a bomb fell on the castle. When we talked about it with great fear, someone from the district party headquarters told us:

"Don't be afraid. Just like grass cannot grow on a palm, the Germans cannot stay here."

On the next day the Russians began enlisting men and also some women. At that time in Pirigantse,[1] 10 km from Voronove, an airport was built, so Dina Kurlansky and I were sent there to work in [unknown word[2]]. On the road there were already a lot of dead and wounded from the German air attacks and when we arrived at the spot there was turmoil. There was no telephone communication with anyone; the

Germans were very close. The Russian officials immediately caught whatever motor vehicle was available and drove away, and [took] Dina with them (by the way she came back later; she wasn't allowed to cross the border to Russia). I stayed. I didn't want to part from my family. The locals of course immediately looted everything there. It was impossible to go straight home so I went, together with several Gentile girls who I had arrived with, to spend a night at a peasant's house. There, all the neighbors gathered and talked about how now they'd have some revenge on the Jews.

The shooting was awful. The sky was red because of fires. They said that Voronove was all up in flames and all the Jews there had been killed. They just ate and drank and for me the night was endless. On the next morning, as soon as the Germans appeared in the village, we started on our way home. They [the Gentile girls] didn't want to be seen with me so I followed behind them. When I came back to town it was not burning.

I found everyone there had fear in their eyes. It was frightening to show oneself in the street, and talk was of how the Germans had appeared suddenly. One thought of the bitter future, but didn't imagine the slaughter. When Batia Finkelshtein arrived with her family from a small town near the Lithuanian border and told us that they were shooting Jews there, nobody believed her. My sister Batia also lived in the same area with her family, in a town called Rudiskes, so we paid a Christian to bring them over to us. They were really happy to hear from us, but their parents who remembered the Germans from WW1 didn't believe the stories and didn't want to leave their house behind... When we sent the Christian for a second time to bring them, he found them being led to the meeting place with suitcases and their little boy with them. She only nodded to him with her head.

All the Jews from there were drowned in the Trakai Lake. And this is a clear fact.

In that way our troubles slowly started. Everybody was desperate. Some were hopeful. Some said that the spirit board had turned to the good side and looked for various other signs, until the action began of going from house to house shooting everyone sick.

After some time they arrested six people: Zerakh, Esther and David Shelovski; Yitzakh Volpianski, Yesheyahu Olkenitski, Gershon Eishishki, and they never came back. There were rumors that in the surrounding towns, and in Lida, there had already occurred a day of slaughter, and that now our day of slaughter would come. When five [more] people were shot: Binyamin Kaplan with his wife, Nionie Grodzenchik, Leyzer Katzenellenbogen, and Gershonovitsh, I came in tears to Rokhl Katzenellenbogen. She said:

"Don't cry. Soon we shall all meet and nobody will cry for us."

She was killed with Yehudith and family.

*

Three days before the slaughter we were not allowed to leave our homes, but we would sneak around to visit each other. I visited the Dlugins. They thought that because Aharon cleaned German houses maybe they'd let them live. So said Ettke Lubetski when she came to me, because her aunt Esther Lichtman knew the chief of headquarters, maybe she'd save them all. But nothing helped them.

[One day] came Itke Olkenitski with Chaya, daughter of the Myadler Rabbi, desperately asking what we planned to do to hide. We said we would hide mostly because of the parents. At that time we lived in Kalmanovitsh's warehouse, where we had been given an apartment by the Russians, because they decided that our previous big house was too big and too good for a Zionist family. They moved us twice, until we were sure we'd be deported to Siberia. Together with us lived a Divenishok family, Blyakher, so we all built a hiding place.

As soon as they begin to drive everyone out to the market place, our neighbors, and the Kletzker Rabbi with his family all began to go out. He used to repair German watches and thought that as a useful Jew he and his family would be saved. His brother Hershl prepared two bottles of gasoline to throw on them and burn everything, but he didn't do it because that would have killed many Jews who were in hiding.

Each Rabbi had his own followers. They didn't get along with each other and lived in disagreement, but in the market place that all changed. Together with them went the Rabbi of Soletchnik and his son, a cripple in a wheelchair. He showed them documents proving that he was injured in WWI fighting for Germany. They take him aside and shoot him. Our other neighbors, Yitzakh Dvilianski, Beyshl and their families, and also the Divenishok families Blyakher, Yankelovitsh and Schneider, barged into our warehouse to prepare a good hidden door. We were 20+ people hiding in this hiding place. From inside we heard people going in and out of the house, clapping on the walls, searching. We sat still. We hugged and kissed little children to keep them calm. Above us, from the attic, they dragged Sheynke Blekherovitsh's brother. They found him hiding in the hay and shot him on the spot. We are trembling from fear for several hours before Dr. Gordon, from Navaradok, who knew about us, tapped on the door to tell us we could go out, and thus we had been saved for now.

*

In the Lida ghetto we often met Voronovers that had survived; with some of them we worked together. The situation becomes worse and worse. The rumors from surrounding towns and villages were of mere slaughter. They said that in the Vilne ghetto the situation was a little better. Rokhl Shevakh, with family, tried to reach Vilne. On the way they were arrested. She ran away and wandered into the forest with the child, and when she returned to the ghetto she was afraid to show herself because they were looking for her. Meanwhile we heard about Bielski's brigade in the forest— a way to save ourselves.

Rokhl Kopelovitsh's brother was waiting to pick her up in the forest, but when it became time for her to go, the baby cried in the cradle and she came back.

My sisters came to the forest with great difficulties. After some time a big raid [on the forest camp] occurred and they had to go back to the ghetto. Feitshe Grodzenchik said that it would be impossible to move around with a baby, so they decided to share their destiny with all the [other] Jews.

We began talking to our neighbors about having to build a hiding place. We dug throughout the nights. With hard work we made a tunnel from the backyard to the outskirts of town. The entrance [was] from the corridor behind a small disguised door.

One morning in September my mother looked outside the window to see what was new in the ghetto. She noticed silhouettes outside the wire fence and exclaimed: "We are already surrounded!" Everybody in the house jumped to their feet; in the ghetto people were already running around like crazy, not knowing what to do, to hide or to be deported "for labor" as it was called. The 15 of us went down into hiding. From above the entrance was disguised by Leybe, a Jew from Baranovich who had already lost his whole family and didn't want to live or join us. In the hiding place [there] was barely [space] to sit, with legs "over us". There was no food or drink, only a piece of bread, but we were too terrified to feel hungry. Lips were burning from dehydration. Luckily we found a shovel and dug a small hole in the ground to find some moisture for the lips. My father fainted several times, so we silently revived him. Upstairs in the house there was constantly someone searching. They used to tie a wooden beam to a horse and run him in the yard. When the beam made an empty sound they knew there was a hiding below and they stopped to catch the Jews. We could hear the voices, the crying, and shots into caught Jews. Thus we suffered for 6 days and nights.

When we couldn't stand this anymore we had to go out. We waited until it was raining and then broke the door. We cut the wires and ran into God's hands. The night was dark and we were almost blind—couldn't see anything. My mother and sisters Rivke and Yaffe ran with Basyeh Poditvianski, her husband and son, who were together with us in the hiding, being sure that my father and sister Khenyeh are running after them. My father's coat got caught in the wires so became cut off from everybody and didn't know where to go. We were terrified and didn't know where we were. My sister said she was going to look around and see where we were. She went, and every minute felt like a year. We were regretting that we had let her go, and when she [finally] returned we were happy. Then my father recognized a hut where he used to pray in the ghetto, far from the cemetery. From there it would be close to Stashevitsh, a Gentile who lived near the Head Commissar, where we used to work, and he was known as an honest Christian. On the way to him we came across a swamp from where we barely managed to pull each other out, without shoes. Then we noticed a policeman who was standing and smoking exactly where we had to pass.

We lay down and raised our heads from time to time to see if he was gone. It was almost morning and he wasn't moving, smoking one cigarette after another. After endless waiting we heard someone calling him. When he went away we dragged ourselves to the cemetery. Then policemen from a nearby house started shooting at us. Apparently they heard movement in the cemetery, but because of the rain they didn't bother to go out and shot from afar. We stretched between the graves. The bullets were flying over us. When it became quiet and at first light, we approached Stashevitsh's stable at the same time she came to milk the cows. She noticed us and exclaimed "Oh Jesus Maria, how did you get here?" We went into the stable. She told us to climb up to the attic and to pull the ladder so that no one could climb up. Later she brought us some hot tea. We put our hands [on the cups] to warm up a bit; we weren't able to hold the cups because our hands were frozen.

They also brought some of their warm, dry clothes and took away our clothes to dry. We lay there trembling from cold and fear, thinking about the destiny of our closest [relatives]. We concluded that we would stay here for several days until we had decided on our future moves. But when it became dark they came up to us with bread and milk, saying that we had to leave immediately because they were afraid. Our pleas to let us stay for the night didn't help. They carried [our] father over a footbridge, showed us the Rashliki Forest. From there we could get to Syagle[3] where partisans could often be found. By the way, we already knew from the sisters who had come back after the raid not to ask shepherds for directions, because they'd betray us. I had a couple hundred of zlotes in my coat so I gave them half. The forest was wet. We clung to each other and sat under a tree, afraid not of animals but of people. We sat for a whole night and then for a whole day wandered back and forth, afraid to ask anyone for directions. When we were already too tired to walk we saw from afar an elderly peasant riding [a horse]. I went out to him and asked for directions. He said that we were 3 km from Lida. We realized that our wandering around was pointless and decided to go straight along the road— whatever will be, will be.

We were walking with me in the front and they following. Everybody is watching us. My father is noticeably Jewish. Then we see from afar a papers checkpoint. We immediately turned to a field and stayed seated. Suddenly a man approaches us and tells us not to be afraid. He knows we are Jews. [He tells us] that in the last days a lot of Jews went through here but the Germans caught them. The patrols already killed a lot. We immediately gave him our last money and asked him to lead us by a side road with he in the front at a distance and we would follow. He walked and we run after him at a distance, until we lost him, and began to wander around by ourselves wishing a bullet would take us all, until we got to Syagle. We saw a house with a burning oven, food cooking, and a young guy walking around. We went into the house and began to warm up and dry our clothes. The Christian [woman] came in and asked us to go away far from the house because sometimes the Germans would come around, and sometimes the partisans. Again we were sitting in the bushes in a field. In the evening we see partisans riding on horses. We ran to them with joy. They were Russians. When they learned from us that we are Jews from the Lida ghetto, they said to us – until now you've spent your time with Germans and now you come to us? You deserve to be shot for this! They forced us to stand against a wall and not to make a move. One of their group felt sorry for us and tried to convince them to set us free. After we stood for quite a long time they told us to go away and not to show ourselves anymore.

On our way we again met several Russian partisans, who pushed Father aside, and told him to go and find the Bielski squad on his own while they would take us into their squad to be their wives. It didn't help to talk to their conscience. Suddenly they heard sounds of shooting from the village. Hearing the approaching shooting, and not knowing who is shooting, they quickly disappeared and left us behind. Apparently the shooters were drunk partisans who thought the Germans are near. We continued further, hoping to meet Jews.

We experienced a lot of fear of Russian partisans. From time to time they threatened to shoot us, but when we told them that we were on our way to Bielski they left us alone. Finally we met a group of Jews from Lida, with them Keileh Rudnik with husband and child. The youngster opened up a gap and disappeared. My father was not able to keep up with Keileh and her family. We went back together. In the evening we went through a village. A peasant was sitting with his family at a black wooden table with boiled potatoes and sour milk [sour cream] on it. They are eating calmly. We thought if only we could at least stay in his warehouse. Later we met a Jew from Lida, Starovolski, who is leading a group of Jews to Bielski, and we were already going together. One time, when I was on a side road, I was surprised by several partisans. When they saw how terrified I was they immediately told me they were Jews. It was Tuvye Bielski with several of his men. I took them to our group – he was happy to see the leader of our group whom he knew from before– and he ordered that everyone be taken to his squad on different roads. Later, now being all together, we went into a village where we found Zusye Bielski, sleeping in a warm bed at a peasant's house. He was happy to see saved Jews and immediately offered his warm bed to my father.

*

We didn't know anything of my mother and sister until Rosh Hashana eve. We are all sitting together near a fire and warming up. Suddenly someone calls our names and says that our mother and sister are here. They had taken a very difficult route together with Batia and her family. This whole time we had been close to each other and didn't know it.

Now we are all together. It is Yom Kippur night and we come to the Patashnia Forest— a gathering of Jews from different towns and shtetls. My father is praying *Kol Nidre* and other prayers from memory while others help him with the bitter tune.

During the day we would rest; at night we used to walk several kilometers. The rags on our feet would freeze during rest periods and it was hard to move around in the snow. Thus we dragged ourselves to Bielski in the Naliboki Forest. There were 2 camps there. They wanted to divide us between the two camps, but Asael Bielski ordered them not to divide families against their will.

In the forest we were among Jews. One could forget how different life had become— as long one isn't seeing any Germans. One day several families made a small fire to boil their clothes [for disinfection]. Exactly at that time a German airplane appeared in the sky and bombed the area. The bucket and everything in it was perforated, but we managed to escape the place.

[Once] Sokolov came for a visit from headquarters. Since he knew me, when he went in with Bielski into the *zemianka*,[4] he asked him to look after us and give us whatever we needed. We never needed anything. We were happy to be among Jews and share our destiny with them.

*

On the day the Red Army liberated us, the Germans were retreating in the forest. [On their way they] attacked our camp and shot 9 people. We had to leave the forest, because lots of them were running through the forest. Bielski led 1,230 saved Jews out of the forest; they had joined him on different roads, knowing that there was a Jewish squad with a Jewish commander who would take in any Jew. We came together with everyone to Navaradok and from there to Voronove. We came back with bitter hearts and deep sorrow, in rags, dirty, wires instead of shoelaces to keep them [on the feet]. In the ruined and exhausted Voronove, in the market place, we looked at the Jewish houses hoping to see someone looking back. Everybody was looking at us as if we had returned from the other world. Suddenly a Jewish major was glad to see us and said that he had been traveling around the neighborhood for a while and we were the first Jews he had met. He was most happy to meet my father with whom he later sat down to remember a *Gemarah* page. He took us to his room, put a loaf of bread on the table, which we didn't see for a long time, gave us food and drink, and found a room for us at Dlugin's. All the Jewish houses were occupied by Russians or ex-servants for whom it was a dream-come-true.

The Jewish soldiers in the Russian military spread the word that there was a Jewish family living near the road, so they would make small packages with food and bring them over to us. Slowly, the few surviving Jews came back to town and scattered around to different parts. They would visit each other, but it was scary to go outside of the town because of the White Poles, who had already managed to kill 2 Jews, Kaplan and Pupko.

Voronove was not for us anymore. It was impossible to walk the streets and see the occupied Jewish homes. As soon as it was possible to leave, we left. We were afraid of being deported to Siberia.

*

One way or another we finally left. In the past, when an *Ole*[5] was going away, everyone would escort him to the train station. When the train stopped everybody would sing Hatikva; all the passengers would look outside the windows. Now, we gathered together to visit the few graves left, then my father made an *Azkara*[6] at the huge mass grave, saying goodbye to the graves. He looked back while passing Benakani, said goodbye to the old Jewish cemetery, to the last Jewish houses, the last Jewish home belonging to Sibirnik, and left forever.

Footnotes

1. Ed. Note: This location has not been identified. In the original text, the place is spelled: pey (or fey)-yud-reysh-yud-gimel-aleph-nun-tsadek-ayen.

2. Ed. Note: The meaning of the word is unknown. In the original text the word is spelled: kuf-vov-pey (or fey)-ayen.

3. Ed. Note: This location has not been identified. In the original text, the place is spelled: samech–yud–aleph–gimel–lamed–ayen.

4. Ed. Note: A trench or dugout.

5. Ed. Note: Emigrant to Israel.

6. Tr. Note: A memorial prayer.

[Pages 346-351]

A Child Partisan

Yekutiel (Kushke) Boyarski

Translation by Emma Karabelnik

Ed. Note: This article appears in both Hebrew and Yiddish in the original Yizkor Book. The following is a translation of the Yiddish text. Photos appearing within the Hebrew version are included here.

On a beautiful day in May of 1942 we saw that the shtetl had been surrounded by a wall of armed hooligans. Jews immediately realized that their slaughter was near. Parents didn't know how to protect their children. The helplessness was awful. My mother said to my father:

"Let Kushke go, at least he will live."

They asked David Menyeh Riva's, who was preparing to leave Voronove, to take me with him. He agreed. He knew that I, a strong and healthy youngster of 16, would not become a burden to him.

We left at night and arrived to Tashmantse[1], about 8 km from Voronove. We went into a Gentile stable; he was a good Gentile. He kept us for 2 days. On the third day he asked us to leave, because it came to his knowledge that a severe punishment awaited anyone hiding Jews. He was simply afraid for his life. David went to another Gentile to ask for help. We remained [in the first stable] to wait for him. When the good Gentile went into his stable and found us, he just went crazy. He was sure that we had left with David. He broke out in panic and asked us to leave immediately.

We had no choice, and on the same night we left to look for David: his wife, his two children, Shayke and Khonke, and I, a boy— all of us helpless. We had to go and we didn't know where David was. Finally we came to the same Gentile that David had gone to see, but he [David] wasn't there anymore, and he [the Gentile] told us that he had returned to us.

The Gentile told us that there has been an action in Voronove, that most of the Jews had been murdered by the Germans and their collaborators. Now the murders had stopped for a while so we could return to Voronove. I proposed to go via Lida. With heavy hearts we went back to the first Gentile, because we didn't know what would happen if we weren't able to reunite with David.

On our way we met a group of Jews who came from the opposite direction. We scared them, and they ran away. I realized that they thought we were Gentiles, so I started shouting to them:

"Jews, don't run, don't be afraid!"

They came back. They were Rochl Dukshtulski, her two brothers, and a little sister.

From there we continued together to look for David and to go back to Voronove.

We came back home early in the morning. The shtetl was already half empty. One part of the Jewish population had been murdered, another part had been deported to Lida. My parents were not there anymore. Of my whole family, only my oldest brother survived. He worked in Bastuni, where he had heard the bitter news. He decided to stay there for the night and thus might survive for who knows how long. With him also was Dudeh Avak's, and together they came back home.

After a short time we were deported to Lida. They locked us up in the ghetto and took us to forced labor. Our work was to dismantle wooden beams and wooden rails, and prepare them for other uses. Dudeh was a carpenter, and his neighbor in the ghetto was a locksmith who worked in the German gun workshops. So this locksmith would bring a part of a rifle every day, until a whole rifle could be assembled. The butt and other wooden parts were built by Dudeh in the carpentry shop, because it was impossible to smuggle those parts into the ghetto.

So we had a whole [functioning] rifle in our possession and continued to undergo risks for more guns.

We made plans for an escape. We felt the ghetto would soon be liquidated, and it would be safer to leave this place as soon as possible.

We planned to go to Natsher[2] Forest. The challenge was to smuggle the rifles. We had 20 rifles, our only hope. We put them in a keg which Zuckerman used to take "*drek*"[3] out of the ghetto. He was a good Jew. He had a good job. He went out into the town every day and managed his life. It was a good job for us too. He took our rifles to the forest, a real life-saving trip.

We walked into the forest separately, at a distance from one another, in order not to be noticed. [Our alibi was] we would be going to work and had decided to spend the night in the forest. Then we took our rifles from the hiding place and went away.

We walked at night. During the day we would hide in the forest, and walk again at night. It was a very hard road. The going exhausted us in a hurry. With us there were a couple of sisters of the Stol family from Benakani. They were extremely exhausted and couldn't continue with us. That night we went to a Gentile, took his horses from the stable, and traveled with horses and wagons all the way to Natsher forest.

*

Here in the forest there were Jewish families organized as a squadron of Jewish fighters. They took over our rifles with gratitude. I was taken into a fighting squad, despite my young age. I was physically well developed; they liked me. I performed military assignments along with everyone and waited for an opportunity to fight.

On the first night we were assigned a watch in the forest. They took me deep into the forest and left me on watch. It was night. I was alone. My shift was from 10pm to 2am. The time passed extremely slowly. I thought they had forgotten to replace me so I went aside, sat down, and fell asleep. When they came to replace me I couldn't be found because my sleep was too heavy, but I had an intuition that they are looking for me and I jumped up. One of the two who had come to replace me wanted to report on me to headquarters, but the other said:

"Think about it. He is still a child. He has time to learn discipline. Let him be."

The next day the same incident happened. Two brothers were on their shift and one of them fell asleep at the post. When his replacement came and found him asleep, he reported him to the commanders. In the morning they court-martialed him and shot him before his brother's eyes. I was shocked by this incident. I thought: they kill Jews here too? I then decided that I would never fall asleep, never.

Since then I was considered one of the guys [an equal]. I was assigned tasks requiring responsibility. I rose in ranks. I spent my life in the forest fighting against Germans. I participated in sabotages, interfered with their military plans, blew up their trains, and destroyed their communication systems. I experienced extraordinary feelings, good feelings of fighting and revenge.

One day a German airplane appeared [in the sky] and took photographs of our camp. The next day there appeared thousands of German soldiers. We noticed them from a distance. They proceeded like a herd of sheep, clinging to each other tightly as they walked. They looked to me like an armored wall. They threw themselves on us by the hundreds. We fired on them first. A combat developed. We had losses, but they paid with hundreds and hundreds of dead and wounded.

Still, we had to retreat because we ran out of ammunition, and they outnumbered us by the hundreds. We went down deep into the forest and divided into groups. In these depths we spread out towards distant points of the endless forest.

Here I met Yankl Konikhovski from our town.

The Germans pursued us. We wandered from place to place, driven by their frequent raids, and tired from the frequent fatal confrontations with them. We usually won. In the depths of the forest we were the strong ones, but then another problem arose. Other White-Polish groups appeared. They were locals. They knew the forest better than anyone. Now we were not the only rulers in the forest, and we had to fight on two fronts.

There was an incident once when a group of six of our men was sent to get food for the squad. We [accidentally] ran into a camp of 200 Poles. From one of the houses a Pole noticed us and cried out:

"Stay still! Who are you?"

Immediately a rain of bullets fell onto us from a watchtower. We managed to kill the guard, but then tens of Polish bandits appeared from every corner. The night was very dark. We managed to kill dozens of them, but we left without food.

That night we had to move to another place in the forest. We went to the Lipiczanska[4] Forest near the Neman [River]. We had a long and hard road ahead, but we made it although hungry and tired for several nights in a row.

*

One day we woke up to find ourselves totally covered with snow. Winter had fallen upon us without warning in the middle of our sleep, and we were totally unprepared for it. Our situation became critical. Winter depressed us. We had to worry more about food, about warm clothes, and about other vital conditions. Hardest was the issue of shoes, made even harder by the wandering in snow and mud. Our vengeful fighting was now burdened by an even harder fight for existence. There are people among our ex-Partisans who remember mostly our heroic acts and combats. I mostly remember the awfully hard living conditions that we had to suffer. Nobody writes about such simple things, but I see in them the greatest heroism of Jewish Partisan life. That difficult winter reflected our hard lives. For a boy who had instantly become a lonely orphan, the solitude became greater during the winter. The hunger was greater and more frequent. The cold exhausted and broke my spirit. To survive a winter in the forest is an extraordinary act of heroism, which only the most dedicated and determined could handle.

One night we were sent to watch the Lipiczanski[5] road. The deep, endless forest was crossed by railway lines. Suddenly we came over 4 Germans who started firing at us with their automatic weapons. We finished them off and silenced them, but we had to change our direction. The way back took us 8 days and 8 nights of maneuvering, shortages, and fighting. We had losses on our side, dear [friends], but the German losses were much more numerous, and after all that was our main purpose and we were proud of it.

We arrived at Lapitshne[6] with not more than 8 people. We stopped at a Russian regiment. They welcomed us as fighters. Here in this regiment a day didn't pass without confronting the Germans, and we fought with them day after day. The Russians regarded us as brave fighters who fought with a feeling of revenge and were highly skilled. They appointed us frequently for difficult military assignments and for acts of sabotage every day.

We ambushed and killed countless numbers of Germans every day. Their corpses were scattered around by the dozens on the roads and in the fields so they would rot and scare their cowardly brothers.

We were also sent to Zhetl to blow up trains [passing] in the area. Here we killed them by the hundreds. They fell down frightened like sheep and in a mass panic. The great heroism which they had showed in the ghettos against starving and unprotected Jews was gone as soon as they confronted a handful of partisans.

*

By the end of 1944 Grodno was already liberated, and so was part of its surroundings. Our commander, who had communication with Moscow, divided us into groups according to its instructions, and we went out in the groups to finish off the remaining Germans and to clean up their last nests [in the area]. We went in the direction of Skidel. We were all supposed to meet there. In my group was the chief commander of our regiment and he appointed me, an 18-year old youngster, to be his representative. There was no one happier than me, obviously I had earned some skills as a fighter.

[Ed. Note: The following section appears only in the Hebrew version of the article in this book.]

When we crossed the Neman and approached the railway lines, [we discovered] mines attached to the rails. We started to dismantle them. Some of them exploded and some of our men were killed. In the morning we arrived in the camp.

Either because of the explosions, or because some farmer noticed us and told the Germans, they appeared in the morning. Our guard noticed them. They proceeded in tight rows with an unstoppable fear.

Before they had time to act we began firing and killed dozens of them. We escaped, but we lost three of our friends.

After two days we were reunited with the squadron. Those were days of revenge and action. The Germans were on the retreat. Every day brought new waves of them and we had no choice but to do the killing. Every day we ambushed them, and every day we killed tens and hundreds. To me those days were full of satisfaction from killing my family's murderers.

At the end of the same 1944 we were released.

We came back to Voronove as [agents of] N.K.V.D. We were sent to a village about 20km from town. We were ordered to arrest two Poles who had collaborated with the Germans. With us traveled two Russians: we were 8 people. We took two peasants and their carriages with us, and we told them where to go. As we approached the forest cabin we saw one running towards the house from behind. Our alertness had waned for a moment and we hadn't noticed that one of the carriage drivers had warned his brother. I called him to stop. He didn't obey so I shot him. Meanwhile six or seven Poles came out against us, armed with automatic weapons, and they covered us with heavy fire. There was no choice so we jumped into a pit. A skirmish developed in which we were protected by the pit and they were better armed. We killed few of them, but we had to retreat.

While retreating, one of our comrades was captured. He was the last victim that I saw in [this] war.

Editor's Footnotes

1. This place is spelled as follows in the original text: tes-aleph-shin-mem-aleph-nun-tsadek-ayen. The exact location of this town has not yet been determined.

2. In the original text the name is spelled: nun-aleph-tes-shin-ayen-reysh. The precise location of the forest is not yet known.

3. Scatological Yiddish term for excrement

4. In the original text the place is spelled: lamed-ayen-pey-tes-shin-vov-nun-kuf-ayen-reysh.

5. In the original text the place is spelled: lamed-ayen-pey-tes-shin-yud-nun-kuf-yud.

6. In the original text the place is spelled: lamed-aleph-pey-yud-tes-shin-nun-ayen

[Pages 352-366]

Under Gentile Regimes

Yitzach Ben–Ami

Translation by Emma Karabelnik

Ed. Note: This article appears in both Hebrew and Yiddish in the original Yizkor Book. The following is a translation of the Yiddish text. Photos appearing within the Hebrew version are included here.

A Jewish Regime

The Poles fled town in a panic as soon as first news arrived of their daily defeats in the battles against the Germans. The town was left without authorities. Everybody was seized with a panic for a while. The Jews felt the smell of chaos, confusion, and danger.

The Gentiles, raised for generations by the Chmielnitsky[1] tradition – always dreaming of anarchy and robbery – immediately decided to come into town, to do pogroms and rob everything that comes by.

The next morning they began to fill the town, arriving in groups: robbers with [big] eyes. They came from various villages. They wandered around town as if without a purpose, but their eyes gave away their darkest thoughts.

The Jews, who usually know how to take advice and make decisions, on this occasion became helpless and passive. They were sure that their lives were unprotected and had no assurances they would be able to get out from this trouble safely. Their pessimism overwhelmed them and they lost their wisdom and initiative.

Suddenly, on one bright day, at midday, Yitzach Olkenitski gathered together several Jewish youngsters and shared his plan with them: how to protect ourselves from murderers. And we accepted his plan.

In minutes the guys stood up ready to strive for the goal: to take the fate of the town into their own hands. They put on firemen uniforms, put thick military belts around themselves, put various casks on their heads, pushed toy revolvers and other guns under their belts, and went out into the streets to give a "warm welcome" to the pogromists. The pogromists had already divided, and by agreed signs had spread out to different predetermined locations.

Our guys came over in groups and began pushing themselves towards the pogromists, shoulder to shoulder, asking them what they were doing here, and advising them to go back to their villages if they loved their lives. The Gentiles realized they had come to the wrong place, that here they'd have to deal with people who wouldn't stand by and were ready for anything.

At night we felt that the Gentile heroes were in a bad mood and depressed. They had no wish to die just in the sake of a robbery and had lost all their courage. We pushed them back with encouraging shouts and drove them out from the town disgraced and humiliated.

We saved the town for several days. We established a Jewish regime of self–defense and life–preservation. Meanwhile the Russians came.

The Germans Are Coming

With the arrival of Russians, great changes took place in the life of the Jews. I began to study in a "10–year" school, a kind of preparatory school towards an academic career. The lives of the youth flew in a promising directions for them. The new regime put its hopes in us, the future generation, and saw us as future representatives of the regime in occupied territories. The regime put effort into holding meetings and took specific actions to organize the social life. They organized balls for us, distributed benefits, and organized various activities that contributed much to the social life.

On June 22, 1941 we were at a dance ball. We danced until dawn and planned to continue dancing. Suddenly we heard the sounds of an explosion, thunder and ringing. No one understood where they were coming from. We were all startled and the dance was abruptly ended. We went back to our homes. The streets were already full of people. The town was in a state of turmoil and depression. Undergoing the most turmoil were the Russians. They, who should have been the first to know of any changes in the political situation, were instead the most surprised.

The town was in total state of chaos and it was growing minute by minute. The older folks ran around terrified and helpless, their uncertainty was great. Only we, the young folks, didn't take it seriously. We ran to the site of the explosion, on the railway line, far out from town, as one might run towards a joyful event.

On the way we saw that the Russians were packing their belongings and getting ready to leave Voronove. The Russians fled in fear and haste. We were [again] lost and confused. Some of us thought we should follow the Russians because the new rulers may see us as representatives of the old hateful regime and cause us trouble. Everybody knew that one doesn't play games with Nazis. But there were others who said:

'Anything but the Russians. They will instantly enroll you in the army and send you to the most horrible frontlines in the greatest danger, and your life will not be safe. While with the Germans it will be hard, you shall be enslaved, but at least our lives will be safe.'

I escaped. I went out on my way with two other guys and we walked in the direction of Russia. When we arrived [nearby] to Devinishok, we hid behind a big house in some village. We spent the night under the blue sky.

In the morning we wanted to continue, but it was not possible anymore. We were told that all the surrounding area is full of Germans. I returned to Voronove unwillingly.

On the way, Germans caught me and took me to their camp, in quite a civil manner. In the camp there were a lots of light tanks, packed with nice young soldiers. At that time, apparently, they were still apprentice murderers, not yet fully experienced. They treated me very nicely. I talked with them in Polish. I explained that I was just walking home. They kept me arrested for a whole day. They didn't interrogate or charge me with anything. They just ordered me to fill all the tanks with gas. After that they fed me well and at night told me: you are finished and free to go.

With Germans in Voronove

When I arrived home Voronove was already full of Germans. In those two days they had already managed to spread fear into everyone. In the morning they dragged the Jews to forced labor. They drove them on foot for kilometers with threats and beatings, and then forced them to extend highways.

One night the Poles made a raid on the 'young Jews who collaborated with bloody communists'. They arrested yesterday's friends in order to find favor with the victor. They arrested me too, me, their former best friend. They kept us in a house built by the Russians. They put about 40 men in a tiny room for a long period; no one knew when this would end. We stayed there for about a month, sleeping upright (standing). Then they brought someone called Zalmen Dukshtulski. He was from Vilne and was staying in Voronove illegally so they caught and arrested him. An interesting fact is that they didn't interrogate us, they didn't touch us, they just kept us isolated with our doubts and fears. They didn't beat us, but they let us know that in 3–4 days we would all be murdered. They didn't give us food. We survived thanks to food brought to us by our parents. Those were the first days of human humiliation.

One time, Kashminsky, a *folksdoitche* [a German citizen] whom we knew, grabbed a package from one of the unfortunate mothers. He specifically picked one from a rich family, knowing that her package would contain good expensive stuff. He brought it to the Germans and told them:

"You see, here is for you what they eat. Even at the times of lack and arrest, they eat better than us."

It was on the day of Yom Kippur. On that same day a group of drunken Poles and Germans approached our room. They wheezed, roared, and shouted threats and accusations about our being a nation known for sucking Christian blood etc., and shortly afterwards they shot at us through the windows. We instinctively bent down and threw ourselves on to the floor, lying on one another, and somehow we all survived.

About a quarter of an hour after the shooting they dragged us out one by one, stripped us of our clothes, and beat us up with a rubber hose on naked backs, as if we were cattle or house–pets. The blows were painful, but more painful was their conduct and the humiliation.

We decided then to escape, to survive, whatever it takes. We pledged it to each other and we meant it with all our intentions. We planned to act on our plans immediately after the arrest ended, but... only two of us survived, Zalmen Dukshtulski and I.

*

In Lida Ghetto

On May 8, 42, when the Jews of Voronove went through the selection: to life or to death, I stood with everyone and awaited my destiny. I was wondering how to save myself when suddenly a German, for whom I used to work in the old days, before those black days, came up to me and cried out:

"This is my locksmith with his family, I need him!"

He pushed me to the right side and I survived.

After few days they took us to Lida Ghetto. There they sent me to work in the workshops which were under the supervision of Head Commandant *Ubershturmfurer* Hemweg. He was a real Nazi who believed that the Jews were a nation of an inferior race, but he was against their extermination. He built the workshops in order to show that the Jews could become productive and useful. He was a real theoretician of "justified slavery" in 20th century. Nevertheless, we had good memories of him. He kept the Ghetto in better condition than others. We also thought of him well later. When they arrested him after the war, as part of the de-nazification, they called us as witnesses to testify against him. We didn't coordinate between ourselves, but none of us said anything bad about him, and he was released. We wanted to live so much that we were grateful to anyone who delayed our death at least for a bit, no matter what his reasons.

In the workshops Jews from different shtetls worked. We didn't know each other [from before], but when we got acquainted some more, we instantly began making plans to escape from there to the forests. First of all we started to collect guns and to repair them, in order to have something to bring with us to the forests.

We found our best opportunity when the same Hemweg sent us to fetch a Russian tank which had been abandoned nearby, in the area where the Germans were afraid to enter. They didn't want to escort us. They were so terrified that they sent us to proceed alone. They, the Jew–murderers, didn't have heavy ammunition. To take care of us light weapons were enough. They despised us, but only as the danger of the partisans grew so did their need for heavy weapons.

We were five men who went, and all of us had hopes of keeping some arms for ourselves. We wanted the weapons to serve us when we were back in ghetto, or when the moment arrived to get out of there into the forest. In this manner we would buy our freedom [and join] the partisans. It was easier to go into the forest with light weapons.

We walked towards the tank without a German escort. They were simply afraid to go with us. One thing I don't understand is how Hemweg trusted us to come back.

The place was an abandoned Russian camp, full of neglected broken weapons and old scrap iron. We took an armored vehicle, filled it with some grenades, some rifles which we thought we could repair, and some unlocked automatic weapons. We covered it all with pieces of metal and started on our way back.

On our way back we intentionally made noise while walking in the forest. We wanted to draw the attention of the partisans who were active in the area. At one place, I think it was Boksht, we came upon some Germans, disheveled, in their underwear, terrified to death, as if a huge catastrophe was approaching. They were unsteady and frightened.

As soon as they realized it was us, "their people", they scolded us: 'why were we walking around unguarded in a place filled with "partisan" dens?'

We proceeded through Ivia. We knew that in this town there was a ghetto. We stopped there to make contact with the youth in the ghetto. But when we went into the ghetto, we found it empty. Where had all the Jews vanished? What had happened here to the whole town?

How did this happen? We were confused. We began talking Yiddish and [suddenly] people got out from their holes. The poor folks got had gotten scared when they saw an armored vehicle with German decoration so they figured that we had came to liquidate them and they hid in their bunkers.

We calmed them down and cheered them up. We told them about the groups of Jews who had formed partisan units. We advised them to get ready because the days of salvation were near. This hope raised their spirits. They wept like little children. They believed and they didn't believe.

In the garage in Lida we immediately started to repair the vehicle, and at the same time prepared the arms for ourselves. We did it simultaneously. At the same time that we prepared the machine for killing partisans we also prepared light guns for these same partisans to use. *Ribono shel Olam*:[2] how mysterious are the ways of self-preservation.

We intentionally worked slowly on the repair of the armored machine. It was our "cover". Thanks to this we managed to prepare five rifles, one machine gun, and about ten hand grenades. The bullet heads were deformed so we built a special machine to straighten them for use with the rifles. We accomplished all this under the noses of the Germans who came to visit day and night. We even worked on the rifles before their very eyes. When we saw them approaching we made such a noise that it would echo everywhere.

The weapons were repaired by specialists: Velvl Krupski from Lida (later he was killed by Russian brother–partisans because they wanted his revolver), Borukh Levine who is here in Israel (as a partisan, he was the biggest specialist in blowing up German wagons), and the author of these lines.

The armored vehicle was repaired by the engineer and his two Jewish assistants. Unfortunately they were killed during the infamous liquidation act.

The engineer was a dear Jew. He did the work of three so we could do our private work. All three of them worked hard doing the job of six.

We Are Looking For a Way to the Partisans

In the winter of 1942 we made contact with partisans. We exchanged messages, made plans of escape together, and prepared everything for escape. Our first encounter was with a Russian officer. He was a POW. He also worked in a train workshop and also wanted to escape to the forest. We found a common language and were looking for a way together. Once we brought him into the ghetto to speak to our friends. It was very dangerous for him but he came to us and he spoke to those assembled in a little house at the outskirts of the ghetto. He told the assembly about the existence of "Iskra", the Lida partisan base. According to his experience, he persuaded us that the matter was quite easy and not very dangerous. We would just have to find the right trails, far from the German routes. He actually revealed to us the road to "Iskra".

That same winter, groups of Jews started leaving the Lida ghetto in the Vilne direction, and thus opening the way for others who wanted to join the partisans. The first group, consisting of Polish ex-soldiers, came upon a German patrol, and most of them were killed in the confrontation. This bitter news caused difficult feelings in our hearts. Doubt crawled into our souls and filled each one of us with fear.

Later more groups assembled together and prepared to go out. They collected everything related to guns: a bullet, a rusty revolver, a sight of a rifle and other small items.

Our group had already possessed a "nice" collection of guns. We had 10 rifles, a machine gun, 2 revolvers and a considerable number of grenades, which seemed to us alive. Most of the weapons were in a state of readiness after being repaired, waiting only to be tried out. This joint endeavor brought us closer together. We felt as one, one body that is preparing for the trial of a lifetime. Every day we had only one goal: to get prepared to go out into the forest under the noses of the Germans.

Day after day we worked together for one purpose only. There were days when we didn't exchange a single word between us. Secrecy and cooperation were our main concerns in life. And so our doubts faded, our sufferings almost belonged to the past, we already lived in the next day.

April 1943

As soon as we heard about Tuvye Bielski's squad, we forgot about "Iskra".

Meanwhile my friends moved to the forests without telling us, and Borukh Levine from Zheludok not only went away, he took our weapons from us. We gathered a group of devoted friends and again began to prepare ourselves for the forests, recovering from the "treason". But here we came upon various obstacles that we hadn't thought of. We were especially concerned about the situation that would result from our escape: we hadn't thought about this and couldn't think about this. It was difficult to leave behind our parents in the ghetto. Not only because of the separation and longing. We knew what would happen after we departed: the Germans would kill them, and also our brothers and sisters, our friends and relatives, and all because of us. Suddenly our escape looked like egotism, selfish thinking, self–preservation at the cost of the lives of others. Among us there were women, one of them later became my wife. We thought they'd weaken us, but they were more realistic and determined than we were. They gave us strength. My wife gave the last shove towards a quick decision. She said that she and her girlfriends were not betraying anyone, but on the contrary our relatives would be happy with the thought that we had been saved.

In the evening I took out my rifle which was hidden, so did my other friends.

At around 11, about 30 people assembled in a preset place, each one carrying more or less nothing. We cut the fence and we left.

Bielski's courier was punctual to the minute. When we crossed the fence he was already there awaiting us. He led us thru deserted paths and after 2 days of danger and fear, of cautiousness and dependency, we all, to the last man, arrived to Bielski's camp, near Stara Huta. The road wasn't burnt into our memories because all our thoughts were focused on our destination, yet I remember the road well.

On the first evening we crossed a small river with awfully cold water. We walked during the night and rested during the day. We lived for whole days without saying a word. On the second night the road was awfully long. We went by a glass factory which was guarded by Germans and Poles. If not for the darkness of the night, we would have endangered ourselves and the partisans. Our guide urged us on. We made most of the way literally running, in order to reach Bielski's camp by early morning.

And so, running, without breath, we came to the camp early in the morning of May 1, 1943.

In Bielski's Camp

First of all Tuvye examined the weapons that we had brought with us. He was very unhappy with the weapons. He expressed himself according to his mood, with full heart and with language without too much culture. He was disappointed. He knew about our "workshop". He needed guns for all his people. We had fooled him, etc., etc.

Then he took us into his own regiment. Everyone had to worry about his own living place within the borders of the camp, and had to build a house for himself. The men were immediately taken to guard duty. This was the highest expression of trust towards us, and a sign of the deepest respect to our value as men.

Thus we merged into partisan life from the first moment. The transition from slavery and helplessness to being fighters against a heavily armed enemy, protectors of those weaker than us, was very quick, without too much thought or hesitation. Thus elevated, although weak and exhausted, we took upon ourselves the night shifts, and stood by this decision.

Bielski's squad was very mobile. It was surrounded by residential nodes, by *chutors*,³ and by forests. From time to time, for our own safety, we had to wander from place to place and cover our trail as soon as we found out or felt that we had been noticed. This had a bad psychological effect: from time to time we felt like hunted animals.

The night of Shavuot I was taking a shift at a guarding point, about 5 km from the camp. My shift ended in the middle of the night of Shavuot and I was replaced by my friend Efroim from Vashilishok. We had worked together in the workshop, were together in the ghetto; our friendship had overcome all these hardships and was very deep. The orders were not to expose oneself, but if one heard the sound of motors, then one would have to stand up, and even shoot into the air. That was the sign for general alarm. I had just laid down to sleep when I heard an alarm shot, and after that firing from a mortar. In several minutes the camp was on guard and ready. The armed ones stood around as a tight fence, the unarmed men and women in the middle. We were ready to protect ourselves and to retreat. Soon several bombs and shrapnel fell inside the camp. We didn't know what the size of the attacking force was so we started a retreat in the direction of Neman. On the opposite bank were other partisan groups.

Our people divided in two. Our group was the smallest in number, and without a commander. We also didn't have enough weapons and were not familiar with the surroundings. We were not sure where we were going, maybe straight into the hands of the enemy. We were our own commanders, stayed calm and cool–headed. We saw that we were going in the right direction. Suddenly, as we came open an open field, we found ourselves in front of the enemy's canons exposed and unprotected. With us was a woman with a baby. She became tired so she gave him to her brother, and the minute we went out into the field he accidentally dropped the baby. As they bent to pick up the baby, the whole convoy slowed down. The Germans noticed us and took the opportunity to fire on us heavily. Half of our people were killed. We pulled ourselves back into the forests under a rain of bullets and shrapnel. The Germans were afraid of the forest and so the rest of us were saved.

At our hiding place we saw that besides the dead we had some wounded, among them Dukshtulski's wife. This weakened and worried us. The moans of the wounded broke our spirit. Suddenly it happened that we broke out into laughter. The rain was becoming stronger and we stayed in place; we couldn't continue. In the meantime Bielski's brother-in-law found us. We saw that his face was painted like a clown's. The colors of his hat had dripped down his face and created a clown's make up. We couldn't resist. The view of this human face with painted broken lines activated all our laughing reflexes. We forgot the whole situation, the sorrows, and burst out into loud laughter. Temporarily this helped.

That night we didn't walk. We didn't know where to go to find our squad. We lay down and considered what to do. Suddenly we heard a human noise. We were sure that the Germans are coming and grabbed our guns. But those were Tuvye's men.

Tuvye's care for people's lives, for saving Jews, was extraordinary, and in all that chaos he remembered to look for us.

We dragged ourselves for a whole night, together with our wounded, until we came to a place in deep forest, in a less populated area, for me a new and unfamiliar situation.

On the next day I was sent to look for my friend Efroim. He hadn't come back to the base. We found him dead at his post. He was shot like can full of holes, all his clothes covered with blood. They shot him from short range. He had saved us. Thanks to his heroism hundreds of Jews survived in this raid.

We felt that this had been a treachery; someone had discovered us and told the Germans. In 2 weeks we found out who had been the informer. We went to this Gentile. We investigated him so harshly that he admitted that his wife had also been an informer. We locked them in their house and set it on fire. We even burnt down the kennel with their horrific dog, in order to teach the Gentiles that Jewish blood would not be *hefker*[4] anymore, and in order to save other Jewish lives. The feeling that we were no longer sheep for slaughter was the best and deepest feeling.

In Naliboker Forests

Tuvye felt that we were noticeable here, and following his extraordinary intuition, he took us to the wide Naliboker Forests.

Again we dug *zemlianki*,[5] again took care of provisioning and buildings for workshops to make clothes and shoes for everyone. Everything started from scratch.

Our group's assignment was to deliver food and provisions for the people. This was an extremely dangerous task. In addition to the German danger, we now encountered Polish groups, traitors and criminals moving around the forest seeking to kill the last remaining Jews.

From time to time we went out to place mines under German military wagons and to fire on them. We blew up railways and telephone stations. Here our military activity expanded. Life was full of action. There was a lot of doing and fighting. In time we were also told to guard the partisans' field–base. It was a well disguised place near Ivenets. From there we made contact with Moscow, and from there we sent our wounded to Russian hospitals, and also received guns and ammunition.

In spite of all the disguising, the Germans found out about the place and began to bother and shoot. Our lives flew by in day–to–day routines, but our mission and the place were so important to Jewish life, that we were able to overcome everything. Here we had to be the initiators. We made their lives miserable. Each time we cut them off from their bases, we cut them off from all means of communication: funny how the surrounding Gentiles enjoyed this. The telegraph pole that we blew up at night, the Gentiles would erect back into place, and the Germans would pay good money for the job.

Summer 1943 – the Huge Raid

The Germans had concentrated about 100,000 soldiers around the dangerous forest in order to exterminate the last of the partisans once and for all.

Before that they had searched all the surrounding villages and locked [the houses], so that not even one partisan could stay or go in there. Then they went into the forest step by step. Our situation turned tighter from minute to minute. We built a bridge in a mountainous area to make way for us to escape the clamshells closing in on us. But at the last moment one Russian partisan betrayed us, and they found out about our bridge. When Tuvye heard this he took out his revolver and ordered us to turn back from the bridge and look for hiding places in the woods. This was the worst situation of our partisan lives. Suddenly we realized, that all the hardship and suffering we had gone through, was for naught, and all hope was lost.

There was an elderly Gentile who floated wooden beams on the river. He knew all the secret paths in the forest, all the deserted stations that only animals know about. He led us out to safety: a good Gentile, a tzadik. Thanks to him the partisans were saved.

Most of the way we made in drainage channels. This took us a week. During the day we lay in the water, and at night we stood up and walked. Our bags were empty of food except for bits of corn seed. The hunger and the humidity wore us out and weakened us. One day someone started a small fire to warm up his soul and we were noticed. Luckily for us, Germans were always afraid of the forest and they didn't want to come too close to us. They only bombarded us from a distance. Thanks to Tuvye's healthy instincts we were saved again. By his order we all had to stay still. The Germans were sure that we had moved and ran to look for us in another place.

The German defeat was total. The great raid they had planned ended up with nothing, and they left. We stayed in the area, but we divided in groups and continued to live and fight.

Our Visit to Lida Ghetto

Our group headed by Meir Shmerkovitsh (Shamir) was the smallest. We decided to go into the Lida ghetto to save Jews. The road was hard and dangerous. In the ghetto horrible things awaited us. We met ex–partisans there who had gotten tired of the raids and had returned to the ghetto. They welcomed us with antagonism and humiliation. They started the old argument again of "See what you look like", "We somehow got by, more or less, and what awaits you?" etc. They did everything to interfere with our talks to the Jews. They simply filled them with fear. Only a small number of Jews left with us, among them two or three Yeshiva boys and Olkenitski.

April 1944

The German retreat march was chaotic. They abandoned all the frontlines and strategic points. Suddenly the roles switched. Now the Germans were looking for secret paths and hiding in the woods. They were hiding during the day and walking at night, and we were pursuing them. Here we met them at their breaking point. We chased, beat, killed and murdered tens and hundreds of them everywhere. We had then 10 days of revenge and 10 days of faith: if one lives one lives all the way to victory.

We chased them and humiliated them, we trampled their dignity. In their own manner and with their own collaborators we drove them to death.

*

In the last few days of the war, one learned so much, more than in years and generations. We'll not forget this lesson, we want everyone to remember:

In the worst of circumstances one has to try to overcome the hardships and live and – most important – outlive the enemy. Arrogance and self–esteem are not a lifetime guarantee for heroism.

In those several days we lost more friends than in 19 months of partisan life, but the urge to fight in any conditions even at the most desperate moments, proved itself.

It had been worth the effort.

Footnotes

1. Ed. Note: "Bogdan Chmielnitsky, leader of the Cossack and peasant uprising against Polish rule in the Ukraine in 1648 which resulted in the destruction of hundreds of Jewish communities; later hetman of autonomous Ukraine and initiator of its unification with Russia…In the annals of the Jewish people, Chmielnitsky is branded as "Chmiel the Wicked," one of the most sinister oppressors of the Jews of all generations, the initiator of the terrible 1648–49 massacres (*gezerot ta ve–tat*). Chmielnitsky has gone down in history as the figure principally responsible for the holocaust of Polish Jewry in the period, even though in reality his control of events was rather limited.", Jewish Virtual Library, "Bogdan Chmielnitsky" http://www.jewishvirtuallibrary.org/chmielnicki–khmelnitski–bogdan–x00b0.

2. Trans. Note: Dear God

3. Trans. Note: Isolated farms

4. Trans. Note: Cheap or unprotected

5. Ed. Note: Residential huts dug into the earth

[Pages 367-368]

Death Before Our Eyes

Rivkeh Konopke–Mayortshik

Translation by Emma Karabelnik

It was Monday, 5pm. I looked outside the window and saw a lot of people running. pale and terrified, from Lida Street. I ran out quickly into the street. I asked what had happened. They answered that the Germans were on Lida Street, near Iyta Olkenitski, rest in peace. Of course, we became "dark in the eyes", as we knew what happened to Jews everywhere as soon as these murderers entered, and that the same would happen to us.

After 6 weeks, at about 2pm, a lot of vehicles arrived and parked near the church. From the vehicles stepped out a lot of Gestapos and began going from house to house, driving out all the men into the market place. Obviously they had a lot of help from Christian folks. The men were kept in fear at the market place for several hours; before they were released home they were heavily beaten. The bandits took six people with them: Yitzakh Antshul, Gershon Eishishki, Yesheyahu Olkenitski and Zerakh, David, and Esther Shelovski, and according to the rumor they were immediately eliminated. We had heard a lot of rumors from other towns about murder, robbery and slaughter, and now that day had come to our shtetl. To Voronove came many people from surrounding towns, Benakani, Soletchnik, Divenishok and others.

On Friday, May 8, at 5pm, I looked outside. Gestapos are walking around in the street with guns. They didn't allow anyone to go to work. Everybody knew that nothing good was awaiting us. Later that day we heard that in Lida there had been a huge slaughter with barely a few Jews surviving.

Yehuda Konopke-
ritual slaughterer and
inspector of Voronove

Our town was surrounded by [local] police and Germans. Some thought to bribe the policemen and get away from the town. We built a secret room and hid there. Twenty–eight people: me, my sister and parents, rest in peace, Moshe Blyakher with daughters Leah and her family, Sara Hindeh and her family, Yitzach Dvilianski and family, Bissel and family, Ankelovitsh's wife and sister–in–law and the Schneider family.

On May 11, a Monday morning, three local bandits from New Plan[2] arrived very drunk, and immediately began driving out and pushing everyone towards the market place. From the market place they took smaller groups, leaving some to live a little longer. The rest were driven to New Plan, near a forest, where there were already pits prepared, and they shot everyone. They brought the few surviving Jews back to the market. At Yitzach Dvilianski's there was a physician from Navaradok (Dr. Gordon). He knew where we were all hiding. He endangered himself and went to the market place. He had medications with him. He was lucky to be left alive. He registered us as survivors and came to tell us that we could go out. With broken hearts we went out to the market place to join the surviving Jews. The head commissioner, Vindish, made a speech and said that we were being kept alive temporarily, and that everything would go as it had in Lida. They forced us all to New Plan. We were at Zalmen Levine's house. On the first day of *Shavues*, it was a Saturday, everybody was told to take packages and we were driven on foot to Bastuni. Those who walked slowly were beaten up on the spot. From the police [station] in Bastuni we were put in wagons and taken to Lida. While traveling in the wagons we thought that it would be wonderful to go on traveling like this forever.

Editorial Footnote

1. 'New Plan' is the name give to the newer section of the town.

[Pages 369-374]

Taking Some More Vengeance

Shmuel Kopelovitsh (Of Blessed Memory)

Translation by Emma Karabelnik

Ed. Note: This article appears in both Hebrew and Yiddish in the original Yizkor Book. The following is a translation of the Yiddish text. Photos appearing within the Hebrew version are included here.

I won't write about my days with Bielski's Partisans. Those were days of sweet, active revenge. While I would like to write more [about those days], a lot has already been written of our doings by others better than me.

Everyone already knows about the vengeance of the Partisans. I am going to tell about a special case of vengeance after the Partisans.

*

On July 10, 1944 Bielski came up with the idea to go out of the woods and to take the whole group to Navaradok.

At 9:00am we all stood arranged into lines. Tuvia Bielski together with the intelligence [scouts], told us that we are leaving the woods. We left with a feeling of joy and sorrow, because here in the forest we had felt the sweet taste of revenge.

It was a hot sunny day and the road was sandy and hard. In the fields and woods there were dozens and dozens of Germans scattered dead and *opgeshindene*.[1] Many woods were burning and from the burnt bodies came an awful repulsive smell that hard to breathe.

Thousands of Red Army soldiers were driving on the roads, with them a lot of captured Germans. The Nazi cowards were afraid of the Partisans' revenge, so they willingly turned themselves in to the Russian military.

In Navaradok there were already other Partisan groups. We all were gathered in a closed park. A Russian mayor–general approached and spoke to us, saying among other things, the following:

"The war is not over yet, and you have to help us to chase the crazy, wounded Nazi wolf back to his den."

After that all the Partisans received their certificates. Some were released and allowed to return home.

For me the question was: where is my home?

Could I return to Voronove, the place of my birthplace where we had all lived our lives, knowing that Voronove had become a mass grave for our most dearly loved people?

We were drawn "home" as a beaver is drawn to his nest after its destruction. We were going home by foot; there was no transportation yet.

On July 18, 1944 a group of 25 people came back to Voronove. As far as I can remember we came through Hermanishok Street at about 3:00pm.

We came into town exhausted, hungry, and in a bad mood.

The town looked dead. The houses stood the same as before, but not a single person could be seen. The several people that we met accidentally opened their eyes wide at us not believing that we were still alive. They were 100% sure that we'd been gotten rid of. Nobody went to his own house; we all stayed together.

In the town there were several Russian "bosses", a representative of the Russian military headquarters, and a couple of assistants.

They were staying in the house of Binyamin Levine. We announced ourselves to them and told them that we were from this town and had been released from the Partisans. Everyone held on to their weapons; we didn't part from them.

The man ordered us to take the house of Goldeh Yehiel's and that we should all stay there together. She had to move out and we took the house. We slept on the floor because we had been used to that for many months. We also didn't have anything to sleep on, but we didn't want to ask the Goyim for bedclothes. However, we did have to ask for food from the nicer Gentiles whom we knew from the town. I found myself eating with a family in Bathhouse Street. The food got stuck in my throat and I lost my appetite when I noticed stolen Jewish furniture in the house and various specific Jewish items. We didn't talk about these things: neither I to them nor they to me.

Later we were given potatoes, bread, and onions, and we started to cook for ourselves at our home. We all ate together.

Our situation was very difficult from a political–security point – even dangerous. Every minute we were at risk of death.

The war was not over yet. The Germans were deserting from the frontlines and with them the Polish Partisans. Both hated the Russians and the Jews, and both were wandering the woods surrounding Voronove. After some time, a reinforcement of Russian soldiers arrived, headed by an NKVD[2] officer, to fight the remnants of the once great forces. They established their headquarters in Hermanisher Street where Vilianski's mill used to be. There they also established a prison.

They caught Germans, brought them to the prison, and we Partisans had to guard them. After 25 murderers were captured we would lead them to Lida where there was a POW camp.

One day I and Yoel Kheifets were on watch shift. My boots were torn. Suddenly I see a German with new boots. I called him to approach and asked him to take off his boots. He thought I was going to shoot him, because that's what they used to do, so he threw himself at my feet and began wailing hysterically. He cried and begged me to let him live. When I took his boots from him and gave him my torn ones, and let him go, he was the happiest man.

After a few weeks Leybke Kaplan, who was a policeman in Vilne, came back to Voronove. He was still wearing his uniform and told us he was going to visit a Gentile in a [nearby] village to retrieve his clothes, which his family had left for him before marching to death. We tried to convince him not to go because the area was full of Polish murderers and it was scary. He wouldn't listen to this call and didn't take our advice. We didn't see him anymore.

The same was the case with Issar Pupko. He went for his furniture and paid with his life, after having survived the Nazis.

*

The Military Headquarters started to enlist Poles to send them to the frontlines, which were still active. But they resisted and there was a special military unit which had to capture them and bring to Voronove. The Russians assigned that task to the Jewish fighters.

But there remained only few of us. The Jewish Partisans had gradually moved to Lida and there remained only me, Moshe Berkovitsh his son Leyzer, and Yudl (Khazn's) Konopke.

We wanted to stay here to take more revenge on our good neighbors, the murderers and their collaborators. We made a list of all the Poles who had helped murder our dear ones and passed it to the NKVD leader, our best friend. I would spend long hours at his office and he wrote everything in the protocol. We purposely emphasized in the protocols that they had murdered Russians [as well]. For Jews alone, nobody would do anything. I signed off on all the details and waited for their reaction.

Thus, pursuant to my signature, in one week they arrested Tekle Bareishes— the shoemaker– and all those who had surrounded the town, who had gathered Jews in the market place, and who had walked around us with the Germans picking out "the communists" and who then shot them in the woods outside the town. They had picked out the children of Shmuel Shelovski, Gershon Eishishki, Yitzach Volpianski and Sheykeh Olkenitski, and with their own hands brought them to death.

We then turned in the Polish teacher Damansky who during German [occupation] became the Mayor of the town and Commandant of the Police. He and many others were arrested immediately.

*

A month later I was called to Baranovich to give testimony; I don't even know for whom.

It was very difficult to get to Baranovich. The transportation and the roads were in bad condition.

In Baranovich I was told to go to the prison. They took me in a big cold room where the investigator from the political crimes department was seated. He tore off a piece of newspaper and started to roll a cigarette from "makhorka"[3], watched me for a good 10–15 minutes, and didn't say a word. Only after that did he start to ask me questions. First, how come I survived while all the Jews were murdered? What did I do for the Germans during German occupation? As if I were the one under suspicion. I proved to him with documents that I had escaped the Ghetto to the woods and joined the Partisans. Finally he asked if I knew Damansky and if I had good relations with him. He wrote down all my answers. He wrote that Damansky, when in the position of Police Commandant, had gathered 265 Jews from Vilne, who had escaped slaughter [and come] to us. He and the Germans took them from the cinema, where they were performing, to a small forest on the way to the railway station and shot them there.

I also added that by his initiative they had searched and caught Russian soldiers who were hiding with us, and shot them.

This had an awful impact on him. He approached me and said he would now call for him [Damansky] and I would have to answer all the questions looking straight into his eyes.

I went out of the room and then they called me back in. Damansky was already there, standing with his face to the wall. I was ordered to sit. After 10 minutes Damansky was told to turn around to us.

When he saw me he recognized me immediately. He opened wide eyes on me and put a finger to his mouth showing that he was hungry. He probably thought that as an acquaintance I'd bring him food. He looked awful, covered with hair, with torn clothes, and house shoes on his feet.

The investigator asked if he knew me and had we ever fought.

He answered that he knew me and my whole family.

Then the investigator asked me if I knew him and what did I have to say.

I looked into Damansky's eyes and told everything about the Vilne Jews and about his collaboration with the Germans.

He lowered his head. He knew what was to be his fate.

Before my leaving he asked me to visit his wife, to tell her where he was, and to ask her to send him packages.

*

A week later I was again called to the Police station. They ordered me to go to Minsk to give testimony in the prison. Again, I didn't know against whom.

Minsk was totally destroyed and it was very hard to navigate. I asked a woman in the street for directions. She instantly recognized me being a Jew. She was a Jewish child and she lived not far away. I had a spare couple of hours so I went to her house. Hew accommodations were awfully poor and small. She was a dentist. She asked me if I knew that today was Pesach. I was surprised. I didn't know so I told the truth that I didn't know. So she took a bit of black flour, mixed it with water, and made *matzoh* on a gas burner— a Jewish soul. I was filled with pride for our people who were born, grew up, and were educated in Yidishkeit[4] – and even in Russia remembered Pesach and to eat *matzoh*. Who can appreciate a Jewish...[sic]

In the prison they took me to a room where the military trial was being held, presided over by a colonel. Here I was told that it was for Tekle Bareishes.

The same game of going out and back in took place. When she was standing with her face to the wall, I approved all the documents that I signed in Voronove.

They asked her if she knew Shmuel Kopelovitsh from Voronove. They asked her again if she felt guilty about collaborating with the Nazis.

She gave negative answers to all the questions. When they told her to turn around and asked if she recognized me, she said – yes!

She became dead-pale when she saw me, and lowered her head.

I also answered that I knew her from my early childhood. I told her to her face all her doings, that she had collaborated with Nazis of her own will, that she knew perfect Yiddish, and understood German.

During my testimony she interrupted several times, but I proved to her simply that she had worked as an anti-communist. For better effect I gave as a fact that she had turned in 2 Russian soldiers that had been hiding in my attic, and then Germans had shot them in her garden, in her presence.

That was enough.

I traveled back to Voronove with a feeling of lightness.

I had revenged our murderers against those killers who had helped exterminate our dear and beloved ones.

Footnotes

1. Ed. Note: In the original text the word is spelled: alef–pey–gimel–ayen–shin–yud–nun–dalet–ayen–nun–ayen. From its context and the root it is most likely a word for the decomposition of human flesh.

2. Ed. Note: The Soviet secret police.

3. Ed. Note: A type of inexpensive tobacco.

4. Tr. Note: Yiddish spirit

[Pages 375-378]

My Miserable Russian Days

Bat Sheba Podisiuk-Kalmanovitsh

Translation by Emma Karabelnik

Ed. Note: This article appears in both Hebrew and Yiddish in the original Yizkor Book. The following is a translation of the Yiddish text. Photos appearing within the Hebrew version are included here.

On April 13, 1940 the Russians deported my mother to Siberia and I went with her by my own will. I wanted to be there with her in those strange surroundings.

We were six little children when our father died and she had brought us up as both a mother and a father. Out of the six, only three were with her now [at the time of deportation]. When the Russians had come my brother Aharon crossed the border and went to Vilne. He wanted to save himself from their vengeance because he had been a founder and commander of Beitar, the "national fascist organization".[1]

They deported Mother though she was innocent and without any jurisdictional charges. Their purpose was to get to Aharon and to please the local communists.

She was sixty years old when she was forced to part from everything that was dear to her in the town and to leave for a strange land.

The Russians let us take with us everything we wanted. And so we traveled to Nikolayevka, a town near Petropavlovsk in Northern Siberia. We were there for two years. We were given a room in a *kolkhoz*[2], but they didn't give us any work. We couldn't take any jobs: my mom because of her age and me because I had to take care of her. We got by from selling our belongings. Luckily there was such a shortage in clothes that we sold our dresses for as much as we wanted to charge, and the price of one piece was enough to feed us for weeks.

In 1942, Sikorsky started organizing the [deported] Polish citizens in order to gather them and bring them back "home" so we two were sent away to work in the railway-building and communication brigades. We lived in the town of Ossul[3] near Karaganda.[4] We were [a group of] seven women. We worked along with the men laying railways. In this way we became Russian citizens.

During our life in the *kolkhozes* we went thru a lot of difficulties. They wouldn't let us work when we wanted and needed work. They said we could earn by selling our goods and could be unemployed for 10 years. Everyone wanted us to live [and pay rent] with them. Actually every apartment consisted of one room, no matter how big the family. We lived in one room with family of ten - bed by bed. We paid our rent with goods. Every morning we would go out [in the street] like peddlers and sell our goods.

We lived in Ossul for 4 years, there mother needed me and my care, so her doctor released me from work. The residents of the village were of quite a good nature, but they couldn't accept that a young woman wasn't working. I felt I wouldn't be able to continue like this for a long time. It was simply becoming too dangerous. So I looked as hard as I could for a position in the collective work, but I was looking for a light work

Among the few Jewish families there was one Svititsky from Slonim, a tailor with his wife who was also an excellent seamstress. She knew about my situation and my need so she offered me to join a sewing brigade. At that time a new brigade was founded, but I had no idea how to sew so she taught me the basics and I started [to work in] the brigade. And so [life] became easier for me.

After a year the [financial] situation of the locals improved. The *kolkhoz* received supplies of clothes [from the government]; my hosts didn't need our dresses anymore so they plainly told us to leave. We didn't have where to go. It was impossible to get an apartment. I was very worried. By chance we got acquainted with a Barash family from Sarna,[5] a family with many children. We decided to buy a "*lepianka*" together, a kind of tiny hut. We paid with two pillows and bedding [cloths] and bought the hut from someone who sold us his old one and built a new one for himself.

We lived together until 1944.

*

One day when I came home in midday for lunch, a soldier from the local police entered the *lepianka* with a bottle in his hands and asked if maybe we have vodka or if maybe we know where to buy some. I felt that there might be a threat for us here, so I answered:

"Here live only women and women don't drink."

He looked around for a while and went away.

Two weeks later, on Shabbat night, two women from Lomzhe, who used to live near us in Ossul, came to us and asked to stay overnight. They used to buy flour in a *sovkhoz*[6] and sell it [in town]. We had let them sleep over several times before. One night we were sitting around talking about what would be after the war ended. We knew that Poland wasn't an option for us anymore, though we didn't know the full [extent of] the disaster. We had thought that the stories about the Nazi despotism were political propaganda. So we sat late into the night and fell asleep very late. As soon as we fallen asleep we heard someone at the door. We asked:

"Who is it?"

Answer:

"NKVD"

I answered:

"Wait a minute, I have to dress up"

Meanwhile I woke the other women and we all put on our clothes. I told them to shut the window and block the door. When we were well protected [barricaded], we all started to scream. They fired a few shots and went away. At about 2 a.m. the shooting stopped and it became quiet. We were afraid to stay in the house. We went out carefully through the window and to the police. The duty policeman wasn't impressed by our fright and told us:

"Go to sleep women, nothing happened."

His answer sounded suspicious to me. I was restless. I had a feeling that something was going to happen— something's up. The next morning I told the story to our Jewish friends at work, but no one had any advice for me. I decided not to sleep in our *lepianka*. I went to [the house of] a Jewish blacksmith, a worker from the area whom we knew, a strong man who had good relations with everyone and knew everyone. I had hoped he would intercede for us but it was too late. He just gave us a room to sleep and we spent the night calmly.

Several days later we heard stories at work about anonymous men who had attacked one of the *lepiankas* at night and killed three people. According to the story, the murderers had made a mistake. They had meant to kill us and killed someone else. Only then did the Russian police wake up and start to investigate. The local population helped them and finally the murderers were arrested.

They were three soldiers. They confessed that they had found out about our "wealth" and so at first they tried to rob us by trick. When that didn't work they simply decided to kill us and thus lay hands on our property. They said they couldn't resist the temptation.

*

My life in Russia was temporary, but in a short period of time I suffered difficulties and want. The Russian regime is an experiment and no one knows how and where it will end. Meanwhile a person is worthless there. I lived my life there in a sea of misery and suffering. The local population born after the revolution had various benefits such as free academic education and right to work, but they lost their worth in depressing poverty and human misery. I denounced my eligibility for citizenship and immigrated with my old mother to Israel.

She had the privilege to live here and died at the age of 88.

Editorial Footnotes

1. Beitar was a Revisionist Zionist youth movement.

2. A collective farm

3. In the original text this place is spelled: aleph-samekh-vov-lamed. The precise location of this town has not yet been determined.

4. Karaganda is in today's Kazakhstan.

5. In the original text the place is spelled: samekh-aleph-reysh-nun-ayen. The location of this place has not yet been determined.

6. A state-owned farm

[Pages 379-381]

In Memory of the Slaughtered Voronove Jews

H. Solodukha

Translation by Emma Karabelnik

Before the War, Voronove was one of the worthiest shtetls in Vilna area. The Jewish population here was exterminated in the most tragic way, exactly as the Jews of other cities and towns during Hitler's bloody occupation.

On September 23, 1941, after the ethnic cleansing of the Jews of Rudomino, I, a 19–year old youngster, together with my 17–year old cousin, escaped from there. After long wandering in the woods, hungry and frozen, we arrived at Divenishok (20 km from Voronove) where good–hearted Jews adopted us. Here we warmed up a bit and regained our strength, but it didn't last for long.

On January 15, 1942 the Head Commissar of the Lida district announced: "All Jews living in the surrounding towns: Divenishok, Soletchnik, Benakani, and the smaller towns – have to move in 5 days time to the Voronove Ghetto."

On January 18, 1942 we, together with the Jews of Divenishok, moved to Voronove. At that time there were about 5,000 Jews. I was given a place to sleep in a small house where 32 people were already living. 125 grams of bread a day, 12 hours a day of hard work cleaning streets – that was our life. But already on the first Sunday since our arrival began the slow liquidation of the Ghetto.

The murderers gathered 25 homeless, elderly Jews and shot them.

Every day brought new victims. One Jew forgot that he is not allowed to walk on the sidewalk, another wore clothes lacking a yellow patch, a third was caught with meat on his plate, somebody else decided to cross the street after curfew hours – they were all shot at the spot.

Voronove's survivors from the woods – at the mass grave

On the 7th of May, quite early in the morning, the oldest Jew in our "house", Reb Pinya[1], a man about 80 years old, told me the town is full of SS and Gestapo men.

On the next day there were already dozens of victims who had failed to escape to the Aryan side. On May 10, a representative of the Head Commissar arrived and he requested the summoning of the "Yudenrat"[2] collaborators and announced to them that: "In Lida, six

Jews had robbed and then murdered a local priest. Five of them had been caught. The sixth's name is Moshe Levine, 40 years old, profession: house–painter. It's a possibility that he is currently in Voronove, that's why in the upcoming days all Jewish documents will be checked. The "Yudenrat" must of course assist, but there is no need, God Forbid, to be afraid. The only one who should be afraid is Moshe the Painter— and the murderer".

What it all meant we understood only on May 11: early in the morning, hundreds of Hitler's hangmen arrived in Voronove and started to go from house to house 'looking for Moshe the murderer'. All Jews were sent out to the marketplace and those that tried to hide were shot on the spot.

At the marketplace people were kept until 2pm under strict watch of course. Then there came an order to be organized into small groups, by family, and at first to march to a place not far from the marketplaced. There, near the crossroad, the groups were stopped. And then, a most horrible process began – the selection. Men to one side, women to the other, and children in the opposite direction. Most of the Jews were concentrated in one place – between them were Zalberg, the Dolmetcher with wife, the "Yudenrat" collaborators, the Commandant of the Jewish Police in the ghetto, and his assistants.

Everybody knew that towards the right meant to prison, towards the left, to the Almighty. The executions were performed at some distance from the railway. Many of those who were sent to the right or to the left would start running immediately. 'Immediately' became the final path for most of the Voronove Jews. About 100 meters behind the shtetl, deep pits had been dug already, where half–naked and shot Jews were thrown. The screams coming from women, children, and men are indescribable. Whoever saw and heard this will never forget.

That's how, on May 11, 1942 all the Voronove Jews died. May these few words be a monument for the slaughtered Jewish settlement.

Editor's[3] remark: This article by Solodukha is an abstract from *Folksshtime*. We publish it – though not all of the details are accurate – to emphasize that the sole surviving record of these events are in the Yizkor books.

Editor's Footnotes

1. In the original text this proper name is spelled using the Hebrew letters: pe–nun–yud–ain. The designation 'Reb' is the equivalent of 'Mr.'.

2. The Yudenrats were Nazi–mandated town Councils composed of Jewish elders and responsible for carrying out Nazi orders upon the Jewish population.

3. This 'Editor's remark' is from the original Yizkor Book text

[Page 382]

This is How My Shtetl Marched to Death

Moshe Kaplan

Translation by Emma Karabelnik

Two Rabbis, the Kletzker and the Myadler are marching to death[1]
They are holding hands with wives and children
They are looking for an answer to a difficult question
In *Torah*, *Gemarah*, *Mishniyot* and *Kabbalah*
Is it possible that there is no answer?
Could they forget the answer?
But there is, there must be
That's how two Rabbis marched to death.

Shaul–Reuven and Minkeh are marching to death
They are on both sides, children in the middle
A tear and another wet the cheeks
They cover the children with their hands

They pull them to their hearts and hug them strongly
Maybe by this they'll protect them
Shaul–Reuven full of dreams of a Jewish state and Zion
Slightly shivers that the dream will not come true
He is not going to Isroel and not to Zion
Instead he is going with his children to his own funeral
That's how Shaul–Reuven and Minke marched to death.

Feivel Baruch–Aharon's, Elya the tailor
And Velvl Mesonznik are marching to death
Grey beards became blurred, white heads disheveled
Actually, they think, under the earth or above it
We live the years given to us as a present
So finish on the way
To recite most of the *Tehilim*, an abstract from *Mishniyot*
Maybe by this privilege will come salvation
We must not lose our faith
Don't lose the faith!
That's how Feivel, Elya and Velvl marched to death.

Yosl and Shtisl are marching to death, Yosef and Shtisl
Fear and hope, mourning and comforting are in the air
Yosl's clever eyes lighten up
Don't be afraid my wife
This is not the last road for our nation
We have a branch in Isroel
They will accomplish our ideals, strike our enemies
That's how Yosl and Shtisl marched to death.

Yankele Avreml's, Dinale Keile's
Beilinke Moltsadski are marching to death
Dina, come and I'll save you
–says a guard – and you'll live
Thank you – says Dinale – I'll stay with father, mother and sisters.
Yankele's fist cracked the guards face
And Beilinke, young and willing to live, goes proudly
Today is the day – she says – to be proud to be a Jew

That's how those three marched proudly to death.

Tsireh–Leah, Keileh, Feigeh, Mineh–Riveh
Sarah–Zloteh, Sarah–Mereh are marching to death
Poor folks are awaiting their support

Poor brides' help before the *chuppeh*[2]
What did you do here, dear God
Poor them, will wait for us while we march
God of mercy, God of revenge, where are you?
We the women, take upon us the verdict, but You, where are You?

That's how Voronove's righteous[3] marched to death.

That's how my *shtetele*[4] marched to death
Saintly faces, lips in prayer, eyes shining
Outcome of a 2000 year mistake
Girls and boys, blooming flowers
Little children, beautiful hearts
Helpless fathers, worried mothers
With doubts about God and belief in their nation:
It will continue living
Fighting and striving
And revenge every soul
Everybody knows
That this is the only consolation.

Editor's Footnotes

1. See: 'The Rabbis and the Rabbinical Dispute' on page 186 for an explication of this line of verse.

2. Bridal canopy

3. Understood from the Yiddish that this refers to Voronove's righteous women

4. Little town

Voronove during a 'Life' march

[Pages 385-391]

Names of Voronove Martyrs
Transliterated by Jack Gottlieb

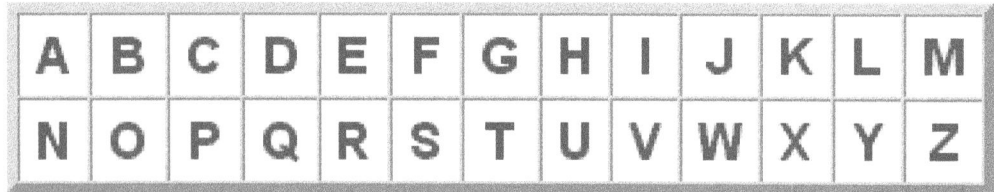

Abramiski, Alter, and wife, Shifra and children

Arkin, Aaron, Margolit, Israel, Haim, Benjaimin, Deborah, Sheena

Arkin, Bluma, Tzvi and daughter

Arkin, Eta-Chana, Beryl and daughter

Balteriski, Aryeh-Lev

Balteriski, Benjamin, Peshya

Balteriski, Haim-Eliahu and wife

Balteriski, Hershel, Faigel

Balteriski, Joseph his wife and children

Balteriski, Pesach his wife and children

Balteriski, Tzvi, Tzvyah and children

Baron, Abraham wife, Rhoda, and Sheena

Basist, Esther

Benunski, Eiziki and wife

Berkovski, Besha-Reina, Yizhak(her son)

Berkovski, Samuel, and wife

Berlovitsh, Feivel wife and children

Benyakonski, Leeba

Benyakonski, Nechama, Mendel, Yoel and family

Bloch, Lazur, wife, Rezel(his mother) and children

Bloch, Shabtai, Reizel(his daughter)

Borski, Hershel, Henia and children

Borski, Zeidel, Bosel, Lev and children

Chafetz, Yesheyahu, Faiga, Feivel, Gisha

Dlugin Shabtai, Tema and children

Dlugin, Shimshon, Krynah, Rephael, Sonya, Chana, Alkah

Dokshtolski, Tzadok, Chanah(his mother)

Dovrov, Alter, wife, Tuvia, Chayim

Dubinski, Israel, Freedel and children

Dublinski, Samuel and wife

Dublinski, Chayim, wife and children

Dudovitsh, Chavah

Dvilianski, Abraham-Elyahu, Motla, Mosya, Benyamin, and children

Dvilianski, Velvel, Judith, Temah

Dvilianski, Yizhak, Esther and children

Eishishki, Gershon, Sheena and chilren

Eishishki, Yechezkiel, Faiga and children

Eishishki, Yitzhak, Mirel, Aaron

Epstien, Yakov, Leah, Faiga and children

Finestein, Moshe, Alta, Monique, and children

Finklestein, Benjamin, Rachel and children

Finklestein, Shema, Chesya, and children

Garbatski, Tzvi(Hershke), Tsiril and children

Gershonovitsh, David, Batya, Joseph, and children

Gershonovitsh, Moshe, Dova, Lev, Chaya, and children

Gershonovitsh, Moshe, Sarah, Abraham, Zalman, Chesya and children

Gobitsh, Chanan, Tovah, and children

Gobitsh, Joseph, Sheena and children

Gobitsh, Tuvia, Reizel

Gol, Joseph, his wife, Chaya(his mother)

Gol, Meyer, Malchah, Chaya, Batya, Mosha

Gorbitsh, Kiza

Gorbitsh, Meyer, Leah, Haim-David and children

Grodznetchik, Yehoshua, Sarah, Grunya

Grodzenchik, Yakov, Chaya, Hayim-Elyahu, Yehuda-Mosha

Grodzenchik, Aaron(Ora), Zelda and children

Grodzenchik, Nachum-Hersh, Sarah-Mara, Yoel, Gisha

Grodzenchik, Pinchas, Judith and daughter

Grodzenchik,, Nachum, Liba(his mother)

Iszkovitsh, Feivel, Chava and children

Itskovitsh, Pesach

Kagan, Yizhak, Leah and children

Kalmanovitsh, Joshua

Kamanetski, Yizhak, Chaya Gittel

Kamitski, Isaac, Nechama and children

Kamiunski, Yakov, Sarah, Henech, Faiga, Gulya

Kaplan, Abba

Kaplan, Benjamin, Riva, and children

Kaplan, Groynim and children

Kaplan, Joseph, Sarah, Lev, Beila, Zalman

Kaplan, Kasriel-bar

Kaplan, Lev, Beila and children

Kaplan, Moshe, Chaya-Bayya, Lev and children

Kaplan, Neta-Elya, Esther, Sarah

Kaplan, Shaul

Kaplan, Yakov, Kreina, Shalom

Kaplan, Yizhak, Chaya and children

Kapli, Yerachmiel-Judah, Rashal and children

Katzenellenbogen, Rachel, Yerachmiel(son), Lazur(son), Zalman(son)

Kolah, Faiga, Judith, Byala and children

Konyachovski, Reizel, Chaina(daughter)

Koplovitsh, Haina, Joseph(her son)

Kosovski, Benzion, Miriam and children

Kovniski, Yakov, Gronya, Miriam, Aharon

Kreshunski i, Moshe, Lyova and children

Kreshunski, Hersch(Sibirnick)

Kreshunski, Judah, Leah, Tzvi, Miriam

Kudlinski, Velvel, Kyla, Dinah, Moshe

Kuropatwa, Chaim Joseph

Kuznets, Lev

Kuznets, Nahum, Sheena

Kuznets, Pesach, Henya, and children

Kuznets, Simcha, wife and children

Kuznets, Yizhak, Bat-sheva and children

Lapidos, Abraham Lazur, Gittel and children

Levine Eyiahu, Tzera-Leah

Levine, Aaron(son of Yakov-Boazo), Sarah and children

Levine, Aaron, Chana and children

Levine, Beerel, Sarah Leah, Shlomo, Shalom, Shimon

Levine, Benyamin and wife, Abraham-Meyer, Beela, Hodas, Chana, Saul, Ephriam

Levine, David, Sarah and children

Levine, Lazur-Hersh, Blume, daughter, Deborah, Abraham

Levine, Mendel, Esther and children

Levine, Motel, Chaya, David, Zelda and children

Levine, Saul-Reuben, Minah and children

Levine, Shlomo and children

Levine, Velveel, 7 year old girl and family children

Levine, Yaakov

Levine, Zalman, Rivka, Meyer(their sons)

Levitovitsh and children

Lefkovitsh , Aaron, Fraidel and children

Lefkovitsh, Heschel, Fraidel and family

Lefkovitsh, Leev-Yechezkiel, Rivka, Pesya

Lipinski, Shimon, Tuvia, Sarah, Abba

Lipinski, Yechezkiel, Fruma, Tzvi, and children

Lipinski, Zissel, Leah-Yentel, Minah

Lobutski, Aaron-Hersh, Leah

Lobutski, Chaim, Edla and children

Lobutski, Shabtai, daughter and children

Magilski, Abraham-Bar, Malcha, Gedalyah and children

Magoliski, Benjamin, Faiga-Rachel, Gedalia, Shmuel, Sheena

Meirrovitsh, Meyer, his wife and children

Meirovitsh, Reuben, Pesya and children

Meirovitsh, Zelta, Bayla and children

Michalovski, Mechla, Siyoma(her son)

Moltsadski, Izaac, Reizel, Belah(their daughters)

Olkenitski, Abraham and wife

Olkenitski, Benjamin wife and children

Olkenitski, Chaim-Yacob, wife and children

Olkenitski, Eta, sons and daughters

Olkenitski, Glika and Velvel

Olkenitski, Joseph, Berta and children

Olkenitski, Shmuel and Bracha

Olkenitski, Yeshyahu, Elka and children

Olkenitski, Yizhak, wife, his mother Ital, and children

Olytovitsh, Yizhak, Faiga and children

Olytovitsh, Zelda-Riva

Pikovski, Motel, Shana, Chaim, Tzvi

Pikovski, Judah, Esther

Plotnick, Ychoshua, Sarah and children

Poditvianski, Abraham, his wife and children

Poditvianski, Abraham, Sarah Leah and children

Pupko, Yerachmiel, Bela-Judith, Abraham, Fraida, Esther, and children

Pupko, Feivel, Esther

Pupko, Joesph, Leah, Issur

Pupko, Joseph, Sarah-Rivkah

Pupko, Motel, Shafrina, Haya-Leah

Pupko, Pinchas, his wife, and Batya

Pupko, Shaul, Miriam, and children,

Pupko, Yakov, Breena

Pupko, Yakov, Loba, Zerach and children

Puziriski, Abraham, Chana, and children

Puziriski, Shlomo, Nechama and children

Rabinovitsh, Noah-Elya and wife

Ribitski, Aharon, wife, Moshe and children

Rivak, Samuel, wife and children

Rodnick, Melach, Rivka, Rodel

Rothman, Velvel, Miriam, Alter and children

Shelovski, Samuel, Faiga-Rachel, David, Esther

Shelovski, Zerach, Pesya

Shiftinski, Chaim, sister

Shiftinski, Nechama, Chya, Henya, Kyla, Shpira Shlomo, Chaya, Byla and children

Shiftinski, Shabtai, Shifra, and children

Shiftinski, Shalom

Shmerkovitsh Bezalel, Batya, Rivka

Shmerkovitsh, Joseph, Shtissel, Meshalom

Shmerkovitsh, Malka, Faiga(sister)

Shmerkovitsh, Meyer(Mytzchik), Dinah and children

Shmerkovitsh, Yakov, Sarah, Chayim, Rachel and children

Shmerkovitsh, Yizhak, Malka

Schneider, Yizhak, Sarah and children

Sifkona, Chaya

Solminski, Mary, Asher(her son), Zelta(her daughter)

Soltchinski, Chaim-Yona, Batya(her daughter) and children

Solts, Berka and children

Solts, Velvel, wife and children

Shtikolshchik, Chaya, Batya(her daughter) and children

Tebashinski, Lev, Edla, and children

Tebashinski, Meyer

Turetski, Yaakov, Esther

Turetski, Yizhak, Faiga-Judith, Fraida and children

Turetski, Gottlieb, Marishal and children

Turetski, Yizhak-Meyer, Deborah, Moshe, Yakov, Rachel, Beirel

Turok, Moshe, Rachel and children

Varsutski, Hinda, Baruch(her son), Dovah(her daughter)

Varsutski, Shlomo, Hodas and children

Vashiliski, Gerson, wife and children

Vellman, Moshe, wife Shabtai and family

Vellman, Nachum, Reizel, Beirel, Yerachmael, Benjamin and family

Volpianski, Anshel, Faigah

Volpianski, Moshe, Loba

Volpianski, Yizhak, Esther and children

Vilinchik, Benjamin(her son)

Vilinski, 'Owner of Flour Mill', wife and children

Viner, Aaron, Rachel and children

Yoselvitsh,(Harav), wife and children

Zhabinski, Lazur, Faigah and children

Ziglnitski, Abraham, wife and children

Zilverman, Levah

Zipkovitsh, (Harav), wife, Chava and children

Zvolotski, Moses, Devrosha and children

[Page 390]

List of Voronove Immigrants to Israel

Transliterated by Judy Petersen

Surname	Given name	Residence	Remarks
AVRAMISKI	Aryeh	Tel Aviv	
AVRAKOVITSH	Yehudit	Petach Tikva	
ALPEROVITSH	Chaim	Yaffo	
ALKONI	Yesheyahu	Beit Alpha	
OLKENITSKI	Moshe	Kibbutz Eilon	
ARBEITER	Chaya	Petach Tikva	
ARKIN	Reuven	Ramat Gan	
ARKIN	Tzvi		
ARKIN	Pesach		
OLKENITSKI	Dov	Haifa	
AVINOAM	Pesya	Kfar Sirkin	
AFLOG	Beila	Nes Tziona	
OLKENITSKI	Meir	Givataim	

OLKENITSKI	Eizik	Tel Aviv	
OLKENITSKI	Shraga	Bnei Brak	
OLKENITSKI	Yakov	Givataim	
AVIEL	Shlomo	Ramat Gan	
OVER	Channah	Ramat Gan	
BLITTER	Henya	Tel Aviv	
BINONSKI	Shmuel	Beersheva	
BLYAKHER	Beila	Petach Tikva	
BERKOVSKI	Yisrael	Tel Aviv	
BILITSKI	Avraham	Akko	and Batya
BAIERSKI	Yekutiel	Kfar Saba	
BLOCH	Yakov	Petach Tikva	
BLOCH	Avraham	Tel Aviv	
BLOCH	Chaya	Kfar Saba	
BEN-SHLOMO	Channah	Haifa	
BALTERISKI	Shalom	Netanya	
GRABETSKI	Baruch	Beersheva	
GINSBURG	Avraham	Yad Eliahu	

GOLNIK	Yaffa	Tel Aviv
GOL	Sarah	Ramat Gan
GIL	Yehoshua	Tel Aviv
GORDON	Daniel	Tel Aviv
GOLDSTEIN	Rivka	Ramat Gan
GERSHONI	Yosef	Ramat Gan
GERSHENOVITSH	Eliahu	Netanya
GINSBURG	Batya	Ramat Gan
DUKSHTULSKI	Zalman	Ramataim
DVILIANSKI	Rakhel	Petach Tikva
DVILIANSKI	Yitzchak	Petach Tikva
DROZNITSKI	Eliezer	Hadera
HERTZ	Osnat	Haifa
HERTZ	Roshka	Hod Hasharon
WEBER	Shulamit	Haifa
WINER	Michael	
WEINER	Sarah	Ramat Yitzchak

ZUPERNER	Rashka	Tel Aviv
ZAHAVI	Avraham	Haifa
COHEN	Yocheved	Kfar Saba
LIPNISKI	Eliahu	Rehovot
LASKIN	Miki	Ashdod
LEVI	Esther	Givataim
LEVINE	Shimon	Petach Tikva
LEPERTIN	Danya	Ramle
MOTZNIK	Mina	Tel Aviv
MAJORCHIK	Rivka	Yad Eliahu
MOLTSADSKI	Avraham	Kibbutz Eilon
MEIRIT	Chava	Ramat Gan
SHTEROSKI	Nechama	Tel Aviv
SOKOLIK	Tzvi	Rishon Letzion
PAZ	Yekutiel	Petach Tikva
PIKOVSKI	Shlomo	Tel Aviv
PODESIUK	Bat-Sheva	Tel Aviv

PUPKO	Hirsch-Yudel	Ramat Gan	
TZUR	Nechama	Tel Aviv	
KRAVTZOV	Henya	Atlit	
KAPLAN	Moshe	Ramat Yitzchak	and Chaya
KAPLAN	Asher	Kiryat Borochov	
KREINER	Masha	Tel Aviv	
KAPLAN	Yitzchak	Zichron Yakov	
KONIKHOVSKI	Yakov	Tel Aviv	
KAPLAN	Zev	Hertzliya	
KAMINETSKI	Gutman	Tel Aviv	
KARNI	Aharon	Tel Aviv	
KONOPKE	Yakov	Ramat Yitzchak	and Hesha
KONOPKE	Ahuva	Tel Aviv	
RUBINOVSKI	Tova	Haifa	
ROTBARD	Chaya	Tel Aviv	
SHAMIR	Meir	Ramat Yitzchak	and Carmela

SHTIKOLSHCHIK	Mordechai	Tel Aviv
SHEINBAUM	Sarah	Petach Tikva
SHOMRONI	Tova	Petach Tikva
SHEMER	Mordechai	Kibbutz Eilon
SHITNITSKI	Chaya-Lieba	Beersheva
SHPATINSKI	Eva	Ashdod

The Soletchnik (Šalčininkai) Book

[Page 394]

Soletchnik Buildings

[Page 397]

The Tiny Town of "Great Soletchnik"

Hirsch Kaplan (Toronto, Canada)

Translation by Emma Karabelnik

At the junction of 4 streets of Soletchnik was the marketplace and at the center of the marketplace stood the big Catholic Church.

Borek the priest, leader of his pasture, was a nice man, and was nice to Jews, but when the position was taken over by a young priest, the situation changed. From time to time local Gentiles gathered in the marketplace, argued, and raised the "Jewish Problem". The essence of the Jewish Problem in their minds and in the town's reality was the question – should they let local Jews graze their cows in the fields near their property or force them to keep the cows in barns, and similar problems.

Every two weeks there was a bazaar day, the biggest in the area, and which was the main income for the town's Jews.

There was a pharmacy close to the church, which was usually rented by Jewish pharmacists.

The family of Zats the pharmacist lived in town for several years and became a vivid part of the community and cultural life.

Near the pharmacy lived the family of Shmuel and Sarah Levine (survived with Partisans, almost all of them are in Israel). The quiet Shmuel and the lively Sarah ran several business trades, and their children were involved in commerce too. During bazaar days they took out a weight-scale: the farmers who came to the bazaar weighed their goods on the scale and paid the children for the service.

Near the Levines lived the Krums. Moshe Yakov Krum, a very religious and honest man, did sewing works in one corner of the house, and in another corner his gentle, quiet wife Fruml sewed clothes. The income from those two exhausting jobs was barely enough for the family. (Sons Yosef and Tzemah live in Israel)

Near them stood a big duplex house called the inn (kretchmeh). In one wing of the house lived two rich, well-established families: the Streletskis, and in the other wing on the side of Vilne Street, the Khlavnovitshes. One was involved in the textile trade and the other, in the shoe trade. Velvl Streletski, the textile merchant, was involved in the political and community life of the town. He was a *gabai* in the synagogue and sang wonderful prayers. Kasriel Khlavnovitsh was a religious scholar, a man of knowledge, and a nice chat-companion, but he was never involved in the community matters.

Over the street lived the Khvayovski[1] family, almost all their children live in Canada. The Khvayovskis owned a liquor house and also sold *yash* [kosher wine]. This last business was managed by the brave wife Khaye, who took upon herself the risks of this forbidden business.

Up Vilne Street, on the way to the market, lived Yosef Valtukh with his family, a tall, tough, and strong Jew who worked his whole life as a wagoner bringing goods from Vilne for the meek. Even the Gentiles admired his strength, telling stories about his power and bravery on many occasions.

In the outskirts, almost at the end of town lived Alter Sheyman with his family. His was the only [Tr. Note: Jewish] family living as farmers. They used to trade in the villages and also to work various crop fields. They came into town only on *Shabbats* and Holidays, in order to pray in the synagogue.

In the center of town, near the Khvayovskis, lived Shimshel Lemelman and Yakov Zhabinski. Both owned large sewing workshops and were considered very rich. Shimshel behaved with great self-importance and called himself Reb Shimshel Lemelman, a sign of his importance.

Near them lived Mutieh Landau, a scholar with broad knowledge. He was the manager of the bank in our town and provided services to other towns in the area. He also owned a textile shop. Because of the bank business, he treated the town residents harshly, and they called him *Amalek*.

Near him was Velvl the shoemaker, head of a large family, and constantly in need. He loved political topics and had great knowledge. His lack of income and bitter poverty didn't affect his good spirits. He was always aware of political changes in the world and was ready for a discussion with anyone on any subject.

Near him lived Mary Levine, a shopkeeper, and her sons who were in the wood business. It was a house filled with joy, and the sound of daughter Khave's (now in Israel) singing came out of the house and filled the grey street with some joyfulness. Across the street lived Khanne-Dvorah Levine who owned a butchery, and her sons were also in the wood business.

At the corner of Vilne and Lida Streets stood two big houses with huge gardens behind them. Those were the houses of the brothers Chaim Moshe Goldanski and Yitzakh Hertz. Those two families were famous for their charity activity, especially Reb Chaim Moshe whose house was always open for passers-by in need, where they could get a meal from his wife's cooking or from the storeroom.

All the town's needy and poor knew the secret of the open house and came to it in the times of want.

During the final days of Soletchnik, the Goldanski household was joined by Khatzkl Luski, Yitzakh Hertz's son-in-law, a big scholar and a progressive, religious Jew. Khatzkl was a gifted merchant and did great community work. Because of his nice voice he used to lead the prayers, especially during High Holidays, and his prayers were lovely.

I remember the *Kol Nidre* night in the Lida ghetto, shortly after the mass murders executed by Nazis in the ghetto. We stayed in the warehouse praying. Khatzkl Luski was singing *Kol Nidre* in the ancient style and his singing was sad, heart breaking, bringing tears to our eyes, and engraved in our memories for life.

After Yitzakh Hertz's house, Moshe Levine, Sonia Goldanski's husband, built a new house near the "big house". In this house was situated the bank and on the other side lived the Katz family. It was a hard working family with new troubles and suffering. Reyzl and Esther did sewing jobs and the rest were bread bakers. All the family members were thirsty for education and kept progressive proletarian views. In 1918 their son Yakov Katz, a promising poet, was arrested by the Germans, tortured, and taken to forced labor. When he was released he died in his home at the age of 22. Shortly after he died, the head of the family - his father-in-law and Khaye's husband, died leaving behind two widows, one of them with two little babies. So after his death they had to come around quickly and take care of their income.

Facing this lived Rabbi Rakovski, shepherd of the tiny community of

Soletchnik— a quiet and modest Jew, poor and depressed. He was not only poor, but also had troubles at home and with his children.

Near the Polish co-operative stood the house of Shlomo the tailor (his daughter Dina is in Israel), after him the house of the Shupians,[2] the richest textile merchants, and close by a tiny short house surrounded by pigpens and inside a large family – this was the house of my childhood. My mother was a goodhearted and laborious woman who lived through a lot of hardships but was always ready to share her possessions with others, and donated money anonymously to those poorer than she. Father tried different trades and businesses but with no success, so mother had to work hard to provide for the family.

One of the biggest houses in town, near the house of Fani Marieh, was occupied by the town's princes of poverty. Except for Shimon the glazier, there were 3-4 families there who were always in need. After this house stood another big house in which the widow Mirl Segal lived, the tailor Ysroel Kotler, Rude the plasterer and Sushka the supervisor. At the end of Lida Street lived Alter the whitewasher with his wife Meira-Yiddis, daughter Zlata and son Beinish. Meira-Yiddis was worried about the street fights at nights: "They will take out each other's eyes, God Forbid!" - she used to say.

*

This is how our town looked and those were its residents. It was a tiny town with a tiny population, but it was a nice warm town with an unexplained magic to it. Its Jews were one big family. Everybody knew each other, knew of each other's troubles, and enjoyed each other's celebrations – together. The town youth, although they were few in numbers, created its own dreams and aspirations, and led a rich cultural and social life. They studied in various educational institutions and belonged to various movements, but joined forces in cultural, Zionist and public activities. They lived a full and content life together with their dear parents in warm houses, united in all their troubles and joys of life. Soletchnik existed as a tiny island of Judaism and peace surrounded by a world of greed and murder.

Until that one autumn day on the last day of *Sukkot*, when the bloody Nazis, and with them the well-known local Yanek Ivashkevitsh, ordered all the Jews of Great-Soletchnik to leave in 24 hours. They moved first to Divenishok and later to Voronova, where they were murdered and deported to deadly ghettos.

They dragged their belongings on tiny wagons, tied in bundles, and left behind, for the cruel world, the houses of their fathers and forefathers.

This Soletchnik in which we happened to live our lives and to dream about a brilliant future, was inherited by the murderers of our dear ones while they, our loved ones, didn't live to see the light and the better future of their dreams.

By telling their story I establish a memorial to those holy martyrs. May their memory be blessed.

On a visit to the Kaplan family in Israel

Editor's Footnotes

1. In the original text this name is spelled: khes-beyz (or veyz)-tsvey yud- beyz (or veyz)-samekh-kuf-yud.

2. In the original text this name is spelled: shin-vov-pey (or fey)-yud-aleph-nun.

[Page 401]

Soletchnik: Small but Great

K. Goldanski

Translation by Emma Karabelnik

The town took its name from the nearby Soletchenka River. This river contributed to its beauty and life, and enriched the lives of Jewish youth there.

The whole town belonged to Count Wagner and his wife, Countess *nee* Pututski. All the houses in town were built on his land and were part of his property. House residents paid an annual tax, like a housing rent. All their property came from him.

The only ones to own their own houses were father and his brother, who became landlords of their houses by chance. All their lands and real estate used to belong to the Post Office. My grandfather was the manager of the Post so he made use of this property. There was a stable near his house, with horses and carriages, in which he cared for all the mail items, and his standard of living was considered extraordinary. Later, a railway was built, and all the mail was moved by trains and from his office. The Post Office then granted him all those lands and property as a compensation for the long years of service, and thus my father became a landowner overnight.

Synagogues

In those times, Jews in town used to pray in the "new" synagogue which was situated on our land. When the old synagogue was disqualified for use because of engineering problems and the Jews had no place to pray, my grandfather donated 10 *dunams* of his land [Tr. Note: 1dunam=1/4 acre]. Others followed with more donations and the prayer house was established. Near the synagogue they built a house for the rabbi, and Soletchnik became a sacred community [Tr. Note: *Kehilat Kodesh*].

The old synagogue was built hundreds of years before the new one and had been disqualified because of cracks in the walls and safety concerns. So there it stood, deserted and bare, and was used as a playground by local children, inspiring their imaginations. It stood in solitude for years and added a mystical atmosphere to the town. Grandfathers told legends about it to subsequent generations, becoming lodged into the memories of fathers and sons. Here is what we found to be true about these stories after verification: in the beginning of 18th century an ancestor of Meir Solts had donated the whole sum of money necessary for the establishment of the synagogue. He also contributed a piece of his land for it. And when the synagogue was built and the community was established, he also contributed a nearby piece of land for a cemetery.

My father used to tell that it was a gorgeous building with a gorgeous Holy Ark standing high up, and one had to climb 10 stairs in order to take out a Torah scroll. My grandfather Reb Monesh was the *gabbai* for many years.

The Soltses

The greatness of the Solts family didn't last for long because of the Meir Solts incident, but it left its good and blessed impact on the town.

Meir's father was a big donor who took care of the community's needs as mentioned before. In the old days he was the Post Office manager, and the General Governor used to rise when he saw him, showing him respect and fondness. As someone honored by the authorities, he was also a proud and respected man in the Jewish community. He sent his son Meir to Moscow University and was forgiven for doing that by the Jewish community. Later, my grandfather Reb Monesh took over the management of the Post. Solts was still rich and well-to-do, but all honors from the Governor were now directed towards my grandfather. For years, people in the community told stories about the Governor stopping his carriage to take Reb Monesh home.

In Moscow Meir Solts met a priest's daughter and started to visit her home. One time he happened to be there for this daughter's birthday and, together with all the guests, he got drunk and fell asleep as Gentiles usually do. When he awoke he noticed the cross that his party friends had painted on his chest. He got scared. He saw an abyss opening up before him and panicked. So what did he do? He sent a telegram to grandfather, Reb Monesh:

'[In Yiddish] Come here, there is trouble. Grandfather left behind all his business and went to Moscow. He found him there all mixed up with the Christians, and he had no choice but to send him away out of Russia. Meir asked to be sent to *Erets Israel*, so with the help of the General Governor he was sent to Israel 3 days after the incident.'[1]

This was 76 years ago, in 1894, and so came the privilege of sending our first representative to make *Aliyah*.

Meir built a wonderful family here, and one of his sons Dr. Elishe Solts OBM was one of the founders of *Maoz Chaim* [Tr. Note: a kibbutz], and the first governor of Nazareth and the Beth Shean district for many years.

Good Memories of Wagner

Carl Wagner was a good Gentile, a friend of the town and its residents who assisted them in different ways. His greatest pride was when his late father's name was mentioned in the synagogue during the prayer for dead souls. Then he began donating large sums of money for the maintenance of the synagogue, enough for a whole year.

There was a Jew in town, Abba Yehuda Soltchnitski. He was 80 years old when he began to bring the post from Benakani and to distribute it in town. He used to bring Wagner's mail to his home, sometimes he had to walk 5km to do this. Wagner had to thank him for this effort so he signed an "Ordinaria", a permanent service fee similar to all his other workers and employees. Every 3 months Wagner's carriage stopped near Abba's house to bring him his fee and also some fruits and vegetables from Wagner's fields.

On this occasion Wagner would also send something to the synagogue. There were other poor folks in town who learned about Wagner's resourcefulness, they used to come to Wagner to show him respect in various ways, and to win his generosity.

Rabbis of Soletchnik

In our times the main Rabbi of Great Soletchnik was Khanokh Sharshevski. He was a scholar and well known in rabbinical circles, not only because of his virtues but also because he was the son of the Gaon "Chofetz Chaim"'s sister. He didn't have sons, and one of his daughters married David Leibovitch who took over after his death.

R. David was a "*parush*" [someone who left his home to study Torah], who migrated from town to town looking for Torah houses until he ended up in Soletchnik, wed, and settled there.

He was a scholar with great knowledge, nice to talk to and a great singer.

They used to tell about him:

When his Katriel couldn't understand why *Aravah* [willow] branches are used if they are wrapped and complicated, he explained to him clearly: Willow [branches] are like human fingers. When they are straight and open, they can even [be used] for Cohanic [Priestly] Blessing, but when they are bent and complicated they can become a punching fist or a fig.

[The matter] became very clear.

When Reb David'l was told that a rich and selfish man had become ill and was taking a long time to die, he said:

'[In Yiddish] When a bad fruit is kept for a long time, it ferments and becomes sweet. Thus his way in the next world will be easier.'

When Rabbi David'l immigrated to America, he was replaced by Rabbi Rakovski who was the last Rabbi of the town and was killed by Nazis together with his flock.

With God's Will Even a Broom is Useful

In 1916 when the regime changed and the Lithuanians took over our region, soldiers gathered near our pharmacy and demanded from us the cognac usually kept for medical use. When we didn't open, they broke into the store at night. They found my mother standing in rags, frightened. They thought she was our maid so they told her:

'Now is your time to have revenge on your rich employers. Take out everything they have in the pharmacy.'

They packed everything, barged into our house, took all our food supply, and demanded we bridle our horses and take them to the destination they'd show us. We knew that we wouldn't be coming back, that in order to hide their actions they'd be getting rid of us on the way. My mother knew it too. She hurried and told my 14 year old brother to take an oven sweeper [Trans. Note: broom], cover it with a sack soaked in oil, and put it burning near the church. When the Gentiles saw the fire in their church, they perceived the danger and ran to put it out. A crowd gathered quickly which the Lithuanians saw prompting them to leave, while all our possessions stayed with us.

Then mother said:

'You see, children, when God wishes, even a broom may start a fire. Mother OBM was so resourceful. She knew how to get out of any awkward situation and to save her family.

Soletchnik Becomes Famous

During World War I, the Germans came to Soletchnik. The width of the local railway didn't fit their trains so they stopped and dismantled the rails in order to change widths. The train was stuck in town and the swollen-from-hunger refugees wandered around town. My father decided to open up a soup kitchen to ease their suffering. He donated the laundry boiler, and good women cooked potatoes and groats from his stock and the milk from his cows. Thus Jewish souls were saved from hunger and its dangers.

When he ran out of stock, he asked for help of "*Yekopo*" in the USA and they sent a large quantity of canned food. The Jews of Soletchnik established a kitchen in the synagogue corridor, and Jewish women took turns cooking for the refugees, until Soletchnik became famous around the whole area, and the refugees grew in quantity. We had to prepare straw mattresses and put them to sleep in the corridor.

The Butcher and his Family

We had a butcher in town. His name was Tuvyeh. His family brought a lot of blessings to our town for its knowledge and *halakha*.[2]

His wife Dobra (Dvora) served as a "*melamed*",[3] she had a *cheder*[4] in which she taught *Gemarah* to youngsters. She loved to study and knew Torah well. Her methods were harsh like all the *melameds,* and she ruled over 15 young scholars as a male would— always with a "*teittl*", a captain's stick, with which scared the disobedient ones, and she knew how to use it.

With time she adopted some methods from Tsarist schools. The punishment for being late to *cheder* or for sloppiness in one's studies was to be put in a corner for a long time. And if the person did it again, he was put in the corner on his knees— the third time, on his knees with a bean under the knees. It was a painful and depressing punishment, but the youngsters found a solution. They cooked the bean until soft and thus made the punishment of the "*melamed*-ess" easier.

In addition to being a *shochet,* Tuvyeh Kagan was also a *chazzan*, and his sons sang with him, assisting him with their voices on notes which his voice couldn't sing.

This is the Soletchnik of old memory. Small and dear, with its good Jews, built by them, and cherished by them. Now its Jews are gone and so is the town.

Footnotes

1. Ed. Note: In the original text this entire paragraph appears within quotation marks, although it seems that only the first sentence is a direct quote.

2. Trans. Note: observance of religious law

3. Ed. Note: Teacher

4. Ed. Note: School house or room

[Page 405]

Soletchnik on the Eve of Shoah

Chaim Kalai (Streletski)

Translation by Emma Karabelnik

[First] Pesach night in 1938. After 5 years in Eretz, I went to Soletchnik. I was a youngster, barely 18, when I left it and I missed it a lot. I wanted to see if it had changed? Developed? Or does it continue its grey dull routine?

My soul was torn from the inner conflict between me and my town that pushed me away, saw me as someone "chasing the winds", and mocked me because I believe in a dream and am obsessed with it. But I am firm in my opinion that there is no future in its existence and its days are short. All the years in Eretz didn't wipe the memory of the conflict, I wanted to return and prove my victory. Moreover I knew that now I am the strong one, that its end is near and I have to save it, and first of all save my parents.

I traveled as if on a mission.

The world was at that time under the threat of the Nazi regime, and I knew that the first to fall will be our brothers Jews. I was impatient and wanted to save my family before it is too late.

Eretz Israel was under Arab siege. We lived under the oppressive mandatory regime and its collaborators – the muftis' gangs. But somehow I didn't think that our lives are in danger. On the contrary, I saw the wire fence around our farm and its gates, locked every night as something temporary, and never doubted our future even in my worst dreams. On the contrary, I wanted my parents to be here with me, my brother and sister and everyone, to be part of the building and developing of a new country.

I entered the town in the middle of the day. Before me I saw the wrecks of the Big Synagogue, between its folds we used to play hide-and-seek, and beside it stood Beth *Midrash* as if embarrassed near its big brother. Although it was the spiritual heart and center of the town, the big synagogue across emphasized its smallness and misery. A substitute is a substitute.

The children ran around excited from [the house of] Rabbi Benya the "podarchik" of the matzos. Again they baked matzos as each year for ages, in the house of Avrom–Itzik, our beloved teacher, and the children competed to be the first to make the holes in the matzos by rolling the barb [??] wheel, "redlen blez". Dear Soletchnik children who later experienced the tragic fate of their parents, together with their parents, were now also full partners with their parents in performing the mitzvah. They didn't pay any attention to me. They argued between themselves, every one described how he put on his kippah, how he washed his hands and said the blessing, how he rolled straight lines of holes, and his young eyes glowed with happiness.

Soletchnik was the same Soletchnik. Do you remember Reb Alter the Yellow, the one whose wife couldn't understand how do they fight at night, when you can accidentally stab an eye and you can't see where to shoot? I found Reb Alter exactly the same, crossing the street with a wide pace to collect the rent money for Mr. Wagner, the owner of the town and surrounding villages.

From the corners of my eye I could see, as always, the town waggoneers leaning on their whips, bored because of lack of work, tailors bending over their sewing machines like yeshiva dancers, shop owners standing in front their shops staring for hours on the puddles of melting snow.

I found Soletchnik exactly how I left it. Sunk in its own world of worries for provision and family sustenance, its several streets were quiet and empty, narrow trails led from the houses to the marketplace, from there to Beth *Midrash*, from Beth *Midrash* to the shops etc. My heart shrunk from sorrow. Dear God, how long will those dear Jews trample in one place and continue from one Shoah to the next, from one decree to the next. How can they live like this?

I urged my father to sell everything and leave town, to make aliya. I couldn't imagine the dimensions of the coming catastrophe, I couldn't imagine the extension of horrors. I just wanted them to be part of our destiny, of sieged Eretz Israel which carried the promise of a safe place for generations to come.

My father, who outlived two wars, in 1905 and in 1914, insisted on his safety:

–Nothing will happen to us. A war is a war, eventually it ends and the Jews continue with their life.

He was a devoted and active Zionist, but was not ready yet to do aliya.

We had a long and bitter argument. I stayed in Soletchnik for approximately 8 months. I was in the center of [Zionist] activity. In the evening hours, a time to think and dream, I told about my Israel, I read [them] letters that I received from Tel Yosef, from my friends there. Hearts trembled, thoughts widened, but that's it. They didn't come any far than that.

Meanwhile I received notice of the first pilot training course in Eretz, and I was very interested [to join], so I parted and left.

I didn't succeed to save my dearest. For many days I wondered – what was the magic of this town, this remote corner of the world that "glued" generations of smart, able and talented Jews, and they couldn't leave it. Until this day I didn't find the answer to this question.

Meanwhile the news arrived of the extinction of Soletchnik together with all Jewish communities in a deadly march of world bullies.

Dear naïve–smart Jews got caught in its enchanting net and now they are gone. And I know that it wasn't their fault or failure. After all, Soletchnik was a sanctuary and a cradle for small dreams of the miserable and haunted. It's not their fault, but the warning is loud and clear, there is no place for Soletchniks in our world, and may all the Jews in the world know that after our town was destroyed, every city in the world is only falsely safe and should be left immediately.

We'll remember Soletchnik and the warning coming from it.

[Page 407]

A Home in Soletchnik

Yosef Krum

Translation by Emma Karabelnik

Our town, which consisted of 35 households, was called Great Soletchnik, as opposed to Small Soletchnick which consisted only of 5-6 houses.

Unlike its neighbor Voronova, which was a town of farmers and craftsmen, our tiny town had mostly tradesmen who traded with local farmers, and a minority of tailors, shoemakers and other servicemen, two or fewer from each profession.

Like all other towns in Poland-Lithuania, it was in constant pursuit of a livelihood and the rejection of Zionism as an alternative. In fact, the anti-Zionism's only purpose was to serve those looking for income instead of idealism. Those [Tr. Note: financial issues] served as an excuse for the parents not to allow their children to leave home and make *aliyah*, and as an opposition to those young people who had started to criticize their parents for being concerned only with money and profit.[1]

In this atmosphere, the good memories are mostly of the Goldanski [Zahavi] family, he being Chaim Moshe and she, Minne Riva.

Theirs was a very wealthy family, considered one of the richest in the area and in town. Their house was a fortress of comfort and prosperity— a house that stood on their own land, behind it their own fields with a private well in the yard.

Their house, which stood at a distance from all the rest of the houses, was a trade house which did commerce only with Gentiles. Because of the physical distance, the family was also a bit detached from the rest of the community. The elders fulfilled all their religious obligations. They were *mitzvah* doers, observing prayers and holidays, but never got involved with community life, and had their own opinions on world affairs, on human relations in the *Golah*,[2] and on the future of the nation and *Eretz* Israel.

Thus their house became special and different from all other houses. It was always filled with various guests, and Zionist emissaries from *Eretz* Israel knew it as a place to stay. Even when they were going some distance from the town, they used to spend a night and rest there.

The store was a tiny supermarket. You could buy [anything] from a sack of grain or flour, to herring and pastry. It was part of the house, so everyone who came to the store, visited the house, and vice versa.

I used to work there as a seller. I was a young boy and wanted to help my parents financially. I quit school with a heavy heart and went to work for others. My mood was difficult, but I fell in love with my work from the first day. I made good connections with people and became a good judge of character. There was an atmosphere of togetherness in the house, with no differences in social status or origin. The boys treated me as one of their own and surrounded me with warm friendship. Many times I have thought about this: this friendship was essential for our besieged nation, meeting a need to keep internal relationships close, unlike in other nations. Trade was conducted under all its rules. The goal was to make profit, but the goods were different: not all were kosher. The Goldanskis preserved their integrity: their business and profit-making ethics were different. They were not interested in capital aggregation and didn't conduct themselves arrogantly. They saw it as a kind of destiny that must be viewed and respected as an obligation, but not as the most important one in life.

And most important, and this is the reason to write a memory about them, was the spirit of practical Zionism in the household. All that they did, or didn't do, was done as if only temporarily, until an opportunity to make *aliyah* would come around.

Reb Chaim Moshe encouraged his sons and daughters to make *aliyah*. His house, which stood on his land along with a cow and a horse, and many businesses and lots of work, needed working hands, but he was ready to give up on this out of an understandable yearning for nationality: they were more needed there.

Thus the Goldanskis were the first in town to make *aliyah*, despite the prosperity at home and the hunger and shortage in *Eretz*. I don't remember the children complaining about their conditions in their letters. I don't remember the parents regretting even once having sent their children away from their table. They had foreseen far ahead and they were correct, but at that time the Goldanskis were considered as being different from the general attitude in Soletchnik.

I worked in this house for seven years. Seven years feeling like one long day of friendship and comradeship. I don't remember if or how my salary was determined. There was some kind of mutual understanding between the two houses because the Goldanskis knew the circumstances of my having taken the job, and knew how to compensate me. They used to bring over wood for heating personally to our cold house, as well as holiday groceries and other stuff. The meaning of their actions was rather that of an act of friendship and comradeship, rather then of financial value, which was obvious and limited.

In my memories of Soletchnik, the house of Chaim Moshe and Minne Riva is that of green garden with a Jewish world-view, where a visionary Jewish camaraderie were kept going until a National revival could be achieved, unique among nations.

Footnotes

1. Tr. Note: In the original text the phrase used is: כסף שערי ט"מ.

2. Ed. Note: exile

[Page 409]

Velvele in Soletchnik

Chava Levine (Lieberman)

Translation by Emma Karabelnik

He was our neighbor, a poor shoemaker with eight children. When I used to come to repair my shoes the whole household was happy. We were rich, or considered rich, while our neighbor Velvele was the poorest of the poor. Yet something drew us to him. His constant joyfulness, the spiritual orientation rather than the corporeal, and the peace and harmony imbuing his whole family filled my heart.

The time was shortly before my *Aliyah*. I had strong and steady opinions about the town's future, its youth, and its Jews with their Judaism. I was worried about one thing only: would I be strong enough to survive the famine in *Erets Israel*? How would I bear the suffering? Could anyone survive the famine? My doubts rose. What should I do? I came to Velvele. I watched his family, hungry for bread but filled with joy, and it made me feel better.

One day I saw him in extraordinarily good mood. When I inquired, he explained:

"You see, we slaughtered a goose, a real goose, who was alive and well. Such a small thing, a goose, and yet we are eating meat for a whole week. [In Yiddish:] Goose–meat, you see, goose–soup. We've become almost like rich men, and it is not finished yet. After a week of eating look what I will still have:"

He opened a drawer, and with great intrigue and pleasure pulled out a gizzard.

"This, you see, will be for dinner today, for all of us."

Velvele enjoyed talking about politics. He had a newspaper which he kept folded in a drawer for three months, and each time he wanted to prove an argument he pulled out the newspaper to prove his point with facts.

He was a good neighbor, an interesting man, so I decided to mention him in this book.

This is How My Mother Blessed Me

Khave Levine (Lieberman)

Translation by Emma Karabelnik

My mother became a widow at the age of 45 and she was left with 5 little children. The oldest was 15. She didn't want to remarry because she didn't want to bring in a stepfather for the children. She remained alone to shoulder the burden of raising the children and taking care of them.

She was known as a smart woman: Meira (Miriam) Levine from Soletchnik, manager of a department store, independent, with solid opinion on public matters and providing for her family all by herself.

She gave us a traditional education and a sense of happiness. In our home we never knew the meaning of orphanage. We were provided with everything we needed, and more. The town's first radio with earphones, was in our house. We loved her and respected her, and were always careful not to hurt her feelings.

In 1936 I felt storm clouds gathering over us. I was her only daughter, with 4 brothers, and my fear was different from theirs. For me anti-Semitism was connected to special fears reserved only for Jewish girls.

I wanted to run away, to make *aliyah*, to be among Jews, but I didn't dare to say this to my mother. *Aliyah* without Messiah didn't fit into my religious education. I was afraid she wouldn't agree and that she'd be against my *aliyah:* I wanted to make *aliyah* and be a good daughter to her at the same time. I confided in my oldest brother. I explained my point of view and my thoughts about the future for Jews in Poland. I said:

Soletchnik says goodbye to first olim: Shoshona and Ysroel Goldanski

'There is a professional school in Vilne. I'll study one of those professions that can bring a salary anywhere anytime. Later, when I am settled, I'll do anything to bring everyone.'

He gave me money without mother's knowledge, because he realized that this would hurt her.

I registered to the school. When I brought her the acceptance letter, she looked at it, thought for a while, and then said:

'If this is what you want, and if your happiness is there, go my daughter, and don't be afraid.'

I promised to help her make *aliyah*, but to my great sorrow this didn't happen.

Dear mother.

[Page 411]

How I Made *Aliyah*

Yosef Krum

Translation by Emma Karabelnik

The "HeKhaluts" branch in our town was like a club for rich children, or to be precise, due to being majority of girls, a club for girls from rich and middle-class families. I, who worked from childhood, wasn't a factor to be heard or considered. I remember my thoughts were always about *aliyah*.

I saw the small town, the misery of its residents, with no chance for improvement in the life of such a small community, and most importantly no hope for the youth. I was looking for ways to go away from there.

In 1932, when I went to *hachshara* [1] in Gorohovo, [2] I was considered a weirdo because I quit a "good" job with a nice family who were very dear to me, and I felt at home in their home. People also couldn't forgive me for leaving my poor parents, which would then lack my help and assistance. But I wasn't forgetting them. I wasn't able to tell others that I planned to suffer for a while and then later bring them over to me, to live like normal people for, better or worse.

The *hachshara* papers came on *Hanukka* 1932. The weather was freezing. People had second thoughts whether "To leave home in such frost?" I put on my coat, parted with a blessing from my parents, and went out. I was upset that my biggest critics were my friends from the branch. Instead of being happy that a friend was making *aliyah*, they mocked and criticized me.

I spent 2 years in Gorohovo in a *hachshara* kibutz before I was approved to make *aliyah*.

Before the approval I had to pass a test in Hebrew. My knowledge came from my teacher Avraham Ledershteyn, and I passed the test.

I returned to town, happy for two reasons: one, because I had succeeded in the hard training and all [the tests], and also because I had overcome my friends' criticism and mockery, those who had established "HeKhaluts" and were its leaders and spokespersons.

Footnotes

1. Trans. Note: training

2. Ed. Note: In the original text this name is spelled: gimel–reysh–vov–khof–vov–veyz (or beyz)

[Page 412]

Because of Wagner's Tractors

By Chaim Kalai [1]

Translation by Emma Karabelnik

Soletchnik was Wagner's private estate. He was a rare descendant of those Germans that Peter the Great brought to Russia in order to improve its industry and enhance its agriculture. In my days his ownership consisted of collecting of rent money from the Jewish houses that either stood on his land or were built with his money.

He worked his fields with his tractors and his hired staff who worked only for a percentage of the income.

You may say that most of the town earned their living from Wagner and his sharecroppers, while the rest from supplying services to residents of the town and its surroundings.

Thus its population differed from other towns. It had several merchants who were very rich and who earned big money, and the rest were shoemakers, tailors and wagon owners.

There were almost no homeowners because most of the Jews lived in Wagner's houses, and there was a Jew nicknamed Reb Alter 'the Yellow' whose job was to collect Wagner's rent payments.

As a child I knew my town well and loved it. I loved the destroyed Big Synagogue, where we played hide–and–seek and dreamt secret dreams of another mysterious world. I loved the broad fields surrounding the town. And we were happy there.

But when I grew up and became a youngster I started to feel suffocated. Yosef Krum and I, and several others, studied Hebrew with teacher Avraham. He, and Byalik's poems, aroused a longing in our hearts for the birds in the broad fields.

I was very attracted to Wagner's tractors. Those huge bugs made of metal and bladed wheels drew my heart when they did their slow loud–conquering–plowing trip through the fields.

I wanted to control them, to be close to them, to drive, and to direct them. I felt that when a person is connected to the tractors, he connects himself to an endless power source. I wanted to study mechanics.

My father convinced me otherwise. He thought that for a youngster deciding to be a craftsman, carpentry would be more appropriate

"Look–" he explained "– carpentry is a clean profession. You take clean wood, you make a piece of furniture, a window, a door. You plane it, and you work with clean material, you plane, you dye, you polish."

I studied carpentry, but I was attracted to Wagner's tractors. With time my father agreed to send me to the Vilne Technion and to abandon the carpentry dream. Only then I did learn why he was so opposed to mechanics.

When I finished my studies, I knew, as my father knew, that there was no future for me in Poland with this profession. A tractor demands wide fields, and for a Jewish boy like me wide fields can be found only in Israel. And this my father didn't want. He was a good Zionist etc. – but still didn't want me to make *aliyah*. 'You are too young.' Eretz Israel is not ready yet for children like you. But I made *aliyah*.

Grandma was crying, mother was sighing, but it didn't help. Wagner's tractor prevailed. Due to them I made *aliyah*, and due to them I learned to love wide open spaces that filled my soul and wouldn't let go.

I could say, according to Byalik's words: Do you know why I made *aliyah*? Thanks to the tractors and fields that filled me with the air of freedom and a homeland.

Footnote

1. Ed. Note: Streletski was his surname before making *aliyah*

[Page 414]

List of Soletchnik People Living in the Diaspora and in Israel

Translation by Judy Petersen

Surname	Given name	Residence	Remarks
CHAVAYEVSKI	Binyamin	Winnipeg, Canada	
CHAVAYEVSKI	Moshe	Winnipeg, Canada	
CHAVAYEVSKI	Sender	Winnipeg, Canada	
CHAVAYEVSKI	Shlomo	Winnipeg, Canada	
MICHALOVSKI	Masha	Winnipeg, Canada	KOTLER
KAPLAN	Hirsch	Toronto, Canada	
KAPLAN	Gitel	Toronto, Canada	
SHEIMAN	Beyrl	New York, USA	
LEVINE	Yisrael	Australia	
SEGAL	Yoel	Germany	
LEVINE	Chaim-Moshe	Siber	
BEN-SHLOMO	Channah-Ita	Netanya, Israel	ZAHAVI
WIZEN	Chesya	Ramat Yitzchak	ZAHAVI

WEISBUM	Moshe	Haifa	SHAIMAN
ZAHAVI	Aryeh	Hadera	
ZAHAVI	Munya	Tel Aviv	
ZAHAVI	Shoshana	Tel Aviv	
ZILBER	Channah	Petach Tikva	KHERMETZ
TEIVEL	Esther	Petach Tikva	KATZ
LUSKI	Meir	Petach Tikva	
LEVINE	Sarah	Petach Tikva	
LEVINE	Meir	Petach Tikva	
LEVINE	Yosef	Ramat Yitzchak	
LEVINE	Alexander	Petach Tikva	
LIEBERMAN	Chava	Tzahala	LEVINE
KALAI	Chaim	Bnei Brak	STRELETSKI
KRUM	Yosef	Ra'anana	
KRUM	Tzemach	Tel Aviv	

[Page 417]

The Great Soletchnik

The Great Soletchnik
(streets, people, memories)

Tzemah Krum

Translation by Emma Karabelnik

In Vilne Province, near the main road to Lida, surrounded by woods and near the river, lay a tiny town called "The Great Soletchnik", with its 30 or so Jewish families.

Four streets were winding in the highest region of the town – Vilne, Lida, Railway, and Mill Streets. The fifth, Swine Street, was a *Goyim*[1] street without any Jews.

The tiny Great Soletchnik

Jews of the area made their living in the markets, not only from Soletchnik. But when the *Goyim* would gather there for bazaars or holidays, the Jews would feel a little or threatened.

Goyim would get drunk and start their murderous scuffles between themselves; the Jews had to be on guard so it won't be taken out on them.

They would drink "beer'le" at Khaye Isha's. She was a woman of valor.[2] She sold illegal vodka and when a policeman would catch her with such a bottle she would grab the bottle and break it on the spot— so he would have no evidence. When the drunken *Goyim* would start scuffling she would throw them out one by one, accompanied by a "black Shmini Atzeret on you".

The Jewish peddlers and the cattle traders did not make a bad living, while the craftsmen worked till late at night and barely earned a living. Although, there was one tailor, Shimshon Lemelman, who managed to live better. He was something of a public figure; when he wanted to say something at an assembly, he would say: "I, Shimshon Lemelman, ask for the word."

Some Jews had a horse and wagon, trading with surrounding villages and noblemen; others were just "vozhaks",[3] like Ishya, Isroel and Valtuch. The *Goyim* would call Valtuch "Yoske vozhak". He was a tall, very strong, and quiet Jew, with a small black beard; he could pick up a huge closet from one side by himself, while from the other side several strong *Goyim* were needed. His small, weak wife, who was afraid of the "evil eye", would add to every sentence 'as I should say': today I baked a little bread, as I should say– and by this meant a big loaf of bread.

Their daughter Libke would tease the neighbor across the street, shouting to her: "No, Reb Rachl Leah, our duck will not go over to your garden."

Their son Yitzick Meir was discharged from the Russian Army

because they couldn't fit shoes for his huge feet.

The official poor folks had their own jobs: two times a year, on *Pesach*[4] and *Hoshana Raba*.[5] On *Pesach* in the *Matzah* bakeries, [they] would sieve, knead, pour flour, pour water wherever needed. On Sukkot [they] sold the Four Species.

In order to help Jews with credit there was a bank in town, serving also the surrounding towns. They [Tr. Note: residents of other towns] did everything to move the bank to them. The Benakani Jews, who had better financial wherewithal than the Soletchnikers, would say: according to our status, our legal standing, we deserve the bank.

Mattea Landau, the bank director would say: 'Gezetz–ketz–shmetz, that's how it is!' And the bank stayed with us.

Mattea would request solid guarantees; he wouldn't approve a loan for everyone. He was an educated Jew, a harsh but straight Jew. Once, my father asked for a loan not knowing what guarantees would be requested. Mattea told him: Moshe Yankl, sign and go, I and Velvl Streletski will be your guarantees. He knew very well that it was going to be hard for Moshe Yankl to make the loan payments.

He called the Rabbi the Rebetzin's husband, would argue with him on law or *peshat*[6], and always had to discuss every point. Because of him, the Rabbi moved to the left side of the street, to live in *Beth Midrash*. Landau's wife would also study *Gemarah* pages during her spare time.

Certain Jews lived in houses belonging to the nobleman Wagner, and the one designated to gather the rent was Alter the Painter, an elderly Jew who always walked around with a golden watch that he got as a present from the nobleman. Guys always asked him about the time; he liked it very much. He liked praying against the cantor's pulpit and he was an honorable house manager. His wife Mereh–Yides, when she saw that in the butcher's shop the *Goyim* could buy "soft" meat for cheap while the Jews got meat with bones for a higher price, she would say: I wish all my enemies were Jewish.

The teacher Leyzer would give private lectures in their house. During the Abyssinian war she came in to the house on a very dark night and said: How do they conduct a war on such a dark night, they will stab one another in the eyes.

Shmuel Levine, who traded leather and [was] a butcher, was also the fiddler of the town. He would play while his wife Sorale and the children would sing along. It was a joyful, warm, dear home.

The most elegant woman in town was Mereh Levine, the widow. Her daughter Khava (now in Israel), a joyful girl, was the main actress in the theatrical plays in Soletchnik. Her son Chaim–Moshe'ke didn't look a big hero, but when the *Goyim* would start a riot in the market, he would grab a wagon shaft and start beating them up in several at a time.

*

The *Gabbai*[7] of the *Beth Midrash* was Velvl Streletski, a handsome Jew of honorable appearance with the looks of a gentleman. [He] was a *Chazan*[8] in better days and sent his children to study in Vilne. He lived on one side of the house and on the other side lived Kasriel Khlavanovitsh, a clever, spiritual Jew.

Another interesting family was the family of Moshe Levi Katz. Theirs was called the Red House. The father was a shoemaker, the mother Beile, a baker, and the children unsuccessful but well–known proletarians with whom the Polish regime would collaborate every May 1st. The daughters Reyzl, Khavah, and Esther [were] very laborious. Esther (now in Israel) took care of the town library. Yakov was a talented poet, and Zerach – a very refined fellow— could be a good speaker except that he pronounced a lamed [Ed. Note: the letter 'L'] as a resh [Ed. Note: the letter 'R'], which played against him.

Velvl Aba Yudes, the shoemaker, used to visit several homes to discuss world politics after the Sabbath prayers. He, meaning his Blumeh, would host the boys and girls, soon to be 'wheels'.[9] They would play *panden*,[10] dance, and have fun. Their daughter Radke would read romances and tell stories to the youngsters in great detail.

The Rabbi's Shamash,[11] Benye, lived in a small house near the *Beth Midrash*, together with his son Avraham Itshe and Khaya–Pesel Kaplan with her husband and their six children. Despite their bitter poverty, they would share the little [they had] with other poor people passing through the town, [they] would sleep on the floor and give others their beds. There was always an orphan stranger staying with them who they kept without [getting] money. Reb Benye always found something to talk about with everyone and loved to chat. When he went out to call a man for minyan, he could forget himself with chatting, and not come back with the man until the *Alenu Leshevach*.[12]

The youth liked to get together at Khana Dvora Levines'. She had a gramophone with records, and two sons and two daughters, and in the yard a big *viltsher*[13] goose and squirrels

Jews would get together in the *Beth Midrash*, pray, spend time together, and study a page of Gemara after the prayer. Here would also appear preachers, *chazzans*, and Hertzl and Trumpeldor advocates.

In cold winter days it was impossible to keep the *Beth Midrash* warm, so everything moved up to *Ezrat Nashim*.[14] The prayers, the *cheder*, the synagogue, the lefties' library, and the meetings of the *liner*[15] and the bank and [social] movements, all was there.

The town was in general Zionist, but there were other organizations [such as] *Mizrahi*, *HeKhalutz*, Zionist Youth, and *Beitar*. I was in *Beitar*, first as a commander, later as culture activist and educator. It's interesting that *Beitar* was a stepson of the town, they would wonder about me, "How is it becoming for Frumale's (my mother) son to be a *Beitarist*."

My mother was the best seamstress in the area. She sewed dresses for noblemen's wives and for members of the government, and the upper gown for the priest. She worked till late at night and always found time to educate her children to become better persons according to her standards. She would react on the spot to any child's misbehavior, the opposite of my father, who was too good to react harshly and immediately. He would collect a big debt and then would give us a big portion of punishment, not proportional to our current sin.

My sister suffered much "shame" because of me. Many would pick on her because her brother was a *Beitarist*, although, as I recall, all the Zionist organizations coexisted not badly at all. They all took care of the library, and conducted plays, social, and other events together. Everyone knew that only togetherness can make wonders.

It's a heartache that our little town is no more and that it's sweet, interesting people perished in such a painful way.

Footnotes

1. Ed. Note: Literally, 'Gentile'

2. Ed. Note: The phrase in Hebrew is 'eshet chayil'

3. Tr. Note: Laborers

4. Ed. Note: The holiday of Passover

5. Ed. Note: The seventh day of the holiday of Sukkot

6. Ed. Note: Form of biblical interpretation involving the literal meaning of the text

7. Ed. Note: Ssynagogue administrator

8. Ed. Note: Cantor in the synagogue

9. Ed. Note: The word in the original text is written: resh–yud–yud–langer fey, which translates literally as tire or hoop; the meaning of this phrase is not yet known

10. Ed. Note: The word in the original text is written: pe–alef–nun–

dalet–nun; the meaning of this word is not yet known

11. Ed. Note: Rabbi's assistant

12. Ed. Note: One of the last prayers of the service

13. Ed. Note: The word in the original text is written: vav–vav–yud–lamed–tet–shin–ain–resh; the meaning of this word is not yet known

14. Tr. Note: Women's area of the synagogue

15. Ed. Note: The word in the original text is written: lamed–yud–yud–nun–ain–resh; the meaning of this word is not yet known

[Page 422]

Generosity in My *Shtetl*
(Characters, Deeds, and Destiny)

Esther Katz (Taibel)

Translation by Emma Karabelnik

Towards the end of the war I was enlisted in Lithuanian brigade, and I returned to Soletchnik together with them. The *shtetl* wasn't there anymore. All the houses were burnt down and the whole Jewish center was dug up. In the open pits our Gentile neighbors were looking for left-behind Jewish items to take for themselves.

The generous-hearted Jewry of Soletchnik had been wiped out.

No more was the warmhearted family of Chaim Moshe Goldanski. The big, open house for all those in need. The Mrs., Mineh Riveh, always busy with the business, but she would not forget every morning to put large pots of food in the big oven for the hungry and the poor. Widows and newly arrived beggars would come in and fetch food for themselves, a portion of a hot meal.

I looked for and I didn't find Reb Vulf Streletski, the handsome always-smiling Jew, full of humor. He was our *Baal Tefila*[1] and the Gabbai[2] of the synagogue. There would be no celebration in the *shtetl*, no wedding, no circumcision without [him]: Streletski had to participate and would imbue all those present at the party with his singing and joyfulness.

And on the contrary, if somebody died or became sick, Reb Vulf was the first to give comfort and to lighten the hearts of those closest.

Totally different, but also a very special product of our sweet *shtetl*, was Reb Moshe Yakov Krum. His whole family always worked extremely hard, from early morning till late night, never knowing luxury nor prosperity, but when you passed by their house you could hear bittersweet melodies of cantorial songs produced by the head of the family singing to himself while working. *Chazanut*[3] were his "weakness". If he heard that in Vilne, on the *Rosh Hodesh Shabbat* or Holidays there would be prayer with a known Cantor, he would go to Vilna by foot to enjoy his "saying"[4] and his heartbreaking Jewish tones. Where else could one see such characters?

But they [the local Gentiles] harbored a hatred for these brilliant

Jewish characters, and when the Nazi murderers came, they added their bloody hands and helped them destroy my *shtetl*, my beloved Jews.

I remember that on the first day of the war we all knew what would be awaiting us. The youth were standing in small groups having decided to flee. For us, Mereh Levine's house was a merry house with sons and daughters. Now, all those children were already married, and she, Mereh, was standing at the window, very sad, resigned from life, in deep silence, as if she didn't care how and where to live out her remaining life. At that moment, a horse and wagon stopped by the house. We ran towards it and saw her youngest son Avrem'l. For months he hadn't come to visit his mom, and now he had came to share her solitude so she would not be alone anymore. Now he was tired, he had to sleep, and tomorrow he would see— maybe he could succeed in convincing her to escape. [Instead] they went together to the slaughter.

*

The worst murderer among our local neighbors was Yanek Pintshe, the Gentile son of a Soletchnik house owner. With his own hands he organized the slaughter of Soletchnik Jewry, and played a major, active role in the destruction of Voronove and its environment. He became famous and took pride in this. When my niece Gitte'le ran to her grandma and grandpa, he caught her with his own hands and shot her. He boasted about his heroism on several occasions.

After the war the hero left the region and moved away from Poland. Later, Hershke Kaplan, after going through a period with the Partisans and the difficulties of war, traveled to America where, together with his two young friends, they recognized Yanek on a train and delivered him to the police.

He was sentenced to only 9 months for illegally crossing of the border. They said that for his other deeds he should be tried in Poland, after being extradited; they had the right to try him only for what he had done here.

The three guys, Hershke with Moshke Rosvayevski and Yoel Segal, broke into the prison, beat him [Pintshe] nearly to death, and they wanted to lynch him, but the prison guards saved him from their hands.

Now probably the criminal walks around free and happy.

Institution for homeless children

Benyeh the shoemaker lived across the street and I knew him well. He lived in a tiny house with one room and a kitchen— he together with his family of five. At the entrance, where Benyeh worked, two goats were always laying about with great dignity— as if they owned the place.

Besides shoemaking, Benyeh had several more businesses: he would call on Jews at night for *Selichot*[5] before *Rosh Hashana*; on *Succot* he would go around to residences with a citron and he would recite the blessing for whomever didn't know it so the person could recite it responsively; he also distributed wedding invitations.

He did these jobs [not only for money] but also for his own pleasure. Along the way he would catch a chat with everyone, tell a story, or discuss politics. When somebody asked him about a story: "When did that happen?" He would say: "Recently...about 15 years ago."

After spending such a day with people Benyeh would sit down at his workbench to do some shoemaking.

His wife Sarah, preoccupied and exhausted, would help him with raising the two goats. She would walk them alone in the fields for pasture. Thus, she had milk for the children and managed to save a couple of glasses for sale. In the summer she would go almost every day to the woods to gather berries, mostly blackberries. She would fry them and preserve them for winter, and she also sometimes sold them. She did everything to give an education to her children, or at least to teach them a trade.

But the main virtue of these two wide–open souls was their love for children, for the unlucky, the poor, the neglected and the crippled children. Sarah from time to time traveled to Vilne and came back with sick, neglected, and miserable children to take care of. She did this for many years. She could devote herself to one child for years until things got back on track.

Once they brought a little girl, limping and retarded, who couldn't move and had to be taken care of constantly. She stayed with them [the children] as long as possible.

Our Soletchnikers in Israel

Towards the end they brought a half-year-old baby who had lost his mother. His name was Chaim. They took care of him as if he was their own child— nobody had the right to offend him. Anyone who did would get a hollering from the "parents" such that the person would want nothing to do with them.

When it was his Bar Mitzvah, they were told that it would be time to tell Chaim'ke his real surname. But they were against that, thinking of what would be best for him. In the end he discovered his origins and even met with his older sister, but he stayed with Benyeh and Sarah where he had a warm home and ... was slaughtered together with them.

Benyeh and Sarah [were] a model of lovingkindness for Jews. [They] saved Jews with love and devotion the lonely orphans made miserable from the cruelty of life.

Footnotes

1. Ed. Note: The reader of the prayers on special occasions ("Ba'al", Marcus Jastrow, Louis Ginzberg, Joseph Jacobs, Kaufmann Kohler in *The Jewish Encyclopedia, New York: Funk & Wagnalls Co.*, 1906, LCCN 16014703:
http://www.jewishencyclopedia.com/articles/2235-ba-al , last accessed 27 November 2017)

2. Ed. Note: Literally 'receiver'; the treasurer of a synagogue ("Gabbai", Executive Committee of the Editorial Board., Joseph Jacobs in *The Jewish Encyclopedia, New York: Funk & Wagnalls Co.*, 1906, LCCN 16014703:
http://www.jewishencyclopedia.com/articles/6444-gabbai , last accessed 27 November 2017)

3. Ed. Note: Cantorial music.

4. Ed. Note: Another word for the prayers led by a cantor.

5. Tr. Note: Prayers of forgiveness

[Page 426]

Yakov Katz – Soletchnik's Poet

A.G. [Glikman]

Translation by Emma Karabelnik

(from the Vilne Journal, February 2, 1926)

On Adar 3, 5678 (February 15, 1918), at the age of 22, after a severe disease, in Great Soletchnik (Vilne Gub.[1]), died Yakov Katz, a talented poet who left behind a collection of writings, beautiful original Jewish poems, and who didn't have the privilege of being published during his lifetime.

Yakov Katz was born on October 15, 1895 in the family of a poor shoemaker, Moshe Levi Katz in Vilne. When he was 4 years old his parents, in order to avoid poverty moved to a small town, Great Soletchnik, where he started the *alef–bet*[2] at the age of five – not in a *cheder*,[3] but with an old Jewish woman who for one gulden per month "taught *Siddur*"[4] to boys from poor homes – one scale lower than a cheder. He studied until his *Bar Mitzvah* with "teachers" who came from Vilne "Katrialivke"[5] to Soletchnik "for conditions" – to work with groups of children. The learning was not bright and not deep, and mostly not normal,[6] but the children would study with desire and achieve better results than all their friends, even better than those who studied with the best known teachers of the shtetl. In the *cheder* he didn't feel comfortable; he didn't enjoy the learning. He strived for education. He would scrutinize books by himself and read a lot. He had a great desire to go to "the city", that is Vilne, to study in "a class", but the bitter poverty of his home almost put an end to his dream: his father sent him as "an apprentice to a *shtepper*.[7] "A class, my son – his father said – is for children of the rich; poor children must work"...

It was the jealousy of several of the little-town "golden" boys, of this "shoemaker's son" who couldn't coexist with local "youth", which was the factor that caused one "bigshot" of the town, who used to collect money from the rich to release them from forced labor, to sell Katz as a "volunteer" to the Germans to work "on the highway".

After a year of doing hard labor for the Germans, Katz returned home broken, totally scrawny, exhausted and enervated. He had neither the will nor the strength to move to the city anymore, and stayed home for the winter of 5678. In these last weeks he had a premonition of death. In January 1918 he became seriously ill; he lay sick for a month and in February he died at the age of 22 and 4 months.

Hebrew-Religious School – in Soletchnik

Yakov Katz didn't live to be published, but his poems show that a poet left this world too early, one who could have with time been discovered, blossomed, and taken an honorable place in Yiddish poetry. Despite of the fact that he was a worker, he didn't write political poems. He devotedly described life in a small town, using no rude writing, and in a totally different manner— totally different from what our poets were doing until then.

Yakov Katz's poems are fruits of a young muse which hadn't yet come to its full power, but they are already marked by the poetic stamp. His style is light and velvety and his rhythm – soft and moderate.

Footnotes

1. Tr. Note: Vilne province

2. Ed. Note: Yiddish word for 'alphabet'

3. Ed. Note: School

4. Tr. Note: A Jewish prayer book.

5. Ed. Note: The meaning of this word is not yet known. The spelling in the original text is: kof–tof (or sof)–reysh–lamed–yud–vov–vov–kof–ayen

6. Tr. Note: The author probably means the teaching was not up to traditional standards.

7. Tr. Note: A cutter and stitcher of shoe–leather

[Page 428]

A Silent Soul
(in memory of my friend Yakov Katz)

A. Glikman

Translation by Emma Karabelnik

From the sky meandered by accident
To Earth a silent soul,
It fluttered, it twirled
On a light–beam of comfort!

It longed, yearned for life,
It dreamt, but only suffered;
Its star of life
Was replaced by sorrow!

Then had this soul
Lost its dreams
Then suddenly it had vanished
In an abyss, and was forever lost.

To Live I Want – to Live!*[1]

Yakov Katz

Translation by Emma Karabelnik

May it be wilder than before —
To live I want — to live!
May blood gush for years —
To live I want — to live!

May the years go by slowly —
To hear I want — to hear
The sound of peace one more time!
Swear, I can — swear

That then I'll die peacefully
Rest, I will — rest...
When peace comes, happy will
Everyone be, happy...

While lying in a quiet tomb,
Ask, I will — ask
That from war, God Almighty
Save us — save!

And great everlasting peace
Will he give — give!
And people will happily
Live their lives — live!

Great Soletchnik (Vilne gub.),
end of December 1917

Footnote

1. His last poem, written 2 weeks before his illness

Flowers

Translation by Emma Karabelnik

I see flowers, beautiful flowers —
I pick a handful;
I can't decide: a blue flower
Or a red one, or a white one.

It doesn't matter, I pick them all,
All are beautiful and gentle!
Sometimes comes a yellow flower.
It is also not so bad!

I pick flowers by the pile
And I lie down between flowers; —
Maybe — Who knows? Never again —
Will another day come.

Will it come? Then again
I'll pick flowers pile by pile!
But I don't care – who needs to worry:
If it comes or doesn't come?

I know only this — I pick now flowers,
I pick flowers by the handful!
Who needs to wonder? Who needs to think?
The years don't stay still, they run...

Great Soletchnik (Vilne gub.), June 12, 1916

[Pages 430-438]

Soletchnik and Soletchniker in Death

Tzemah Krum

Translation by Emma Karabelnik

The Red Messiah

When the war broke in 1939 the Russians occupied Soletchnik. They proclaimed that they had come to save us from war, oppression and anti-Semitism.

They called everybody to watch a film in a Polish barrack. Before the film a political commissar gave a political speech and told how Russia had once suffered for its ideals.

"But now" – he finished – "we have everything, even salt and matches are available in Soviet Russia."

The audience clearly heard "salt and matches" and thought that the speaker was joking, because these two items were [in the homes of] even the poorest refugees from Poland.

Later we asked a Jewish Red soldier what was meant. He looked around to check that nobody was listening and said:

"Guys, you will have more than enough trouble" – and went away.

They expropriated Israel Levine's house and turned it into a club. They took the fortepiano from Wagner and placed it in the club. Gentile youngsters would bounce on it with their paws and get excited like little children and [make a] racket. All the tables were full with newspapers, chessboards, and lotto. The youth were instantly co-opted, especially the younger ones with real socialist origins. They had to "force" an audience to [come] to the meetings. At the beginning people would attend, but later everybody knew exactly what the speaker would say, and everybody, everybody, was fed up. Even the most enthusiastic communists in the town were disappointed by this land of their dreams. The Russians would tempt the locals. They would scatter promises of things they would bring from Russia. Among other things, the speaker said:

"They will bring as much pepper from Russia as you want."

In the audience sat an old Gentile woman. She would burp loudly and the clownish youngsters had brought her there to have a laugh. The speaker asked the grannie:

"How much pepper for example do you need, grandma?"

She replied:

"Life is bitterer than pepper. What more do I need?"

The poverty and the shortages in Soviet Russia were the result of their policies. When they came to us [to our town], the officers wives bought everything [in our shops]. Old fashioned dresses, which the shop owners lost hope to sell, they grabbed them as if they were the latest word of fashion.

Kasriel Khlavnovitsh, who managed to sell all the leather from his shop, told me:

"You know what I think, Tzemah? I think they have nothing. Because if they don't have leather, they don't have cattle, they have no milk and no butter and cheese. And if so, they don't have any meat and no wool. So what DO they have?"

Meanwhile all the stocks of food and goods were emptied, and Jews began to worry about the near future. But fear of Siberia and fear of their treatment of [what they called] democracy's enemies, scared everyone. They [the Russians] started to bring goods for distribution, but one had to stand in line until midnight to get any.

It seemed that this was Stalin's secret: to keep people occupied 24 hours a day with concern for food and keep their minds away from politics, thus giving the regime quiet time.

Soletchnik Jews worked during the day and stood in lines for some food at night; or families would split in two groups: one would work and the other stand in lines; or [they would] sniff around and grab from here and there. The situation was awful. Worries over simple things, food, clothes, heating and shoes, became so hard that people wished for [something] worse but [which was] at least different, meaning to say:

"Anyway we didn't gain any freedom with this regime; at least in another country we'll have what to eat."

The Nazis Arrive

Early in the morning we heard that the Germans had entered Russia, and already on the next day the Russians fled like cowards and left the town to itself.

Part of the youth, especially those who were active in the Russian regime, fled with them, but most remained for Hitler.

The first days were tensely quiet. But the moment the [Russian] military was gone, and the first German officers appeared, they immediately began organizing a local brigade among the Gentiles and started tormenting Jews.

The first decree was the yellow patch which had to be worn by every Jew, whose blood and lives were [now] worthless. Later they began recruiting us for forced labor which consisted of the most shameful jobs, for which we got crumbs.

Aba Yudke, Velvl Soletchniker's son, once went out without the yellow patch; they shot him on the spot in the middle of town. Before that he managed to beat up a Polish collaborating hooligan. My father went with a sack of corn to the mill. There a Polish policeman beat him up so hard that Gentiles who witnessed it cried.

The Polish hooligans did their best to please their Nazi masters and outdid them in their Jew-hated and murderousness. Once they captured me, Velvl Goldanski and Dr. Levine, and forced us to be harnessed as horses to a wagon carrying stones, and to drag it quickly like horses. They beat us nearly to death with sticks, and Yanushek, Wagner's servant and later a communist activist, shouted:

"Your good life is finished, you dismal hedonists!"

After a few weeks, when Hitler's murderers had sated the local hooligans with Jewish blood, they then allowed able-bodied [Jewish] men and women to work in Wagner's fields. The commandant was a Nazi, a big German guy with a red face, and a murderer. He would scream and intimidate us without a reason, just for his own pleasure. Rokhele Levine, a very pretty girl, on one occasion couldn't stand his ox-like kicking and ruddy grimacing, and so she started laughing. He ran after her and beat her, and then she was gone for having laughed.

The work in the fields was very hard, but at least it was close to the town.

In the Ghettos

Awful news came from Vilne. Life for Jews there had become unbearable. They were beaten, shamed, humiliated, and thousands of them had been taken to death. The ghetto was like a cage in which all victims were trapped; the slaughterer then comes whenever he wants, extracts, and slaughters.

On Yom Kippur, when we were told that we would be concentrated in a ghetto, the wailing, the sobbing, and devastation were indescribable. Jews at the *Beit Midrash*, big minds, independent and experienced with trouble – became totally broken, helpless and desperate.

Every family hired a wagon, put in a few of their belongings, seated the children, the elders, and the weak, and drove to Divenishok, a town 21 km from us. On the way out of the town Polish police performed a wagon search and took whatever they wanted.

After arriving from Voronove, we were divided into the houses of local Jewish families, and that's how we lived. But, before we had time to look around, new information arrived that the ghetto had been surrounded. We knew what it meant because all the news about slaughter-"actions" started with the surrounding of the ghetto...

I remember that my first reaction to this news was that if I don't run away [escape], I'll go crazy. Only thanks to these thoughts of escape could I handle all those awful news. I began organizing a group that would, together with me, look for ways to escape, but unfortunately we didn't escape.

Meanwhile the days during which we were encircled by cannibals went on for years.

One afternoon we were driven out of our homes to the market [place]. Armed Gentiles, amidst unarmed Jews, took high positions so they could see every Jew and anyone from running and saving himself.

That was on May 11th, 1941. After a hard winter of hunger and cold, of diseases, pain, and blood, a beautiful May light had finally arrived as a precursor of spring. But for us Jews it was one of the darkest of days. In the middle of the marketplace [was] a table. There were sitting those who would decide whether we were to live or die. Here, Jews were sorted: left, right or straight. Everyone went in the direction ordered. First they had to leave all their most expensive and dear possessions, and then they went left, right or straight.

Straight was to death.

Those who were left alive heard the bullets killing their dear ones and then were again ordered to be concentrated in the marketplace. We were counted again. Now we were a handful, only a few dozen remained from hundreds.

The staff commander from Lida made a speech before us, explaining to us that because Jews had always hated Germany so much, it was now [time for] revenge and these would be acts of world justice. In the middle of his speech, the horses and wagons came back, filled with the possessions of the murdered. We, the unfortunate survivors. had to watch and recognize the clothes, which only minutes before had been on the bodies of our dear ones. Hearts were crying. And what's next...

After the speech we all scattered to our homes. There, heartbreaking scenes took place. We suddenly understood our disaster. It became crystal clear who would not be with us any more; our [feelings of] insignificance, loneliness, and helplessness grew [quickly].

Some Jews wanted to convoke a "minyan", to pray "minha", to say "kadish", but there was no one to join in the "amen".

After a few more days, all the survivors, except for several men with professions, were sent to the Lida ghetto. Here we met acquaintances from surrounding towns. Their stories about the cruelty of the criminals in the ghettos frosted the blood in our veins. The biggest criminal, Vashoikevitsh, who had helped in the selections of Jews during actions and in the ghettos, and here in Lida had played a big part in the horrific deeds, was himself from Soletchnik— from a respectful Christian family. We were good friends in school. He would frequently come to our house, and I go to his. Sender Levine. Who worked in his yard, told him that I and my family were here [in the Lida ghetto]. Minutes later he called the engineer Altman and told him to take 3 persons from my family to work in the sewing workshop. Altman told this to the *Yudenrat*. He located us, even before we were registered in his [records], and we were immediately sent to the sewing workshop.

On the next morning, some Jews were really afraid of us. We didn't understand what was happening, but later it became clear: to this "good" work were taken only those who had paid well for this "life-promising" working place... or who knows, maybe for another kind of fee. We were there without any fee or any other mediation. To us it was clear; later other people also understood.

In the Forest

Hundreds of Jews worked in the workshops, on a big square surrounded by fences. There was no access here for the Polish and German murderers. Here, nobody was beaten up, here you could have a talk from your heart. Here Jews prayed in "minyans". From time to time people could do a job for themselves. Here they started making gun parts for themselves and for others. Here we started to prepare our escape to the forests.

The "practical" Altman and his assistant Alpershtein would gather us from time to time and try to convince us not to escape to the woods: this, they explained, would bring trouble to those who stayed behind in the ghetto, a.a.v., but I was drawn to the forest.

Here we worked without direct German supervision, even the gate guards were Jews, and they would warn us if somebody from outside was approaching. One time the Head Commissar arrived, and the guards didn't have time to warn everyone. He went straight into the mechanics department and noticed that one Jew was repairing a revolver. The Jew started running and he [ran] after him. The mechanic jumped over the high fence and disappeared into the ghetto. The German stopped chasing and kept the incident silent, but [since then] Jews were more afraid.

I was the biggest agitator to run to the forests, because I couldn't see any other outcome. I made them understand that the good situation here [in the workshops] could "sucker" us in, and then it would be too late.

I used to have special meetings with the Soletchnikers, and a separate meeting with Kasriel Khlavonovitsh. We used to talk, walk, think, gripe, and [just] be silent. When I told him:

"Be well, I am going to see how my [folks] doing."

He would ask me to stay for a bit more:

"Wait, Tzemah, let's be silent for a little longer."

In the ghetto we lived in a small, unfinished room with double beds for sleeping. Together with us in the same room lived the Schneider family from Vilne. It was very crowded with no air to breathe, but we suffered the most from the bedbugs. They helped the Germans to shorten our lives. The nights were tormenting; at night one would think and overthink our situation.

It was clear that we were being kept in the ghetto in order to be exterminated, and meanwhile we were being used as workers. Later would come the slaughtering.

Life outside work became unbearable. Every sound of an engine from outside the ghetto, every scream from afar would freeze the blood and stretch the nerves as by pinpoint, as by needle. I thought again that I'd lose my mind if I didn't run away.

Once, on a very cold winter day, during a "normal" panic in the ghetto, when a rumor spread that an "action" is coming, my mother also went out into the street to "hear" and "see", and she caught a cold, got sick with pneumonia and died. People gathered around her death-bed and cried bitterly. Everyone was jealous that she had been privileged with such a natural, good death.

But nobody thought to commit suicide. Maybe some didn't have the courage, maybe some were too apathetic, or maybe some wanted to live to the day of revenge. Nobody knows how great is the taste of revenge for people-animals.

Only few committed suicide. There was a Jew, Graby, who was a collaborator with the Divenishok *Yudenrat*. He worked for the Germans in a gas station. [Once] he lit a cigarette, threw away the burning match, and the whole station went up in flames together with the Germans. When they ran to look for him they found him hanging in a place not far from there. Maybe it should be considered an act of heroism.

After my mother's death, as soon as the 30 days [of mourning] were over, I told my father, sister, and brother that I was leaving for the woods. They tried to talk me out of it. It was known in the ghetto that Jewish Partisans suffered from hunger, raids, and Russian anti-Semitism, and my family wanted to save me from all this. I survived only due to the dream of escaping to the woods, but I didn't have someone to run with.

One day from the woods came Moshe Khvayovski, a compatriot from Soletchnik, a good fellow. He was hiding in our attic and waited [for an opportunity] to take guys to the woods.

I spoke with him, and he took me with him. [Together with us] escaped Moshe's parents and the Levine family. Only a few had guns. The leader of the group, higher up than Moshe, was Perets, the second in command in the forest. It bothered him that we didn't have guns. He picked on me to go back to the ghetto and threatened to shoot me, but I continued with them until, after hard nights of fear and dangers, we came to Bielski and to the Jewish Partisan squad.

Bielski Squad – a Jewish Shtetl

Tuvia made a strong impression with his wild appearance and calm behavior. He didn't expel anyone— even those who didn't have guns. The man felt he had a mission given to him by fate, and he would perform it with real Jewish heartiness. The squad was in Budkevitser forest. Everybody lived in huts [made] of rods, slept on forest leaves scattered on the ground, did exercises and night shifts, and ate from the common kitchen.

Life there was sweet because the feeling of freedom and the opportunity for revenge made our souls sweet. But, we lived in constant fear of German raids, in constant alert, and we had, from time to time, to wander and move the squad from place to place.

Only in Galibaker Forest, in the deep, dense everlasting woods, did we get a real feeling of stability. [From there] we would go out for sabotage actions against the Germans— cutting off their trains, railways, and other means of communication. We built a camp similar to a Jewish shtetl, with workshops for craftsmen, shoemakers, tailors, hatters, watchmakers, carpenters and mechanics. We built a mill and a bakery, and we even made a tannery. Russian Partisans would bring their cattle to us to make sausages, and left the leather for us. There was even a place for public prayer and we even delivered babies. A bath that we built was not worse than a bath in a bigger town. There were pots with cold and hot water, buckets to wash ourselves, benches to sweat, and in the middle – a hermetically closed room were we used to disinfect our clothes in a temperature of $120^{\circ}C$. We made our own soap. People enjoyed the facility and came to bathe frequently.

Thus we fought diseases and prevented typhus epidemics, but we also had a hospital in the forest with two doctors and with an isolation ward for typhus patients in a separate "*zemlianka*". A few dozen milk-cows gave us milk for the sick, the weak and the children – and for the privileged.

We had dozens of horses with harnesses and wagon drivers who took care of provision and goods that were brought from the outside.

With time, our squad became an address for Jews who wanted to save themselves from the ghettos, from hiding with Gentiles, and from the anti-Semitism of Russian Partisans in the mixed squads. The number of Partisans grew every day as did the number of those who depended on them. People began to regain their lives. Near the kitchen, with the warmth of its fire, Jews would sit around and sing sad songs, and hold parties to raise morale. The performer at the parties was the artist Munyek Shepirski.

News came from the frontlines of Red victories. The Germans began to retreat and they fell straight into our hands, and we had the good feeling of life and survival.

Before the squad dissolved some repressive deeds occurred which showed Bielski to be a vengeful and vindictive person, as if a drink of power had "gone to his head", but in general I remember the squad, and Tuvia himself, as positive memories. He created a safe harbor and rescue conditions for helplessly desperate Jews. Hundreds and hundreds of Jews who survived in Galibaker Forest [to see] victory, and are alive today, owe their lives to Tuvia Bielski.

*

The last assembly of the squad occurred in Navaradok. Everybody received a Partisan certificate and everybody continued on their way.

Among Soletchnikers who returned from different squads: Khaveh Khvayovski with her children Moshe and Sender (Yehoshua died in the woods), the Levine family, husband, wife and the children, Hirsh Kaplan, Berke Sheynman and Yitzach Meir Valtukh.

Died during attacks on German groups in the forests following Soletchnikers: Leybke Kaplan (Hirsh's brother), Ysroel Streletski (Chaim Keile's brother), Sender Sheynman (Berke's brother).

[Page 439]

Names of Soletchnik Martyrs

Transliterated by Judy Petersen

Surname	Given name	Other family	Remarks
OZREIER	Lieba		
BRENCHIK	Gitel		
BRENCHIK	Avraham	Tzviya (wife), Chaya	
GOL	Yehuda	Moshe, Sarah	
GOLDENSKI	Chaim Moshe	Manya Riva	
GOLDENSKI	Velvil	Ita (wife), children	
GOLDENSKI	Yitzchak-Hertz		
HOCHMAN	Yitzchak	wife	
ZHAVINSKI	Riva-Leah		
ZHAVINSKI	Reizel		STRELETSKI
ZILBERKVIT	Alter	Zlate	
CHAVAYEVSKI	Yeshaya	Leib	
CHALBENOVITSH	Katriel	Channah, Shmuel, Dina	
KATZ	Aharon	Nechama, children	
KATZ	Lieba		
KATZ		wife, Boris, mother	manager of Wagner sawmill
KATZ	Reizel		
LEVINE	Avraham	Sonya, children	

LEVINE	Rakhel'e	Channah-Devora, Taibe, Batya, Eliahu	
LEVINE	Mira		
LEVINE	Nachum-Yona	Frida, children	
LUSKI	Chetzkel	Batya, children	
LEMELMAN	Shimshon	Michaela, and their son	
LEMELMAN	Lieba		
LANDA	Mordechai	Lieba	
SEGAL	Miriam		
SEGAL	Feigele		
STRELETSKI	Velvil	Riva (Rivka), Yisrael	
SELTZNITSKI	Velvil	Bluma, Rodel, Nechama, father Yudel.	
PERETSKI	Chaya	Gita, Shulamit	KATZ
TZELSKI	Shimon-Leib		
TZELSKI	Chaim-Moshe	Riva	
KAPLAN	Bentzion	wife, children	
KOTLER	Yisrael	Sarah, children	
KAPLAN	Yisrael	Chaya-Pessel, Malka, Tzviya, Leib	
KRUM	Moshe-Yakov	Frumel, Alte, Ora-Hershel	
KARCZMER	Reuven	Nadia	
RUDNIK	Shmuel	wife, children	

RUDNIK	Chaya	Sonya	
RAKOVSKI		wife, Beyrl, Rivka, Chaya	Rabbi
SHUSTER	Chaim	Binya, Avraham Itsche the teacher	
SHOFFMAN	Avraham	Chaya-Sarah	
SHOFFMAN	Yitzchak	Yocha (STRELETSKI), Bluma, Rivka	
SHEIMAN	Alter	Rivka, Sender, Fruma	

[Page 440]

List of Soletchnik Residents Who Died in Israel

Transliterated by Judy Petersen

Surname	Given name	Remarks
ORENSKI	Rakhel	
ZAHAVI	Yosef	GOLDANSKY
ZAHAVI	Sarah	GOLDANSKY
ZAHAVI	Yisrael	GOLDANSKY
CHAVAYEVSKI	Chaya	died in Canada
KATZ	Zerach	died in Vilna
LEVINE	Batya	TZELSKY
LEVINE	Shmuel	
LANDA	Masha	COHEN
LANDA	Moshe	

INDEX OF NAMES AND PLACES
(**bold**=places)

A

Abramiski, 232, 426, 511
Aflog, 435, 511
Alkoni, 435, 511
Alperovitsh, 435, 511
Alpershtein, 493, 511
Alsorishok, 156
Altman, 492, 493, 511
Amotz, 266, 511
Ankelovitsh, 406, 511
Antshul, 405, 511
Aran, 343
Arbeiter, 435, 511
Arkin, 62, 90, 238, 426, 435, 511
Arkov, 87, 93, 511
Arluk, 121, 132, 511
Arshulki, 81, 511
Ashbal, 238, 511
Auschwitz, 244
Avak, 381, 511
Aviel, 6, 7, 17, 19, 20, 34, 185, 201, 207, 226, 227, 250, 277, 291, 435, 511
Avinoam, 435, 511
Avrakovitsh, 435
Avrakowitz, 511
Avramiski, 435, 511
Azovski, 86, 511

B

Bad Reichenhall, 183
Baierski, 435, 511
Baksht, 140
Balteriski, 66, 426, 435, 511
Bankover, 7, 234, 511
Baranovitsh, 242, 357
Bareishes, 411, 413, 511
Baron, 27, 426, 511
Bartnovsa Forest, 11
Basist, 426, 511
Bastuni, 62, 67, 82, 85, 117, 364, 366, 381, 406
Beitar, 64, 65, 66, 67, 78, 79, 415, 418, 473
Benakani, 24, 25, 158, 378, 382, 405, 419, 450, 471
Ben-Ami, 6, 162, 511
Ben-Shlomo, 435, 467, 511
Benunski, 426
Benunsky, 511
Benyakonski, 5, 121, 427, 511
Berezhno, 136, 146
Berkovitsh, 410, 511
Berkovski, 68, 80, 84, 191, 231, 237, 240, 426, 435, 511
Berlin, 83, 182, 335
Berlovitsh, 427
Bernshteyn, 328, 511
Beth Shean, 449
Bhykvit, 328, 511

Biale Voki, 348, 351, 353, 362
Bialystok, 255, 334
Bibik, 95, 511
Bielski, 74, 76, 77, 123, 124, 126, 131, 139, 143, 144, 147, 151, 152, 153, 160, 161, 168, 173, 372, 375, 376, 377, 396, 397, 399, 407, 495, 496, 511
Bilitski, 435, 511
Binonski, 435
Birkenau, 244
Bissel, 406, 511
Bistriski, 40, 511
Blatt, 356, 511
Blekherovitsh, 372, 511
Blitter, 63, 435, 511
Bloch, 230, 232, 276, 427, 435, 511
Blyakher, 160, 164, 371, 372, 406, 435, 511
Boksht, 393
Bonk, 340, 341, 511
Borisha, 199, 511
Borski, 427, 511
Boyarski, 6, 8, 146, 155, 158, 251, 379, 511
Brenchik, 498, 511
Burshu, 95, 511
Bworonov, 157, 511
Bykhvit, 324, 511

C

Chaikin, 238, 511
Chalbenovitsh, 498
Chavayevski, 467, 498, 501, 511
Chernovitsh, 139, 141, 146
Chmielnitsky, 403, 511
Cohen, 276, 360, 435, 501, 512
Cuba, 279

D

Daikhovski, 156, 512
Damanski, 512
Dayem, 328, 512
Der Galech, 43
Der Mark, 43
Di Brick, 43
Di Lanke, 43
Di Prasadis, 43
Dikson, 8, 328, 329, 330, 512
Divenishok, 160, 233, 254, 364, 371, 372, 405, 419, 446, 491, 494
Dlugin, 68, 96, 97, 106, 112, 159, 232, 237, 328, 378, 427, 512
Dokshtolski, 427, 512
Dovilinski, 512
Dovrov, 427, 512
Drosknik, 343
Drozhets, 328, 512
Droznitski, 435, 512
Dubinski, 255, 427, 512
Dublinski, 427, 512
Dudovitsh, 427, 512
Dukshtulski, 6, 8, 17, 82, 105, 155, 158, 276, 330, 347, 381, 391, 392, 399, 435, 512
Dutchshiyok, 158, 159
Dvilianski, 6, 40, 68, 112, 158, 159, 181, 191, 192, 231, 249, 250, 276, 281, 317, 324, 348, 359, 360, 372, 406, 427, 435, 512
Dzerzhinski, 337

E

Ein Ganim, 284
Eishishki, 66, 158, 371, 405, 411, 427, 512
Epstein, 512
Eshishuk, 231, 233, 338, 351, 352

Eyseltchok, 95, 512

F

Finestein, 427, 512
Finklestein, 427, 512
Fleig, 185, 512
Fried, 341, 512

G

Galibaker Forest, 495, 497
Galitsia, 257
Garbatski, 158, 428, 512
Gelgort, 256, 512
Gerda, 360
Germanishki Street, 111
Gershoni, 435, 512
Gershonovitsh, 87, 88, 93, 158, 159, 160, 371, 428, 512
Gil, 435, 512
Gindlin, 251, 512
Ginsburg, 8, 27, 309, 435, 512
Ginzberg, 181, 480, 512
Givataim, 281, 435
Glikman, 8, 481, 484, 512
Gobitsh, 428
Godenski, 512
Gol, 8, 65, 70, 193, 276, 279, 317, 321, 324, 428, 435, 498, 512
Gold, 328, 512
Goldanski, 8, 444, 447, 457, 462, 476, 490, 512
Goldberg, 203, 249, 250, 512
Goldenski, 498
Goldfaden, 245, 512
Goldstein, 157, 435, 512
Golnik, 435, 512
Gorbitsh, 428

Gordon, 45, 372, 406, 435, 512
Gordznetchik, 512
Goren, 201, 277, 512
Gottlieb, 1, 4, 7, 191, 291, 292, 293, 426, 433, 512
Grabetski, 435, 512
Grodne, 231, 232, 255, 343, 346
Grodzenchik, 6, 8, 69, 80, 94, 99, 103, 106, 109, 112, 158, 159, 201, 226, 227, 231, 232, 277, 310, 332, 368, 371, 372, 428, 512
Gtzvitz, 158, 159, 512
Gurvits, 97, 120, 256, 280, 317, 324, 351, 512

H

Haifa, 256, 285, 362, 435, 468
Halperin, 238, 513
Hamelamed, 513
Hamorashti, 513
Hamyadler, 513
Harkabi, 25, 513
Hemweg, 392, 393, 513
Herminishok, 233
Hertz, 275, 276, 435, 444, 498, 513
Herzliya, 86
Heydul, 303, 513
Hlibolinski, 24, 513
Hochman, 498, 513
Holon, 256

I

Igolski, 254, 255, 513
Itskovitsh, 232, 339, 428, 513
Ivashkevitsh, 446, 513
Ivenets, 400
Ivia, 91, 135, 141, 144, 233, 336, 338, 344, 393

J

Jabotinski, 513
Jacobs, 480, 513
Jastrow, 480, 513

K

Kaczerginski, 355, 513
Kagan, 136, 428, 453, 513
Kaganovitsh, 344, 513
Kalai, 8, 453, 464, 468, 513
Kalika, 324, 513
Kalmanovitsh, 6, 8, 64, 169, 231, 237, 240, 371, 414, 428, 513
Kalwaria, 219
Kaminetski, 7, 17, 71, 214, 217, 328, 435, 513
Kamitski, 428
Kamiunski, 255, 259, 428, 513
Kaplan, 6, 8, 17, 68, 79, 81, 106, 156, 157, 158, 160, 175, 178, 232, 233, 276, 324, 325, 332, 349, 350, 359, 371, 378, 410, 422, 428, 429, 435, 441, 446, 467, 473, 477, 497, 499, 513
Kapli, 429, 513
Karaganda, 415, 419
Karczmer, 254, 499, 513
Karni, 7, 222, 287, 435, 513
Kastel, 184
Katsev, 162, 513
Katz, 4, 8, 9, 17, 93, 331, 352, 444, 468, 472, 475, 481, 482, 483, 484, 485, 498, 499, 501, 513
Katzenellenbogen, 106, 158, 159, 237, 371, 429, 513
Katznelson, 25, 513
Kessler, 146, 147, 513
Khadrovich, 159, 513
Khayot, 86, 87, 513
Kheifets, 410, 513
Khermetz, 513
Khlavnovitsh, 442, 488, 513
Khvayovski, 495, 497, 513
Klausner, 6, 162, 170, 513
Klei, 17, 513
Kletzk, 157, 213
Kletzker, 30, 213, 371, 422, 513
Klisov, 242
Kltkin, 156
Kohler, 480, 513
Koidenav, 337
Kolah, 429, 513
Konikhovski, 6, 7, 8, 67, 97, 199, 222, 231, 275, 291, 333, 352, 362, 363, 383, 435, 513
Konopke, 6, 7, 8, 63, 73, 113, 148, 161, 231, 237, 275, 310, 334, 369, 404, 405, 410, 435, 513
Konopki, 217
Kopelovitsh, 6, 8, 174, 372, 407, 413, 513
Korvo, 87, 513
Kosovski, 429, 513
Kotler, 300, 445, 467, 499, 513
Kovner, 353, 513
Kovniski, 429, 513
Krani, 6, 23, 199, 513
Krashanski, 334, 335, 513
Kravtzov, 435, 514
Kreiner, 435, 514
Kreshunski, 429, 514
Krum, 468, 499
Krupski, 394, 514
Kudlianski, 514
Kudlinski, 429, 514
Kulvitski, 514
Kuropatwa, 429, 514
Kutcher, 357, 514
Kuznets, 7, 8, 80, 230, 284, 289, 299, 306, 317, 429, 514

L

Landa, 499, 501, 514

Landau, 443, 471, 514

Lapidos, 430, 514

Laskin, 435, 514

Lazduny, 144

Laze, 354, 514

Lefkovitsh, 232, 430, 514

Leibovitch, 450, 514

Lemelevin, 253, 254, 514

Lemelman, 443, 470, 499, 514

Leninsky Komsomol, 345, 353

Lepertin, 435, 514

Levi, 435, 472, 481, 514

Levine, 6, 7, 8, 17, 22, 68, 71, 97, 141, 142, 194, 203, 211, 218, 231, 237, 238, 240, 241, 244, 253, 258, 272, 275, 276, 286, 314, 320, 328, 364, 394, 396, 406, 409, 421, 430, 435, 442, 443, 444, 460, 461, 467, 468, 472, 477, 488, 490, 492, 495, 497, 498, 499, 501, 514

Levitovitsh, 430

Levy, 69, 514

Liamberg, 303, 514

Lichtman, 257, 349, 350, 371, 514

Lida, 11, 18, 24, 25, 26, 47, 58, 67, 72, 77, 82, 83, 84, 85, 86, 98, 107, 110, 114, 117, 118, 119, 120, 121, 125, 126, 128, 146, 147, 148, 159, 160, 164, 165, 166, 167, 168, 175, 195, 231, 233, 237, 255, 257, 290, 307, 310, 321, 322, 340, 349, 363, 366, 367, 371, 372, 375, 376, 380, 381, 392, 394, 395, 402, 404, 405, 406, 410, 419, 420, 444, 445, 469, 492

Lida Street, 83, 84, 114, 307, 404, 444, 445

Lieberman, 8, 460, 461, 468, 514

Lipinski, 430, 514

Lipnishok, 233, 335

Lipniski, 231, 237, 238, 435, 514

Lisorski, 6, 8, 155, 363, 514

Litman, 184, 514

Lobutski, 430

Lodz, 90, 346

Lomzhe, 255, 417

Lubetski, 371, 514

Lublin, 74

Lubtsch, 139, 336, 337

Lunka, 354, 514

Luski, 189, 212, 213, 256, 272, 444, 468, 499, 514

Lutsk, 211

M

Mages, 6, 514

Magid, 357, 514

Magilski, 431, 514

Mainz, 175, 176, 177, 178, 181

Majdenek, 148

Majorchik, 435, 514

Mansfeld, 97, 338, 514

Manski, 123, 514

Marieh, 445, 514

Martsishants, 343

Masteikiai, 344

Maulkenik, 117, 514

Mayortshik, 8, 404, 514

Meirit, 435, 514

Meirovitsh, 70, 232, 431, 514

Meliboki, 169

Memel, 50

Mesonznik, 422, 514

Michalovski, 431, 467, 514

Mikelkuni, 238

Mill Street, 469

Miller, 189, 322, 514

Minsk, 337, 412, 413

Mirmelshteyn, 257, 514

Mishkovitsh, 136, 142, 514

Mishkuvski, 212, 319, 324, 514

Mishori, 292, 514

Moltsadski, 7, 21, 226, 232, 269, 276, 422, 431, 435, 514

Monesh, 448, 449, 514

Monk, 180, 514

Moschitski, 251, 514

Motznik, 435, 515

Movelitski, 328, 515

Mutshnik, 8, 369, 515

Myadl, 213, 253, 306, 357

Myadler, 30, 213, 304, 371, 422, 515

N

Nadvorna, 238, 240, 242

Naliboki, 131, 135, 138, 143, 144, 146, 161, 165, 166, 353, 357, 377

Naliboki Forest, 377

Naliboki Plains, 161

Narach, 356

Natscher Forest, 351

Natsie, 340

Navaradok, 124, 126, 127, 195, 372, 377, 406, 407, 408, 497

Nazareth, 449

Neman River, 124

Netanya, 359, 435, 467

Newe-Kibush, 282

Nikolay, 318, 515

Nikolayevka, 415

Novakanski, 317, 515

Nyer Mark, 43

Nyer Plan, 43

O

Olken, 328, 515

Olkenik, 233

Olkenitski, 6, 7, 11, 62, 64, 66, 67, 99, 111, 113, 161, 162, 170, 173, 191, 226, 231, 237, 238, 250, 255, 257, 318, 324, 334, 338, 371, 388, 402, 404, 405, 411, 431, 435, 515

Olytovitsh, 431, 515

Orenski, 501, 515

Oshmene, 238

Ossul, 416, 417

Ostrin, 345

Ostrinski, 328, 515

Ostrovlya, 127

Over, 124, 251, 435, 442, 515

Ozreier, 498, 515

P

Patashnia Forest, 376

Paz, 435

Pepeshni Forest, 91

Peretski, 499, 515

Perlshteyn, 350, 351, 515

Petchikowski, 171, 515

Petersen, 275, 435, 467, 498, 501, 515

Petrokani Forest, 91

Petropavlovsk, 415

Peyrovitsh, 23, 515

Peysah, 334, 515

Pikovski, 6, 7, 41, 80, 82, 85, 241, 431, 435, 515

Pirigantse, 369

Piskovski, 232, 515

Plotnick, 431, 515

Podesiuk, 6, 169, 435, 515

Poditvianski, 66, 191, 373, 431, 515

Poletskishki, 345

Polinski, 256, 515
Ponar, 104
Postov, 355
Poz, 6, 7, 17, 21, 189, 223, 224, 276, 515
Poznan, 48
Pupko, 91, 152, 158, 204, 276, 378, 410, 431, 432, 435, 515
Puziriski, 6, 7, 17, 189, 223, 224, 249, 250, 317, 432, 515

R

Rabin, 1, 4, 6, 24, 515
Rabinovitsh, 432, 515
Radin, 338, 339, 340, 341, 351
Railway Street, 82, 83
Rakovski, 444, 451, 500, 515
Rashliki Forest, 374
Ribitski, 432, 515
Rivak, 432, 515
Rodnick, 432, 515
Rosvayevski, 478, 515
Rotbard, 435
Rothbart, 7, 17, 22, 218, 237, 515
Rothman, 338, 432, 515
Rubinovitsh, 324, 515
Rubinovski, 435, 515
Rudiskes, 370
Rudnik, 353, 376, 499, 500, 515
Rudomino, 419

S

Sadeh, 351, 515
Sarna, 416
Schneider, 372, 406, 433, 494, 515
Segal, 445, 467, 478, 499, 515
Seltshnik, 160

Seltznitski, 499, 515
Shaiman, 515
Shamir, 6, 10, 17, 19, 46, 94, 99, 160, 161, 165, 169, 250, 332, 346, 359, 368, 402, 435, 515
Shapira, 7, 8, 17, 190, 193, 263, 314, 315, 316, 322, 516
Shapiro, 68, 231, 245, 250, 262, 267, 516
Sharid, 7, 226, 516
Sharshevski, 450, 516
Sheiman, 467, 500, 516
Sheinbaum, 435, 516
Shelovski, 81, 102, 157, 204, 267, 310, 322, 338, 371, 405, 411, 432, 516
Shemer, 435, 516
Shevakh, 372, 516
Sheyman, 443, 516
Sheynman, 497, 516
Shiftinski, 432, 516
Shirs, 354, 357, 359, 516
Shitnitski, 435, 516
Shlohim, 25, 34, 516
Shmerkovitsh, 6, 7, 17, 19, 34, 46, 69, 99, 100, 128, 160, 161, 185, 191, 207, 231, 232, 250, 263, 265, 310, 322, 402, 432, 516
Shoffman, 500, 516
Shombakh, 218, 516
Shomroni, 7, 8, 19, 249, 256, 261, 263, 276, 283, 289, 295, 302, 314, 435, 516
Shpatinski, 435, 516
Shteroski, 435, 516
Shtikolshchik, 433, 435, 516
Shupians, 445, 516
Shur, 193, 516
Shuster, 500, 516
Shvanbakh, 11, 162, 194, 307, 516
Siberia, 67, 68, 162, 163, 245, 246, 247, 286, 336, 371, 378, 415, 489

Sifkona, 433, 516
Skidel, 385
Slonim, 416
Smoliarnia, 43
Smuk Forest, 104
Sodovski, 516
Sokolik, 238, 334, 435, 516
Sokolka, 47, 48
Soletchnik, 8, 9, 17, 88, 141, 364, 365, 372, 405, 419, 441, 444, 445, 446, 447, 448, 450, 452, 453, 454, 455, 456, 459, 460, 461, 462, 464, 467, 469, 470, 472, 476, 477, 481, 482, 485, 486, 487, 489, 492, 495, 498, 501
Solminsky, 516
Solodukha, 8, 419, 421, 516
Soltchinski, 433, 516
Soltchnitski, 450, 516
Solts, 117, 118, 433, 448, 449, 516
Soroki Tatarov, 351
Sorotzkin, 211, 212, 516
Stankevitsh, 152
Starovolski, 376, 516
Stelmakhs, 246, 516
Stephan Street, 56
Stol, 382, 516
Streletski, 8, 442, 453, 466, 468, 471, 472, 476, 497, 498, 499, 500, 516
Sutzkever, 355, 516
Svolik, 259, 516
Swine Street, 114, 198, 469
Syagle, 375

T

Taibel, 8, 475, 516
Tebashinski, 433, 516
Teivel, 468, 516

Terk, 303, 516
Tlopp, 256, 516
Trakai Lake, 370
Trotski, 191, 246, 303, 324, 328, 334, 516
Tsalel, 303, 516
Tscherniachovski, 516
Tsikovski, 87, 89, 92, 516
Tsikovskies, 87, 516
Tsipkovitsh, 213, 250, 516
Tsirinski, 328, 516
Tsunzer, 245, 248, 516
Tsur, 17, 516
Turetski, 433, 516
Turok, 433, 516
Tzelski, 499, 516
Tzemel, 249, 516
Tzur, 435, 516

U

Ulanovski, 89, 90, 92, 93, 516

V

Valtukh, 443, 497, 517
Varsutski, 433, 517
Vashiliski, 433, 517
Vasilishok, 143
Vellman, 433, 517
Vickry, 176, 517
Vidlenski, 246, 517
Vileyka, 355
Vilinchik, 433, 517
Vilinski, 433, 517
Vilne, 11, 34, 47, 49, 50, 53, 54, 57, 65, 70, 81, 82, 103, 104, 105, 119, 158, 196, 201, 216, 219, 232, 233, 235, 236, 237, 242, 249, 250, 254, 255, 256, 297, 300, 301, 302, 306, 310, 314, 321, 322, 323,

343, 344, 348, 349, 350, 353, 354, 357, 359, 362, 372, 391, 395, 410, 411, 412, 415, 442, 443, 444, 462, 465, 469, 472, 476, 479, 481, 483, 485, 486, 490, 494

Vilne Street, 11, 254, 297, 306, 442, 443

Vilne Technion, 103, 465

Viner, 433, 517

Virshudski, 246, 324, 517

Volfianov, 360, 517

Volozhin, 212, 242

Volpianski, 81, 85, 102, 157, 231, 328, 338, 371, 411, 433, 517

Vronki, 247

W

Wagner, 8, 447, 449, 450, 455, 464, 465, 466, 471, 488, 490, 498, 517

Warner, 85, 517

Warsaw, 48, 192, 217

Weber, 435, 517

Weiner, 97, 103, 324, 435, 517

Weinshteyn, 354, 517

Weisbum, 468, 517

Weiss, 254, 517

Weitzman, 359, 517

Weksler, 256, 517

Werner, 73, 517

Winer, 435, 517

Wizen, 467, 517

Y

Yachka, 230, 517

Yankelovitsh, 372, 517

Yasinov Forest, 141

Yavniel, 286

Yehiel, 409, 517

Yoselvitsh, 433

Yudes, 472, 517

Yustman, 215, 517

Z

Zahavi, 435, 457, 467, 468, 501, 517

Zalberg, 421, 517

Zamak Veldel, 43

Zats, 442, 517

Zawolna Street, 53

Zerakh, 81, 157, 158, 371, 405, 517

Zhabinski, 257, 318, 328, 434, 443, 517

Zhavinski, 498

Zheludok, 396

Zhetl, 385

Zhuravelniki, 143

Zhyrmun, 118, 349

Ziglnitski, 434, 517

Zilber, 468, 517

Zilberkvit, 498, 517

Zilverman, 434, 517

Zocharkin, 338, 517

Zubrove, 343

Zuperner, 435, 517

Zvolotski, 434, 517